£21-50

THE MEDIEVAL TOWN

Europe in the Middle Ages
Selected Studies

Volume 15

General Editor
RICHARD VAUGHAN
University of Hull

NORTH-HOLLAND PUBLISHING COMPANY – AMSTERDAM · NEW YORK · OXFORD

THE MEDIEVAL TOWN

By
EDITH ENNEN

Translated by
Natalie Fryde

1979

NORTH-HOLLAND PUBLISHING COMPANY – AMSTERDAM · NEW YORK · OXFORD

North-Holland ISBN 0-444-85133-X

Published by:
North-Holland Publishing Company – Amsterdam/New York/Oxford

Distributors for the U.S.A. and Canada:
Elsevier North-Holland, Inc.
52 Vanderbilt Avenue, New York, N.Y. 10017

Library of Congress Cataloging in Publication Data

Ennen, Edith.
    The Medieval town.

    (Europe in the Middle Ages selected studies ; v. 15)
    Translation of Die europäische Stadt des Mittelalters.
    Bibliography: p.
    Includes index.
    1. Cities and towns--Europe--History. 2. Cities
and towns, Medieval--Europe. I. Title. II. Series:
Europe in the Middle Ages ; v. 15.
HT131.E5613   301.36'3'094   79-1362
ISBN 0-444-85133-X

This book was originally published in German in 1972 under the title *Die europäische Stadt des Mittelalters* by Vandenhoeck & Ruprecht, Göttingen
© Vandenhoeck & Ruprecht, Göttingen

Printed in The Netherlands

2\8 59 2

General Editor's note

This English translation of Edith Ennen's *Die europäische Stadt des Mittelalters*, which appeared in German in 1972, provides the first and only general account in English of the flourishing European cities of the Middle Ages. The author, who is an acknowledged expert in the field, having published some twenty books and papers on the subject, has revised and approved this translation herself. She has preferred to keep notes and bibliography as in the German edition; the index, which is new, is the work of the translator.

August 1978   Richard Vaughan

Contents

List of figures

INTRODUCTION

What is a town?

The question 'what is a town?' can easily be answered in a plausible manner for the medieval period. As a compact silhouette, the skyline of a medieval town, densely built up, surrounded by a wall, dominated by churches and its fortress, stood in sharp contrast to the surrounding countryside. It was very different in all these respects from the sprawling urban settlements of our own day. The wall served not only as a means of fortification; it also delineated an area of special urban law, that is the far-reaching legal equality of the townsfolk, which was in marked contrast to the hierarchical and lordly order which prevailed outside the walls. The towns enjoyed a type of constitution in which their free burgesses participated in the business of running the town and even, in some cases, achieved autonomy against intervention by the town's overlord. This state of affairs, by planting the seed of the civic equality of our own day, was to make any separate and distinctive town freedom superfluous in modern times when the condition of medieval townsmen became the norm for society in general.

The medieval town wall enclosed a population which differed from the outside world not only in its civic freedom but also in its freedom of movement, and in the specialized and richly assorted variety of occupations carried on by it within the town's walls. Concentrated there, was the industrial side of the economy of the day which the town authorities controlled and directed; it was in the towns that the merchants were based, who threw a network of commercial alliances across the whole of Europe and who had further links in the Near East and in North Africa. They determined the fate of the town through the town council and they were carrying out economic policies in an age when kings and princes, fully preoccupied as they were in imposing their wills on their vassals and in building modern institutionalized states, were scarcely in a position to carry through deliberate and systematic policies throughout their different territories.

The focal point of the business life of the town was its market, where a variety of goods from different areas of production were exchanged. By means of its market, the town was able to dominate the area around it while also acting as the central point of all economic life. Its traditional cultural as well as its political and economic standing in the region aided this centralizing tendency. Any settled localities which fell behind the towns in their facilities or in their ability to serve as sophisticated, hierarchical and clearly-defined units, ceased to be able to compete. This centralizing function acts as one of the most consistent essential ingredients of the town.

The intention of present-day historians is not so much to establish a rigid definition of 'what is a town' as to try to adopt a compound bundle of criteria whose make-up varies according to time and place. Such criteria can then be modified, further developed or added to and the order of priorities can be adjusted. We are indebted to C. Haase for providing this enlightening break-through into such a compound notion of the town. His 'bundle of elements' always includes such criteria as: external form and appearance of the town; its deliberate or gradual settlement; its lay-out, inner structure, stratification of society, division of labour and, occasionally, as was the case in the Middle Ages, its special legal status.[1] We also need to take into account the town's functional aspect and, as part of it, its contribution as the centralizing element in many spheres of life. Structure and function, while they always exist side by side, never recurred twice in the same combination. In the particular variant of one time and place, they created the marked individuality which every town possessed. We must also take into account the awareness of contemporaries of these factors and their way of expressing them in the terminology of their own day.

Even the most loosely-knit and flexible concept of a town, however, must only be used as a framework or an aid to reconstruction if it is to be worthwhile. It can help us to portray the fascinating variety in the towns' appearance which otherwise the fragmentary survival of tradition and evidence would make it difficult to define. Such a concept can also help us to distinguish and to differentiate functions; to provide a lively and exact idea of the great medieval towns and their distinct surrounding territories, both in their interrelationships and their chronology.

What kind of urban culture emerges from the Middle Ages? Urban history does not begin with the Middle Ages. Why else should we use the term 'Middle Ages'? By it, we have come to understand the years between about 500 and 1500 A.D., although such divisions into distinct periods are always questionable. They can serve only as devices to bring under the historian's control the uninterrupted flow of time. We should treat the ill-defined time barriers and the overlapping features which mark the period between 500 and 900 A.D. as an age of transition from Antiquity to the Middle Ages, and the period from 1350 to 1500 as the transitional age between medieval and modern times.

Can we really say that there was any urban culture at all in this period from 500 to 1500 A.D. designated by us as the Middle Ages? Were not the early and high Middle Ages an epoch of agrarian economies, dominated by landlords within an aristocratic hierarchy, with the king at the head and his subjects stratified into various levels of subservience beneath him?

In the first chapter, we shall give a detailed reply to the question of continuity of culture from Antiquity into the Middle Ages; here we shall concentrate on establishing the place of medieval urban culture in the general historical scheme. The earliest enclosed settlements of an urban type come from a period before the introduction of pottery. Taking a wider view, the transition to a predominantly urban culture took place in the Near East as early as the seventh millenium B.C.[2] The various regions of Europe were urbanized at different times. Here, urbanization began in the eastern Mediterranean in the second millenium B.C. but reached the Rhine by the first century of the Christian era. The town in Antiquity, which embodied both the Greek *polis* and the Roman *civitas*, formed the basis of organization of public life, providing the permanent headquarters of both priest and magistrate. With its surrounding district it provided a unit in which the countryside formed only an appendage, lacking its own ruling class. This dominance of the whole fabric of life[3] by the town was preserved in the Middle Ages only by the Mediterranean and, above all, by the Italian urban settlements.

On the other side of the Alps, the countryside retained its political and cultural importance. This manifested itself in the solitary castles of noblemen, in country estates, and in churches and monasteries which were sited far from towns but which also served as religious and cultural centres. Those who wielded secular power could not overlook their descent from the old Germanic lords of the countryside and the town was never a favoured place of residence for the nobility in north-western Europe. The sharp contrast between town and countryside, a special urban law, and the exclusive concentration of trade and industry in towns, are all typical medieval features. Moreover, the relative smallness of medieval towns is an indication that they had lost the important position which they had held in Antiquity.

During the emergence of the Middle Ages from Antiquity, areas of Europe without urban culture existed alongside other European regions with very ancient urban traditions. The part of Europe which remained outside the boundaries of the Roman world possessed no towns. The expansion of the Roman Empire was accomplished by means of urbanization but at very variable levels of intensity. The *civitas* was the usual form of arrangement. With a few exceptions, it formed the lowest political unit. This urbanization united the world from the Antonine Wall in Britain as far as the Euphrates in a manner which would never be achieved again.

Within the Roman Empire, we can distinguish a number of regional economic areas.

(1) Italy, together with Sicily, Sardinia, Corsica and the southern Alpine region.

(2) Spain, Gaul and western Germany with Britain as an outlying area and Scotland and Ireland falling under Roman influence.

(3) The central and eastern Alpine region, the northern and central Balkans as far as the Danube delta on the Black Sea, linked, after Trajan's time with transdanubian Dacia (modern Rumania).

(4) Roman North Africa from Morocco to Tripoli.

In addition to these four Latinized regions, three can be added which remained largely Greek:

(1) The Greek motherland in the southern Balkans together with the almost fully Hellenized Near East and the populous area of Asia Minor, incorporating in addition Crete and Cyrenaica, the Crimea, southern Russia between roughly Kiev and the Black Sea with Armenia and the Caucasus as outlying areas.

(2) Syria, Palestine, north-western Arabia and northern Mesopotamia formed another Hellenized area.

(3) Egypt was perhaps the richest and, at any rate financially the

most well consolidated region, closely bound up with Nubia and Cyrenaica.[4]

To understand the situation at the beginning of the Middle Ages, we must consider mainly the first two zones mentioned above as well as the border area of the third. Italy declined under the emperors while the provinces came to the fore. The leading families of Italy disintegrated. The ancient cities of Italy have been incorrectly depicted as basically consumer towns,[5] but Rome, in imperial times, might justifiably come within this category. Annually 400,000 tons of grain were distributed amongst its population besides the festivals and games which were provided for it. Provincial cities also proved costly centres of civilization. Rich citizens erected triumphal arches, theatres, arenas, temples, baths and aqueducts. The economy expanded on the basis of consumption and luxury, and technical changes tended to confirm this. The number of slaves diminished while the legal position of those remaining improved. The remainder of the great mass of free citizens of the state developed into the *humiliores* of Roman law. In the second century A.D., although the town settlements of the Empire were becoming smaller, particularly in Italy and in the old Greek settlement area, they maintained the ancient way of life for a long time. Nevertheless, the Emperor Hadrian was already finding it necessary to attach certain economic groups in the towns permanently to their occupations. The means of transport were developed or neglected at the whim of the state bureaucracy. In banking, the greatest achievements of the past were undone: the *tesserae nummulariae*, the tokens which guaranteed the security of deposit arrangements of the Italian private banks fell into disuse in the course of the first century A.D. The ideal notable of Roman society was the great landowner, resident in the town, who saw his life's purpose fulfilled in an official career in state service and in a life otherwise occupied with politics, literature and sport.

The *civitas* of the imperial age was an organized unit composed of a town linked with an area of surrounding countryside – *territorium est universitas agrorum intra fines cuiusque civitatis* ("a territory is constituted by the totality of lands within the boundaries of each *civitas*"), as the Digest puts it. The citizens of these *civitates* were those who were either descended from citizens, or were adopted, or who were freedmen, or finally those who were granted citizenship by special privilege, irrespective of whether they dwelt in the town or in the countryside belonging to it. Their organs of government were their popular assemblies whose influence was diminishing in imperial times, the *curia* and the magistrates. The *curia* was run by the rich landowners who dwelt in the towns but possessed great estates in the surrounding countryside. Only in relatively few towns, for instance in Ostia, the port of Rome, or in Alexandria of Palmyra, did merchants belong to this upper group. Merchants and craftsmen had their meeting-places in the *collegia* (corporations). Many of these corporations possessed their own temples and assembly halls.[6]

The western provinces add certain nuances to this picture.[7] Whoever agrees with Max Weber in using the term ancient 'coastal culture' does not simply mean by it restricted coastal districts but also has in mind the formation of a whole region, the dependence of one part on the other, and the whole network of connections in the entire Mediterranean Basin. In the Mediterranean, communications radiated in every direction, whereas in the Atlantic they were reduced to a restricted, linear pattern. With its acquisition of Gaul and Spain, the Roman Empire not only pushed to the shores of the Atlantic but also obtained in the huge interiors of these countries great navigable rivers of a sort which, apart from the Nile, it had previously lacked: the Baetis (Guadalquivir), the Danube, the Rhine and the Rhône. Gaul, in particular, was enclosed by its rivers which flowed out from the interior and surrounded it. On the route from Narbonne to Bordeaux, one came, after a short journey, to the watershed between the Tyrrhenian Sea and the Ocean. The Rhône valley, with the Saône, provided the main trade route penetrating Gaul. It was through it that Lyons achieved its position of central importance, both in trade and administration and finally as a foothold for missionary activities in the western German provinces. From the Saône, many roads stretched out, with Britain as their final destination. The shortest overland route went into the Loire valley. The Seine reached in the direction of Britain and from early imperial times the rich *nautae Parisiaci* were active here. The upper Rhône, traversable along the valley, linked the waterways of the Aare, Doubs and Moselle with the boats travelling from Toul, thus providing the link between the Rhône and the Rhine. Into these greater rivers flowed smaller tributaries which established further links with inland areas. By means of the canals, harbours and bridges which they erected, the Romans improved the possibilities of this transport network. As far as land transport was concerned, they were able to utilize the possibilities of the successful tradition of horse breeding in Gaul and Germany as well as putting to good use the well-developed cart tracks of Gaul.

In its *oppida*, like for example Bibracte, situated on four high hills, southern and central Gaul already contained in the pre-Roman period centres of craftmanship, from which goods were despatched over the country roads. The artistic crafts of Gaul, above all in metalwork, were of excellent quality and formed part of a tradition which continued unbroken from Celtic to Roman times. South-eastern Germany also possessed Celtic *oppida*. One whose existence has been fully confirmed, and which has been more thoroughly investigated since the war, is that of Manching near Ingolstadt. Its walls enclosed an area of 380 hectares and it was an important political, economic and cultural centre in the late La Tène period.[8] Another such example is Stradonitz in Bohemia. The pre-Roman metal industry of Noricum gave Magdalensberg its great importance.

In north-eastern Gaul and western Germany such types of urban *oppida* did not exist. On the banks of the Rhine, the Romans established great troop concentrations for offensive action in order to defend the Rhine frontier after the defeat in the Teutoburg Forest. Here their appearance marked an epoch; in a short period of time, the left bank of the Rhine experienced a huge development which was not of indigenous origin. The urban civilization which was created here at this time was the product of the tremendous investment of a world empire with all the possibilities which that brought.

Such opportunities gave the transport system of the Roman west the chance to develop. It reached into Britain and by way of the North Sea coast and the estuaries of the Ems and Weser penetrated into the non-Roman German territories and ultimately reached as far as Scandinavia. The Roman tendency to skirt the Atlantic coast until entering the North Sea meant that they encountered vessels in the Rhine estuary coming from the opposite direction, from inner Gaul and the Rhineland. Britain, Germany and France were thereby linked together and a transport zone was created which almost foreshadowed that of the age of the Hanse.

This transport network could be used by native industry, and once the army removed its grip from the private sector, economic development became possible. This happened in 69–70 A.D., after the crushing of the Batavian revolt brought peace and the end of colonial status, at least in its economic aspects. As an example, one can observe with very great precision the progress eastwards of *terra sigillata* pottery. Twenty years later it had moved to southern Gaul and ninety years later to eastern Gaul, present-day Lorraine and the Saar. In the second century A.D. it reached Trier and the Rhine, Rheinzabern, Sinzig, Remagen and ultimately beyond the Roman frontier (*limes*).

In the middle of the first century, pottery began to be manufactured in an artistic fashion in Cologne, the chief town of lower Germany and, at the end of the century, terracotta began to be made. Probably, the brass and bronze industry which had been transplanted to the area between Aachen and Liège from Capua, began about 80 A.D., its raw materials coming from Gressenich. The glass industry of Cologne goes back to the first century A.D. By the end of the second century, perfume bottles were already being manufactured here and the dried-up remains of their contents have actually been preserved. From 150 A.D. there existed in Cologne a workshop producing a specialized form of blown glass which achieved the highest peak of ancient artistic glasswork, for instance a great flask with handles which were covered in rosettes and garlands in white, red, blue and gold thread. From the third and fourth centuries survive engraved glasses, among them the famous Circus Bowl, the largest and best preserved example of figurative cut-glass from Antiquity, produced in Cologne some time between 320 and 340 A.D. The most beautiful surviving Cologne *Netz-Diatret* glass was found in a grave of the early fourth century. Cologne glass has been found as far afield as Scotland.

Gallic cloth making by ordinary households but with centrally-organized distribution existed in the north from the sea to the Moselle, namely in the region of the Nervi and Atrebati as well as of the Treveri. The Secundini at Igel near Trier were cloth manufacturers of this sort and have become famous for their imposing gravestone which still stands in Igel.

A standard Rhineland product was wine, perhaps already found under cultivation by the Romans and certainly encouraged by them. Demand for goods from the Roman Empire did not, however, cease but only diminished: certain types of wine, grapes, oil and olives, papyrus and the products of the luxury and art industries, spices, salves, semi-precious stones and pearls were imported and oriental dealers came into the area. The demand for imported luxury goods reached its greatest height when from the late third century onwards, the imperial palace at Trier was being splendidly furnished and, soon afterwards, when the Christian Church was developing its cult. These imports were partly financed by the taxes of the whole Empire, lavished here for emperor, court, army and officialdom. If we treat this area of the Rhine frontier in isolation from the economy of the Roman Empire as a whole, the flow of these tax revenues into it constituted an important element in its balance of payments. Moreover, parts of the frontier area were able to compensate for their imports with very important exports. The balance of trade began to stabilize. Cloth played the major role here. Perhaps the lower costs of cloth production in this province provided the foundation for its successful export. In comparison with Gaul and western Germany, the *agri decumates* on the eastern bank of the Rhine and the Danube region, with the exception of Noricum, remained colonial lands which were in part supplied from eastern Gaul and later primarily from centres in the Rhineland.

The intensity with which Roman civilization was imposed naturally varied. It reached its culminating point in the great *civitates* like Cologne, places of considerable industrial wealth and with trading links which reached as far as Britain. Another example is Paris where the island on the Seine, site of the pre-Roman *oppidum* of Lutetia, soon became too small and where fashionable quarters in the Roman style were erected on both banks of the river, reaching as far as the summit of Mont Saint-Geneviève where the Pantheon stands today. Here, on the left bank, there came to an end the road which stretched from Rome via Autun, the Roman town built at the foot of the old Celtic settlement of Bibracte, and via Orleans to Paris. The left bank of the Seine also provided the solid type of ground suitable for the central heating systems beloved of the Roman architects. The contour of Mont-Saint-Geneviève was adapted to create an amphitheatre. The left bank also had a good water supply. The aqueduct ended at the site where even today one can see twelfth-century ruins, which still bear the name of the Palais des Thermes.

Paris belonged to the region known as *Gallia Lugdunensis*. The capital of *Belgica Secunda* was Durocortorum, present-day Rheims. Nemetacum, the later Atrebatum or Arras, was the centre of the northern Gallic cloth industry. Sources from the time of Diocletian name *birri* (mantles) and *saga* (gowns with sleeves) as articles for which Arras was famed, and they were equal in quality to Egyptian and Asiatic textiles. Diocletian's tariff of maximum prices mentions

birri from Cambrai and textiles from Amiens, the ancient Samaro-
briva which was another well laid out provincial town.

Trier provided both the base for the imperial policy of aggression
against the Germans, east of the Rhine, and for the urbanization of
Gaul. It was its greatest commercial centre and the capital of Belgica
Prima. In the valley of the Moselle, near Trier, the roads from the
south by way of Lyons and Metz, those from inner Gaul by way of
Rheims and those from the Rhine all converged. The ancient ford at
Trier was already in 70 A.D. furnished with a strong bridge. A series
of public buildings, including an amphitheatre estimated to hold
30,000 spectators as well as fabulously laid out private houses, bear
witness to Trier's golden age in the second century. Inscriptions show
that there were Trier merchants active in Carnuntum, Regensburg,
Bordeaux and Lyons and finally among them a merchant who was
trading over the Alps, a member of the famous *Corpus Cisalpinorum*
and *Transalpinorum*. This man was a ship-owner and a wine and
pottery dealer. Beasts of burden carrying bales of cloth appear on the
Igel pillar. They are crossing a mountain range, perhaps the Alps. The
cloth production of this Trier region was a centrally organized industry of the first importance. In the city the ancient culture was
promoted by *grammatici latini* and *graeci*.

Splendid public works provided for the needs of these great
settlements, assuring above all the supply of drinking water. One can
still today see the Mainz water system at Zahlbach, the remains of
that which served Cologne and Bonn from the Eifel, as well as the
aqueduct belonging to the Metz water system which crosses the
Moselle at Jouy-aux-Arches. Metz was another flourishing town with
an amphitheatre and merchants and craftsmen organized into industrial colleges, among them the *holitores* and the *nautae mosallici*,
with their *tabularius*, their secretary. The Metz doctors are also a
well-attested body. At the junction of the route between Metz and
Rheims and that between Trier and Lyons lay the less important town
of Toul, at the end of the navigable stretch of the Moselle.

A special feature of the border provinces are the great military
headquarters which developed the characteristics of towns. On the
Rhine, Mainz, Bonn, Neuss and Xanten are in this category. They
developed from fortified camps into the *canabae legionis* (legionary
huts) which attracted industry – the army workshops were also inhabited by traders dealing with the non-Romanized Germans – and
finally into the civilian *vicus* (settlement).

In addition to the great fortresses and garrisons, there were also many small towns or urbanized villages, the *vici*. They straddled the roads and possessed fine buildings, traditional theatres, temples, Mithraea and included among their prosperous population leading citizens, industrialists and some merchants. The *vicus* of Schwarzenecker in the Saar, which was never later built over, has now been made accessible after large-scale archaeological investigations. In the extent of its buildings, the rich furnishing of its houses and the high quality of the ancient works of art found there, it provides an interesting example of one of these *vici*. The prosperity of the place was founded on its position as a staging post for provisioning the garrisons on the Rhine. A cloth-making establishment, a *fullonica*, has been discovered there. *Terra sigillata* pottery was also manufactured in the vicinity and was exported to Britain and the Danube region.

Augsburg, Regensburg, Passau, Juvavum-Salzburg and Carnuntum were the most important towns and settlements of the Danube region. In Pannonia, as in southern Gaul, infiltration by Italian merchants preceded the Roman conquest. Carnuntum was the centre for the amber trade. From the end of the first century A.D. trading connections linked it with south, north and west. It played an important role as an intermediary point in the export of Gallic and Rhenish wares and we know that a Trier citizen set himself up as a merchant in the hut settlement at Carnuntum. From the beginning of the second century merchants from Cologne banded themselves together in a league of fellow citizens in neighbouring Aquincum. Hadrian created a Roman *municipium* at Carnuntum but only seldom in its history did this town, lying on the outer frontier of the Empire, experience either security or prosperity.[9]

As part of her highly developed civilization, Rome brought her speech, her spiritual life – including a whole heaven full of gods – into the new Roman provinces. Celtic remained in use for a long time[10] as the language of home and neighbourhood in the province of Belgica. Latin was already, however, not unknown in the Trier region in Caesar's time because the transport system, which we have already mentioned, made communications with the Mediterranean possible. Trier's citizens, trading there, brought back their knowledge of the language with them. The fact that Latin was the language of war played the major part in contributing to its spread. Inscriptions reveal that Latin was both written and read among a wide segment of the

Trier population in the second and third centuries and it is the natives who were using it on their tombs and buildings and in sacred inscriptions. Occasionally, one finds a father with a Celtic name whose son's name is Latin. Weisgeber showed that a surprisingly large proportion of the personal names in the Trier region can be explained neither by Latin nor by Celtic origins but belonged to some unknown local group. He further went on to prove that the names ascribed to the Germanic Rhineland people by the Romans included, in addition to the Celtic element, an element of pre-Germanic provenance.[11] The contention, still accepted by Aubin, that in Caesar's time the whole of the right bank of the Rhine from Basel to the Rhine-Meuse delta was settled by Germanic peoples, as well as the left bank deep into the Netherlands, has been completely disproved.

As far as the left bank of the Rhine is concerned, we must reckon with various native elements in the population: Celtic in the south and west, with perhaps elsewhere a population neither Celtic nor Germanic[12] or Germanic only in the widest sense, a population doubtless augmented by immigrating Germans (*Elbgermanen*). Superimposed upon these were the Romans, who were themselves not of uniform ethnic origin. This variegated population was welded together by more or less superficial Romanization. Religious practices show this very clearly.

The 'Roman Peace' (*Pax romana*), which was never again to be attained in Europe's history, collapsed in the crisis of the third century,[13] which was a military and political crisis as well as an economic and monetary one. After 224 A.D. Persia under its Sassanid rulers developed into a powerful and ambitious world power which permanently threatened Rome. In 252 the Goths invaded Asia Minor. In 256 the Germans conquered all the fortresses of the German *limes*. The Alemanni pushed forward temporarily into the Auvergne while the Franks reached Spain. The *Colonia Julia Faventia Paterna Barcino*, that is Barcelona, was destroyed in 260. A decline in population and production, price crises both inflationary and deflationary, shattered the economy. The landowning upper class abandoned their town houses and retreated to their villas on their great estates. These third-century estates amounted to small lordships within the state, with their own soldiers and industries, numerous farm-workers and dependent peasants. They enjoyed far-reaching tax privileges and strove after self-sufficiency rather than any longer being market orientated. On the estate of Ausonius, there were not only slaves and dependent peasants (*coloni*), but also carpenters, masons and smiths.

All this represented a sharp set-back for urbanization. The barbarian invasions had brought about the permanent destruction of many important places and a contraction in urban settlements. Small urban centres, the *civitates*, and the open *vici* were hastily walled about, and altar stones and sculpture from the peaceful days now gone by were taken and built into the walls, such was the need for hewn stone. These constricted walled towns ceased to be comfortable places in which to live. The Emperor Julian, who lived for a long time in Paris, made the best of things when he wrote to his friends that he liked being in the small town of Lutetia, situated on an island and connected to the other river bank by two wooden bridges. The island lacked its own spring so that water had to be tapped from the river, but the permanent level of the water facilitated this and its glitter was pleasing to the eye.[14]

In general, the northern Gallic *civitates* now had an area of from 10 to 30 hectares. The towns of Provence were not reduced in this way, and Toulouse too remained between 80 to 90 hectares in size.[15] The most outstanding exception was Trier. In the age of Constantine its walls enclosed some 285 hectares and the population in the fourth century A.D. amounted to about 60,000 inhabitants. Many of the great buildings of Trier, as of Cologne, date from this later period. In Trier the basilica, imperial baths and the enormous granary on the bank of the Moselle, and in Cologne the imposing praetorium jutting onto the Rhine and the Rhine Bridge, all belonged to this epoch. In the *civitates*, which were not able to take part in such a boom, we can also trace changes. The second golden age of Trier differentiated itself from the first by the considerable contribution which the state made to it, a fundamental factor from the outset. Here, as in Arles, Lyons, Rheims, Tournai, and Autun (later replaced by Metz) we find state manufactures, above all in the textile industry.[16] Control by the state was the price which had to be paid for the further survival of the Empire.

The hereditary obligation to remain either in an urban occupation or tied to the soil came into being after the rich *curiales* withdrew to their estates and only the less prosperous remained in the towns. Administration and the collection of taxes fell upon their shoulders and many tried to avoid the burden by fleeing from the towns. The urban *curia* lost ever more importance and its place was taken by the

Figure 1. Town plan of Roman Trier showing contours and important buildings.

defensor civitatis, the *curator rei publicae* and finally by the *comes civitatis*. By the beginning of the fifth century many towns had ceased to be under the authority of urban senates. They shrank to the level of walled military encampments which were now cut off from their surrounding territories not *de iure* but *de facto*, both by their walls and by the loss of their upper class to the countryside. The classical unity of town and land in the *civitas* and the character of the town as the residence of the great estate owners was gone; the towns thereby lost much of their significance.

The world ceased to be ruled from Rome. In 381 Constantinople was designated the new Rome. The palace of the emperor, whose authority no longer had a legal but a religious base, became the heart of Byzantium. The substitution of apportioned taxes in place of assessed taxes which Diocletian began, provided the prerequisite for a state economic policy. The gold coin of the era of Constantine, the *solidus*, remained current in Byzantium, while north of the Alps there was a changeover to silver coinage. It was not until 1070 that this Byzantine gold *solidus*, the *besant*, was debased, evidence that stability was again achieved here.

The Christian Church provided a counterbalance to the general move of notables into the countryside. The church linked its organization to that of the state and the urban centres, the *civitates*, provided both bases for Christian missionary activity and seats for its bishops. When the *territorium* around the town was placed under the control of the bishop, this militated against the further loosening of the bonds between town and country. The transfer and adoption of obligations which had previously been exercised by the state, even civil and arbitrationary authority, in addition to the acquisition of considerable wealth and estates, for which they obtained immunity, all served to strengthen the power and standing of the bishops in the towns of late Antiquity.

The collapse of central control in the chaos of the fifth century, together with the breakdown of state administration and the disappearance of the office of *defensor*, inevitably transformed the bishop into the actual lord of the *civitas* and set in motion the development which would lead to the episcopal town lordship of the Middle Ages. Already in the second century Christianity was pushing forward into the Germanic provinces of the Roman Empire. An episcopal organization also developed here in late Antiquity while many Christian communities flourished in the *civitates* and *castella*. Archaeological discoveries are all the time producing further evidence of the widespread dissemination of Christianity. Inscriptions and grave goods reveal the penetration of Christian beliefs into everyday life. From Trier alone, 800 Christian grave inscriptions survive from Antiquity.[17] In 326 A.D. the state room of the palace was demolished. On its site the great double church grew up whose area is today covered by the cathedral and church of Our Lady. Jerome, Athanasius and Lactantius all spent time in the ancient episcopal city and consulted the important library there. In front of the Rhenish *civitates* and *castra*, outside the Ulpia Trajana on the lower Rhine, at Cologne, Bonn and Mainz, the Christians erected cemetery chapels for their burial places as well as churches dedicated to their martyrs and pious bishops, among them that "marvel of imperial quality"

(Doppelfeld), the church of St Gereon in Cologne. Churches for the community, such as the recently discovered baptistry found under Boppard parish church, put to use what was once a Roman military bath.[18]

These features, namely the whittling away of ancient urban civilization and the formation of large estates in the countryside as the new centres, not only of economic but also of social and political influence, the advance of Christendom and with it the increasing power and wealth of the Christian Church, must be borne in mind when we come to consider the links between the ancient and medieval urban cultures.

CHAPTER 1

The legacy of Rome

Only a brief summary of the considerable scholarly controversy on the subject of the cultural continuity between Antiquity and the Middle Ages can be made here. In the nineteenth century, an attempt was made to find one single year which might be said to mark the boundary between the two epochs. Nowadays, since we take into account constitutional, social, and economic factors, we appreciate that such an attempt to find a decisive turning-point must prove illusory.

It is no accident that it was the cultural and economic historians, Dopsch, Aubin and Pirenne, who were the ones who opened up the question of continuity between Antiquity and the Middle Ages and put it in its widest setting. Dopsch certainly went too far when he denied the existence of any definite breach in the whole process of "European cultural development from Caesar to Charlemagne". Aubin came nearer to the truth when he used the conclusions developed from his researches on the Rhineland to reappraise carefully the facts known at the time. He was, however, working within the limits of the then known archaeological evidence. Pirenne's theory that it was the influence of the Arab invasions and not the movements of Germanic tribes which first disrupted the inner cohesion of the Mediterranean Basin and sealed the fate of the Ancient World, must be countered with the objection of Lombard that Arabic money contributed to a new upsurge in urban life in the early Middle Ages. Every swing of the pendulum in this controversy has provided an abundance of material, opened up new aspects of the picture and finally brought in sight a consensus of agreement which now enables us to produce a general review which the archaeologists will no doubt continue to amplify.[19]

We can grasp only certain chronological and regional differences in the problem of the cultural survival of Antiquity into the Middle Ages. The real problem does not begin with the Germanic invasions of Italy. The rise of the eastern Germans, which began in the middle of the fifth and came to an end in the middle of the sixth century, was only an episode in the tale of the demise of Antiquity rather than the beginning of a new epoch. These kingdoms differed from one another in detail but followed a similar general pattern. They came into being in the late Roman period, their Germanic subjects were closely akin to each other and comprised only a small minority within them, for they remained overwhelmingly Roman in population. They were marked by an element of duality in their organization which was transcended only by sole allegiance to the king at the top; otherwise there was a sharp division between Aryan Germans and Catholic Romans. Stroheker was correct when he pointed out that "the foundation of Germanic kingdoms in the fifth century coincided with the growth of political provincialism in the west of the Roman Empire". The new kingdoms, moreover, encompassed areas which had already experienced independent developments and there are significant examples of direct collaboration between local forces and the Germanic tribes who were taking control of the same districts. An example is the aristocracy of Gaul which, after the middle of the fifth century, allied itself with the Visigoths and the Burgundians. In this way, a centrifugal movement prevailed which, although it had its roots far back in the late Roman period, had been repressed until finally invasions by alien tribes overwhelmed the Roman Empire.[20] Stroheker correctly laid emphasis on the part played by the Germanic tribes in this development and it was not the western Germanic tribes of Alemanni and Franks who constituted this threat but the allied tribes of eastern Germanic origin.

How these developments in the kingdoms of the eastern Germanic tribes reached their culmination can best be viewed by using legal evidence. Ernst Levy's fundamental research has opened up the true meaning of the folk law (*Vulgarrecht*).[21] This law grew out of provincial usage and deviated from the ancient classical juristic law which it simplified and popularized. In Byzantium classical concepts were victorious in the *Corpus iuris* of Justinian which was never binding for the west. Thirty years earlier the *Lex romana* of the Visigoths, the *Breviarum alaricianum*, which drew overwhelmingly on the *folk law*, had come into use. This *Lex romana* of Alaric II, influenced by popular legal forms, was later adopted in France and remained the authoritative record of Roman law for the west until the high Middle Ages. The folk law also determined the largely Roman element in the oldest Germanic legal codes headed by the Visigothic laws codified in 475 into the *Codex Euricianus*.

These Germanic states represent the first breach in the unity of the Mediterranean region and one which took place before the breakaway caused by Islam. Only merchants and envoys could from now on easily travel between these different states, for there was no longer any unified territory which stretched over the whole Mediterranean area. The provisioning of Rome with grain continued to function under the Ostrogothic kings but it was primarily grain from Apulia, since the connection with Africa was severed. The destruction of Rome during the sixth-century Gothic wars removed any hope of a return to earlier conditions and Justinian, after his victory, made no attempt to restore the city. One consequence of this break-up was to create a 'lost Italy' consisting of the islands of Sardinia and Corsica, which carried on in their own way outside the main course of events. Dalmatia was also a victim of these developments and after 600 the Slavs blockaded Salona, which was eventually destroyed by the Avars in 614.

Goths, Vandals and Burgundians held onto Roman ways, especially in economic matters; in preserving a money economy and foreign trade and in the survival of great landed estates, maintained by the exploitation of slaves or *coloni*. The Romans preserved their own upper class, the senatorial nobles, who continued to live in the towns. The majority of Germans preferred to live in the countryside but their kings did possess town palaces: Theodoric developed Ravenna and made it his capital and his palace was a copy of imperial Roman buildings; the Visigoths resided at Bordeaux and Toulouse, Barcelona and Toledo; the Burgundians in Geneva. The kingdoms of Euric, Geiseric, Theodoric and Gundobald still belong to Antiquity but those of the Merovingian Clovis, of the Visigoth Reccared and the Lombard Rothari belong to the Middle Ages.

Before we tackle the problem of the survival and development of urban culture, a moment's consideration of methodology is necessary. Why, for decades, has embittered discussion, costly archaeological investigations and searches after the minutest piece of evidence taken place in order to determine the arguments for and against the continuity of civilization as between Antiquity and the Middle Ages?

A great deal is involved here. Continuity is a question which is basic to all history. One seeks to find "a manageable vantage point to view the unending march of time" (Droysen).[22] It is only from such a vantage point, separated from the actual event by some centuries, that one can see breaks in this progress; from our own day perhaps we see events in proportion only when we go back to around 1800; from the age of the French Revolution one had a similarly good perspective back to about 500 and the age of the tribal movements. From this latter turning-point we can bring into focus the wider period between the fifth and ninth centuries when the survival of an urban way of life lies at the centre of the question of continuity. For centuries the men of the Mediterranean world had been accustomed to settle in towns, to dwell in them, to carry out their religious observances in them and to use them as their political centres. Partly through a simple dissemination of culture, which can spread without actual movement of people, and partly through political and military expansion, the urban way of life was taken from the Near East to the Rhine and Danube regions. Where would it go next? Would the Franks, Alemanni and Lombards change their old rural way of life and build a new one upon the ruins of Antiquity or would there only be a 'continuity of ruins'? This would make the urban development of central Europe a new beginning and would confirm the idea that every nation was bound to develop urban culture when it had reached a certain point of maturity.

'The town' – and here we mean the medieval town – with its market was an 'invention' which helped to solve the early problem of co-ordinating division of labour in the economy and thus it made possible far-reaching specialization by the producers in the secondary and tertiary sectors. This is the way that modern national economists[23] have pictured a purposeful economic development moving towards the industrial society of our own day, and the town is treated as serving as an important stepping stone in this process of advance. This notion, worthy as it is of consideration, can and will not wholly enable us to understand the complex phenomenon of the town. Nor is it a purely economic question. Did the urbanization north of the Alps in Roman times have the significance simply of a passing episode or was it an effective influence upon medieval developments there? Was there, apart from such direct continuity, also indirect continuity, in the shape of influences coming from southern European areas where town culture had survived into the

Middle Ages? Did not all these influences, including the Roman legacy in Christian form as a southern French, Spanish and Italian influence on the one hand, combine with the new central European innovations and developments? Is it not true that a cultural legacy can only be taken up given sufficient readiness and ability of the heirs to accept it? It is not so much reluctance to take a decisive stand as understanding of the complexity of the fundamental historical processes involved in medieval town development that prompts caution when viewing all the possible lines of development.

The problem can be resolved most strikingly in the middle region where the legacy of Rome was partly but not entirely dissipated, that is in the Frankish Empire between the Seine and the Rhine. In *Germania germanicissima* one can speak of an indirect and approximate continuity. In general, where Romans formed the prevailing proportion of the population, in Spain, southern and southwestern France and, in spite of both Lombard invasions and Frankish immigration,[24] certainly also in northern Italy, urban life carried on in its old way for a large number of people.

Without actually destroying the Roman Empire, it is clear that this veritable earthquake created by the tribal migrations, did not allow it to continue unimpaired. Under pressure by the barbarians on all of Rome's frontiers from the third century onwards, there were changes in the abovementioned superstructure of society which meant a reduction in urban culture. The rigid system of controls introduced by the centralized and oppressive Late Roman Empire made trade and transport part of the state organization. This collapsed during the age of tribal migrations in the whole of the Western Empire. In many cases initiative on the part of the townspeople ceased, and a section of the leading citizens retired to the countryside. The severity of the blow to urban life even in Italy is revealed by the fact that here too many ancient towns ceased to exist, especially in the south, which Sestan described as a "real cemetery of cities".[25] Other towns changed their location, whether they were situated inland or on the coast; this was often the consequence of war or malaria. At any rate, the result is a notable regrouping of urban centres. The reduction in the area of Italian towns was not as great as was proved by F. Lot for French towns.[26] Bologna certainly decreased in size from 70 to 25 hectares but again reached 100 hectares in the eleventh century. Topographical continuity varies considerably from town to town: in Verona the network of streets continued to coincide with that of ancient times; in Padua, which was destroyed in 603, rebuilding following an irregular pattern occurred. Municipal organizations[27] also finally disappeared in Italy. However, King Rothari offered some protection to the *civitas* in Clause 39 of his Edict which included a special peace. This placing of the town under a special peace certainly proves the legal standing of the town but evidently, in comparison to the "immense majesty of the Roman peace", this reduction to a special peace brings out the lack of an imperial town law or of any substitute Germanic conception of this sort.

The town thus remained a legally differentiated and limited settlement. It is certain that the Italian towns remained the seat of political, judicial and administrative authority even into Lombard and Frankish times. The *duces* and *gastaldi* resided in towns. The towns also possessed dependent regions which they themselves administered. Lombard settlements based around a castle, such as the area of Seprio studied by Bognetti,[28] which was carved out of the old territorial possessions of the cities of Milan and Como, sometimes disrupted the Roman problem of towns and their surrounding territories. According to the Lombards, too, the town was above all a fortress. However, the impression which the towns had made on the land was so ingrained that even these rustic conquerors were not able to make fundamental changes. Violante[29] has shown how, in the Po valley, economic and social developments continued in an unbroken pattern. Professional traders, moneyers and non-servile handworkers continued to exist and to reside in towns. Evidence survives in Italy in another important instance of the typical ancient town-country relationship: the ancient *civitates* became bishoprics. Northern and central Italian dioceses remained unchanged in their lay-out until the thirteenth century. They were relatively small – their smallness strikes the traveller in Italy even today – so that they were very easily dominated from an urban central point while, on the other hand, the inhabitants of the diocese could recognize the episcopal city as their natural centre. The significance of the bishoprics for the development of the city states of northern Italy arises from this and it is thus a relationship which echoes the situation which prevailed in Antiquity.

North of the Alps the diocese was much too large to serve as the basis of city-state development. Here the land assumed its own separate place in ecclesiastical organization. H.F. Schmidt has described the legacy of the Roman spirit of security under the law within medieval Italian urban development.[30] He saw it primarily in the separation of administration and justice which came to fruition early in the Middle Ages in the juxtaposition of consules *de communi* and *de placitis*. He also found it in the development of record keeping in the towns which grew out of the notarial records which in their turn were a direct continuation of the late Roman tabellionage records. Thus, the practice evolved of registering private legal business in public registers. Indirect continuity came in the form of adaptation of Roman concepts. The more marked survival of literacy in Italy – in contrast to northern Europe where literacy became a clerical monopoly – is also a sign of the certain survival of urban life.

For Spain Dietrich Claude[31] has challenged Sanchez-Albornoz and sought to prove the survival of the *ius civitatis* into the sixth and seventh centuries. He uses as evidence a Visigothic town creation which was built onto an older settlement, Reccopolis, founded by Leowgild in 578 and named after his son Reccared. Claude suggests that Leowgild was there conferring Roman civic law, although such law was ceasing to be administered in practice. Barcelona's Roman background has been revealed by considerable excavations and the findings from these are exhibited in the Roman museum. After the Frankish attack of 260 the *Colonia Barcino cognomine Faventia* turned to utilizing its old religious and burial monuments and other pieces of masonry – as happened time and time again – to build a strong fortress which would suffice until the thirteenth century. This fortress and its fertile surrounding area were responsible for giving the town the status of a ruler's residence for the first time in its history in the fifth century under Athaulf and Galla Placidia. However, the town suffered from some degree of depopulation during this period as is proved by the existence of a Visigothic burial place within the area of the Roman town. The first evidence of episcopal organization comes from the fourth century. As always seems to be the case, the bishop played an extremely important part here in preserving an element of continuity. Under Bishops Quirico (656–683) and Idalio (683–689) Barcelona shared in the progress experienced by the Iberian peninsula in the seventh century. The first established relations with Ildefons of Toledo and with Tajon of Zaragoza, the second with Braulio of Zaragoza and with Julian of Toledo. The activities of its mints provide the evidence of continuity and even of increased activity. The eighth century brought this to a halt with the Islamic conquest. The break in continuity in Spain comes with the collapse of the Visigothic Empire. Islam and the Reconquista put their special stamp on the next phase of Spanish urban development.

What was the situation in Gaul, one of the provinces of the Roman Empire which had been richest in its urban life?[32] There were already in Gaul definite boundaries which separated the region of Gallo-Roman occupation from the predominantly Frankish areas. Because of this, the degree of continuity varied between different regions. The work of Joachim Werner[33] on the dissemination of the products of different mints and the discovery of scales for weighing gold in the Merovingian Empire reflects this. The whole of the area covered by the Merovingian Empire lacked the broad foundation of a small coinage which could be used in ordinary market transactions. After the collapse of the Roman frontier on the Rhine in the years 406–407 the mints of Gaul turned to producing copper coins. In Italy money of small denominations first disappeared in the seventh century. What remained in existence and developed in the Middle Ages was a very shrunken superstructure of money, the minting only of precious metals, gold and silver. This restriction to minting only precious metals, as practised by the Merovingians, Visigoths and Lombards, can only signify a reduced money economy. Money certainly continued to provide a standard of value but actual coins were used only in large transactions of foreign trade or else were hoarded. Basically, the precious metal itself was alone used as a standard of reckoning. In the Merovingian state south of the Seine, the ancient monetary system was still dominant as long as royally approved mintmasters coined from royal treasure a gold coinage of uniform weight and size and of an approximately equal purity which could be used for payments and mutual exchanges.

The situation in the Austrasian part of Merovingian France was different. There, coinage was rare and while money was also coined from precious metal, coinages of different date and provenance circulated side by side. It was not the nominal value of the currency which mattered here but its actual intrinsic value, which everyone had to test for himself. For this men needed scales, weights and standard ingots of precious metals. These are found widely as grave goods, particularly in the Frankish region of northern Gaul to the north of the Seine, in the Walloon areas and in the Rhineland. The regions where scales for weighing money are found and the areas of numerous Merovingian minting places appear on the map opposite. We can thus differentiate between a region of southern Gaul which

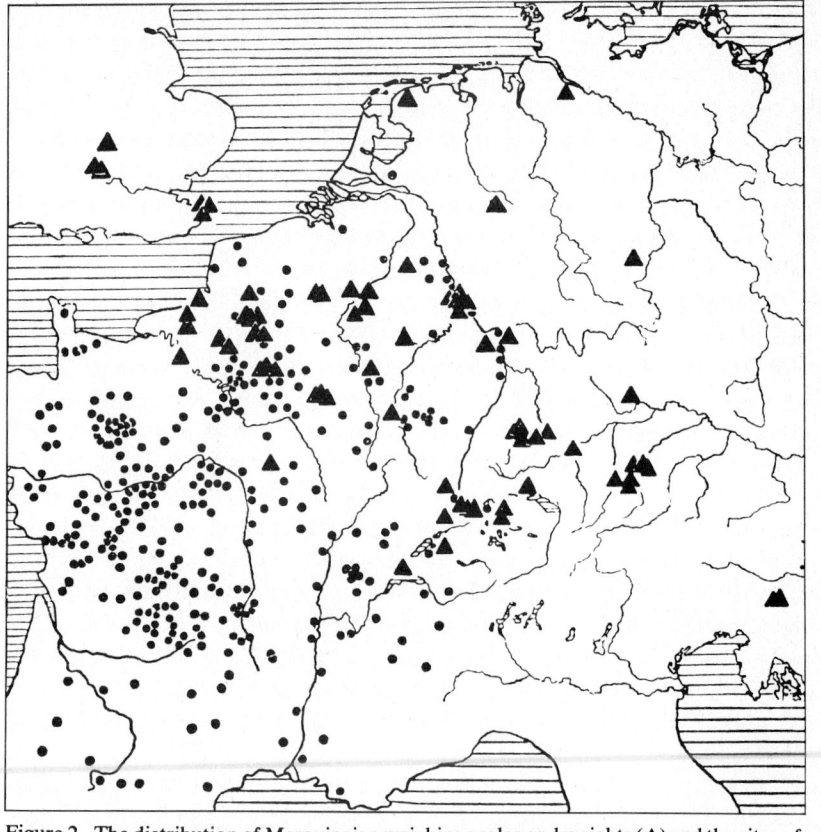

Figure 2. The distribution of Merovingian weighing scales and weights (▲) and the sites of Merovingian mints (●).

still had an active money economy and another, the north-western region extending into England, which did not.

Sources from the seventh and eighth centuries have proved the existence of old-established Merovingian royal customs offices, linked with warehouses, in Marseilles and Fos.[34] Ships came here from Italy, Byzantium and the Near East bringing spices, luxury articles and papyrus which the royal chancery was still using in the seventh century, as well as oil which the Church used in great quantity for lighting. Because of this traffic, it is recorded, the inhabitants of Dijon could afford to drink the wine of Ascalon in the sixth century if they did not care for their own Burgundian variety.

In south-western France, especially in Auvergne, the social structure still reveals features of late Antiquity. We can trace here in the sixth century the family connections between Gallic senators, active in ecclesiastical and imperial administration under Frankish rule, and the former late Roman senatorial aristocracy.[35] Gregory of Tours, the great sixth-century historian, is an example. It was altogether a small upper group, but it also knew how to maintain undivided control over its landed properties. Its understanding of ancient culture and civilization had otherwise become rather tenuous.

Many incidents in Gregory of Tours' *History of the Franks* and in the contemporary lives of the saints give evidence of urban life. In complete contrast to the cliché-ridden descriptions of the saints themselves, the remarks about their backgrounds are genuine and plausible. Belgian researchers have used them to particular effect.[36] Gregory of Tours described Dijon[37] from first hand with its strong walls, four city gates, and thirty-three towers. These Roman walls served to protect the city until the twelfth century. This is likewise true of the walls of Bourges and Poitiers, both cities with a continuous life from a Celtic-Roman as well as a Romano-Merovingian past.[38] Here dwelt rich landowners who possessed town houses and granaries, a testimony to the preservation of the social structure of Antiquity. At Angers, there was a house with three floors, a sign of shortage of space and dense building which was also a feature of Paris.

These towns were the heart of economic life. Gregory mentions that in 583 Leudast, count of Tours, when he was staying in Paris, visited the merchants' houses, searched through their wares, cast his eye on various pieces of silver and said that he would buy this and that since he still had a great deal of gold and silver. Gregory also mentions a merchant called Christophorus who travelled to Orleans because he had heard that a great quantity of wine was available there. When he had bought up the wine and transported it to his boat, he left for home with a huge sum of money which he had received from his father-in-law and travelled on horseback with two Saxon servants. From the Life of one of the bishops of Angers, written about 620, we know that merchant ships were constantly sailing up the River Loire. The Life also mentions the slave trade and this is likewise well-documented from other sources. The traffic in luxuries and, above all, the spice trade was chiefly concentrated in the hands of Syrians and Jews.

Royal authority, as well as comital and episcopal administration, all influenced the development of towns. When Bishop Desiderius of Cahors fortified his episcopal town in the seventh century, built churches within it, commissioned buildings from well-hewn stone and set-up a water system, or when King Chilperic rebuilt the arenas of Paris and Soissons, they were acting no differently from the way the emperors and great *curiales* had acted earlier on. The growth in power of the bishops in the sixth and seventh centuries is unmistakable. The break between Antiquity and the Middle Ages comes late in southern and south-western France if it is to be discerned at all clearly in the light of assured evidence. For example at Bordeaux it occurred in the eighth century.[39]

We also find foreign trade and industry if we cross the Seine. Verdun was described as a city of rich merchants in the time of Gregory of Tours. In the Rhenish episcopal towns of Mainz and Cologne, professional merchants are traceable from the eighth century onwards. The Roman routes over the Alps were still being used for trade. Coptic bronze vessels were taken by Lombards through Italy to southern Germany and up to the Rhine to England, as extensive finds of them there have shown.[40] Bowls of mother-of-pearl edged with bronze from Merovingian graves of the late fifth and sixth centuries seem to be the native work of wandering craftsmen. Immigrant craftsmen can also be shown to have existed from written evidence. For example, Bishop Nicetius of Trier, the last Roman to hold the see, had stonemasons for rebuilding Trier cathedral brought from Italy through Switzerland. In the seventh century an English abbot similarly had glass workers brought from France to make windows for his monastery. This provides evidence of an industrial activity which was no longer restricted to its town of origin and of industrial products of rare quality. Industry had not simply sunk to the level of household crafts. The glass industry of northern France and Belgium, the pottery in the Argonne as well as that of the Rhenish hills and of the Eifel, the basalt industry of the lower Eifel which distributed its mill-stones along the Rhine, are all important examples of industries with particular local connections in Merovingian times. The purely urban location of industry often disappeared. Trade came to rely on the rivers rather than the overgrown and dangerous Roman roads.

If we now turn to the towns themselves,[41] we have to rely very heavily upon archaeological evidence. As we move further and further east, written sources become scarcer and appear at a later date. We are thus dependent on the co-operation of the archaeologists for results and the scholarly responsibility for dating and interpreting finds lies chiefly with them. It is always worth remembering, however, that archaeological evidence can be as defective as written material.

Within the Meuse, Rhine and Moselle area, we can observe a further regional variation. The districts around the estuary of the Rhine experienced no continuity of urban civilization. Here, as in the *Agri decumates* east of the Rhine, the crisis of the third century marks a decisive break. On the Lower Rhine the old *Colonia Trajana* (Xanten), the second largest town of the Roman province of lower Germany, was completely abandoned about the middle of the fifth century. The cemetery and memorial over the grave of two slaughtered Christian martyrs formed the link here with the Carolingian ecclesiastical foundation around which a city grew in the high Middle Ages. Elements of continuity increase along the Rhine upstream from Xanten and along the Meuse upwards from Maastricht.

The present-day cathedral in Cologne stands on the site of the episcopal church of late Antiquity.[42] The splendid Roman governor's palace, which lies under the rebuilt city hall, was used by the Merovingians as their residence. The Roman siting of buildings here had an extraordinary measure of continuity. The area covered by the Roman *civitas Agrippinensium* continued as a *pagus* that is the *Terra Ribuarium*, which is largely identical with the later bishopric of Cologne. The kingdom of the Merovingian, Sigibert, reached southwards, past the former Cologne *civitas*. It was not this Frankish kingdom of Cologne, but the Roman territorial divisions, which determined the area of the Ripuarii within the wider Merovingian realm.

A striking phenomenon is the change in the precise location of settlements within the same localities, especially noticeable in the Frankish kingdom. Aubin was the first to point it out and he assumed that it proved that there had been destruction. His classic example was Bonn, where the cemetery church on the site of the present-day minster provided the starting-point for the town, while the site of the old legionary headquarters remained outside the medieval walls. This change of site took place very gradually. Documentary sources reveal that in 691 the church of St Cassius is described as adjoining the fortified town of Bonn (*sub oppido castro Bonna*) that is to say in the suburb of Bonn, the town itself being then identified with the fortified enclosure which at that time alone bore the name of Bonn. In the ninth century the same church was still described as sited outside the walls of the fortified Bonn (*foras muros castro Bonnense*). In the sources of the early eleventh century it is the other way round. The Dietkirche, the original old parish church in the south-west of the former fortified camp, was now described as in the suburb of Bonn (*in suburbio Bonnae*). The concept of what constituted the suburb had been completely reversed. We know today that south of the Bonn legionary camp lay the Roman civilian settlement and that the cemetery of a Christian Gallic population existed from early Frankish times near the church of the martyrs. In other words, the surviving Gallo-Roman population apparently moved to the neighbourhood of the church of the Christian martyrs.

Neuss provides a parallel case. The late Roman legionary settlement lay far from the medieval town which grew up around the Roman civilian settlement town of St Quirinus. The latest excavations have provided evidence in support of the Roman origin of this church. The great importance and attraction of the cemetery churches, built outside the Roman walls, is completely borne out. In Cologne we know that St Severin, St Gereon, and the church dedicated to St Ursula, have their foundations in religious buildings of late Antiquity. In Maastricht, the cemetery church of St Servatius was of greater importance than the church of Our Lady, itself built into a corner of the Roman castle.

Continuity of settlement is as frequent in the neighbourhoods of the *castella* on the middle Meuse as it was on the middle Rhine. The shrinking and walling of the *civitates* had blotted out the distinction between them and the Roman legionary camps, the *castra*, so that the latter could also serve as the basis of medieval towns. The very size of the ancient *civitas* might stand in the way of its survival into Frankish times. Frankish warriors had no place for huge stone ruins. They could neither restore them nor defend them. They were more accustomed to maintaining and defending small, fortified settlements or castles. Preference for water-transport over the road system which fell into neglect as a result, also favoured these castle districts. Consequently, places which lay on the old Roman road system, for example from Cologne via Bavai to Boulogne, were abandoned.

Full proof of the persistence of the ancient framework can be seen at Namur on the Meuse. On the middle Rhine, considerable continuity of settlement is to be found at Andernach, Koblenz and Boppard. We have already mentioned that at Boppard a church for the community was erected in the military baths of the Roman castle after the troops had left. The Roman fortifications survived longer, and it was not until somewhere between 1200 and 1250 that the walls were repaired and some expansion of the town centre became necessary. Boppard continued its life as a royal estate. Early Christian and early Frankish gravestones prove the permanence of the settlement.

In the case of Mainz and Speyer, we can demonstrate the shift in the main area of settlement. The first Germanic settlement primarily affected the outer districts, and for some considerable time the inner urban area remained relatively unpopulated. However, the population did return there. In Mainz[43] the great late Roman walled enclosure of 105 hectares managed to encompass the whole population of the city throughout the Middle Ages. Only on the bank of the Rhine itself was a small but important addition made to the town's area. Speyer,[44] on the other hand, was considerably enlarged in the eleventh century. The change in location of the main area of the town is revealed by the importance of the churches which were later to be found only in the suburbs. The measures of Bishop Sidonius of Mainz to deal with the rise of the Rhine's water level are an example of how a sixth-century bishop assumed the responsibility of lord of the city. Worms seems to have suffered less than Mainz from destruction in the fifth century, and in the seventh and eighth centuries it assumed the role of administrative capital of the province of southern Germany.[45] Cemeteries and religious centres are the surest proofs in all three towns of the links between Roman and Merovingian times.

The peculiarity of the Moselle area lay in the exceptional position of Trier, and in this area there is plenty of archaeological evidence of proved and unbroken habitation in the country settlements as well. In Trier, Metz, Toul and in the Saarburg area of Lorraine a Gallo-Roman population survived. There is pottery and glass of certain local provenance from Trier in the fifth and sixth centuries. The Trier Register of the Poor (*Armenmatrikel*) of the seventh and eighth centuries proves the survival of an urban lower class. Until 560 the bishops of Trier remained Romans, and we still find members of the Roman aristocracy in Trier in the seventh century; the continuous list of its bishops shows the survival of both a Christian community and of an episcopal organization there. The bishop took over the public business of the old *curia*: care of buildings and of the poor, as Venantius Fortunatus reveals that Bishop Nicetius did. In Nicetius' position as episcopal lord of Trier we can grasp the substantial element of administrative continuity between the late Roman and early medieval periods, although Trier's population had very much diminished. The huge walls, which still only enclosed one main unit of settlement, could no longer be defended. This was fatally demonstrated by the Norse raid of 882. Subsequently, the main area of habitation around the cathedral was enclosed by a palisade which arbitrarily cut across the chessboard formation of the Roman street pattern. It was now, for the first time, that Trier turned her back on her Roman past.

Metz appears in Frankish times as an episcopal seat and religious centre, rich in churches. As capital of Austrasia she now possessed greater political importance than Trier. Toul decreased in importance although its Gallo-Roman population remained and its bishops continued to be drawn from senatorial families as was Lupus of Troyes, who was born in Toul.

In the land of the Alemanni, the links with Antiquity were more tenuous, and this was also true of the populated parts of Bavaria.[46] A certain topographical continuity in Strasbourg, Augsburg and Regensburg is indisputable. Here the episcopal organization was transformed in a far more radical manner than in the Rhine and Moselle regions. At Augsburg the bishop apparently abandoned the city for Saeben-Brixen in the time of tribal migration, and the bishopric of Augsburg was then refounded by Dagobert. It thus lost its direct link with the traditions of late Antiquity. The Augsburg grave of Afra apparently survived as a religious centre. In Regensburg the cemetery of St Emmeran remained in continuous use. From the end of the seventh century at the latest, Regensburg became the centre of the duchy of Bavaria and also both an ecclesiastical and religious centre. Chur can be shown from archaeological evidence to have had an episcopal church lying within a late Roman castle, and it exhibits a similar maintenance of Roman survivals which is also confirmed by linguistic evidence from this area. Down the Danube, from Regensburg onwards, one can find no further examples of topographical continuity. The history of the lands of the Danube region in this period of transition was very much stormier and more disastrous than that of the Rhine and Moselle areas where Roman civilization had had a wider and more profound impact.

We have already noted that the Christian Church provided the surest bridge between the ages, and this is generally accepted. The number of churches also determined the outward appearance of the urban type of settlement Frankish times. French researchers speak of the 'holy Merovingian city' (*ville sainte mérovingienne*) and have excavated the various layers beneath many cathedrals. Metz has around forty Christian sites, Paris has twenty-six, Rheims has twenty-two, Trier has twenty, Lyons has eighteen and Bordeaux has between nine and eleven. For Cologne, Mainz and Besançon, the number is still more considerable.[47]

It was under the shadow of the churches that the urban way of life was preserved in the Middle Ages. According to canon law a bishop might only reside in a town. Liège is an example of this and at the same time an illustration of the strength of the respect for martyrs and saints in Frankish times. In this case, the seat of the bishop moved away from the earlier Roman *civitas* of Tongres, firstly to the burial church of St Servatius in Maastricht and after that to the burial church of St Lambert at the unimportant *villa* of Liège. We also encounter fortified episcopal sees or great religious houses as the original cores of medieval towns east of the Rhine in Germany – another example of the penetration of ancient urban ways here too.

"In contrast to the situation in Gaul", says Loyn in his survey of English developments, "the break in the continuity of town-life and villa-life was sharp and dramatic . . . This is not to deny the possibility of continuity in habitation sites at places such as London, York or Cambridge . . . Canterbury, although it changed its name from Durovernum, is one attested site for continuity". The same is true of Dorchester. At *Venta Belgarum* (Winchester), where intensive excavation of the city centre began in 1960, Biddle has located the breakdown of urban life in the fifth century and presupposed only a 'thread of continuity' to the 'early capital' of the seventh century.[48]

Areas of more varied development provide a nuanced picture of stability and then one of complete change. Topographic links of a general sort – in actual details every case differed – mean a great deal in the history of these towns but still provide little evidence of cultural continuity in the wider sense. The careful search which has been made for elements of continuity and which has illuminated the early history of our towns can be summed up in the following list of significant features and types of evidence. We start with continuity of ruins, continuity of burial places, adaption of Roman imperial residences (*regia*) as Merovingian palaces, frequently the continued existence of old Christian episcopal sees and religious centres. As additional types of evidence, we can look for the survival of a Gallo-Roman population under new lordship, the persistence of foreign trade, some industrial exports although now mostly without an urban base, the existence at a diminished level of a market economy in the old *civitates* under episcopal control. Lastly, while the old Roman cities underwent a transformation in their political status and Trier lost its preeminent place to Metz and Mainz to Worms, yet there are indirect indications that they were of some importance to their rulers.

The last echoes of Antiquity and the first signs of new beginnings often touch and even encroach upon each other so that we can speak of an age of transition rather than of an abrupt break. Most important of all are the pieces of evidence which point to the survival of an urban Gallo-Roman population, because it is that which carried the urban way of life into the age of confusion and transition. Decisive for the future structure of society will be the attitude of the new ruling class which, from the sixth century onwards, also occupied the leading positions in the Church. The question was whether its members would choose to reside in the towns and to make use of them.

If we turn our attention to the Carolingian period, and more specifically to the essential features of Carolingian society, we must recognize that the former Roman centres have turned into islands amidst a world which has become predominantly rural. That would remain for a long time the fate of the towns of central Europe. The town as a residential centre had survived the age of tribal migrations in some particularly important sites of the Rhine, Meuse and Moselle valleys, but the distinctively urban way of life with its special contributions to civilization had not survived. We should not forget that the decline in the urban way of life had already set in during late Antiquity, but what was then the expression of a permanent crisis afterwards simply became the normal state of affairs.

The countryside assumes its own separate significance. To begin with only in the suburbs of the former *civitates* but afterwards in lonely isolated districts, religious houses developed as places of higher education and culture; also as the centres of great estates, such as were owned by the nobility too, and which we can presume to have existed in France in the sixth century.[49] Industrial activity continued on these great estates. Religious houses not only moved about considerable quantities of goods within their huge possessions, often scattered over wide areas, but also participated in trade. In the seventh century the abbey of Saint-Denis was already obtaining freedom from customs at Marseilles for its oil and other products. Chlothar III gave income from the customs of Fos as a gift to the abbey of Corbie and the abbey received these in kind, in the form of goods coming from the *cellarium fisci* at Fos. According to a reckoning contained in a charter of Chilperic, Corbie received from Fos 10,000 pounds of oil, various spices in amounts varying from one to 150 pounds, much fruit from the south – olives, almonds, figs, dates and pistachios – and fifty volumes of papyrus. Saint-Germain-des-Prés, whose wine production was six times what it needed for its own consumption,[50] in 779 obtained a royal privilege permitting the abbey's traders (*negotiantes ipsius sancti loci*) to trade where they wished on both sides of the Loire so that they could obtain oil for lighting. The lord could set up a market, for there were still no regalian controls over markets. These do not appear until the second half of the ninth century, although the rights of minting and collecting customs had been regalian rights since time immemorial. Many of these markets, set up by estate owners, subsequently disappeared, but it was not only insignificant market centres which were involved. At Saint-Denis there grew up the famous market at which Anglo-Saxons and Frisians, who in the eighth century approached the Syrians and Jews in importance as traders, came to buy wine. It was apparently difficult to find as much wine as one needed on the market. The religious houses of northern France, Belgium, Westphalia and lower Saxony took care to keep in their possession some vineyards suitable for wine production.[51] The great estate-owners strove after self-sufficiency; they were not particularly market-oriented.

We have seen how the *civitas Agrippinensium* continued to exist in the Frankish Empire as the land of the Ripuarii. This survival of Roman regional divisions within the Frankish state is not an isolated example. When Chilperic ordered the dukes and counts who had been conquering Aquitaine to withdraw into the towns at the approach of the army of Guntram, he presupposed that most of these dukes and counts were living in the countryside although this was a region with plenty of towns where they might have lived. The town was not in this case their only centre.[52]

Research into the siting of Frankish palaces reveals direct continuity between Roman and Merovingian times,[53] not only in Cologne but in many other places as well. That the Merovingians continued to use palaces built by the Romans may only mean that they were unable to build new ones for financial or other reasons. Nevertheless, they aimed at establishing permanent residences. In Carolingian times, the movement of lords from one palace to another began, as did the rebuilding of some of them. Aachen and Worms under Charlemagne, Frankfurt and Regensburg under Louis the German, were all favourite stopping places, not so much real residences as the chief centres of the kingdom.

The group of men who had really become permanently resident in the towns were the bishops. In spite of all the shrinking back, one can recognize in the Roman and Romano-Christian inheritance in the area between the Seine and the Rhine a spiritual strength which influenced the Middle Ages as well as a certain material basis which was to be significant in the revival of urban life.

CHAPTER 2

New beginnings

The legacy from Rome was only one of the sources of strength of medieval urban development. New settlements of non-agrarian character created in Frankish times, business emporia chiefly on the coast, castles and markets, all reveal separate individual forms of organization, bearing at the very least within them the seeds of urban life.

This new awakening was based upon a combination of activity in the north linked to the rise of the Austrasians within the Frankish state. The appearance of Anglo-Saxons and Frisians at the fairs of Saint-Denis is an illustration of this. We must reckon with influences other than economic ones, like alterations in trade routes, as well as the political developments which accompanied the rise to power of Austrasia within the Frankish kingdom. Invasions by nomadic tribes from the steppe, the Huns at the end of the fourth century, and later of the Avars in the sixth century, destroyed links between the Black Sea and the lower Vistula and with Italy by way of Aquileia, Carnuntum and the Moravian gateway towards the Oder and the Vistula. On the other hand, the trade route which ran from the Roman centres on the lower Rhine to the coastal regions of the North Sea and across the Jutland peninsula into the western Baltic was never completely severed. After a period in the doldrums from around 500 A.D. onwards, these links between west and east revived in the seventh century although the traffic never recovered the momentum which it had had in Antiquity.

The mighty force which produced this increase in momentum in the seventh century was that of the youthful German tribes. After the end of the age of tribal migration and of far-flung conquests, with the coming of greater political stability, they turned their attention throughout the Frankish state to the peaceful activities of land reclamation and cultivation and the semi-peaceful activity of trading, which in its earliest forms was often combined with robbery. Northern European links with southern and central Gaul, which were more tenuous than those with the north, that is with England and Scandinavia, increased in importance. As new methods of organizing trade developed in coastal areas, new commercial centres sprang up from the Somme to the Baltic, and they appear in the sources as *portus*, *vicus* or *wik*. The latest researches of L. Schütte have revealed that a *wik* may not have been restricted to being a trading centre, but may have served as an agricultural settlement too. The most important of these *wiks* were Quentowic on the River Canche; secondly, a *wik* which was sited near Domburg on the island of Walcheren and which we only know from excavations; thirdly Dorestad at the junction between the Rhine and the Lek; fourthly Haithabu, a later development, which lay on the southern bank of the River Schlei; and finally Birka on Lake Mälaren in Sweden.[54]

The first certain mention of Quentowic dates from around 670. After 864 it disappears from the records. It is specifically described as the customary mainland harbour for the Anglo-Saxons journeying to Rome. It was also the harbour for Anglo-French trade and, together with Rouen, Amiens, Maastricht and Dorestad, it was among the most important of the Carolingian customs and minting places. Traders from Quentowic visited the fairs of Saint-Denis, bringing with them wine, oil and madder. Dorestad, conquered by Pippin at the end of the seventh century, became rich and famous in the eighth century and then in the second half of the ninth century lost its importance, partly because of plundering by Norsemen but also because of a succession of floods caused by the rising level of the River Rhine. Near the market place from which overseas trade was conducted, there was a fortress (*castrum*) and a church of St Martin, occasionally used by the bishops of Utrecht as a palace. Dorestad was the terminal point for links between Rhineland traders and the north. To judge from discoveries of coins, it was also closely bound up with the Frisian coastal trade. The merchant-peasants of Frisia came to Dorestad. In the winter they stayed at home on their farms and created artificial barriers to protect their settlements in an age before the permanent dykes were created, and during this season they sold their goods in and around their own neighbourhoods.

The trading routes which stretched out from this northern Frankish centre over the North Sea and up the west coast of Jutland joined there a trade route which crossed Jutland and then passed over the Baltic and through Gotland to Lake Mälaren. This was the cultural centre of the Swedish countryside then, as it is today. Its trading centre of Helgö,[55] which lay on a small island on Lake Mälaren, has yielded archaeological evidence which goes back mostly to the fifth and sixth centuries. It had a well-developed metal industry, a survival of the fine craftsmanship of the Western Empire during Antiquity. Helgö forms a link in the chain between Antiquity and the Middle Ages. In its pattern of settlement it was not a town but a collection of large farms. Later its place was taken by Birka, the central market for the countryside whose harbour was the regular meeting place for all the ships of Danes, Norsemen, Slavs and Samländers and of all the peoples of the northern Baltic. It disappeared in 970 and its role in its turn was taken over by Sigtuna until finally Stockholm developed as the main centre of this area.

Powerful Swedish royal families like the Inglings, as well as great noble families, could afford costly imported goods and fine-wrought metal work. They participated in the increasingly active trade with Western Europe. The Viking period began in the eighth century: attacks on England and Wales were largely Norwegian expeditions while it was the Danes who attacked the Frankish state. The Norwegians and Danes were primarily seeking land but commercial interests predominated for the Swedish Varangians. In 839 A.D. the Swedes appeared outside Constantinople. The first wave of Viking expansion lasted until 930.

Birka and Haithabu were the commercial centres of importance of the Viking era. In the ninth century Haithabu was the depot which bridged the transport networks of the Rhineland and Scandinavia. Its hey-day began about 900 and its decline set in about one hundred years later, while its complete elimination from being a place of any importance took place in the confusion of war in the middle of the eleventh century. Its successor was Schleswig, standing on the north bank of the River Schlei. Haithabu covered an area of some ten hectares in the ninth century, and of some 24 hectares in the tenth century. Birka was scarcely half the size. Both were in their later stages surrounded by semi-circular walls.

These *wiks* were neither primarily simply stopping places nor were they just centres for the transhipment of goods abroad, as one was earlier inclined to believe. They did grow out of the needs of foreign traders but they also had a permanently resident population, even if it were one which was being constantly augmented by immigrants from far and wide. The excavation of cemetery sites in Haithabu has clearly shown that there was a population which was both socially differentiated and specialized in different occupations. In addition to tradesmen there were also craftsmen; as well as rich merchants there were also poor people. These *wiks* also served certain centralizing functions, as both market places and religious centres. If we turn to their trade, upon which their wealth was based, it was mainly in luxury goods from abroad – wine, Rhenish pottery and glass. Haithabu was the easterly terminus for the trade in basalt from the Eifel region, and it also acted as the centre for distributing imported goods further into Sweden. The slave trade was part of this activity at this time, and Haithabu was the point of despatch for Christian slaves into Scandinavia, who were exchanged for furs. Discoveries of fine woolen cloths in graves at Birka and Kaupang in Skiringsaal, as well as at Haithabu, support the supposition that Frisian woollens were being imported. Kaupang owed its importance to the soft soapstone from which household goods could easily be made. These soapstone vessels were northern exports. Amber and iron were brought to Haithabu from the east and it then served as a centre for further distribution. Slag heaps found in this *wik* show that iron ore imported by sea from Sweden was being used as the raw material in iron production. An oven for glass-manufacture has also been found, and there is further evidence of potters and makers of wool combs. Jewellery came from the Frankish lands and from Britain and the manufacture of weapons was of great importance in the Viking period.

The foreign traders who formed the leading group in the *wiks* did not conduct their business from the *wik* itself but actually travelled with their goods so that they have come to be known as 'itinerant merchants'. This is not meant to imply that they were constantly on the move and possessed neither house nor farm, wife nor children. They did possess them, either in the *wik* itself or in the countryside, for not all of them resided in the *wik*. Some only came there to trade and divided their time between that and large-scale farming. Seasonal trading by peasants remained a feature of Norwegian life until well into the Middle Ages. One Norwegian merchant who lived on the land is well known. He was Ottar from Heligoland, who travelled to the court of the learned English king, Alfred the Great, and provided a description of the northern lands for Alfred's translation of Orosius.[56] Ottar's prosperity did not depend upon his relatively small farm where he had twenty cows, twenty sheep, and twenty pigs, nor upon the small amount of ploughed land which he worked himself with his horses. It depended on his large herds, which he hired out, for he possessed 600 domestic beasts as well as six costly hunting beasts used as decoys. He also relied upon the Finnish tribute levied in animals' hides, birds' feathers, whale-bones and ships' ropes, made of whale-skin or sealskin bound together. He could not himself use the whole of this Finnish tribute and so he brought the surplus to market. He sailed along the west coast of Norway to Skiringsaal and from there further to Haithabu; his second major market was in England. He also made regular voyages of discovery and reached the White Sea; as he said, his purpose was partly to discover how far north the land remained inhabited but he was probably also in search of opportunities for buying furs. He also went on pilgrimage. This Ottar was thus far from being resident in a *wik*.

Haithabu must have presented a colourful picture when the merchants were newly arriving and the great caravans were appearing in the *wik*. As well as Norwegians and Anglo-Saxons, an Arab merchant from Spain is known to have visited it. Many of the regular visitors certainly had special places to stay in the *wik* even if they did not actually live there. These foreign merchants were always ready for adventure and were well-prepared to take risks; they knew as well how to wield a sword as to steer a ship, could converse in different languages and knew many lands and tribes. It was a Frankish merchant, Samo, a political adventurer, who managed to found a Slav state.

These traders were freemen, either northern peasants or lesser notables. The Frankish merchants in Dorestad were liable to the royal officials neither for the usual hospitality renders nor for customary death duties. This was laid down in a charter of Louis the Pious for merchants going to Dorestad. These exemptions were also enjoyed by the men of the church (*homines ecclesie*) of St Martin of Utrecht, though they were free from these dues owing to royal officials because of the immunity of their church.

Apparently the kings did have possessions as well as certain rights in the *wiks*. They established an official there, known as the *wikgrave* or *wik* prefect, as we know from evidence from Birka, Haithabu and Quentowic. The *wikgrave* was a high official. For instance Hergeir, the prefect of Birka, was a trusted royal councillor. At Quentowic, the *illuster vir*, or illustrious lord, Gripo was the official, and Charles the Bald entrusted him with diplomatic missions to the Anglo-Saxon court. Quentowic and Dorestad were important to the rulers as royal customs places. There are already signs of a special mercantile law in Carolingian times, for the kings assured the legal standing of their merchants in foreign lands by bi-partite agreements with the rulers of those lands.[57] However, this royal lordship over the *wik*, exercised not by the ruler in person but delegated to the *wikgrave*, affected neither the merchant's freedom of movement nor his independence. He conducted trade at his own risk and enjoyed the profits from it. In the north, royal control was especially hedged about with limitations: customarily "a decision was taken on each public question more in accordance with the common will of the people than as the consequence of royal authority" (*quodcumque negotium publicum magis in populi unanimi voluntate quam in regia constet potestate*). This was the comment of Rimbert, biographer of Ansgar, about a revealing incident on one of Ansgar's Swedish journeys.[58]

What is more, these merchants had organized themselves.[59] They travelled in convoy and within the *wik* itself they were organized into guilds. A rune stone provides evidence that the merchants of Hai-thabu were meeting together before undertaking commercial ventures. A guild of Frisian merchants at Sigtuna certainly goes back to at least the tenth century. Prohibitions of guild associations in the Capitulary of Herstal of 779; in the Capitulary of Thionville of 805; in the Capitulary of Louis for Italy of 822; in Carloman's Edict of 884 and in the Statutes of Hincmar of Rheims of 852, all provide evidence of their existence in the Frankish Empire. Scandinavia and northern Germany also had peasant guilds.[60] Specialization of occupation was not, as we have already mentioned, so well developed in the north. The Germanic guilds specified which group of relatives, left behind at home, would extend their protection to a travelling member, or they offered him the protection of a lord. It was a purely fraternal relationship in contrast to the one which bound the followers of a lord to their master. It was more than an extended blood-brotherhood relationship although an element of blood-brotherhood did enter into it. It was also a ritualistic and social grouping and the guild banquet was an expression of this. Banquets played a large part in guild life and appear in a Christianized form in the eleventh century. An essential element in the guild banquet was to honour the dead, which was a combination of both the obligation inherent in the blood-brotherhood relationship and also of the religious needs of the group. The guild, while it was certainly centrally bound fast by oath-swearing, was otherwise loosely organized. It consisted of a head, aldermen and the guild assembly. It was an exclusive personal association and the acceptance of a member was dependent upon the assent of all the guildsmen. Its chief means of punishment or pressure was expulsion from the guild.

The assembly called the *thing* in the *wik* of Birka appears to have had nothing to do with the guild. We have therefore to reckon with three separate authorities in the *wik*: the royal official, the *thing* (*placitum*) and the guild. How the constitution of the *wik* functioned in detail and how the authority was divided between the royal *wikgrave* and the guild, as well as the relationship between the *thing* and the population, is obscure because written evidence is so scanty. In this case, the archaeologists likewise can give us no further help.

It is significant that this group of foreign merchants, whether peasants, or notables engaged in trade or resident dealers under the *wikgraves'* authority and royal protection, is clearly distinguishable from the unfree population, the great estate owners and above all from the clerical landowners who were organizing long-distance commercial enterprises. The residents in the *wik* thus represented a first step in the emergence of traders, destined ultimately to develop into a professional merchant class.

Where should we place the *wik* in the story of the development of the medieval town? The problem which we must now face is that of their disappearance. The rise, hey-day and decline of the *wik* can be compressed into two centuries. They had their successors: Quentowic was replaced by Montreuil, Dorestad mainly by Tiel and to some degree by Utrecht and Deventer, Haithabu by Schleswig and Birka by Sigtuna, but the rupture is too complete to permit us to speak of a transplanting of the settlement, apart perhaps from the case of Haithabu. When Quentowic and Dorestad disappeared, there remained the neighbouring customs' centres of Rouen, Amiens and Maastricht and in the ninth century a new series of places sprang up – Deventer, Tiel, Bruges, Ghent, Antwerp and Valenciennes.[61]

About 800 A.D. Emden came into existence. It was excavated after the last war[62] and was found to be a settlement consisting of one main street occupied by craftsmen and tradesmen, similar to that found on the island of Walcheren and too small to have been a farming centre.

The settlement also possessed a wooden church, and an artificial mound built for security on a marsh. Both hill and settlement were extended in the tenth century. Here, the merchants of Frisia possessed their own non-agricultural centre and they traded in their own wares. Mentions in written sources of the import of textiles from Frisia by the abbeys of Fulda and Werden has been interpreted, in the light of archaeological evidence, as referring to trade in Frisian cloth and not to the distribution by Frisians of Flemish products. Excavations by Feddersen Wierde also suggest that, early on, farmers at Emden filled out their work day with crafts and trade and indeed that the people of the poor northern areas were dependent upon such extra activities for survival.[63]

Continuity in Emden, where the present Pelzstrasse (Fur street) corresponds to the old main street of the earliest settlement, should serve as a warning against drawing exaggerated conclusions from the disappearance of the other *wiks*. Disasters provide only part of the explanation. Natural catastrophes, and the destruction caused by war played their part in the disappearance of Haithabu and Dorestad but were a much rarer cause of the final disappearance of a settlement than superficial consideration would suggest. The disappearance of so many *wiks* suggests that this early urban phenomenon of the business emporium represented a first tentative step in bringing new towns into existence which did not always prove successful. What was lacking in these *wiks* which disappeared was the stability which larger and more prosperous settlements enjoyed and which helped towns to survive periods of depression. The *wiks* did not possess great communal buildings. While they were able to offer their inhabitants only limited protection, their wealth was nevertheless sufficient to attract plunderers. When the exiled Swedish king, Anund, sought to recover his crown with Danish aid, he offered his allies rich gains in return for their help; he would take them to Birka where there were many rich merchants and an abundance of goods and treasure. The prefect of the *wik*, Hergeir, had only the traders and local people available for defence. Full of terror, they fled to the nearby castle and immediately ransomed their *wik* for one hundred silver pounds. The same story was told of the merchants of Tiel in the eleventh century who surrendered their *wik* under similar circumstances "because they were merchants" (*quia mercatores erant*), confirming by this remark the poor opinion of the ecclesiastical chroniclers for merchants.

The irregular and wandering life of these leading merchants meant that they were not so firmly bound to the *wik* as later town dwellers were to be to their settlements, or as the survivors of the Gallo-Roman population were, who continued to dwell within the ruinous but still grandiose Roman towns. The *wiks* lacked such a tradition, and they also lacked solid foundation within the surrounding countryside. Dhondt attributed deeper and more conclusive causes to the disappearance of Quentowic than simply coastline changes, alteration in trade routes or even plundering by the Vikings.

First of all we have to note the absence of deep roots in the case of these Merovingian mushroom towns. They do not seem solidly anchored to the soil. These emporia constituted alien enclaves within the Carolingian world rather than organically belonging to it.

Since they came into existence as trading centres, they were dependent on the fate of the trade routes and reacted sharply to changes in them. This was true of Quentowic, which declined in importance with the revival of the transcontinental route from the Baltic to Byzantium. The trading emporia remained too one-sidedly non-agrarian, one-purpose settlements in spite of the beginnings of industrial activity in them and of their centralizing functions. As in the parallel case of hill towns, as one-purpose settlements they were extremely susceptible to collapse. We can perhaps by now better appreciate the significance of the purely topographical continuity in the urban settlements of Roman origin.

There was a much greater chance of survival for those trading centres which lay near earlier Roman settlements: namely the Merovingian *vici* of Namur, Huy, Dinant and Maastricht on the middle Meuse, which in Carolingian times all had the name *portus*, as well as those of Tournai and Metz, the Merovingian minting centres Marsal, Vic s. Seille, Moyenvic and Dieuze in the Moselle-Seille region, and lastly the later settlements of Frisian merchants at Cologne, Mainz and Worms, who also met in these episcopal towns groups of native traders. The Meuse centres profited from the strategic position of the Meuse-Moselle area under the Carolingians,[64] and from their siting at the junction of river and crossroads at a time when river transport was becoming increasingly important. We must also take into account, as Despy's[65] findings have shown, the links between the towns and countryside around them and their functions as a market centre as early as the Carolingian period. The estate survey of Prüm of 893 shows that the hinterland there experienced a sharp increase in population which, since the dues remained static, meant a certain amount of prosperity for the peasantry. They had their own wares –

wool, linen and pig-iron – which they brought to market. In addition to the 'ports' (*portus*) on the Meuse, which were all destined to develop into medieval industrial towns, there existed also the market centres which would never manage to become towns like the pilgrimage centre dedicated to St Hubert in the Ardennes. As we shall see, among early medieval market places as well as among trading emporia, similar processes of selection will operate to determine which of them will ultimately develop into towns.

If we turn to the inland areas east of the Rhine, we arrive at the question of the relationship between castle and town.[66] We must not fall into the error of seeing the development of the castle solely in relationship to that of the town. Castles had also played a major role in the development of purely rural settlements since the early middle Ages. The uncertain situation in the ninth and first half of the tenth centuries created by the Viking, Saracen and Hungarian invasions, had brought about, in rather a haphazard way, an increase in the number of fortified places of the most diverse kind. A major step was the reconstruction of old Roman walls. There is evidence of this in north-eastern France, on the Rhine, in the Danube region and in northern Italy. Abbeys and palaces were fortified and refuge-places were erected anew, and the tenth-century Henrician castles in Germany belong to this last category.[67] Castle building in central Europe is, however, much older. Mention may be made here of the Germanic fortified places (*oppida*) with their links with the Celts, which were not specifically urban in character. The *caput gentis Mattium* in Hesse was a Germanic *oppidum* of this kind, abandoned after the destruction wrought by Germanicus. These fortified centres reveal that the Germans were accustomed to living in defended enclosures before they were familiar with towns. The Franks and Alemanni thought of the Roman towns as castles and spoke of Kolnaburg, Strasbourg, Augsburg and so on. Dannenbauer's notion of a Germanic aristocracy resident in towns has never been substantiated by archaeological evidence.[68] A passage from Gregory of Tours[69] illustrates this point, in which he reports on the campaign of King Childebert against the Frankish magnates Ursio and Bertefred. The king ordered his army to break into the refuge which the two had fortified:

In Woëvregau there was a farmhouse (*villa in pago*) (*Vabrense*) dominated by a steep hill. On its summit was a church dedicated to St Martin. Here, long ago, there had been a castle (*ibi castrum antiquitus fuisse*) but now the place was no longer defended by human constructions but solely by its position. The defenders now had to barricade themselves into this church with their possessions, women and servants.

Such actions are hardly suggestive of nobles accustomed to castles.

We must not overlook the links connecting the Germanic *oppida* with the various types of Carolingian fortress. One often finds a fortified settlement of the double type, consisting of a castle proper and a suburb outside it. The fortresses of Saxony, which played a part in the wars against the Franks, are examples of this type of construction. One can name as instances investigated by Schuchhardt: Iburg near Driburg, Eresburg (Obermarsberg), Hohensyburg, Braunsberg near Höxter and the Herlingburg (Skidroburg) near Schieder. They consisted of high fortresses ringed with large walls. Widukind described such Saxon fortresses which consisted of a castle, and a civic settlement, that is of *urbs* and *suburbium*, and he calls them *oppida*. Whether these *suburbia* consisted of anything more than outer fortifications, whether craftsmen or traders occupied them and whether markets were held there, it is impossible to say with any certainty. The Saxon fortress of Eresburg continued its existence incorporated within the medieval town of Obermarsberg. At its foot, around 900, was the market centre of Horhausen, present-day Niedermarsberg. Louis the Child granted the abbey of Corvey the market, customs and minting rights of 'Horohuson', and this early medieval market belonging to the abbey, under the protection of the old Saxon fortress, lies at the heart of the early medieval town of Horhausen, whose further development failed to live up to its early promise.

The Franks had at their disposal, in the face of Saxon attacks, former Roman towns, *castella*, like Deutz which the Saxons were already threatening in 557 or Utrecht, whose existence as a *castellum* is mentioned from the sixth century. In non-Romanized Germany Büraberg near Fritzlar was accounted a great Frankish fortress. On his mission to Hesse in 723 Boniface came to the *Donareiche* in Geismar and built the wooden church of St Peter in Fritzlar. He made Büraberg, which he termed an *oppidum*, into an episcopal seat. At the highest point in Büraberg today there remains a chapel with a cemetery which is still in use. Büraberg, to judge from most recent excavations, had the lay-out of a town: a fortress covering an extensive area with a permanent settlement within it, and with a mixed agricultural-industrial outer settlement.[70] It was abandoned as a fortress about 850. The bishopric of Büraberg was perpetuated as an ecclesiastical district within the archdeaconry of the abbey of St Peter of Fritzlar. Fritzlar took over Büraberg's ecclesiastical position and here, where in Carolingian times there had been a market settlement, an abbey with a royal palace and finally a fortress, there grew up the medieval town.

The Frankish *curtes* formed another type of fortified settlement of medium size found chiefly in Hesse and Westphalia. Stengel and Görich[71] see in them the origin of the medieval towns east of the Rhine but they were never more than just settled localities.

According to Schlesinger,[72] Erfurt and Würzburg represent significant early urban forms of development between the Rhine and the Elbe. As well as being the centre of the Thuringian countryside, Erfurt also lay from early times at the junction of ancient international trade routes. Its development proceeds from a pre-Frankish fortress on the Petersberg within which was built a royal hall and the royal abbey of St Peter. Erfurt was also temporarily designated as a bishopric and remained an important ecclesiastical centre. In the Capitulary of Thionville, of 805, it appears as a border post trading with the Slavs. Its oldest merchants' quarter lay at the foot of the Petersberg and under its protection. A second merchant colony lay on the right bank of the Gera. In Würzburg, too, development began with a fortress, namely with the old ducal castle combined with the church of St Mary on the left bank of the River Main. The church of St Mary began as an episcopal church but in the eighth century the bishop's seat was removed to the right bank of the Main where a trading settlement then sprang up. The Capitulary of Thionville also mentions Bardowiek near the later medieval towns of Lüneburg and Magdeburg. At Magdeburg, on the site of an older pre-Carolingian castle within the great fortified episcopal enclosure, Charlemagne erected a new castle. Castle and merchants' settlement formed the beginnings of the development which was to give Magdeburg its age of major development under the Ottonian emperors.

This link between castle and merchants' settlement was a common pattern in the area between the Rhine and the Elbe. But we must take into account an alien, Mediterranean element in this, namely a notable religious institution in the shape of an episcopal see or abbey.

The extent to which these elements cut across one another can be illustrated from the case of the coastal port of Hamburg.[73] The 'Hammaburg' was erected here under the aegis of the baptismal and

missionary church of Archbishop Ansgar. In 845 it was destroyed by
the Vikings:

The surprising swiftness of this event allowed no time for the men from the surrounding area to assemble (*pagenses congregandi*). What is more, the count who was the
commander of the place, the noble lord Bernhar, was not at hand. When the lord bishop
first heard of the appearance of the enemy, he first of all wanted to defend the place
using the inhabitants of the castle and of the unfortified *wik* (*in suburbio*) until
reinforcements arrived. However, the heathens attacked and the castle was already
encircled. He now appreciated the importance of defending the outer areas and
pondered how he might save the holy relics entrusted to his care ... also the people
who could escape from the castle rushed about in confusion. Most had a narrow
escape, some were captured and very many were slain. After they had entered, the
enemy thoroughly plundered the fortified city (*civitas*) and the neighbouring *wik* (*vicus
proximus*); they made their appearance in the evening and remained that night and the
following day and night. After completely ransacking the place and putting it to the
flame, they disappeared again. The church which had been rich in artistic objects and
the wonderful monastery erected by the bishop were burned to the ground. Together
with numerous other books, the splendid bible given to our father by the noble
emperor, was destroyed. Everything which Ansgar possessed there, church vessels as
well as other valuable objects, was lost, either robbed or burnt during the enemy's
raid.[74]

The fortified enclosure remained abandoned and the bishopric was
transferred to Bremen but the former *wik* settlement continued to
exist and expanded further in the second half of the ninth and tenth
centuries. Economic survival was clearly not too dependent on the
fortified city.

We can sense from Rimbert's report the terrible shock which the
appearance of the Vikings had caused, but although it started by
being devastating, the long-term effect of contact with the Vikings
was a stimulating one. It was not only that they revived the need for
realizing the importance of town fortifications: their travels far and
wide also brought distant regions into commercial contact with the
west. Numismatics provide telling evidence of this. Silver dirhems,
struck in Iran or Turkestan, flooded Scandinavia. About 80,000 have
been found in Sweden, half of them in Gotland alone, 4000 in
Denmark and 400 in Norway. How much was booty, how much
tribute, ransom or the result of commercial transactions it is impossible to say.

There were also foreign trade links to the south and east. Regens-
burg and Lorsch are both mentioned in the Capitulary of Thionville.
Detailed information about the situation on the border between
Bavaria and the Slav lands is available in the toll list of Raffelstetten

(903–905), a place which has now disappeared. This document was the subject of a masterly study by Ganshof.[75] As the result of a variety of complaints about unlawful tolls, Louis the Child ordered a special meeting of the local court (*placitum*) to be held at Raffelstetten under the jurisdiction of the margrave. At the meeting of the court the local notables were to testify about the tolls as they had validly been operating earlier on. The first three clauses deal with the Bavarians who travelled down the Danube from the Forest of Passau to the Bohemian Forest. Their main interest was in the salt trade. Any salt which they transported for their own household use was exempt from customs as long as the ship-owner confirmed this on oath. If anyone sailed to a lawful market (*mercatum legitimum*) without either paying anything or making a declaration, he was liable to the confiscation of both vessel and cargo. If a serf came, he was to be detained until his lord came and paid. We have here another instance of trade being conducted by landowners using their unfree tenants. The salt shipped was Reichenhall salt and the lords possessed either salt-pits or shares in a salt mine. Slaves, mainly Slav prisoners of war, were also used in trading by these people. The Bavarians were allowed to buy and sell and hold a market wherever they wished. Two places are named as having been particularly favoured by them, Rosdorf in the Aschach basin, which no longer exists, and Linz. Whoever paid his salt toll at Linz could proceed further without paying again.

The second part of the document refers to people who took the land route through the Traungau, especially those from Bavaria and the 'Slavs of that land' (*sclavi istius patriae*), that is the Slovenes from southern and south-eastern Bavaria. They came with their slaves, horses, oxen and household goods and could buy whatever they needed throughout the area without being liable to pay tolls. They could market their goods without being arrested as long as they kept to the middle of the street. If they preferred to make their purchases in the market, they could do so on as favourable terms as possible but would then be obliged to pay tolls. Perhaps in spite of the tolls, it was still advantageous to buy in the market where there was a more comprehensive and regular supply of goods. This toll was a market toll. Stipulations about favourable prices offered a protection against the toll collector as the toll rose with the price of the goods. Salt carts which took the lawful route (*strata legitima*) along the Enns were obliged to pay a transit toll in salt. Boats from the Traungau could transport salt from the warehouse on the Traun as well as from

Steyr on the Enns. If they came from Traungau itself they were free of tolls.

The third part of the document, except for the last sentence, deals with the Slavs who were not resident in Bavaria and who were thus regarded as foreigners. They came from Bohemia and Old Russia by the route through Kiev, Krackow, and Prague in order to trade. They paid tolls on their imported goods which they then sold: wax, slaves and horses. The rate of toll was laid down. The Bavarians and Bavarian Slavs, as the last sentence confirms, paid nothing. They were allowed to buy imported goods freely and to sell their own wares, chiefly salt, to foreigners as they pleased. The fourth part of the document again deals with the Bavarians who chiefly shipped their salt on the Danube and so reached beyond the Danube and beyond any of the places mentioned in the first part of the document. The owners of these salt boats were not permitted, after they had passed through the Bohemian Forest, to land anywhere, nor to buy or sell until they reached Eperasburg (Ybbs?). There they paid the duty of three bushels of salt for every "lawful vessel" (*navis legitima*). This meant every boat of a specific customary size, manned by three people; after that they could proceed to Mautern, opposite Krems, or to any other salt market. There, they again paid three bushels which thereafter gave them the right to buy and sell at the best price they could get without fear of any further interference either by the count or by anyone else. The salt trade operated in this region under strict regulations, and could only be carried on in the officially sanctioned markets. This was intended to prevent dealers from defrauding the tolls. The fifth section concerns the Bavarians who traded in the Great Moravian state. For them, there was a sort of export duty. There was also, of course, the question of what customs the Moravian ruler would levy.

The sixth and concluding section of the Rafelstetten toll list deals with the truly professional merchants (*mercatores*), the Jews and others who came from Bavaria and from outside it. They paid the just dues (*iustum teloneum*) as before. The Bavarians who were trading, and whom we have already met, were not professional merchants and were not described as merchants. They were big and small landowners exploiting the salt mines and pits and who chiefly dealt in salt, although they occasionally also traded in slaves and other wares. They enjoyed far-reaching toll privileges and consequently what they owed had to be strictly defined. In the case of the professional merchants it was simpler.

They paid tolls according to legally enacted tariffs. Thus, the document clearly differentiated between professional merchants and landowners engaged in trade, a distinction which we have already met in the northern parts of the Frankish state. It reveals also the strict regulation of market organization as well as the significance of the markets to society.

We should now consider these markets.[76] While trading *wiks* and castles were becoming linked together within a single settlement, the market might also have no permanent location but be held fleetingly in some street or other. We need to distinguish between the annual market and the fair (*feria*), which was an annual market of particular importance, and the weekly and daily markets. The latter were closely bound up with life in the settlement, played a part in the town's development and helped to keep it going. Naturally, markets were held in the *wiks* and, even if to a lesser extent, also in the old *civitates*. Otherwise we hear little about them. The reform synod of 744 made it the duty of the bishop to supervise the use of the correct weights and measures as well as to ensure the proper regulation of the market (*legitimos foros et mensuras*). The term forum employed for the market in late Antiquity was abandoned in France in the eighth century in favour of *mercatus/mercatum*. Forum, however, reappeared in the Meuse area in the tenth century. Many new markets came into existence in Carolingian times. Finally, the king had to assume responsibility for those visiting the market and control over the market itself. In the eastern Frankish state, where there was a considerable need for new markets, the market regalian right came into existence in the second half of the ninth century. Already in 833, when the abbey of Corvey sought a royal privilege because it lacked a market in the vicinity, it was conceded a mint. Corvey and Würzburg are the first minting places east of the Rhine. In 861, however, they were joined by Prüm which, because it was too distant from either mint or market, was granted both a market and the right to strike coins for its estate of Rommersheim, while the market toll was assigned to the abbey. Here, there is already evidence of a particular need for a market – *mercatum more humano* – which would become narrowly defined in the charters of later periods. When Louis the German confirmed to the abbey of Saint-Denis the existing market near its dependent cell at Esslingen on the Neckar, a very favourable location from the point of view of transport, he also bestowed his protection on the market. The link was established between market and immunity, which was important because it brought a territorial element into the market privilege. In 898 King Zwentibold granted the abbey of Münstereifel a market, royal mint and two-thirds of the market tolls. A tri-partite concession, already classical, comprising market, toll and mint as well as the conception of a public market appeared in 900 in Louis the Child's privilege to the abbey of Corvey for its *villa* of Horhausen at the foot of the Eresburg. The bailiff of the abbey could, under threat of royal punishment, demand payment of customary market tolls from those coming to transact business. In 908 the bishop of Eichstätt was permitted, at his own request, to have a market and mint and to levy tolls as was customary in a market place and to build fortifications against Hungarian raiding (*urbem construire*). In 911 Charles the Simple granted Bishop Stephen of Cambrai the right to fortify his palace on his hereditary domain of Lisdorf, today incorporated into the town of Saarlouis, and also granted the rights to hold a market and erect a mint. There is no evidence, however, that any development actually took place. It was again Charles the Simple who bestowed upon the abbey of Prüm in 919 the right to establish one market in a suitable place of its choice within the abbey's lands (*si rectores eius loci utile judicarint, mercatum statuant in quocumque potestatis sue loco voluerint*). No regalian rights over markets developed in the kingdom of the western Franks, partly because there were already sufficient old markets in existence and partly because the power of the king was very weak.[77] East of the Rhine, the development set in train in the ninth century continued without set-backs to Ottonian times. The link between market and landowner remained strong; it was he who controlled all privileges. The organization of the market remained subordinated to territorial lordship.

What types of early towns did the Slavs develop? Here, recent research in Bohemia-Moravia and in Poland has produced surprising results. [78] The situation in the western Slav region has something in common with the early forms of towns in central Europe, namely with the castle-market towns of the area between the Rhine and the Elbe. In the so-called Great Moravian state, the nobility possessed strong castles in the Moravian hills and in western Czechoslovakia. The interesting Moravian sites are those of Mikulčice, near the town of Hodonin or Göding, and Stare Město, that is the Old City, near the town of Uherské Hradiště or Hradisch in Hungarian). They display levels of settlement going back to the time of the Great Moravian state. The excavations in Mikulčice have produced finds which reveal far-reaching trade links as well as the existence of specialized crafts-manship. It seems to have been a large-scale settlement, having something of the character of a town with a population which was socially differentiated and specialized according to occupation. The remains of a palace as well as of four or five churches and the elaborate lay-out of a dozen graves reveal it as an important centre of political and religious life with a population of about 1,000 in-habitants. It possessed at least one fortified suburb. Frankish, Irish-Scottish and Byzantine influences can all be traced here. The presence of German clergy was also not without significance. Stare Město was a settlement covering the very considerable area of two hundred hectares but with its buildings laid out in a rather scattered pattern; it consisted in fact of several fortified centres with craftsmen grouped around each of them. The whole conglomeration amounted to being at most an urban village. These settlements in Great Moravia still pose many unresolved questions. With the collapse of the state of Great Moravia in 906 they disappeared, being either wholly aban-doned or reduced to the level of mere villages. When urban life reappeared in Moravia, it was as the result of the increasing im-portance of the Bohemian state to which Moravia became linked.

Secure within its protection of mountains, Bohemia stood fast against the Hungarian invasions which toppled the state of Great Moravia. It experienced a swift economic development, concentrated in the first place in Prague where the seat of the prince was transfer-red in the late ninth century. The country was christianized under the rule of St Wenceslas between 915 and 929. Arab travel reports picture Prague as it was in the tenth century.

The city is built of stone and chalk and it is the great trading centre of the land. Russians come here from Krakow as do the Slavs with their wares. From the land of the Turks (Hungarians), Moslems, Jews and Turks come with their wares and with minted coins. They export slaves, tin and various hides. Their land is the best of the northern lands and the richest in life's necessities. One can buy enough wheat for a penny to last a month, and for another penny one can buy enough barley to maintain a riding horse for forty days. Ten hens cost a penny. They manufacture saddles, bridles, and solid shields in the city which are used in these lands. A thin, loosely woven cloth like net is also manufactured which has no real practical use. They fix its price at ten cloths for one penny. They both trade in it and use it for payment and possess it by the trunkful, for it is accounted wealth and one can buy the costliest things with it: wheat, slaves, horses, gold, silver, everything possible. It is curious that the inhabitants of

Bohemia are brown-skinned and dark-haired and one seldom encounters anyone of the blond type.[79]

This text reveals Prague as an already populous town in which the streams of foreign and local trade converged. Some features, if they are correct, suggest certain archaic survivals, for example the use of the fine, small cloths as money. Prague was also at that time a centre of political life and an episcopal see. Archaeological finds confirm what this report says, with the exception of some details, for example the exaggeration of the number of stone buildings. In the second half of the tenth century, Prague consisted of a castle and a number of suburbs. We do not know the site of the market. There were in any case at least two, one in a Prague suburb and one in the *wik* of Wyshegrad (*in suburbio Pragensi et vico Vissegradensi*). Its foreign trade grew up primarily along the route from Regensburg via Prague to Krakow and Kiev.

Study of castle walls has been instructive in helping us to understand the situation in Bohemia outside Prague. The old walled castles, especially in eastern Bohemia, were similar to the fortifications in the state of Great Moravia. The new sites of the tenth century were small, about two to five hectares in size. While part of the older wall system collapsed, another part shrank to a small proportion of its former size. The privileged status of a small number of people dwelling within these castles has always been appreciated. With their help, the great lords, like the Premyslids, maintained their power. The castles became centres of districts, with more recent settlements becoming centres of the subdivisions of these districts.

The two phases of development which we have sketched here have been clearly shown by Gieysztor to have been phenomena common to the Slav peoples. He traced the foundations of the Pomeranian towns of Wollin, Kolberg, Stettin and Kammin to the mighty fortresses of the ninth-century state of Great Moravia, as well as the Polish centres of Gniezno, Stradow and Chodlik, and also Russian centres like Kiev, Smolensk, Ladoga, Pskow and perhaps Novgorod. He also mentioned the very localized emporium of Reric on the Baltic, but attributed to it a position of special importance.

In general, and in comparison with the second phase, these ninth-century castle sites were not numerous. The concentration of political power was less clearly marked than it was to be later on. There were still many freemen who stood in opposition to the lords of the castles and they had a right to intervene in public affairs. This changed in the course of the tenth and eleventh centuries, which saw overwhelming power being concentrated more and more into the hands of the nobility and of the state. Thus, Gieysztor applies the term "castle towns" (*villes d'état*) to the defensive towns of the second phase, distinguishing them from the earlier sites, which he denoted "magnate towns" (*villes des grands*). The castle towns were numerous: ten in Moravia, fifteen in Bohemia and sixty in Poland within present-day frontiers. One is bound to admire both the industry and the sagacity of the Polish researchers who discovered them. These were central points dominating a limited region. They consisted of the *suburbium* belonging to the castle and of the castle (*castrum*) itself – in Poland the mighty constructions of timber and stone with a lattice pattern reveal further developments in the techniques of using timber at a time when the west was beginning to turn to stone building. The suburb could perhaps best be described as a fortified craftsman's settlement. The castle was the seat of the prince or of his deputy with his following of clergy and laymen and the castle servants. From the economic point of view it formed a centre of consumption. How was it provided with goods for its daily needs? Apparently a free market and commercial movement of goods between the castle and surrounding countryside did not operate. Rather was it the case that the granary was filled with the dues delivered in kind by the unfree peasantry of the castle-district. The fact that there were villages of craftsmen in the neighbourhood of the *suburbium* seems to indicate that industrial production had not reached a very high level. The craftsmen in the suburb were not freemen who worked for wages or to sell their goods in the market; they belonged to the lordly organization centred on the castle, and received from the lord a paltry proportion of the dues of the unfree peasantry. An eleventh-century Czech source shows that men were forced to leave the land to work as craftsmen in the suburb. In addition, they had themselves to contribute to their own main-tenance for which they worked allotments around the castle; their way of life in the suburb was therefore that of craftsmen-peasants. As major centres of consumption, the castles assured their supplies not through economic means but through their power to compel suburbs and villages to minister to their needs. They obtained dues in the form of industrial goods as well as of farm produce. The craftsmen in the suburbs were dependent upon this lordly class in the castles for whom they worked. The lords, for their part, were able to accumulate wealth and thus the means to buy luxury foreign goods. The merchant group still largely consisted not of professional merchants, but of members of the class of wealthy landowners. There were also foreign merchants, only a few of them German but either Jewish or, as in the settlements along the coast in the tenth century, Scandinavians.

With the coming of Christianity to Poland, some of these castle-centres also became bases of ecclesiastical organization. Gniezno and Poznan are both examples of this. The clergy were of foreign extraction, Rhinelanders, Bavarians, Saxons and Irish, and the Church brought with it the first admixture of western culture. In general, indigenous development still lay in the future. In Poznan, for instance,[80] the Slav castles lay on the right bank of the River Warta. An early ninth-century castle with a small suburb was destroyed in 950 but was soon rebuilt and in 968 became an episcopal see. This settlement was in its turn destroyed in 1039 and at the end of the eleventh century a new castle was built on the site now occupied by the Romanesque cathedral, and two suburbs were created. In the thirteenth century the main economic and political centre shifted to the left bank of the Warta, where the development of the community was strongly influenced by the presence of foreign merchants from western Europe.

The castle towns of Old Russia also had Slav origins. The Varangians saw Russia as the land of fortified settlements, as a realm of towns. Much of the early history of these places has been the subject of controversy between Scandinavian and Russian scholars. It is true that Kiev, by the end of the tenth century, was already an urban settlement with stone buildings, but when Thietmar of Merseburg spoke of four hundred churches and eight markets in Kiev, he was most certainly exaggerating. The existence of numerous churches did, however, remain characteristic of Russia and, as we shall see, also of Scandinavia.

The situation in Hungary[81] is far from clear. While Szekely maintains that towns first really came into existence with the appearance of urban craftsmen in the twelfth century, Fügedi pushed the presence of early towns further back, although he did not deny the importance of the changes in the twelfth century. Fügedi makes a distinction for the tenth and eleventh centuries between the castles and suburbs like the episcopal fortresses of Raab, Neutra and Waitzen, and agglomerated settlements grouped around a market like Fünfkirchen. In that locality the market formed the central point for several settlements which included the site of the cathedral built over a former Roman cemetery. According to Fügedi, Stuhlweissenburg and Gran are transitional types. In Gran, south of the bishop's castle where a royal tower controlled the river crossing, the market was surrounded by various small groups of settlements. Independent developments certainly took place here before the immigration from the Holy Roman Empire in the twelfth century.

The northern cultural zone, to which England belonged before the Norman Conquest, has already been described using the examples of the important early, but subsequently abandoned, towns of Haithabu and Birka with their western European links. We can also trace here from the ninth century onwards the development of permanent towns. The Danish Ribe, which appears in the Life of Ansgar as a *wik* with a church and in the eleventh century as an episcopal see; Roskilde on Zealand which is first mentioned after 860, was described by Adam of Bremen as a "great city and the seat of the Danish kings" (*civitas maxima sedes regia danorum*); Viborg in Jutland, known as a trading centre from 960 onwards, became an episcopal see in 1065. Trading links joined it with England, Iceland, Sweden, Norway and the Rhine estuary and finally through Stade with Germany and Italy.

The old capital of Schonen is Lund, which Cnut the Great founded on the model of London. The Anglo-Saxon model is also imitated on the coins minted here. In Norway, Tönsberg on Oslo Fjord, probably the successor of Skiringsaal, Drontheim and Bergen must be mentioned. Research on the town centre of Bergen has been producing material for a century now.[81a] Its links were with the west, as evidenced by the Rhenish pottery, found at all levels from the eleventh century onwards. Adam of Bremen also reported that Birka had deen abandoned so that there are hardly any traces of the city (*in solitudinem redacta est, ita ut vestigia civitatis vix appareant*) but he called Sigtuna a "great city". Sigtuna today is a small town on Lake Mälaren whose main street corresponds to the old single-road settlement of the eleventh century;[82] from this street wattle paths ran to the river bank. On the land side the mighty Romanesque church delineated the limits of the settlement. This was one of the so-called merchants' churches, that is churches frequented by foreign merchants which as God's houses served both as religious and social centres of merchant society and as secure warehouses. Johansen has summarized the information about these Baltic merchants' churches. A similar concentration of merchants' churches and a large street running right through the town as at Sigtuna, are also to be found at Viborg and Lund. The churches of Sigtuna were probably used by Frisians, Englishmen and Russians as well as by other commercial visitors. In Old Wisby, where in the pre-Hanseatic period there were already many church buildings made of wood and stone, there was a St Clement of the Danes, St Lars of the Russians and a St Olaf of the mainland Swedes. Apparently in the eleventh and twelfth centuries each of the different groups of foreign merchants travelling in the Baltic founded their own churches in the towns frequented by them, standing on their own land, controlled by themselves. However, these trading places still remained only fair towns for seasonal trading which were only full when the foreign merchants were in residence. Johansen[83] sees the prototype of the northern town in the merchant town of England, where the Vikings first built on the foundations of the highly developed culture of the Romano-British zone. Vikings and Anglo-Saxons together created the five Danish towns of Lincoln, Stamford, Leicester, Derby and Nottingham.

The solution of the problem of the origins of urban development in Anglo-Saxon England must centre on the relationship between the fortified *burhs* and later boroughs.[84] The *burhs* go back to the time of Alfred the Great and his son, Edward. Each consisted of a large enclosure which could be occupied by a sizeable body of men and which were comparable with the late Carolingian and Ottonian fortress on the continent and also, to some extent, with the German castles of Henry I. Sometimes the Roman walls were used, sometimes earthworks and sometimes new stone walls were made. Almost all the *burhs* served as minting places and no money was struck in the tenth and eleventh centuries outside them. These fortresses were not necessarily incipient towns; they represented rather a group of settlements out of which towns might grow so that when there was a combination of *burh* and market, a borough could develop. Then its future existence as a medieval town was assured. The creation of markets was a royal prerogative. Almost all boroughs in Anglo-Saxon times were royal, the non-royal ones being exceptional. After the sharp break in development brought about by the Anglo-Saxon invasions, urban life stirred at the end of the sixth century in favourable locations, mostly places with a Roman past: at London, an emporium with a market and halls for displaying goods and a place frequented by foreign merchants; in Canterbury which developed into the religious capital of the island; in Rochester with its market, harbour and ancient bishopric which in the seventh century finally broke away from its Roman past. The *cnithengild* is mentioned in Canterbury in 858. New places came into existence like Hamwik, today forming part of Southampton but which then served both as a harbour for foreign trade and as an outlet to the sea for Winchester. Winchester itself, with its royal palace and religious buildings, noble houses and market street displayed the features of an early capital. After 892 when its fortifications were rebuilt, notable developments took place.

Statistical evidence is available at an earlier date for England than for the continent. Domesday Book mirrors the significance of the urban centres of Anglo-Saxon England in the age of the Norman Conquest of 1066. London possessed around 12,000 inhabitants, York 8,000, Norwich and Lincoln 5,000 each, Thetford 4,000, Oxford 3,500, Colchester 2,000, Cambridge 1,600 and Ipswich 1,300. Winchester, with a ground area of seventeen hectares may have had a population of 8,000 inhabitants. Towns of such an order of magnitude had obviously ceased to be self-sufficient. They needed imports of agricultural produce. An ever decreasing proportion of their population continued to live by agriculture. The inhabitants of Cambridge were still, however, required to lend their ploughs three times a year to the sheriff.

Arab traders and Arab coins also appeared in the north. The first warlike advances of Islam towards the west set in with the completion of the conquest of Egypt about the middle of the seventh century; in 711 it began to attack the Visigothic kingdom of Spain. Although in North Africa there was still bitter opposition from the Berbers, Spain fell easily to Islam and became the foothold for far-reaching Moslem expansion. The Spanish Umayyads, who regarded the Abbasid dynasty as usurpers, cultivated· their links with the Byzantine Empire, the Abbasids' natural enemy. However, Andalusia still remained within Baghdad's radiating sphere of influence. After being shaken by a severe crisis in the ninth century the Umayyads in Spain enjoyed a golden age in the tenth. When one looks at the poor and rustic way of life in the Europe of the day, the Moslem Orient and Spain seem by comparison rich and highly civilized.

The Arab world was an urban civilization.[85] Towns were centres of religion and craftsmanship. Craftsmen worked for the local market; only the luxury industries were of more international importance: the carpet weavers of Armenia and the leather workers of Spain, where Cordoba became synonymous with fine leatherwork; the metalware of Toledo. The paper industry was introduced from China. Found in the ninth century in Samarkand, in the tenth century it had reached Damascus and Palestine and in the eleventh century Valencia in Spain. The earliest merchants of the Moslem world were Jews. When competition from Arabs and Persians began, they held their pre-eminent position in all types of banking activity. They instituted the credit instruments of *suftajah* (exchange) and *sacc* which we have come to know as the cheque.

The caliphate of Cordoba,[86] which had its apogee in the tenth century, was an ethnic melting-pot. As well as Moslem immigrants like Berbers and Arabs, there were negroes from the Sudan and slaves of Slav origin. The Moslem population of Andalusia consisted, as it did throughout Islam, of freemen, freedmen and slaves. Below the mass of freemen were to be found the *Uhassa*, which were differentiated from the *Amma*. It was the families of Arabic origin who formed the core of the aristocracy but it was the middle classes, rich traders, who were responsible for the economic and cultural upsurge of the tenth century. Industries and markets were concentrated in the towns. Market dues and halls were rented out. From the ninth century onwards we have evidence of the existence of free industrial undertakings grouped together in different corporations. Most industries were to be found in the Suk which lay in the neighbourhood of the great mosque. The luxury industries occupied fairly roomy houses, surrounded by arcades which sheltered shops. The wholesalers had their own warehouse: the *fondaco*, and traded on commission both in the wares which native industry produced and in imported goods. In the tenth century the luxury trade began to rival that of Baghdad. The textile industry, with its abundance of raw materials at hand, was of the first importance. The textiles were manufactured in establishments belonging to the ruling caliph. In other towns the famous silk industry of Spain was to be found. Furriers and leather workers flourished in this land of harder winters than the ones to which the Moslems were accustomed. Ceramics, crystal glass, jewellery making, parchment and paper manufacture were all important and slaves also played a significant role as a commodity. The greatest export harbours were Algeciras, Malaga and Almeria. There was also a specialized carrying trade.

A characteristic of Andalusia in the tenth century was the considerable number of its urban centres. Many were already displaying in the age of the caliphate their present-day agrarian character – village towns or urban villages. Networks of irrigation canals determined the permanent distribution of the Berber population on the land but in districts without such facilities the population was concentrated in larger settlements.

The Moslem towns all possessed a central quarter in the immediate neighbourhood of the great mosque. From this centre the large main streets radiated out to the city gates and between the streets lay the various town quarters in double rows. There were often also settlements outside the walls. The street network was built with confusing irregularity.

After the capital, Cordoba, Seville was the most important Moslem town in Spain. The quantitative evidence is unfortunately very contradictory, and in one place Cordoba is stated to have had 471 mosques and in another 1,600. In the tenth century the population must have been between a half and one million, at any rate far in excess of the other western urban centres of the day. The Madina of Cordoba with its seven gates corresponded to the old Roman town and its walls rested on the foundations of the ancient Roman walls. It had the shape of a rough parallelogram whose shorter side ran along the Guadalquivir. The Roman town became too small for the population. The bridge over the Guadalquivir was famous: 223 metres long and resting on sixteen arches. A walled quay ran the length of the river as far as the mill. The great mosque, after the Christian Reconquest transformed into the cathedral, covered an area of 180 by 130 metres, and is the largest in the world after the mosque at Mecca. Pillars were incorporated into the design. It has some 850 of these as well as utilizing parts of the early Visigothic church. Jasper, agate and alabaster from the East were used in great abundance. Most of the 4,000 lamps were made from bells which had been pillaged.

The Christian Reconquista proceeded slowly and suffered many set-backs. It began in 718 with the revolt in the Asturias and ended in 1492. Its progress is systematically bound up with the creation of new settlements. Security was provided for the reconquered and depopulated land by a combination of Christian military might with economic progress. The great northern Spanish estate owners procured new settlements with far-reaching grants of freedom in the *carta de población*. This forms the first wave of new European town foundations.[87]

CHAPTER 3

The emergence of the medieval town

The population of Europe increased from the seventh century onwards. This upsurge in population made both possible and necessary an increase in the area under cultivation. We can set the first period of land clearance in Europe between the seventh and the tenth centuries with slack interludes during this time. In the tenth century there was a pause before the great colonization period of the high Middle Ages began. Already in the ninth and tenth centuries we can find islands of denser settlement, for example around Paris, in the vine-growing area of the middle Moselle, and also in the Ardennes and Pyrenees, that is to say also in areas which were not very fertile. Technological improvements, by intensifying exploitation, contributed to the reclamation of new arable land: better tools, ploughs and harrows, flails, as well as the spread of water mills which, in contrast to the situation in southern Europe, could depend for continuous water power on summer rains; better methods of harnessing draught animals. All these changes improved production. On the great estates of the northern Frankish religious houses, they began to divide the arable into three equal parts on their directly exploited seigneurial land, so-called Salic land. These parts were then sown in rotation with winter and spring crops and in the third instance left fallow. This was the beginning of the three field system of agriculture and it meant a significant increase in the production of corn which in turn meant more bread for more people. However, the system had the disadvantage that a third of the land still remained fallow, seed was sown haphazardly, and arable farming needed not only a disproportionate amount of labour but also required a great deal of land. Yields, according to modern standards, were ridiculously low and the population generally lived on the brink of famine. Each bad harvest could conjure up such a disaster because for a long time no sufficient surpluses could be accumulated from season to season or distributed from one locality to another.

The forest was still important in men's lives and they were aware of this. It was not only the hunting reserve of kings and noblemen, its wild beasts adding some variety to the medieval menu, it also produced wild fruits and honey, the material for all possible tools, for house-building, fence-building, even for the building of the earliest castles and churches as well as ships. It served to provide fuel for heating and for industries, like the metal industry and the production of salt from salt-springs, where processes were dependent on heat. Its clearings provided pasture for animals because there were few meadows: on the domains of the abbey of Saint Germain-des-Prés there were 213 hectares of meadow as against 11,000 hectares of arable land. The forest was especially indispensable for pig-rearing and on the lands of the same abbey 153 hectares served to maintain 100 pigs.[88]

We must place the development of the medieval European urban economy, based on markets and the transportation of goods, within its agrarian background and see it in relation to the agrarian side of the economy. Our so-called Industrial Revolution was also preceded by an agricultural one. There were not only economic factors but also social ones. Land reclamation, although it was certainly organized by the nobility, could not have been accomplished without the hard labour of the unfree peasantry. The colonizing peasants were offered many privileges. A new type of freedom became associated with colonized land. The increase in population made it possible for the countryside to send its surplus inhabitants into the towns; throughout the Middle Ages the towns were dependent on immigrants for growth. The gradually improving position of the peasantry left behind in the countryside enlivened the economic relationship between town and country. The country population provided a market for industrial goods and paid for them with surplus agricultural produce. It was no longer mainly demand for luxury goods by a small lay and clerical upper class which kept trade going. The peasant, too, managed to fulfill his own needs by selling his surplus produce to traders and craftsmen. The *wiks* and markets as they increased in population came to include inhabitants who were becoming dependent for their provisioning on the countryside. In the towns, for their part, crafts came into being which provided essential goods.

These processes cannot be conveyed in neat statistics. Source materials, with the exception of England, do not provide them. According to the information in Domesday Book (1086) the population of England at that time amounted to 1,100,000 inhabitants, and we can reckon on 3,700,000 inhabitants in 1346. Otherwise scraps of evidence must suffice. They are not always as explicit as that of a charter of 1181 of the provost of St Severin's in Cologne. It concerns the case of a young man who preferred the life of a shopkeeper to tilling the soil and, as he himself attested, was so fond of town life that he could no longer bear to live in the country and considered selling rent charges secured on his land – naturally to get together capital to begin his new career in the town.[89] The comital law of the town of Dinant in the middle of the eleventh century regulated the legal status of outsiders who were attracted into the town and wished to stay there. Among them were dependent tenants of the abbey of St Hubert and of the bishopric of Liège.[90] When Duke Godfrey I of Brabant and the abbot of Gembloux built together a church on the desolate but easily defensible Mont-Saint-Guibert, many came, attracted by the fact that the place was free, and built houses there.[91] In this case an early town was founded. In another case, what else could the poor or oppressed folk who had sold their land to the church of Paderborn do but go with the proceeds into the growing town of Paderborn itself, which was under the control of their energetic bishop, Meinwerk?[92] Men hoped for a freer and easier life, greater security and a better chance to achieve something, more company, the splendid spectacles during church festivals or those afforded by visits of the court and princes. So great was the attraction of town life that landowners were forced to limit emigration there by force or with concessions.

The increased amount of active exchange between town and country led to an increase in the number of market settlements. The tenth century saw further developments in the ninth-century German market law. In the charter of the abbot of Corvey granted to Meppen in 946, the king's peace was assured to all who visited the market, both on their outward and return journeys. After his Hungarian campaign, Otto I granted a series of markets along the Bergstrasse and in Alsace. Together with his trusted friend, Bishop Adaldag of Hamburg, he transformed the economic position of northern and eastern Germany. In particular, he reformed the mercantile arrangements at Magdeburg. The merchants of Magdeburg received from the Ottonian

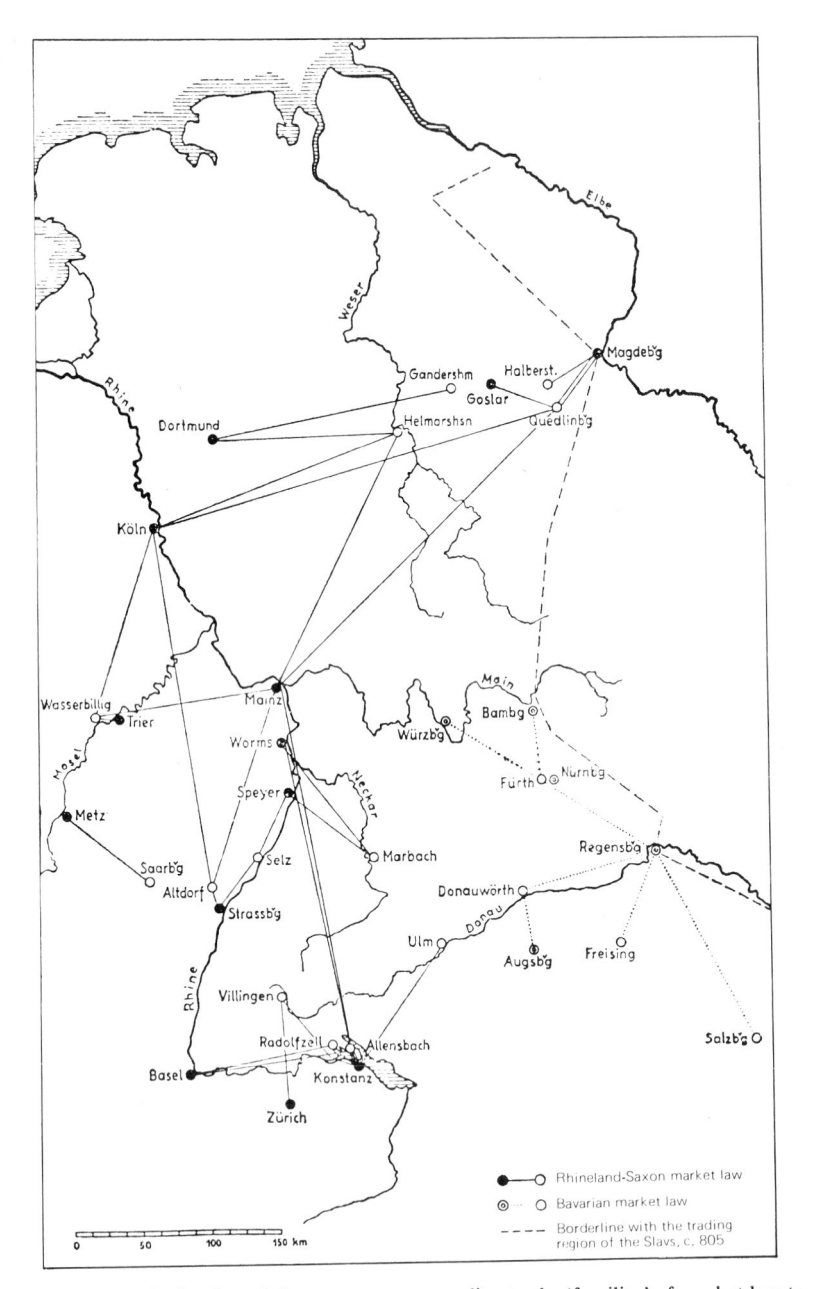

Figure 3. The distribution of German towns according to the 'families' of market law to which they belonged.

emperors freedom from customs throughout the Empire, with the exception of the continued liability to pay tolls at Mainz, Cologne, Tiel in the Betuwe, and Bardowiek. Under Otto III the royal market charters reached a new stage of development. Certain places were designated as having a special new market law and their markets were to serve as prototypes. These chosen places were ancient market centres which, because of the frequency of markets and prestige of their standing, became models for other places. They deserve naming. Among them Mainz occupies the first place because its market custom reached as far away as Lake Constance and Saxony; then comes Cologne, whose laws were adopted as far away as the Elbe and Moselle; Bavaria formed its own zone of market law under the primacy of Regensburg. Dortmund in the north-west and Zürich and Constance in the south-west were market centres of secondary rank. In the eleventh century, while royal power declined, the market places east of the Rhine continued to increase in importance. Market settlements with special market churches grew out of old one-street mercantile colonies.[93] This happened at Hamburg, Osnabrück, Minden, Münster, Paderborn, Hildesheim, Goslar, Quedlinburg, Halberstadt, Stade, Bardowiek and Brunswick. In the twelfth century, in the region of the middle Elbe, market settlements no longer originated in royal concessions of markets but through the grants of privileged market law, *ius fori* by territorial lords. An example is Jüterbog which in 1174 was granted privileges by Archbishop Wichmann of Magdeburg.[94]

While in Carolingian times the Meuse-Moselle formed the major trading axis, this was now replaced by the Rhine, a fact which is reflected in the oldest Koblenz customs' tariff which dates from the middle of the eleventh century.[95] Since the tolls were often paid in kind out of the boat's cargo, they provide welcome information about the character of trade. The Rhine trade was linked with the north Italian towns by the agency of merchants from Constance and Zürich using the Swiss mountain passes, while Regensburg merchants provided similar links with the south-east. The Meuse was an important adjoining axis, especially the middle stretch comprising Dinant, Namur, Huy and Liège. Then comes the Moselle with Metz, Toul and Trier. The important centre on the river Main was Würzburg, on the Scheldt was Antwerp, and on the Ijssel, Deventer.

Only slaves, swords and hunting falcons are directly mentioned as trading commodities in the Koblenz tariff. Sheepskin for saddle covers from Flanders, cheese and salmon from the Netherlands, salted herrings and eels, wine and wax, and brass vessels and pans from the Meuse appear among the commodities delivered in payment of customs, that is many articles in ordinary daily usage and industrial goods. The brass industry of the Meuse region brought its merchants onto the great west-east route via Cologne and Dortmund to the rich copper deposits of the Harz at Goslar. There is documentary evidence of this trade in 1103. In 1005 the Emperor Henry II granted to the church of St Adalbert at Aachen a tenth part of all royal revenues in Walcheren, Dortmund and Goslar. The combination of these three places again turns on their importance as trading centres, and the trade in iron ore certainly went via Walcheren to England. The trading links between Cologne, Tiel and London date at the latest from 1000.

The north-western economic zone, whose right flank was becoming more prosperous in the tenth and eleventh centuries, stretched southward along the Rhine. Wares from the Orient were brought back along the same route. A report of an embassy to the Emperor Otto's court by Ibrahim ibn Ahmed al-Tartuschi mentions with wonder that "there were to be found here [at Mainz] spices normally to be found only in the Far East, though Mainz lies far in the west, among them being pepper, ginger, cloves, spikenard, *costus* and *gargant*. They are imported from India where they are available in great quantities." He called Mainz "a very large city, populated in part but with open spaces. It . . . is rich in wheat, barley, spelt, vineyards and fruit." The Frisian traders went up the Rhine with cloth, bringing wine in return down the river. At Worms, tolls were paid by merchants, Frisians and craftsmen.

Growth in industrial production is particularly significant. The existence of a group of enterprising tradesmen who were prepared to travel far and take risks, guaranteed the market for these goods. Free craft production, free because it was not controlled by lordly interests, sought the proximity of traders and of markets in the *civitas* or *portus*. The concentration of industries and crafts in towns led to improvements in quality, which was a condition of progress at a time when illiterate tradesmen were not yet capable of regulating the industrial production of their entire territorial districts. In the eleventh century the urbanization of north-western Europe accelerated and the cloth industry developed. We have evidence of wool imports into Cologne and Ghent in 1000, in 1024 the cloth industry already existed in Arras and in 1043 in Saint-Omer. Occasionally in the eleventh century and regularly in the twelfth century, cloth was exported over the Alps and Pyrenees to Italy and Spain. In the twelfth century, the linen industry developed in the Lake Constance area and southern Swabia, and in the first decades of the thirteenth century its products were to be found in Italy. The wealth of written evidence from the Mediterranean region, above all in the notarial registers, made it possible for H. Laurent and H. Ammann to trace the foreign marketing of these products.[96]

Italy possessed an advantage through the continuous preservation of many towns. Several things combined to pave the way for a free development of Italian commerce: the settling in towns of the majority of the great landowners who early on engaged in trading ventures; the long-standing links with Byzantium kept open opportunities which could be put to fuller use after the victory of Otto I over the Hungarians at the Lechfeld in 955; the Byzantine conquest of Crete in 960 and the conquest of Sardinia by Pisa and Genoa in 1015–1016 which opened the way for Italian trade[97].

A new town, Venice,[98] was the earliest and most successful in building up a commercial empire. In the Middle Ages, Venice embodied best the ideal of a city state, completely free from all feudal influences and instructions. The Annals of Fulda show that already in the ninth century even north of the Alps men knew of regular travels of merchants to Venice. In the same century the ruling class of Venice was engaged in sea trade. Thus the Doge Giustiniano Partecipazio mentioned in his will 1,200 pounds of silver described as *laboratorii solidi*, that is money invested in sea trade, and he made a bequest of one sack of pepper to a relative, Orso Partecipazio. The river traffic on the small coastal rivers, along the Adige to Verona and the Po to Lombardy, already appears in the tenth century as an active traffic linking the Italian hinterland with maritime trade. Its fleet made Venice an essential ally of the rulers of Italy and Byzantium. Thanks to its position, it was able to mediate between Constantinople, the greatest city in the world of that time, centre of unheard of refinements, of art, and of the art industries, and the Slav world of the Balkans and the west. Liutprand of Cremona, the negotiator of the marriage of Otto II at the Byzantine court, wrote a description of his travels. Filled with malice against the Byzantines, he described how the clever Venetians and men of Amalfi smuggled out purple and silk goods, although export was prohibited under imperial law. Venice also imported spices and textiles from the Orient and North Africa and brought the products of the western metal industries as well as slaves and timber from the Slav lands and Istria back to the Orient, where the Saracens urgently needed timber for ship-building. It also offered its own products, fish and salt from the salt pans. Under Doge Peter II Orseolo (991–1009) the expansion into Dalmatia began. Already in 992 Venice was able to secure important privileges for its trade from the Byzantine rulers. During the crisis caused by the Norman attack on the Byzantine Empire in 1082, it obtained the Golden Bull which marked the end of the first stage of its rise. This brought freedom from all dues throughout the Byzantine Empire and gave the Venetians a series of warehouses and shops in the best trading areas, and three landing berths in the Byzantine capital, where they already possessed a church.

At this time Amalfi fell back to a position of secondary importance in the oriental trade. Like Venice it belonged to the Byzantine Empire but in practice enjoyed independence. It possessed a fleet which, in the ninth century, was the most formidable in the Tyrrhenian Sea. The merchants of Amalfi had important interests in Naples, colonies in Constantinople, Antioch, Jerusalem, Egypt and maintained trading links with Muslim Spain. For a small town, cut off from its hinterland by rocky mountains, it was a remarkable but also exhausting period of expansion. Amalfi, it was said, is not in Amalfi. The leading role in this golden age of Amalfi was taken by its statesmen and entrepreneurs, Mauro and his son Pantaleone di Mauro. Mauro imported silk and works of art from Constantinople and set up hospitals for his fellow-countrymen in Antioch and Jerusalem. His son bestowed bronze doors on the church of St Paul Outside the Walls in Rome. In the face of the Norman threat, he tried to create an alliance between the pope, the emperor Henry IV, Gisulph of Salerno and the Greek emperor Constantine X. The Norman Conquest of Amalfi did indeed mark a decisive turning-point. The Amalfitan quarter in Constantinople was merged with that of Venice, while settlements at Durazzo, Ravenna and Bari as well as those in Egypt and Syria survived at a reduced level. Nevertheless, the merchants of Amalfi continued to be found in every harbour of the Tyrrhenian coast. When the war between Pisa and Genoa started, Amalfi allied with Pisa.

Naples, one of Italy's oldest cities, and the centre of a fertile plain, left it to the Amalfitans and Pisans to develop the commercial potential of its position as a harbour while its own inhabitants remained purely property owners. The same was true of Salerno despite the mention in the early eleventh-century record of the privileges of Pavia called the *Honorantiae civitatis Papie* of men of Salerno bringing oriental textiles to Pavia. Gaeta had a commercial fleet, some silk industry and helped to supply Rome with food. It possessed links with Genoa and had a settlement in Constantinople, although the city was in no way comparable to Amalfi.

Apulia was exposed to Saracen attack over a long period of time. Siponto was taken by them in 927, Taranto in 976 and Bari was only saved from the same fate in 1002 by the intervention of the Venetians. On the other hand, Byzantium also clung tenaciously to this region whose centre, Bari, was the residence of the Byzantine catepan, whose harsh rule was bitterly resented by the local population. Already in 1064 the population of Bari bound itself by oath to support Robert Guiscard, and in 1071 the city finally fell to the Normans. The coastal cities of Apulia were favoured havens for pilgrims travelling to the Holy Land and certainly also commercial centres. Bari is the best documented of them. When the chronicle of the bishops of Cambrai reported on the miraculous rescue of the emperor, it narrated how he escaped drowning by swimming to a foreign ship and giving out that he was a rich merchant from Bari. The tale is certainly untrue but it shows that Bari was regarded as a rich commercial centre even far away. The first Golden Bull granted to Venice in 992 forbad the Venetians to take Amalfitans, Jews and Lombards, that is the non-Greek inhabitants of Bari on their ships, which would enable them to enjoy the advantage of reduced tolls which these ships enjoyed. This angered the Bari merchants but did not injure the active commerce between Bari and Byzantium. Trade with the Levant survived the Norman Conquest of southern Italy. There was a momentous episode in the 1080s when ships from Bari on the return journey from Antioch stole the relics of St Nicholas from Myra and brought them home on 9 May 1087. In 1089 Pope Urban II consecrated the magnificent church of St Nicholas in Bari.

Rome had little foreign trade because of the presence of the papal curia but remained, as it had been in Antiquity, a considerable importer of goods. It was one of the greatest pilgrimage centres of Christendom, and pilgrims and merchants are often to be found together. Anglo-Saxons, Frisians, Franks, Lombards, Hungarians (after 1001) all possessed their own churches with their own hospices and cemeteries in the Holy City. In the district known as the Leonine city, there was a special *burgus Saxonum* or *Anglorum* and a *burgus*

Frisonorum. As early as 1052 the site of the Roman money exchange is mentioned. The Romans had a reputation for avarice: "the Roman people, according to their custom pursue money grubbing as if it were a canonical rule" (*populus Romanus, suo more nummorum canones secutus*). Its terrible plundering at the hands of the Normans in 1084 was extremely detrimental to the city's development.

The rise of Pisa began in the eleventh century with its successful expeditions against the Saracens. They brought Pisa the lordship of Sardinia and an important base in the centre of northern Africa. In southern Italy the Pisans had a colony in Naples. They overtook their Genoese rivals in Corsica, enjoyed trading privileges in Rome, as well as along the coast between Gaeta and Luni and on the Arno.

Genoa followed close upon Pisa in its importance.[99] In the charter which the Italian kings, Berengar and Adalbert, granted to the Genoese in 958, the city appears primarily as a residence for landowners whose main concern was to remain in undisturbed possession of their lands both within and outside the town. The precise legal character of the land tenure and its other special features must be defined more closely. The document is partly concerned with leaseholds. Land was exploited for the benefit of landlords. The part of the charter describing possessions names serfs of both sexes. The legal validity of various titles to property is guaranteed: the titles under customary law, by written deeds and through inheritance. The possessory section also mentions mills, fishing rights, vineyards and salt pans, that is products of the land which could be traded. Already at that time the needs of trade, especially maritime trade, determined the lay-out of the town. Genoa did not possess such convenient links with the hinterland as Pisa. A report of 1065 reveals the involvement of the Genoese in regular commercial activity on the Syrian coast. The landowners of the tenth century are the viscounts (*vicecomites*) and the church advocates (*defensores ecclesiae*) and the *gastaldi* to whom had passed a large proportion of the episcopal and religious properties. They are the great leaseholders of church property which they further sub-rented. The customary law of the Genoese of 1056 already reveals extensive exploitation of landed property in order to procure commercial capital as the nobles resident in the towns turned to large-scale commercial enterprise.[100]

We also find in Italy traces of increasing growth in markets and industry. A charter of Otto I to Milan in 952 described the public market (*mercatus publicus*), which had stalls with benches laid out in front of them (*stationes in ibi banculos ante se habentes*). We know the names of people owning adjoining plots of land and there are merchants among them. Trade in Lucca had an industrial basis from the very beginning, rooted in many techniques which had survived from Antiquity. The art of beating gold and silver into fine sheets as well as the various arts of gilding which were already being practised in ninth-century Lucca both belonged to such unbroken traditions. Gold thread was an Italian export of some importance. Later, Pisa became a centre of the leather industry, Milan of the arms industry, while Venice secured a virtual monopoly of certain types of fine glass manufacture. Cloth, woven from a mixture of cotton and linen, was already being exported from Piacenza via the port of Genoa in the twelfth century. Florence was a finishing centre for textiles from north-western Europe. The silk industry spread from Sicily, where its centre was in Palermo, to Tuscany, while Venice owed its swiftly flourishing silk manufacture to its Byzantine links. Lucca became the leading centre of Tuscan silk manufacture.

Southern France and the Spanish March suffered terribly under Saracen onslaught in the ninth century. In 838 Marseilles was suddenly attacked; Barcelona was taken in 852 and 985. In the 880s the Spanish Saracens secured a strong foothold between Hyères and Fraxinetum near Fréjus and plundered from here throughout the hinterland. Only in 973 could Count William of Arles take and destroy Fraxinetum. Economic life was able to recover in the eleventh century. A harbour fortress and fortified towers were erected at this time to protect Barcelona. Slave traders from the city were usually present at the Genoese market and in 1009 a merchant called Robert appeared in the city (*in civitate Barchenona advenit quidam homo nomine Roberto negociatore*) who, as scholars have discovered, was a Flemish cloth merchant.[101] The route to Spain was already known in Ottonian times to the rich slave dealers of Verdun but the "certain Robert" was nevertheless a solitary pioneer along this route.

This "renaissance of long-distance trade" was studied by Pirenne. To him long-distance trade was a characteristic sign of economic development and he saw a direct link between the *renaissance économique* and the beginnings of urban life: *L'origine des villes du moyen âge se rattache directement comme un effet à sa cause à la renaissance commerciale*. This is naturally too one-sided a view. We must not look at the medieval town solely from the vantage point of the Rialto, the port of Genoa, Cologne or the belfries of the Flemish

towns. This one-sided and provocative thesis of Pirenne, Planitz and
Rörig[102] was the product of a justifiable reaction to the theses of
Rudolf Sohm and Georg von Below. Sohm overestimated the importance of the royal concessions of market rights while Georg von
Below overemphasized the significance of areas rich in industry from
which market centres drew their products. In its turn, the reaction
against the three great urban historians has become almost too sharp.
We need to amplify the work of these great researchers and to
appreciate the rôle of trade within a more nuanced picture. We must
make it clear that eleventh-century trade was already quite different
from the foreign trade of the period between the eighth and tenth
centuries. It was now based upon export industries in the towns and
this developed in the following centuries. Trade and the practice of
crafts were now overwhelmingly urban professions. The seasonal
traders, landowning traders as well as manufacturers on great estates,
were in decline if they had not completely disappeared. The division
of labour between town and country began to break down. The town
market played an important rôle in this process. It was not foreign
trade but markets which made the towns into the centres of economic
life. The increase in market settlements, especially east of the Rhine,
the intensification of market life in old *civitates* as in the "permanent
market" of Milan (Lopez), are further indications of the progress of
the urban way of life.

In addition to the "renaissance in large-scale commerce" we must
take into account "the renaissance associated with rural revival."
Higounet has described in detail how the slow revival of Bordeaux,
where urban life had sunk to its lowest ebb in the ninth century, was
due in the tenth and eleventh centuries not to the initiative of
merchants engaged in foreign trade but to the upsurge in rural life,
above all the increase in the rural population. "The expansion of
agriculture restored Bordeaux' position as a market. Before it took
back its place in the mainstream of great commerce, it had found in
the tenth and eleventh century the forces of its salvation in the land
of the Garonne and in Gascony." But even this approach to the
shaping of urban growth is still one-sided. It is too exclusively
concerned with economic factors, with treating the progress of towns
as merely a matter of increasing division of labour.

The medieval towns were also centres of power and administration
although north of the Alps, not within a city state setting but a feudal
one. Aachen remained the "royal town and principal royal seat" (*urbs*

Aquensis urbs regalis sedes regni principalis). In 876 Regino of Prüm called Frankfurt "chief seat of the eastern kingdom" (*principalis sedes regni orientalis*) and from the ninth to the beginning of the eleventh century it was one of the places most often named on royal itineraries as a stopping place. Just as Aachen became important during the later years of Charlemagne's rule, so under Louis the German Frankfurt consolidated its rôle as the chief centre of the ruler and place of residence of the court. Between October 833 and August 876 Louis the German visited Frankfurt thirty-three times, including many long stays, four of them lasting over the winter.[103]

Regensburg, which we have already mentioned a number of times as a centre for foreign trade, was an episcopal seat and a Bavarian ducal residence. Under Louis the German and Arnulf of Carinthia it became an important royal seat of the eastern Franks.[104] Rheims had a comparable position as a capital within the western Frankish kingdom in the ninth century as did Laon in the tenth century. In contrast to the Merovingian's desire for town palaces, which really represented a last echo of Antiquity, in Carolingian times royal palaces were frequently moved out of the towns to a site near the abbey outside the walls. Under Otto the Great, Magdeburg, like Regensburg, experienced a similar combination of serving as a centre for foreign trade and being a royal residence, and it became the Aachen of the north.[105] A Frankish or Saxon royal palace does not, indeed, in itself amount to a town, and important sites of palaces like Ingelheim or Tribur, Werla and Tilleda never developed into towns.

Town palaces first reappear with the Staufer emperors. Of the known cases, in Aachen and Frankfurt the palaces formed the old heart of the town which developed around them. Magdeburg and Regensburg already had urban features before their palaces were built. This is especially true of Regensburg. Aloys Schulte compared Regensburg with Pavia.[106] The Roman Ticinum, Ostrogothic bulwark against Byzantium, after the murder of Alboin in 572 was the political centre of Lombardy and its chief minting place. It remained the capital of the kingdom of Italy after it was conquered by the Franks, although a capital which was certainly prone to rebellion. Pavia served as an administrative, financial and judicial centre. It was there, rather than in nearby populous Milan, that the hospices (*cellae*) and town houses (*curtes*) of the churches and abbeys of central and northern Italy and of France sprang up. The bishops of Milan, Lodi, Cremona, Bergamo, Tortona, Genoa, Piacenza and Reggio and the abbeys of St Ambrose in Milan, of Bobbio, St Giulia, Nonantola, St Martin at Tours and Cluny all had their town cells (*cella, curtis* or *xenodochium*). They took advantage of the economic activity in the town, the availability of luxury goods there and the congregation of merchants. The early economy of Pavia, controlled by royal officials, was described in the famous *Instituta regalia et ministeria Camerae regum Langobardorum et honorantiae civitatis Papiae* "The regalian institutions and offices of the Chamber of the Lombard kings and of the noble city of Pavia," dating from about 1010–1020. This document lays down the payments due to royal chamberlains from the Venetian, Salernitan, Gaetan and Amalfitan merchants as well as from the Anglo-Saxons and other merchants from north of the Alps. It also enumerates those due from the craftsmen, organized into *ministeria*, butchers, fishmongers, tanners and silk weavers, and reveals the organization of the mint. Everything was designed to provision the court. This impressive organization was already in process of decay when it was so described. Many of the rights of the Chamber had been granted, or wasted, away. In northern Italy the great communes eliminated royal control over their economies, and, early on, Venice, Amalfi and Genoa loosened their links with their old masters in Byzantium. This should serve as a reminder not to exaggerate the part played by the kings and other territorial lords in urban development. Nevertheless, the influence of the ruler's power on urban development persisted, except where it became fossilized within the archaic structures of the Ottonian Empire. In cases where the state was in advance of its day or had a strong basis in Antiquity it was particularly effective. The county of Flanders provides a striking example of the first situation and the episcopal cities of the second.

The earliest features of the modern state north of the Alps appear in the north-west, in Flanders, the French royal domain and Normandy. Flanders provides a particularly early prototype. Not only concentrated there, but throughout the whole of the southern Netherlands and sporadically elsewhere too, there grew up comital residential castles which were the embryos of the great Flemish towns.[107] Count Baldwin II, who had taken over his land as a wilderness laid waste by the Vikings, brought this area between the coast, the River Scheldt and Artois under his control in a succession of terrible wars between 898 and 918, and he built castles on the coast and on the banks of the Scheldt and Lys to defend his country of Flanders against them. These Flemish comital castles,[108] of which Bruges is the oldest, are really also palaces, though certainly not in the sense that the count of Flanders had his fixed place of abode in any single one of them. He, like other lords, remained on the move – *ambulantes*. These castles do, however, have something of the character of palaces in their lay-out. As well as the castle itself, a secure place of residence for the count, the whole complex also provided places to live for the people who worked in the castle, and a granary. Bruges also had a collegiate foundation dedicated to Our Lady and St Donatian, whose church was modelled on the abbey of St Mary at Aachen. This reveals the self-assurance of a dynasty which had Carolingian blood in its veins. A combination of a residence for the lord and a religious foundation is typical of royal palaces and was emulated by the higher nobility.

In the same way as the counts of Flanders and other rulers of the southern Netherlands, the Conradins in the Lahn valley set up castles in Limburg, Weilburg and Wetzlar which had their own religious foundations. Towns grew out of these complexes and Wetzlar in fact became an imperial city. Warburg in Westphalia belongs in the same category. At Ghent the gloomy comital castle (the Steen) and the abbey of St Pharaildis, which no longer exists, had a settlement of craftsmen where leather workers, among others, fulfilled the needs of the castle. At both Bruges and Ghent a colony of merchants grew up outside the comital residence. In Ghent the comital castle and abbey of St Pharaildis lay in the centre between the Vorburg with its Cordwainers' Street and the *portus* separated from this main complex by the river. Later these Flemish comital castles became the legal, administrative and domanial centres of castle districts, and this Flemish organization of administrative districts controlled from comital castles made the towns dominated by the castles centres of administration. There are many detailed questions about the topography and chronology of early Bruges and Ghent which still remain controversial. The chief feature revealed by research has been a dualism represented by a comital residence, protected by water, and a separate mercantile *portus* set apart across the river. In Ghent this *portus* included a craftsmen's quarter and here the great abbeys of St Peter and St Bavo formed the bases for further settlements.

A comparable dual situation existed in the episcopal towns. This comprised the bishop's seat, established within the Roman walls and the merchants' settlement which grew up in its shadow. In Cologne this commercial area grew up around a great market place, in

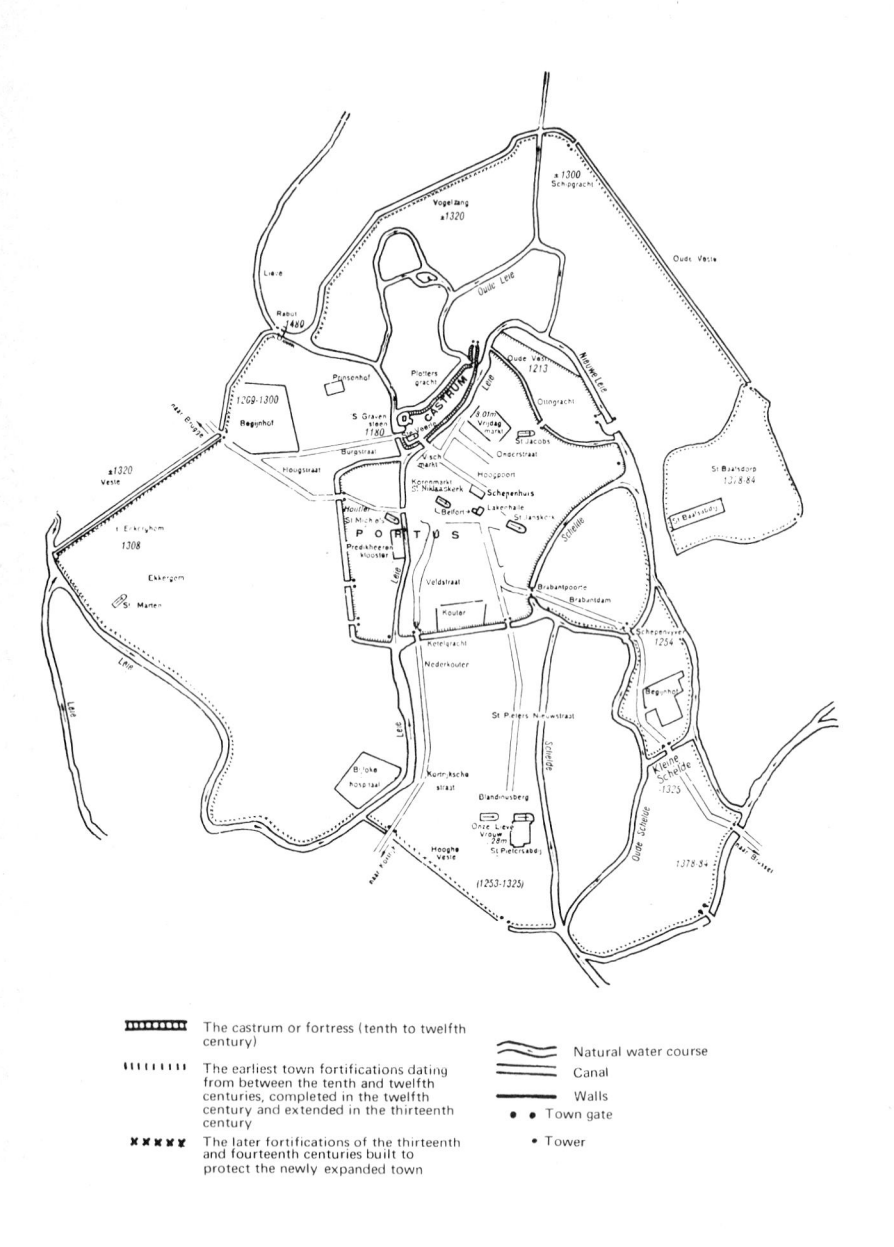

Figure 4a. Town plan of medieval Ghent.

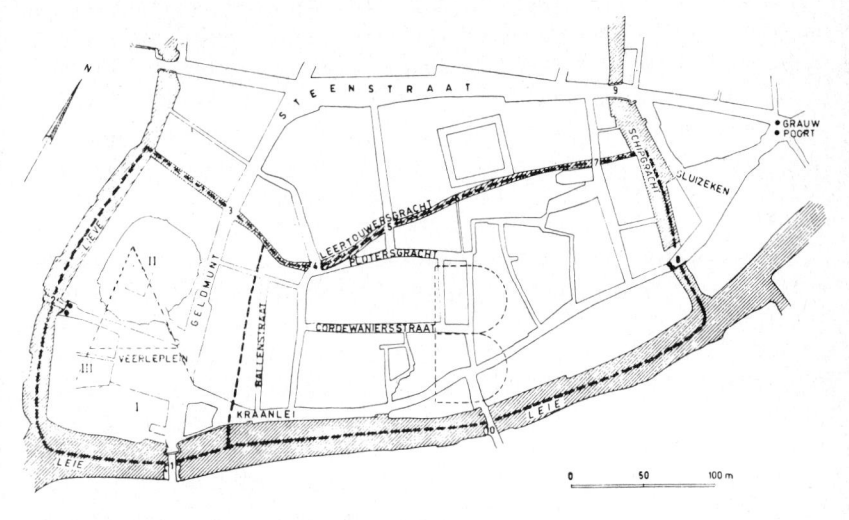

Figure 4b. Plan of the comital castle at Ghent.

Trier[109] within a walled area controlled by the bishop and immune from outside jurisdiction or, as another special variant, in Speyer, as a merchants' quarter near both royal palace and episcopal town. The topography of these towns therefore is based upon a very simple ground plan. In these cases, the bishop's seat plays a part equivalent to the comital castle although it is not only much older but also entirely different in origin, going right back to Antiquity. The elevated status of bishops in the Empire increased the importance of towns which developed out of episcopal seats.

In Cologne the new upsurge in the city began after its destruction by the Norsemen in 881–882. Precise information about the extent of this destruction is lacking. Two years later houses were rebuilt and the fortress had been restored. In 891 churches were being restored and in the first thirty years of the tenth century new churches appeared in districts which had never before been inhabited. It is clear therefore that new settlement was taking place outside the ruins. The town grew markedly during its rule by the king's brother, Archbishop Bruno (953–965). As *archidux*, *tutor* and *provisor* in the west of the Ottonian Empire, he made Cologne into the centre of Old Lotharingia. In 953 the revolt of the magnates of Lotharingia broke out here. The situation in western France was also controlled from

Cologne. Many fled from the Norsemen to Bruno as "the safest harbour" (*tutissimum portum*). The Whitsun festival of 965 was a memorable day in Cologne, a family feast of the Ottonians and a court and imperial celebration. Still basking in the glory of his coronation in 962, Otto I returned to Cologne from Italy bringing with him his mother Matilda, his sister Gerberga, queen of France, with her sons, Lothar and Charles. As host, Bruno presided over the destinies of Lotharingia and western France.

An expansion in Cologne's economic life began about this time. Its foreign trade rested on foundations quite independent of Cologne's status as an episcopal seat, although this was not an unimportant factor in its economic development as a whole. Already in 967 there is a mention of an Easter meeting of the faithful in Cologne, perhaps an indication that the traditional Cologne Easter Fair was already in existence. Archbishop Bruno's acquisition of St Peter's chains certainly gave an impetus to the second fair, which took place on the feast of St Peter in Chains. The third fair took place at the end of October, the feast of the holy Cologne bishop, St Severin.

What the Ottonian emperors did for Cologne, the Salians emperors did for Speyer. Expansion of the town followed the rebuilding of the huge cathedral in the eleventh century and the building of the town walls, which took place in several stages.

In addition to all the other developments which we have already mentioned and illustrated, the powerful religious spirit of the Middle Ages also contributed to the upsurge in urban life. It was not only a question of fairs and markets being closely connected with religious festivals. Free settlements, the French *salvitates*, lined the pilgrim route to Santiago de Compostela; pilgrimages were responsible for bringing towns into existence or making those which already existed prosperous. We need only think of medieval pilgrim towns like Le Puy and Chartres. In the course of the eleventh century the church of Chartres became France's chief centre of pilgrimage. A relic of the Virgin was kept there which had been of service in the wars against the Norsemen and had helped in an epidemic of some feverish illness. The Romanesque church was already as big as the present-day cathedral. By 1100, in addition to the cathedral, some twenty churches filled the hills and the valley and the economy was powerfully influenced by the pilgrims: taverns, shops, bakeries, butchers and money-changers were doing profitable business only because of the pilgrimage trade. Otherwise Chartres was a cloth town belonging to the Isle de France section of the northern French region of textile production. It also already had an excellent school in the eleventh century, like the French cathedral schools at Orleans and Paris, which also excelled in the eleventh century.

In the southern Netherlands, Liège had an important school in Ottonian and Salian times. Religious houses continued to provide additional important centres of literary and artistic life, and they were also occasionally starting-points for the growth of towns like Saint-Trond in the Low Countries, where the development of economic life coincided with its increase in importance as a centre of pilgrimage. The chronicle of the abbey of Saint-Trond shows this clearly.[110]

Towns had always been religious centres; this was the essential nature of the legacy from Rome. Now they again became cultural centres in competition with religious houses and castles.

"The towns both expanded their old fortifications and filled out within them" (Aubin). Naples, enclosed within its ancient walls, in the tenth century grew around the *junctura nova* and, in the time of Roger II, who conquered it in 1140, it had 30,000 inhabitants. Genoa, fortified by Rothari in 642, was refortified in 952. The wall enclosed the suburb belonging to a margrave and the episcopal seat as *castrum* and *civitas*, but the *burgus* remained outside this system of fortification and was only walled in 1156. Venice's first city walls date from 900. The city grew out of the *civitas Rivoalti*, soon to become the *civitas Veneciarum*. In 1084, the division of the town into quarters known as *confinia* began. Seventy-two of them are mentioned in the *Liber plegiorum* (1224–1228) and they almost all had their own churches. Milan grew up in a series of concentric rings, as we know from the description of Bonvicinus de Ripa, *De magnalibus urbis Mediolani*, of 1288. It already had 12,500 houses by that date.

Urban development between the Loire and the Rhine followed the pattern of the topographical duality of an ancient urban centre and an early market or merchant settlement, as we have already shown.[111] We must also allow for the existence of other less important embryonic urban developments and for the presence of numerous variants in the main two elements themselves and in their mutual relationship. The old urban centre can be an episcopal see within Roman walls – east of the Rhine within early medieval fortifications – a royal palace or a noble's castle, a fortified religious house or an abbey; in general one can describe them as the fortified seats of either spiritual or lay lords. The *suburbium* growing up around this seigneurial or royal seat might be an early merchants' colony, a *vicus*, a *portus*, *emporium* or *negotiatorium claustrum* or it might be a market settlement. Two examples may serve to illustrate this – Verdun and Bonn. For Verdun we have Richer's description of 955, based on his own knowledge of the place. First of all he describes the *civitas*, the fortified episcopal see which stood on a tree-covered plateau falling steeply to the

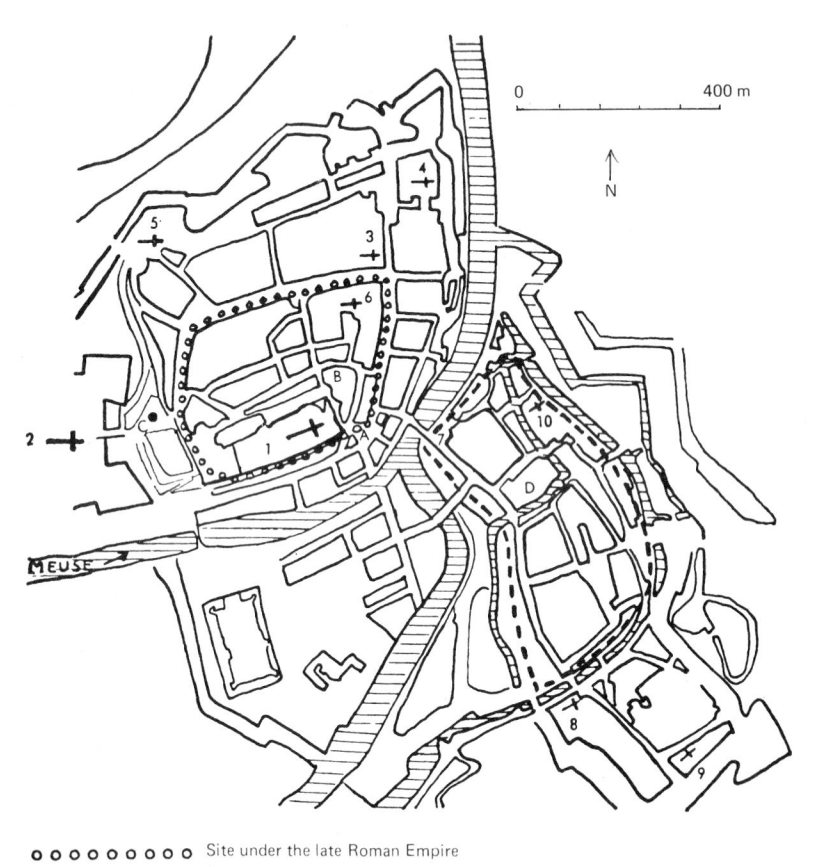

○ ○ ○ ○ ○ ○ ○ ○ ○   Site under the late Roman Empire

— — — — — — — —   Probable line of the fortifications of the early town
(eleventh to thirteenth century ?)

1 Cathedral	5 Saint-Maur	9 Saint-Victor	A Place Mazel
2 Saint-Vanne	6 La Madeleine	10 Saint-Sauveur	B Rue Châtel
3 Saint-Pierre	7 Sainte-Croix		C Tour le Voué
4 Saint-Paul	8 Saint-Airy		D Braceolum

Figure 5. Town plan of Verdun.

Meuse and extremely difficult to capture, and then he describes the well-fortified merchants' colony associated with it but separated from the *civitas* by the Meuse and linked to it only by two bridges.

The merchants of Verdun, who created a fortress so early on, are already known to us as the rich slave traders of Ottonian times. Slav prisoners of war, brought from Magdeburg by way of Cologne, were castrated in Verdun and sold as bodyguards to the caliphs of Cordoba.[112] The profit from this trade, which stopped about 980, was "immense". Verdun also had an eastern trade, as is shown by a treaty concluded by its merchants with those of Cologne. For the merchants of Verdun, too, Cologne was a post on the way to obtaining the copper of the Harz mountains which they used in their metal industry of high artistic quality. They brought spices to Cologne and probably also other Mediterranean products. The Champagne fairs also gave them contacts with Italy and in the thirteenth century business agreements made by them appear in the Genoese notarial records.

The situation in Bonn was quite different from that in Verdun, a centre of foreign trade whose place was taken in the thirteenth century by Metz. In ninth-century Bonn a merchants' colony grew up along a single street in the shadow of an already existing settlement around the abbey of St Cassius, that is to say at the very heart of the old urban settlement. Norse raids severely undermined it. In the eleventh century a market place sprang up in front of the unfortified abbey settlement; it is possible that the remains of the old merchants' colony were incorporated into it – topographical details make this seem likely. The great market place, which corresponds to the present one, was occupied by a considerable number of market stalls; rows of terraced houses with their rectangular ground plans adhered to a uniform pattern. This was an unfortified market settlement. It was first walled after 1244 on the order of the rulers of the town. The case of Bonn beautifully illustrates the fact that town growth is a long drawn out process, though not without its decisive moments of deliberate planning, or of fresh foundations, forming part of this slow development.

One can describe these towns between the Loire and the Rhine as slowly evolving towns, in contrast both to those created by a single act of foundation and to those south of the Loire and Alps which remained completely enclosed within their ancient walls. Naturally, all the big cities, in process of time, received fresh stimuli for growth.[113] While the cities of eastern Germany, especially those east

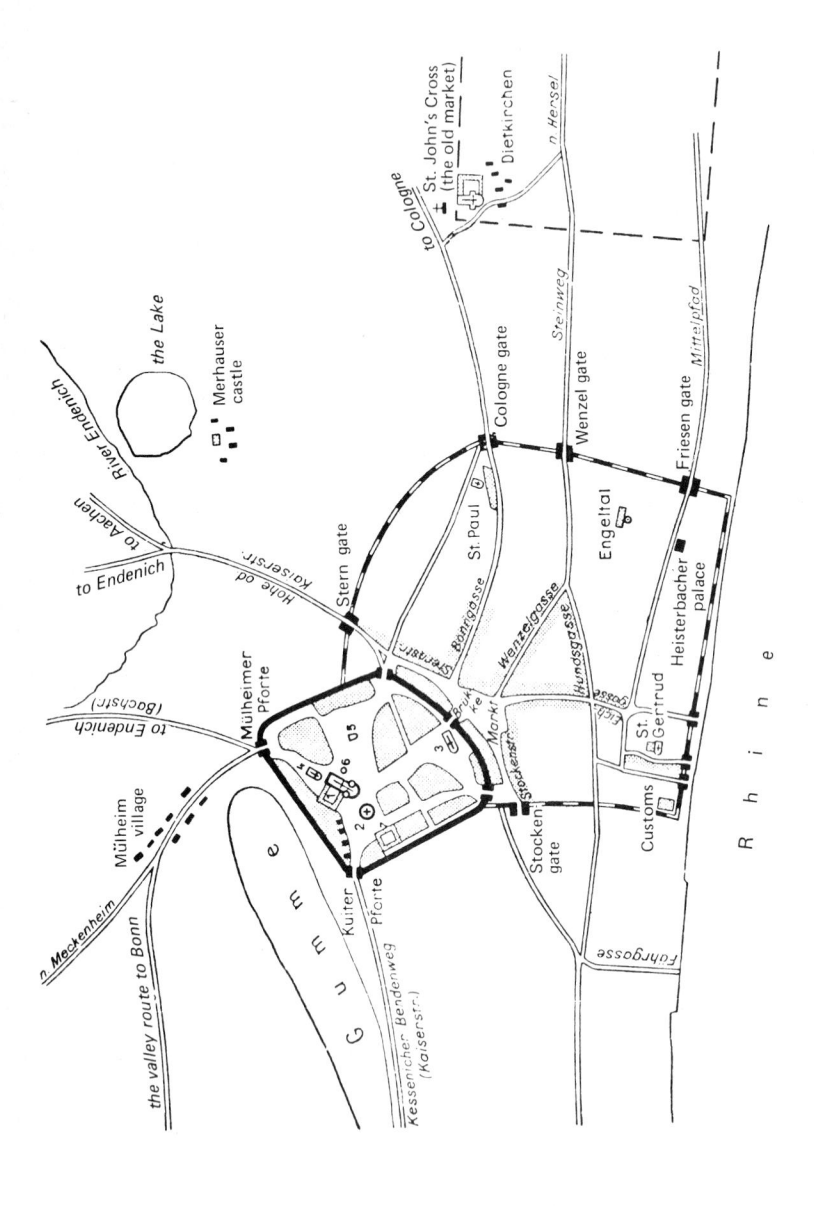

Figure 6. Town plan of Bonn in the twelfth and thirteenth centuries.

of the Elbe, had previously been ascribed to deliberate foundation policy, archaeological as well as historical research has revealed the existence of earlier types of urban settlement. A new and interesting, though unconfirmed, thesis has discerned a topographical duality comprising the castle on the one hand and merchants' quarter on the other in the eastern part of central Europe.[114] The spread of these merchant settlements can be traced in the twelfth century by the location of churches dedicated to St Nicholas, which are characteristic of such urban centres. The significance of this thesis may be that these merchants' quarters may provide the missing link between the castle towns of indigenous Slav provenance and the eastern towns governed by German law which were of a later date. Thus, elements of gradual growth and deliberate foundation are also found in the east and reveal the following types. (1) The old southern *civitas* comprising a single unit of settlement. (2) The double settlement consisting of lord's residence and commercial and economic centre. (3) The deliberate urban foundation. We must bear in mind that settlement which belongs only to one of these categories and is a pure type is rare. As we have already established in the discussion of continuity, no two cases are alike in the process of medieval urban development. Each town has its own individual character.

From the tenth century onwards, when their walls were built, the towns took on their typical medieval outward appearance. The wall was naturally not a romantic gesture but the result of bitter necessity in a time which was really desperate for peace but did not achieve it. The relatively small size of lordships, town communes, and principalities meant that peace was disturbed more by chronic feuding than by major warfare especially since, until 1495, the feud in Germany was a permitted means of legal dispute – with certain limitations. The Roman wall, newly repaired, or the lord's castle, had sufficed as a refuge place in the emergencies of the Norse, Hungarian and Saracen raiding, but they were no longer sufficient to protect the suburbs lying beyond them with their greatly increased population. The Roman walls were therefore extended to incorporate the merchants' settlement or to provide for growth within the original *civitas*, as happened in the twelfth century at Bourges, Poitiers and Dijon; or newly-erected walls now protected suburbs and enclosed both lord's residence and merchants' market suburb within the same wall system. The duality of the town was thus ended. Stone walls took the place of earth walls and palisades. In Cambrai, for example, bishop and burgesses were jointly responsible in about 1090 for erecting stone walls where before the town had been protected only by wooden ramparts. "The bishop, with the help of the citizens, in place of the previous wooden rampart surrounding the town, fortified it more strongly with a wooden wall" (*unde eisdem civibus auxiliantibus totam in circuitu civitatem vallo ligneo prius compositam ipse eqiscopus munivit muro lapideo fortius*). The cathedral fortress within the city was still given a separate fortification: "Also he fortified the inner ecclesiastical city with an excellent wall where there was both the church of the blessed mother of God and the monastery of St Autbertus, built on a raised and formidable castle mound." (*Castellum etiam infra civitatem, in quo erat et aecclesia b. genetricis Dei et coenobium sancti Autberti muro excelso firmavit, fossato relevato alto et terribili.*) With the introduction of building in stone from the Mediterranean area into north-western Europe, we encounter one of those profound currents which both initiated and accompanied central European urban development.

Stone was first used again north of the Alps in the post-Roman period for the special protection of the lord's residence, for castles, for the buildings of privileged notables and for great religious buildings, but also for smaller, fortified churches. The erection of stone walls by trading and industrial centres is a sure criterion of their renewed importance. The superior rank of certain towns was also reflected in stone buildings, which varied from place to place according to local cultural peculiarities. Two main types of medieval noble building grew up – tower houses and hall-houses (*Saalgeschosshaus*), the basic elements of which have their origins in the Mediterranean area in late Antiquity, and which began to influence the buildings of the upper classes of northern Europe in the eleventh century.[115] Metz and Trier, on the edge of the Lorraine stone-building region, were notable for the number of their tower houses. The stretch of the Rhine as far as Utrecht is straddled by tower houses or monumental castellated mansions. There are also plenty of stone buildings in the Meuse area from early on, as also in Flanders, while French Burgundy, the Loire Valley and Britanny have many urban timber and plaster buildings (*Fachwerkbauten*). The hall-house contributed more to the noble way of life than the tower house. It had a stronger influence still on the houses of townspeople and even of the peasantry of western and central Europe.

In the early Middle Ages the hall-house was limited to imperial palaces, the castles of great princely dynasties, bishops' palaces and abbeys. It took the form of a long two- or three-storey building. A high hall was usually situated above the lower ground floor. The presence of the living quarters on the upper floors is a decisive feature and still remains a characteristic of the town houses of more prosperous people down to the twentieth century.

Stone walls sharply divided the densely built-up and complex lay-out of the town from the surrounding countryside, although there were exceptions to this. Almost all the towns in the Tyrol were without walls,[116] while in south-western Germany there were villages which were fortified. But, in general, the wall is a characteristic of the town in the Middle Ages. Its erection was one of the most burden-some communal obligations of medieval townsfolk. It was the achievement of a population which had come into these centres to work from far and near and which otherwise lacked any unified character – whether local, legal or communal. The walls bound them together into a unified social entity, a self-confident bourgeoisie. The right to erect fortifications was often a cause of major dispute between the lord of the town and the inhabitants, for example at Cologne. The town wall played an important part in the economy of the town; in the towns of autonomous territorial lords, the prince was naturally an interested party, because these towns were the main fortified places of the principality. He was prepared to compensate the townsfolk for their duty to maintain the wall either by allowances in taxation or by permitting them to levy an excise or purchase tax. This excise duty became a major source of income of many towns. Most towns acquired their walls in the twelfth century, some pioneers already in the tenth century, while in the central region of early town formation, the Rhine, Meuse, and Scheldt towns were mostly walled in the eleventh century.

What name should we use for these settlements now expanded into towns and what should we call their inhabitants?[117] Contemporary sources are written entirely in Latin, and translation is not easy because the historians and chroniclers of the time and the chancery clerks who drew up the official records were compelled to employ ancient terminology to describe the settlements of their own day. This classical nomenclature often thereby took on a quite new meaning. For example, the Latin word, *civitas*, in the early Middle Ages came to mean no more than a fortified settlement, most often a fortified episcopal see, while a walled abbey will be described as *lapidea civitas*, and in the end *civitas* also became synonymous with *castrum*. The German term for town, recorded by poets in glossaries, was *burg*. The Roman centres were given the name of *burg* – *Kolnaburg*. This is the term which remains in use today. "On the castle wall" in present-day speech in Cologne, means "on the town wall". Hence one also speaks of *castrum Bonna* – Bonnaburg. The *Annolied*, written between 1080 and 1100, in general continued to use the term *burg* and only seldom the newer *stat*. On the other hand the Legend of St Servatius, written by Henry von Veldeke about 1170, used *stat* exclusively. The modern word *Stadt* for town thus first appears in the eleventh century.

No one name was given exclusively to townspeople. The Latin terms *cives* and *urbani* are not unequivocal. *Civis* can simply mean any town inhabitant or a layman as opposed to a cleric. When Notker of St Gall translated *civis* as *burgliute* ("castle people") about 1000, he may in this case have been thinking of the people of Constance and thus have meant townsfolk, but a clear distinction between people of a *burg* (castle) and of a *Stadt* (town) is as unlikely as a clear distinction between castle and town themselves. The etymology of the medieval Latin *burgus* and *burgensis* is revealing, but also highly controversial. *Burgus* can mean a fortress, but also a more or less unfortified settlement. The second meaning was already employed widely in the fourth century, and on a larger scale in the ninth and tenth centuries *burgus* was used for settlements in the Saône, Rhône and Loire valleys. From this region the term *burgus* for settlement spread to France at the end of the tenth century, especially to southern France, and from there to northern Italy and northern Spain. We are indebted to Liutprand of Cremona for an explanation of the term: "they call a collection of houses not enclosed with a wall a *burgus*" (*ipsi domorum congregationem quae muro non clauditur, burgum vocant*). Thus *burgus* meant a built-up, unfortified settlement. In German-speaking areas – Brabant and Flanders as well as southern Germany – *burgus* was first employed with this meaning at the end of the eleventh century and in the twelfth. The word *burgensis* grew out of the term *burgus*. It appeared at any rate after the eleventh century in the Rhône-Saône-Loire area and designated the inhabitants of a *burgus*. Subsequently, when *burgi* became priviliged places, as will be discussed later on, the word *burgensis* will come to denote the inhabitants of a privileged, freed settlement. From this point of departure, *burgensis* came to be used in German-speaking areas for men living under town law, who in German were called *burgaere* and in the Germanic languages of the Netherlands, using a derivation from *portus*, *poorter*. In Germany there was a development in the reverse direction: the word *burg* came to be replaced by *Stadt* if a town is meant, and finally *burgus* was used only in the limited sense of merely a fortified site. On the other hand *burgaere* came to mean less and less often the inhabitant of a castle and was finally used exclusively for a townsman who enjoyed a special legal standing. One can only speculate whether the medieval Latin *burgensis* contributed to the development of the term *burgher*. What matters is that in the eleventh century the terms still in use today first make their appearance. A new self-awareness revealed itself in the changes of nomenclature.

Specially founded towns now sprung up everywhere. In Spain, the *poblaciones* represent such a wave of foundations. In eleventh-century France, especially in the south and south-west, privileges setting up *burgi* and *salvitates* make their appearance. In 1007 the count of Anjou built an abbey with a *burgus* on his allodial estates. He granted it to the abbey of Beaulieu and explained that "whoever inhabited this town could never be charged with the infamy of being a serf, but all its inhabitants will be free" (*in quo burgo quicumque habitabit nusquam poterit de crimine servitutis infamari, sed omnes eius habitatores erunt liberi*).[118] Freedom was assured to the new inhabitants and nobody might accuse them of being servile, unfree, dependent men. The famous legal principle that 'town air makes free' is already apparent here. The *salvitates* were wide-spread in the duchy of Gascony and the county of Toulouse, lining the pilgrim route to Santiago. They offered the protection of better peace, favoured the cultivation of land, and were also occasionally market centres. The dukes of Gascony assured to the *salvitas* of the abbey of La Sauve-Majeure security on the route for pilgrims who came to pray there and for merchants coming to the annual and weekly markets. Within the boundaries of the *salvitas* – designated by crosses – everyone was to enjoy security: knights, peasants and merchants; just as the burgesses living in the *burgus* enjoyed unlimited security. The flood of people into the *salvitas* grew so large that further settlements, each with its own parish church, grew up. In the eleventh century new foundations began in Flan-ders,[119] although the act of foundation must be inferred, because no documentary records exist. The barren and uncultivated area of inner

Flanders between the coastline and the River Lys, which ran almost parallel with it, was provided with towns by the endeavours of Counts Baldwin V (1037–1067) and Robert the Frisian (1071–1091): Thourout, Lille, Messines, Aire, and Cassel were their creations. The founding of castles as the centres of administrative districts with religious houses of canons and fairs – Torhout, Ypres, Messines and Lille all became great Flemish fair towns – was the achievement of the counts, but they only attained their great success with the co-operation of merchants. Through these foundations the counts linked the coast with the Scheldt area. We have already mentioned the oldest foundation of the dukes of Brabant, Mont-Saint-Guibert, dating from 1116. Their most important foundation, however, was 's Hertogenbosch, described in 1196 as "the new *civitas* by the wood" (*nova civitas apud silvam*). Its undated charter of franchise goes back to the time of Duke Henry I, the most notable founder of towns among the Brabantine dukes.

In England under the Norman kings it was as often a question of expanding the old English towns as of founding new ones; most new foundations were in the Welsh march. The greatest number of town foundations occurred in the twelfth century, including those by feudal lords, especially in backward and underpopulated areas like Lancashire, Devon and Cornwall. The wave of these foundations ebbed away in the second half of the thirteenth century.

In Germany, the high water-mark in the creation of new towns occurred later. The foundation of Freiburg (*burgum liberum*) by the Zahringer dukes took place in the early twelfth century. Freiburg has been likened to a fanfare which heralded a new era in German urban development. In its charter of foundation[120] Conrad von Zähringen explained that he had set up a market on his own soil – *forum constitui* – at Freiburg, and the foundation of a market turned into the foundation of a town. He had further seen to the summoning of well-to-do merchants from all over the place and these constituted a sworn association with the town's founder. Leaving aside for the moment the constitutional side of the question, let us establish now that the market privilege was issued for the benefit, not of the lord, but of the market settlers. Each newcomer received a piece of land of fifty by a hundred feet on which to build a house in hereditary tenure for a payment of a rent charge of one shilling per annum. The Staufer established towns in Alsace, Swabia and Pleissenland.[121] In northern Germany Lübeck was the most important new town; in 1158–1159

Henry the Lion[122] finally took over and completed its foundation, which had been begun by the Schauenburgs in 1143. This foundation had behind it the strength of the mercantile experience of Cologne and Westphalia. In Westphalia, the era of foundations began in 1185 with the successful creation of Lippstadt. The purpose of these early German foundations was to set up commercial and industrial centres on favourable trading routes. These towns became important or at least middle ranking centres. The younger town foundations were due to the initiative of the modern types of states, the Italian communes, the French monarchy, and the principalities within the German Empire.

Borghi franchi[123] appeared in scattered places in Venetia and Liguria, more frequently in Emilia, and were numerous in Lombardy and Piedmont from the middle of the twelfth century. They were the foundations of the great communes, which used this means to impose their regional policies upon neighbouring towns or feudal lords. The *borghi franchi* served as footholds to control a road, crossroads, a ford, or the way out of a valley, as the centre point of a mining region, as a means of opening an area up to cultivation, or to assure a route into an underdeveloped area. The commune of Brescia, for instance, in 1179 resolved to rebuild the castle of Casaloldo, erected a market there that year, and granted the inhabitants of *castrum* and *suburbium* certain privileges. They should pay no higher taxes than the citizens of Brescia, and enjoy the same freedom, in return for occupying the castle with troops and keeping faith with the commune of Brescia. A charter of 1210 illustrates how such a new fortified settlement came into existence. The commune of Vercelli was to be responsible for building the new *burgum*, digging trenches and setting up four fortified gates with a gate tower and a church – all at its own expense. A market and a road which would connect it with other localities was to be made, and every inhabitant was to receive a building-plot; taxes should not be higher than in Vercelli. Gina Fasoli had at her disposal rich documentary sources, which in many cases she quoted in detail in the original form, to reveal the policies of the communes concerning town foundations, the building of the *borghi*, and the legal standing of their inhabitants.

Just as the *borghi franchi* provided strong points for consolidating the city states, so the town foundations of the German territorial princes provided the effective cores around which would be organized the growth of their states, created originally out of an assemblage of uncoordinated districts acquired through a variety of legal titles. This princely urban policy not only consisted of creating towns but also included the development of existing towns or of places about to become towns. On the borders of territorial lordships and in areas which were particularly divided amongst many lords, new foundations were especially numerous. To a special group belong places given privileges by lords but which never achieved the status of towns – places endowed with urban law: *villes neuves* in France and in the French-speaking parts of the Empire; *Freiheiten, Täler* and *Weichsbilde* in Germany. The *poblaciones, salvitates, burgi liberi, bastides* and *borghi franchi* have something approaching this legal structure. In Lorraine, the movement for freedom begins with the charter of 1177–1178, unfortunately not surviving in the original, granted by the bishop of Toul to the inhabitants of the newly-built fortress of Liverdun. The movement was modelled above all, however, on the Law of Beaumont of 1182. Taking over this law in many cases meant only freeing from serfdom the inhabitants of a village without granting further town law. Occasionally the foundation of a new town is also purely fictional. In one case an agreement was made between two parties for the pooling of goods and the division of liabilities so as to combine into a *nova villa* as a way out of an embroiled and complex legal situation.[124] French kings used such *pariage* agreements to extend their influence. The *bastides* of south and south-western France of the thirteenth and fourteenth centuries were instruments of royal or baronial policy and were connected with changes in agrarian structure. The *bastides* of Gascony were frequently erected on the land of Cistercian or Premonstratensian granges after their direct cultivation by the abbeys had been abandoned. The Cistercians were glad to conclude agreements with the kings of France or Gascon barons for the erection of such *bastides* on their land. The seignorial *bastides* were deliberate counter-foundations to the royal *bastides*.[125]

The distinction between freeing villages, creating areas of urban law and creating towns was an exceedingly fluid one. *Hanc libertatem dedi* is the summing up in a statement of the episcopal privilege of Liverdun; and the town law of Huy of 1066 contained the term *libertas villae*. However, the term embraced two entirely different types of settlement, both at the moment of receiving the privilege and later on.

Leon in Spain is a town. Saarbrücken or Elberfeld, which make their appearance as *Freiheiten*, became important towns, even if only in modern times. Blankenberg on the Sieg, raised in 1245 to the level of a town by Count Henry III of Sayn, is today one of the smallest titular towns of Germany, and it is only in its pattern of settlement that it reminds us of its urban hey-day. A real town economy could never have developed here. From the very beginning its function as a stronghold and administrative centre was more important than its economic role. Many foundations by German territorial lords were centres for official control over the lords' lands and survived into the nineteenth century as district and bureaucratic centres. Every territorial lord, however small his lands, wanted 'his' town or a couple of towns as symbols of prestige and from fear that otherwise too many enterprising people would depart into the towns of neighbouring lords. The result was that many mini-towns came into existence. Many were nothing more than walled villages, others showed some degree of social differentiation arising out of business life and a mercantile economy, which earned them the unfortunate name of "one-acre burgher towns".[126] It is impossible to portray the full variety of this chapter in urban history.[127] This discussion has confronted us with legal and constitutional questions, to which we must now turn.

CHAPTER 4

Town rule and the communes

The eleventh century was not only the epoch of the renaissance in trade and a time of decisive change in a market-orientated economy based upon the division of labour, it was also a time which, in its powerful and sometimes revolutionary movements, brought demands for peace and freedom. Peace was a particular prerequisite for trade and business; it was necessary for the travelling merchant, for the fair-goer and for the townsman with his wealth and wares in his house and in his town. The Church strove after freedom and made a first bid to free itself from the restrictions of the aristocratic world of the early Middle Ages. Freedom was also the desire of both the burgesses and of the peasantry.

The early medieval period was an age of lordship. There is an essential contrast between our modern state with its whole apparatus and machinery of government and our modern society with its pressures, and the lordly social order of the early Middle Ages where rule was based upon personal submission and upon the slowly developing reciprocal obligations between ruler and ruled. This social structure, which allowed greater scope for self-help and freedom from control, has been much discussed in the last decade. It is not necessary to do more than mention it here.

The ruler, at that time, faced not so much isolated individuals as communities. Schlesinger remarks that "it is not the ruler alone who produced and shaped the medieval political order. No less effective in this process is the community. In all governmental arrangements there is also a co-operative element and one cannot say that lordship was the indispensable factor in the creation of organized communities. On the contrary, it is truer to say that the communities sprang from their own independent roots."[128] Forms of government are as diverse as are types of community. We are going to examine one particular medieval form of government and society, namely urban government and the communes which grew out of urban societies. They are mutually interdependent from the very beginning.

It is necessary to begin by discussing the pre-communal period of medieval town organization. By this is meant the time when the lordly element dominated the public one. In many towns the internal conflict between ruler and community brought into existence a sharply defined degree of independence or even led to full public autonomy. In the latter case, the voice of the populace replaced that of the ruler and, in so doing, took over his authority to rule. It would be wrong to assume that organized communities merely emerged through struggles with lords and that no communal organization existed before such struggles occurred.

There has been a great deal of controversy about how the communes came into being.[129] The multiplicity of forces which underlay the creation of town organizations and the variety of their different forms should serve to warn us against seeking one single root cause for the development of the medieval commune. It is a unique creation of the Middle Ages and something quite new. The survival of many ancient towns cannot presuppose continuity in their institutional history. Rudiments of the town constitutions of Antiquity may have survived in Italy; episcopal government provides a connecting link between Antiquity and the Middle Ages; the legal thought of Antiquity survived. All such things, however, became absolutely woven into medieval constitutional forms. The examination of one single brick should not distort our impression of the whole new building, for these single elements may often have served quite different purposes in their medieval context. Certainly, we can no longer regard the existence of town law as providing the absolute criterion for defining the medieval town. The older generation of scholars who did take this view, in so doing uncovered real evidence of the significance of the special town law in the development of the medieval town. By its very nature, however, the development of the commune was also intrinsically dependent upon the social structure within the town or group of towns. Planitz was correct when he pointed to the common features which lay behind the legal and constitutional relationships in the business centres of north-western Europe. He was wrong, however, when he made this the basis for generalizations.

A special feature of north-western Europe is the very early merchant guild, which appears in the records from the early eleventh century onwards. Alpert of Metz, a monk from the diocese of Utrecht, in a work composed about the year 1020,[130] described the merchant guild of Tiel, a town which had succeeded ruined Dorestad and become for a time the most important trading centre between England and the Rhine valley. The pious monk expressed his indignation that the hard-headed folk of Tiel did not administer their law according to the custom of the land but according to their own will, and he maintained that this procedure was permitted by the emperor. He was unable to understand that, as merchants under royal protection, they were in fact proceeding according to special merchant law. The common land law of the early Middle Ages was the law of an agrarian society and did not meet the peculiar needs of a merchant community. This was particularly true of the rules for recovering debts. In this case, as in others, the medieval procedure was proof by the judgement of God and, above all, the ordeal by single combat. This procedure was an exceedingly troublesome undertaking for a merchant who was often in the position of having to prove or contest a debt. The inhabitants of Tiel were freed from this process. They could clear themselves by oath from charges of debt. In Huy, the charter of privileges of 1066 similarly replaced the trial by single combat with the taking of an oath.[131] The inhabitants could declare themselves guiltless of a debt by taking an oath supported by three 'oath-helpers'. Alien merchants, who could not so quickly find oath-helpers in Huy, could clear themselves by a personal oath and by the symbolic procedure of *exfestucacio*. The guild statutes of Saint-Omer of about 1100 stress that, if a man were challenged to single combat, he could turn for support to a guild only if he himself were a member. About the year 1070, Baldwin of Flanders freed the inhabitants of Grammont from the obligation to undergo the ordeal. In 1116 Count Baldwin VI freed the burgesses of Ypres from trial by single combat, by ordeal of hot irons and of water; instead they could clear themselves by oath with the aid of four oath-helpers. In northwestern Europe, in Flanders, on the French royal domain and in Normandy, once the ordeal had been abolished, the reform by rulers of the medieval penal laws began.[132] In 1127 William Clito, count of Flanders, explicitly laid down in the statutes of Saint-Omer that the burgesses of Saint-Omer would not be required to undergo single combat in any market town of Flanders but only to stand trial by the court (*Schöffen*). In 1173, the emperor Frederick Barbarossa granted a charter of privilege to Flemish merchants in the German Empire: nobody could challenge a Flemish merchant to single combat; if anybody wished to bring an action, then an oath was to be acceptable without bringing a challenge (*vare*). Finally, in 1178, the merchants of Verdun succeeded in obtaining from the city of Cologne their freedom from trial by combat and from any sort of ordeal.

This principle of law merchant would become an important part of the law of many towns. It was merchants' law which also established the right to free testamentary disposition, for under general legal practice the lord had the right to the goods of a deceased alien; freedom from the law of the shore (*Standrecht*) and security for vessels laden with cargo are other examples.

To return to the Tiel guild. Alpert goes on to say that the merchants of Tiel established a common fund which they used at specified times to defray the cost of a splendid banquet. This, he believed, was simply an invitation to get drunk; it was in fact the guild banquet, where members certainly caroused but where they also commemorated the guild's deceased members. The statutes of the merchant guild of Saint-Omer provide a detailed picture of this event. There was a rigorous procedure intended to ensure that the banquet proceeded peacefully; one member must not hit another with a fist, with bread or stones (there being no other weapons to hand). It was also laid down that after the banquet and when all its costs had been met, any remaining money in the guild coffer should be used for public purposes, for the streets, town gates and fortifications.

For Cologne a list of newly-enrolled guild members survives for the years 1135–1170.[133] We can learn much from this. The number of guild members must have been between two and three hundred. They were, as a rule, both burgesses and inhabitants of the Rheinvorstadt or suburban district of St Martin on the Rhine. As in England, no guild member could come from outside the town. The members were merchants in the narrowest sense of the word, wholesale traders. Naturally, they were also active in the profitable retail trade. Already by the twelfth century the dealers in cloth, iron, salt and victuals had their special stalls in the Cologne market where the cloth-sellers were the first to take up their positions. The humbler retailers, grocers, poulterers, cheese and wool dealers did not belong to the guild. According to the details of their places of origin, seventy-one per cent of the new guild members were immigrants from other towns; the *Schreinskarten* (deeds registering transfers of property in Cologne) of the middle of the twelfth century give evidence of only fifty-one per cent. There is no evidence of activity by the guilds among the community at large. The general merchant guild organization goes back at least to the eleventh century, and it survived until the middle of the thirteenth century.

The merchant guilds of northern France, Flanders, the Low Countries, England and northern Germany, which are not to be confused with the craft fraternities or *Zünfte*, appear as a powerful force in the town. A leading circle of townsmen joined together for mutual and unconditional support. For the guild brethren of Saint-Omer membership afforded them help if they were involved in difficulties. The men of Schleswig bloodily avenged the murder of an alderman of their guild, Cnut Laward, son of King Eric of Denmark; when the father of the murderer, King Nicholas, appeared as a fugitive before the gates of Schleswig, on 25 June 1134, he was permitted to enter, although his companions tried in vain to warn him of the danger. Suddenly, all the bells rang out and he and his companions were slain in front of the cathedral. However, even allowing for the gaps in the research which has been done, as well as in the evidence which survives, it remains clear that there were many towns in the northwest of Europe which never possessed any kind of guild; they were only possible in important trading centres.

The guild was, and remained, an exclusive personal grouping. It never comprised more than a limited number of townsmen. Neither the merchants' law nor the guild law had well-drawn lines of demarcation. "One is misunderstanding the cohesive strength and strongly defined character of a group of men if one forgets that beneath the common links of the majority of members there existed deep personal and local differences." Such was the judgment of Kroeschell on the relationship between the guild and the commune. The guild did not possess the power to pressurize non-members. On the other hand, the guild statutes of Saint-Omer state forcefully that any merchant resident in the city who did not become a member could not expect its assistance. This was the only way of persuading a merchant to join. The merchant guild has left no lasting trace of its influence on the development of the town commune. It was not a corner-stone for the development of the commune. It did, however, have some influence on the growth of the idea that the community should organize itself to the extent of providing a meeting place. This had the effect of strengthening the town's position against its rulers.

In the lower Franconian towns the guild by no means represented the only example of town organization. In the Rhine, Meuse and Moselle towns, the *Schöffenkolleg* or college of echevins, a judicial organ, was the oldest legal and administrative assembly. Towards the west as well as to the east, however, echevins gradually dwindle in importance. In the north, around Schleswig, we find no such assembly. This was also true of the newly-founded towns of lower Germany where it did not operate as an administrative body before the town councils came into being. In Cologne, even in the agreement of 1258 between the city and Archbishop Conrad von Hochstaden, it was specifically laid down that the Cologne echevins were obliged under oath to observe the law of the Church and of the city. They also had to admit that they had always governed the city with the agreement of the archbishop. The echevins were thus nominated by the lord of the city and bound by oath. Their jurisdiction extended in the first instance over the town and over a well-defined area of land around it. As soon as the town jurisdiction becomes separated from the larger surrounding judicial districts (a phenomenon which becomes apparent in the tenth century but which can appear much later), and as soon as the *Gerichtschöffen* began to be chosen from among and by the townsmen, they came to constitute a separate administrative unit. To some extent, the Franconian legal system provided a prototype for medieval urban constitutions but it had to be modified for this purpose. If the *Schöffenkolleg* were to fulfil the requirements of a town's judicial system and administration, it had to be staffed by men who understood something of the law and of the economic life of the town. We can indeed sometimes glean from the rather scanty source material that the town *Schöffen* were often engaged in business.

In many towns we meet as another organ of judicial administration the ancient *ungebotene Ding*. This institution appears in the town law of Augsburg, Regensburg and Ulm and was an ancient judicial assembly at which attendance was compulsory. It has also been proved to have existed in Worms, Boppard, Koblenz, Bonn, Siegburg, Cologne, Neuss, Trier, Metz, Toul, Verdun and Dinant. Occasionally, in a very decayed form, we can still find it surviving at the time of the French Revolution. In north Germany one finds the old *Echteding*, often synonymous with the *Bursprake*.[134] This was a gathering of associated members to deal with matters of common concern. It is found from Utrecht to Dorpat but these *Burspraken* did not take hold beyond the Rhine. In many parts of south Germany the townsfolk assembled on the day of the swearing-in of the new town council.[135] In addition, in almost every town, there existed assemblies without institutional basis or defined composition which convened to deal with affairs in unusual situations.

A primitive phenomenon which it is not possible to trace further, but which existed in all sorts of agrarian as well as urban societies, was the *Nachbarschaft* or association of neighbours, *Geburen*, *vicini*. It can be traced throughout Europe, in Cologne and Soest as well as Genoa, where it became the basis of the special wards or districts in the town. The inner divisions in the towns frequently had their roots in the countryside. Here we find earliest the feature which German scholars, above all, increasingly stress: the existence of close connections between the development of urban and rural communities. Steinbach saw too one-sidedly the Cologne *Sondergemeinde* as a product of the decentralization of urban judicial developments. The process is more complex. Alongside the importance of neighbourhood groupings, we must also take into account the rôle of the Church, especially of the parish boundaries, in forming territorial entities.

Kroeschell has thrown important new light on one controversial area by explaining the importance of the territorial distinctions within the commune. He brought out the similarities between the founding of the towns and the colonization of villages within forest areas (*Rodungsdörfe*). He also pointed to the similarity between rules of free tenure in town and country. The colonization movement to him was "the communal settlement of equally entitled associates" which formed a "prelude to the establishment of law". He attributed to colonization a particularly important part in the development of urban law. To him the founding of a town involved far more than the rational imitation of an established urban pattern. In the Westphalian Wikbold area, which he studied, he discovered "forms of free settlement which could not be fitted into a pattern of contrasts between town and country communities". Here he was quite correct. The German free districts and valleys, the *villes neuves*, and the like, have always been seen as the legal links between town and village, as 'town law places' and never as mercantile creations. Because the larger, older towns often grew by swallowing up their suburbs, in the process of taking over what was noble land they thereby also adopted its freer tenure. Kroeschell's ideas are also important for the type of town settlement where the act of founding the urban settlement was important, in at least a part of the town, in cementing a sense of community. R. von Keller, using southern and western European evidence, has demonstrated the part played by the colonization movement in inaugurating personal freedom and freedom of owner-ship.[136] Yet it is Kroeschell's achievement to have revived the discussion of this question. In his study of the Wikbolden, he revealed one regional type which was well worth investigating. His fundamental argument demonstrated the one-sidedness of Planitz's view that the communal idea developed out of a sworn association. However, he rather overstated his case. One cannot use the example of the Westphalian Wikbolden to undermine the well-grounded notion that foreign merchants played an important part in the development of towns. For instance, Münster does not belong in this category, as Westphalian research has shown. "Only the well-trained, world-experienced and world-travelled merchant could have conceived the complicated and subtle legal concepts of the Münster merchant law and it is upon him in particular that Planitz bases his theory" (Engel). Kroeschell never straightforwardly posed the question of how far municipal law (*Weichbildrecht*) controlled the practical and essential functioning of town life. In the last resort, he made the same mistake as Planitz, of underestimating the differences in types of towns and only a detailed typological discussion could correct this.

It was the combined forces of lord and settler which brought the town communities into existence. Many market settlements came into being in this way. What is the importance of the market in the development of town law and the community? Market law, in its developed form became, as Schlesinger stressed,[137] simply the law of the whole locality around the market. Basing his work especially on the example of Halberstadt and using the topographical studies of Stoob on the towns of lower Saxony, he viewed town law as the fusion of merchant law with market law. This is true, although perhaps one should emphasize more strongly than he does the smooth transition and overlap between the merchant's trading post and the market settlement.

From this variety of forms and notions belonging to native law, and by process of adapting traditional institutions, the German towns developed their own peculiar substantive law and their own constitutional structure at a time when they were still under seigneurial rule. We must consider two further points. Were there influences from other European areas? And how, when, where and by what means did communal forces get the upper hand over the town rulers? The development of the town commune is not purely a matter of legal evolution. Its constitutional development is closely interwoven with the political events and spiritual ideas of the age. The eleventh century brought considerable unrest in the towns because of substantially increased immigration, especially the influx of dependents of uncertain legal status who poured in. The stimulus of the movements for introducing God's peace and more communal freedom excited unrest. The lively discussion of church reform, heresy and the investiture contest also played their part in stirring unrest, especially in the last years of the tenth century, predominantly in Aquitaine in south-western France where the central government was particularly weak and anarchy especially widespread. The peace movement adopted a number of institutionalized forms, though the medieval terminology is imprecise. The initiative for the oldest peace leagues, *pax Dei* or God's peace as they were later called, came from the clergy, especially from the episcopate who were able to enforce them by using ecclesiastical sanctions. The movement was to the advantage of the poorer element in the population. After the Council of Charroux in about 989 its aim was the protection of the Church and the weak, and the suppression of violence. In the eleventh century it received new impetus from the *Treuga Dei*, the imposition of truces for specified periods. The use of the oath as a device to strengthen provisions for peace is specifically mentioned as part of the proceedings which took place on the meadows of St Germanus at Le Puy. Merchants were among those whose protection was laid down. We do not know how far the movement enjoyed much practical success. The feuds of the great continued to occur through the eleventh century but, on the other hand, we do not know how many were actually prevented. But this movement, directed against the *potentes* on behalf of the *inermes pauperes*, was also supported by the general mass of the poor. In France, the development of diocesan and urban sworn associations was closely linked with it.[138] In other respects the movement moved very sharply away from ecclesiastical control and in the towns it was a lay movement which often developed into a force opposing clerical overlordship.

The peace movement appeared relatively late in Germany. It was about 1082 that a 'God's Peace' was first proclaimed at Liège; from there the movement certainly spread to Cologne. In 1083 a Cologne synod under Archbishop Sigewin proclaimed a God's Peace. Two years later, at Mainz, the imperial episcopate declared it binding throughout the Empire. In 1103 the German emperor ordained an imperial peace of four year's duration "for the Church, clerics, monks, laymen, merchants and women". The delay in the appearance of the peace movement in Germany may be connected with the greater security which the country had enjoyed under Ottonian rule. However, some such measures, in the meantime, became necessary, as is shown strikingly in the *Hofrecht* of Bishop Burchard of Worms: for the years 1023–1025 there is mention of almost daily capital crimes in the records, of bloody fights "fought in a bestial manner and arising out of nothing but drunkenness or bravado". In one single year in Worms, thirty-five people met their deaths from such causes. The movement for God's Peace and peace in the country became the province of the government. Herein lies its significance. It contributed enormously to the transformation of the penal code. It is easy to distinguish it from the urban sworn associations; but in its aim and in the methods employed – the use of an oath to assert their objective – the two movements were similar.

The convergence of clerical, governmental and urban movements also brought into focus the conflict over freedom. In eleventh-century France the relationship between the spiritual and the temporal world was being reconsidered. The attempt to remove lay control from the monastery and from the whole spiritual province produced a heightened religious feeling; reform and heresy lay dangerously side by side here in what was a desire to emulate Christ's poverty. France is the home of the reformed cloisters of Cluny and Fontevrault and of the reformed religious orders of the eleventh century – the Carthusians, Cistercians and Premonstratensians. The French church's relationship with the state was burdened neither by the tradition of an imperial church policy nor by a problem like that of Germany's involvement in Italian politics. The result is that the clerical inspiration of the investiture contests and their religious rather than political origins stood out more sharply than in Germany or Italy.

In Germany, however, the investiture contest became a political struggle which divided the Church and reduced its power in favour of the lay princes. The towns became involved in this struggle, taking sides and imposing their own conditions on the different parties. The population took up the cry for reform and turned it into an attack on simony and a demand for the stricter observance of a truly spiritual life. The towns along the Rhine provided the battleground for the decisive struggles between emperor and pope. It was at Worms that the deposition of Pope Gregory VII was proclaimed – twenty-four of the thirty-eight German bishops appeared at Henry IV's invitation. It was at Utrecht, on Easter Sunday 1076, that Bishop William pronounced the anathema against the pope. While Utrecht remained a secure imperial bastion until 1112, in the imperial town of Cambrai an episcopal schism developed which promoted a political expansion of Flanders into the Empire as well as bringing civic unrest. The first sworn association of townsmen was broken up in Cambrai in 1077. During the episcopal schism there in 1102, however, the pro-papal Robert, count of Flanders, invaded the territory of Cambrai and the pro-imperial bishop had, of necessity, to recognize the commune of the burgesses. The Emperor Henry IV's campaign there in 1103 resulted in Count Robert agreeing, at a solemn imperial assembly, to support the emperor's candidate for the see of Cambrai. The commune was naturally dissolved by the pro-imperial bishop during the emperor's new expedition against Flanders in 1107. In 1122, the lordship of Cambrai was seized from the emperor by Count Charles the Good of Flanders, to the joy of the city. This was because the count "was feared by all the bands of robbers like the thunder and lightning". The region of lower Lorraine remained for the most part loyal to the emperor. Bishop Otbert of Liège sheltered Henry IV from the attacks of his son. It was from here that the emperor organized his resistance. Supported by a contingent of the townsmen of Liège, he was able to resist Henry V as he attempted to cross the River Meuse at Visé.

In Cologne, 1074 was the year of the merchants' rebellion against Archbishop Anno. The archbishop's confiscation of a boat belonging to a merchant proved the last straw and he himself escaped the enraged population with only a moment to spare. The revolt ended in the bloody subjugation of the city. When Anno's fourth successor, Frederick, who had come to Cologne with imperial backing, went over to the camp of the emperor's son in 1106, the city (this was after the victory at Visé) took the opposite side and stayed in the imperial camp. The archbishop was driven out and the city strengthened and extended its fortifications. It adopted its own policy, sometimes supporting its overlord and sometimes opposing him. In the great revolt on the lower Rhine in 1114, it took his side, perhaps because of his earlier adoption of the Oath for Peace which had been promulgated in Cologne in 1112. Under the Emperor Frederick I, Cologne received its first seal, one of the oldest civic seals in the whole of Germany.[139] In 1149 and 1178 Cologne quite independently concluded two treaties with Trier and Verdun. However, episcopal overlordship lasted *de facto* until 1288 and *de iure* even longer.

In 1119 a schism also developed in the see of Liège in which the *ministeriales* of the Liège church and the city of Liège took different sides. In 1122, during the emperor's visit to Utrecht at Whitsun, there was a conspiracy of the episcopal *ministerials* against him, and the bishop was imprisoned on a charge of treason. A strongly pro-imperial party now appeared among the citizens. On 2 June, the emperor confirmed to the inhabitants of Utrecht and Muiden a charter of Bishop Godebald on condition that they took an oath of fealty to him. In it, the townsmen, who wanted to fortify the city of Utrecht with a wall, were granted freedom from tolls. In upper Lorraine, Trier remained pro-imperial while the bishops of Metz, Toul and Verdun followed no consistent policy. Here too, the cities of Metz, Toul and Verdun took the side of the emperor in direct opposition to their episcopal overlords. The Gregorian supporter, Theotger, abbot of St George's in the Black Forest, was elected bishop of Metz in 1118. But he was never able to obtain control of his bishopric because of the strong opposition in the city, and he died at Cluny. Henry of Winchester, a protégé of Henry V, who changed to the papal side, only obtained control of the bishopric of Verdun by armed force. By contrast, in 1115 the citizens of Mainz persuaded Henry V to free their archbishop, Adalbert. When, in 1119–1120, the archbishop then granted the inhabitants of Mainz freedom from alien laws and dues, he specifically named the *cives* among those who had interceded for him with the emperor. They had received him like "true sons of their father" when he had been released, half-dead, from prison. The townsmen had become a political factor in their own right.

But was there already a united, free bourgeoisie living under the same law? This was by no means true in the tenth and eleventh centuries. The town population was socially stratified and subject to a variety of different laws. The members of the merchant guild whom we have already discussed formed one such group. Some of them came into the town from far away. Merchants belonged to the upper strata of urban society and they appeared both in large and small towns around 1100 under the names of *optimi, prudentiores* or *meliores*. To this upper strata also belonged the group known as *ministeriales* who were in the service of either the town's overlord or of some other nobleman. They were particularly numerous and influential in episcopal and royal towns. It rarely happened that they remained continuously on the side of the town's overlords, for they developed their own collective awareness which could bring them into sharp opposition to their masters. An impressive example of this was the conspiracy (*fortissima coniuratio*) by the *ministeriales* of Utrecht against their bishop in 1159. The relationship between *ministeriales* and townsmen[140] has also been and is likely to remain the subject of weighty discussion among historians. A high proportion of the leading men of the towns came from the ranks of the *ministeriales*. In the last resort, the important distinction is between the south German cities, where the *ministeriales* became a town nobility, and a place like twelfth-century Cologne where commercial interests dominated both *ministeriales* and townsmen alike so that they cannot be distinguished.

To the middle *stratum* of urban society belonged the many *Zensualen*, people who had risen from servitude; among these were dependents who often remained subject to their lords and who thus gave a foothold in the town to alien non-urban legal rules. The alternative was that the fugitive bondsmen sought to break their bonds with their lords, and the lord's reaction to this was to threaten the town's peace. The situation was an extremely uncertain and mobile one. Eleventh- and twelfth-century society was characterized by its striving for social advancement. The *ministeriales*, for instance, rose from servile status in this way. Economic and political standing, wealth and influence, cease to reflect the status of a person under the law. Real tragedies, litigation and even civil strife, could result when the freedom of an important individual was in question. The famous saying that 'town air makes free' was vindicated in the towns although there were naturally considerable variations and exceptions. The Charter of Lorris (Art. 18), which comes from the first half of the twelfth century, already expressed the classic maxim: if a man managed to stay unmolested by his master in a town for a year and a day, he could carry on living there, free and without restrictions. One finds this statement in Flemish, English and German town law of the twelfth century.[141] How did it come about and how was the time-honoured legal control of the overlord removed? In north-western Europe we encounter the first attempt by an unfree population to obtain their freedom in the towns of Dinant and Huy in the Meuse valley. In Dinant the problem of immigrants was resolved by the comital overlord, who proclaimed that all immigrants, with the exception of people from three particular lordships, should be subject directly to him. The old saying that the air gave a man his free status had the meaning here of giving the townsmen common standing before the law. But the citizens wanted more than legal equality, they wanted freedom. In 1066 the citizenry of Huy bought the freedom of their city (*libertas ville*) from the bishop of Liège with a considerable sum of money. The charter of privilege, which is very badly preserved, is the oldest known recorded statement of town law surviving for the area north of the Alps. It regulated three important groups of problems: debts under merchant law which we have already discussed; the law governing new citizens; and, thirdly, local territorial law. The maxim that 'town law makes free' had not yet been conceived. In Huy immigrant bondmen remained subject to their lord. However, the burden of proving servile status remained with the lord, and the legal procedure governing this proof was a long drawn-out one. A serf could be given back only into the custody of a man who could show that he was a good and just lord; a bondman whom the lord had burdened with services over and above what was customary was allowed to remain unmolested. Huy developed a far-reaching right of asylum. Anyone who committed homicide outside the boundary of the town and managed to reach its territory could not be touched as long as he was prepared to appear before a court. He was thus preserved from private acts of vengeance. Similarly, anyone who inflicted an open wound on another and then fled into a house, could remain there in peace until he was summoned before the local court. Such legal provisions had already appeared earlier in the *burgi* and *salvitates* of south-western France. It seems evident that this movement for *libertas*, as well as the terms *burgi* and *burgenses*, reached the Meuse from this region of south-western France. These concepts of freedom often have their origin in the earlier colonization and represent the 'law of a new settlement'. One wonders whether the Spanish *poblaciones* may not be a source of this process of legal development. For years I have pointed to the privilege of Cardona of 986 as proof of this,[142] since it assured freedom for everyone, including the evil-doer. There is plenty of evidence of considerable cultural influence moving from south and south-western France into central Europe, just as there is of the close cultural relationship between south-western France and Spain in the Middle Ages. Detailed research remains to be done here. We must repeat at this point the question put to Kroeschell, namely how far the little settlements with their own particular status could be a model for the huge, developed cities? The settlers or inhabitants might develop from such an example their own concept of freedom. The later development of the urban constitution, however, naturally varied according to the size, the political and economic importance and the social structure of the settlement. The townsmen could only actually make a contribution to the development of this law[143] once they had established their own personal freedom and that of their property.

Urban law with its flexibility, predominance of written, deliberately introduced and uniform rules, prevailed over the old customary law. Calculability and rationality characterized the merchant spirit. The rigidity of the old form of the law, the *vare*, was readily laid aside in the twelfth century in the town laws. Apart from the special free rights of burgesses, originally the privilege only of sworn burgesses and excluding day-workers, maids, servants and apprentices, the town slowly evolved a far-reaching equality before the law and in the courts; equality in the exercise of political power was generally missing. The towns sought to protect their burgesses from the jurisdiction of outside courts. Distinctions in legal status were replaced by differentiation between rich and poor while oppression by the lord of the town was replaced by the oppression of its own patriciate. In Cologne, in 1258, there was a complaint that rich and powerful burgesses were forcing ordinary people to become their dependents, *Muntleuten* (literally 'mouthpeople'), which led to perversion of the legal system. Also, conflict between natives and immigrants became more pronounced. Trade between towns meant that a special law for outsiders became necessary, one capable of providing swift remedies. The laws governing urban trading monopolies were in many ways disadvantageous to an outsider as was also the prohibition of direct trading between aliens.

On the whole, by the end of the Middle Ages, the walls of the town enclosed a territory with its own jurisdiction and its own simple and clearly differentiated administration. Equality and uniformity of law was extended when the law of what one might call a 'mother' town was adopted by a chain of 'daughter' towns. This was never, however, consistently carried out. About the middle of the twelfth century we can distinguish two different types of legal system existing in towns on the Meuse: the law of Namur and the law of Liège, and they corresponded to the areas controlled by the overlords of these two towns. In the second half of the twelfth century we already find many newly-founded towns following the law of Magdeburg. In 1188–1189 the town of Hamburg was founded, with its law based on that of Lübeck. At the beginning of the thirteenth century, Speyer law became a widespread model. These 'families' of towns following the same urban code are a widespread European phenomenon. In Spain, Jaca formed such a 'mother' town and in England the same was true of Oxford, which in its turn was an offshoot of London.

In the towns, from the twelfth century onwards, the power of the politically involved mercantile bourgeoisie evolved through the sworn associations. We can better learn what part this played in the development of the commune if we look at the region of northern France and Flanders rather than that between the Rhine and the Moselle. In the latter, imperial bans restricted the movement's growth. We can see this in Trier although the evidence is scanty, also in Cologne and more ambiguously in Freiburg im Breisgau.[144] In Flanders, autonomy was achieved by the townsmen combined together under oath, led by the guild merchants.[145] In 1127 special political circumstances, namely the conflict over a successor to the murdered and childless Count Charles the Good, gave the patriciates the excuse to combine under oath with the *cives meliores* of the Flemish cities for joint action on the question of the succession. Such was the trust and friendship between the townsmen that they only wanted to act collectively (*nam ex civitatibus Flandriae et castris burgensis stabant in eadem securitate et amicitia ad invicem, ut nihil in electione nisi communiter consentirent aut contradicerent*). The count's notary, Galbert of Bruges, who was a participant in these events and observed them with a sharp eye for reality, has left us a report of what happened. He reveals the maturity which public life in Flanders had already achieved by this time. William of Normandy, originally the most successful candidate for the succession, had made concessions to the towns whose united stand had made them an important political factor. He granted them substantial privileges; in one such privilege for Saint-Omer, where we have the original document, many favours were conferred and, above all, the sworn association of the burgesses was recognized. This was modelled on the sworn association of Aire on the River Lys which Count Robert had recognized in 1100. The strength of the sworn association at Saint-Omer by 1164 is shown by another document which never obtained the force of law but which, Ganshof believed, reflected the aspirations of its townsmen. In it the *communio*, the *Eidgenossenschaft* or sworn association, was to play a decisive role: the *iurati communionis* ("jurymen of the commune"), elected without any participation of the town's overlord the count, were to act as the representatives and members of a town court quite alien to the *Schöffengericht* (the old urban court controlled by the town lord). This corresponded to a commune of the northern French type. In Tournai and Compiègne the mayor and *iurati* were administering the towns by themselves; in Saint-Quentin, Laon, Chauny, Corbie, Roye, Braye-sur-Somme, Péronne and Athis the *iurati* had rather to accommodate themselves to the old arrangements within the college of echevins. In Flanders a constitution based on the sworn associations had not developed, and the echevins rather than the sworn leagues remained in control of the towns. William Clito, in the *cartula convencionis*, as the privilege for Bruges is called, gave the townsmen the right to change their law in their own assembly as new circumstances dictated (*comes superaddidit eis [civibus] ut potestative et licenter consuetudinarias leges suas de die in diem corrigerent et in melius commutarent secundum qualitatem temporis et loci*). This arrangement did not survive the rule of the energetic counts of the house of Alsace. But the towns managed in general to maintain their self-government and this had the advantage that early on in Flanders modern systems of law and government developed. From Galbert's own attitudes we can see clearly the great extent to which the Flemish bourgeoisie felt themselves responsible for the state of *terra Flandriae*. We find a similar feeling of responsibility for events in areas outside their own walls in the Rhenish towns from 1254 onwards.

From its very beginning the communal movement in France also displayed a revolutionary character. We first find written evidence of this in Le Mans in the year 1070; *facta itaque conspiracione quam communionem vocabant*, as it is put in the *Actus pontificum Cenomannis in urbe degentium*. This movement really had urban roots although it assumed a regional character and had many similarities to diocesan communes. In Le Mans, before the revolt of 1070, there was besides *civitatis consuetudines atque iustitie*, a special customary law of the town.[146] In the twelfth century, the king of France took the movement in hand and eventually became its sole guarantor, and it now represented a single type of commune.

In northern France the sworn association of burgesses amounted to being the same thing as the community at large. It was territorial.

According to the wording of a document of Philip Augustus for Amiens, dating from 1190, the commune is defined both as a district and as an association of burgesses. In a confirmatory charter for the commune of Soissons of 1189 it is enacted that all the inhabitants of the city and its suburbs should swear an oath to the commune (*universi homines infra murum civitatis et extra in suburbio commorantes... communionem jurent*). This indeed amounted to being the fundamental act of creation of the Soissons commune, which included all the permanently resident menfolk of the town *nos* [= *rex*] *in civitatem Suessionensem communiam constituisse de hominibus illis, qui ea die domum aut plateam habebant infra terminos urbis et suburbiorum eius.* Clerks and knights were excluded. Care was also taken that serfs were not enabled, by some roundabout means like marriage, to evade their lords. But here also, after a year, 'town air made men free'. In Amiens the burgesses collectively were designated *iurati.* Their reciprocal obligations to give loyalty and help were laid down in the first article of the charter (*unusquisque iurato suo fidem, auxilium consiliumque per omnia iuste observabit*). Often, however, we can take the term *iurati* to mean the sworn assembly which had been elected. Alongside it was the assembly of the commune which could be summoned by the stroke of a bell. The commune also had subordinate organs of government of an executive nature; for example in Amiens the *dekanes* or *servientes communie.* Their highest duty was the maintenance of peace. *Pax* and *communia* were almost synonymous.

Maintenance of order in the town lay at the root of the harsh penal codes which the towns developed and enforced, above all the community's penalty of the destruction of a miscreant's house which, at the same time, symbolized his expulsion from society. This penalty was also used in Amiens against an injured person who attempted to take justice into his own hands and who was not content with the rigid system of compensation ordained by the official body of the commune itself. The overlords of the towns, whether king or bishop, were not completely excluded from authority when the commune formally came into existence. The king could not only give his seal of approval to the commune, he could also annul it. In Amiens the king was represented by a *prepositus* and *bailli*; there were defined limitations to his rights of intervention in legal matters as opposed to those of the *major* and *scabini* or *iudices*, as the governing committee of the Amiens commune was known. Of particular value to the king was the income from judicial dues, of which a certain proportion was destined for him. When, in Hesdin, somebody redeemed their house from destruction by a fine, half went to the king and the other half for the town fortifications. In the important cloth town of Amiens, merchants and their trade are mentioned in the charter. Particular care was taken for their security and speedy legal assistance was given to an alien merchant if a debtor defaulted. The old merchant's edict about exemption from fighting the judicial duel was carefully defined territorially and it was forbidden in the commune to employ a hired champion. The echevins were the established authority for attesting to the legality of documents and their existence made proofs by ordeal superfluous. Older structures survived into the constitutional period of the commune. In Amiens there were still three *ungebotene Dinge*. But it is not possible to go any further here into the considerable variations of law and constitution which existed in the northern French communes.[147] The urban sworn assembly is here not only a revolutionary episode, in that it represented a break-through to greater freedom for the community, it was also in its formative stage a constitutional type in its own right. At its basis lay the sworn brotherhood which encompassed all areas of medieval life including the clerical and feudal. It had an importance in achieving greater independence for the townsmen far and above the broad area of the constitution. It was not without reason that it aroused decisive opposition. The town sworn assembly, in recognition by King John of London's sworn association in 1191, was described as *tumor plebi, timor regni, terror sacerdotii* – a running sore among the people, a terror to the kingdom, a horror for the clergy.[148] Planitz was right when he saw the sworn association as a powerful driving force which characterized the formation of the constitution in the great medieval towns. He failed, however, to differentiate it fully from the guild and did not distinguish sufficiently between the formation of the community and the development of a free or even autonomous constitution. Nor did he separate the purely legal from the constitutional process, and he is too careless and sweeping in his study of the dissemination of the sworn assembly. The northern French type of commune, constituted on the basis of the sworn assembly, was the equivalent to the sworn confederations in Cologne, Trier and the Flemish towns as well as elsewhere.

In the Mediterranean area, to which we shall now turn, there were comparable stages in communal constitutional development. It is not possible to examine every regional variation over this huge area. Venice's exceptional position, as a city which never belonged to any feudal state, has already been mentioned. Max Weber described[149] the arbitrary nature of the doge's power as "thoroughly patrimonial in character, a sort of city king". The doge's authority was followed by a growth in power of the patrician families who lived around the Rialto. In the twelfth century, alongside the doge there grew up the Council of the Wise (*Sapientes*). The role of the people, gathered in the *placitum*, was limited to declaring its assent (*collaudatio*) to what the Council had decided. As Max Weber forcibly emphasized, the financial needs of the community, which were created by its warlike commercial and colonial policies, were a powerful element in the creation of a patrician oligarchy. After 1164 the city, because of its part in the town league against the Staufer, could only meet its financial obligations with the help of a credit consortium. Eight of these were the so-called tribunician nobles, the *tribuni* being originally the heads of the separate islands. Four members were drawn from 'new' families who had become wealthy through commerce. Among these was a Ziani who was a member of a proverbially rich family which owned enormous properties both within twelfth-century Venice and outside it.[150] The existence of an assembly of the populace, of the Great Council and the Small Council, the division of the city correspondingly into *confinia* or *còntrade, trentacie* and *sestieri*, the method of electing the doge using forty electors chosen by four *probi homines*, the well established form of the oath administered to the doge who became the first official in the city, all show how systematically the constitution had been set up by the patricians. According to Max Weber:

The constitutional and administrative methods of Venice are famous because of the success of this tyranny, both patrimonial and governmental, in controlling a vast area of land and sea by the strict limitations in their freedom of action which the noble families imposed upon themselves. Their control was maintained because they held together the whole machinery of power through such a rigid system of secret controls, the like of which had never been seen before. This was possible because every member of the group, which was dominated by powerful monopolistic interests, had daily before his eyes a basic solidarity of interests within and without the group which made it possible to absorb individual interests in the collective tyranny. It was actually managed in this way: power was divided between competing authorities at the centre. Various 'colleges' in charge of specific administrative tasks, almost all invested with legal and administrative powers, competed among themselves for control; the administration was divided into many branches, all staffed by noblemen while legal, military and financial affairs were divided amongst various officials; officials held office only for a brief time and were under strict control during their tenure of office; from the fourteenth century onwards, there came into existence a political court of enquiry, the Council of Ten. As an instrument of terror this was directed chiefly against the nobility. On the other hand, it was by far the most popular body among the populace, who were excluded from political power, because it was the single but effective means of successfully prosecuting the patrician officials.

The situation in other Italian towns was far removed from that in Venice with its inner cohesion. At the beginning of the constitutional development of the port of Genoa lies the privilege of 958, which we have already mentioned. It deserves our attention as one of the oldest town charters in Europe. It was, as the notable Munich historian, Eduard Hlavitschka has shown, granted by King Berengar II and Adalbert under special political circumstances. Berengar lived in permanent fear of the Emperor Otto I. In 950/51 he had effectively redrawn the frontier of the border area of Obertenga, of which Genoa was a part, but Margrave Obert gave the actual exercise of power in Genoa to a viscount from one of Genoa's old Roman families. In 952 the viscount was Ido, from whose son, Obert, three branches of the Genose family of Visconti were descended. Margrave Obert, who in 945 was adviser to Berengar's opponent Lothar at the court of Pavia, was among the Italian magnates who fled to Germany in 960 to seek Otto's aid against the 'tyrant', Berengar. It was in these circumstances that King Berengar tried to assure himself of Genoa's support by a grant of privileges.

After its conquest by Rothari in 642–644 the walls of Genoa had been destroyed and it had been degraded into a mere *vicus*. But it was now refortified. Thanks to its defences, it offered a safe refuge for people fleeing from the constant attacks of the Saracens. The walls, which enclosed the castle with the church of S. Maria al Castello as well as the city with the cathedral of S. Lorenzo, did not however include the *burgus* with the old cathedral of San Siro. The privilege does not mention this tri-partite division of Genoa, which however is mentioned in other twelfth-century documents. The charter is concerned solely with the inhabitants of the *civitas*, and mentions neither the margrave nor the archbishop. By *civitas* it here means the whole city, not in the closely defined sense but in the wider sense of the word, encompassing *castrum* as well as city in the narrow sense and *burgus*. One would like to believe that the bestowal of a privilege on the inhabitants of *civitas Januensis* presupposes a businesslike entity capable of accepting and promulgating a charter. But, as we have seen, it was particular political necessity which

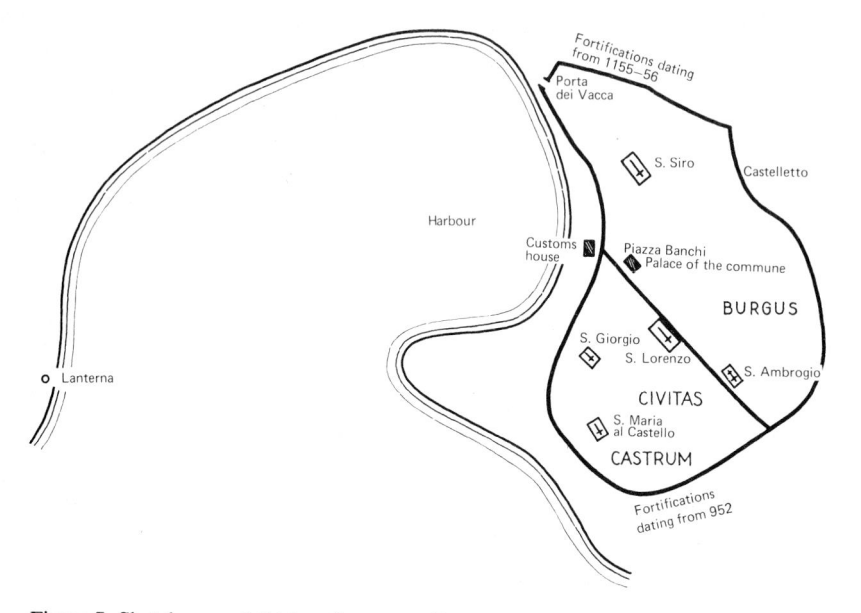

Figure 7. Sketch-map of thirteenth-century Genoa.

compelled the king to turn directly to the population of the city. Nothing is said about their organization, and one could believe that they were organized on an improvised basis to meet these special circumstances if it were not that the document specifically confirms the citizens' customary law as well as guaranteeing their undisturbed possession of their property. R. Keller has already surmised that these customs were part of the law surviving from the time of the first foundation of Genoa. A distinct foundation is also proved by the existence of the *burgus*. This clarification, confirmed by the close relationship between Genoa's privilege and the Spanish *poblaciones*, seems to me more plausible than the view of Vito Vitale,[151] who believed in the survival of Romano-Byzantine legal customs. Against any idea that there was continuity with Antiquity, we must consider the evidence of findings in upper Italy as well as Genoa's own dramatic history and, above all, the topography of the town which reveals considerable immigration in the tenth century, perhaps even already in the ninth. Above all, the privileges of free shelter for strangers and house-peace are included in the 958 privilege. The sum of the individual 'house-peaces' created the city peace in Genoa; in this, the privilege followed lines laid down in Lombard times, and the town appeared as the sphere of an enhanced and special peace.

The importance of the medieval institution of immunity, by no means limited to Genoa, is a valuable confirmation of the presence of "a local element in the evolution of the commune" (Dilcher). Genoese society at the time of the settlement had developed into a real community in this protected area and one which was now recognized by the king and given its freedom. Such a freed community of people is seldom encountered in Italy in this form, especially not in big cities. This is the consequence of the gradual, unequal growth of towns being a more frequent phenomenon than growth by absorbing a suburb which had been a site of new settlement. Most new settlements are only *borghi*.

One of the early forms of Italian Lombard settlement, to which the Frankfurt legal historian Dilcher draws particular attention, is the creation of the town as an area with its own constitutional rules, still under the rule of the bishop, and distinct from the surrounding countryside. The result of this was that the town dwellers as *concives episcopi* collectively enjoyed the privileged standing of the episcopal church. Dilcher hinted that this implied a new concept of *districtus civitatis* which made possible a typical urban constitutional law. He stressed that, between 800 and 1000 A.D., town dwellers were forming a more cohesive society. Genoa provides a particular example of such a development. Dilcher attributed to the church a considerable contribution in passing on a tradition of public law from the ruler. H.F. Schmid, however, pictures the bishops simply in their rôle as figureheads for their towns and has shown that laymen played a part in the administration of ecclesiastical property; "there existed in all episcopal cities a circle of men qualified in law and business, a literate and prosperous upper *stratum*. This class produced, as well as popes and bishops, consuls and *podestàs* and, above all, the *iudices* and *notarii* who were so numerous in the medieval Italian towns". Dilcher also stressed that the bishops never achieved the position of liege or seigneurial authority over the town. The difference in status between bishops and leading citizens was certainly smaller than in northern Europe where the bishop and richer merchants belonged to different spheres of life.

In Italy, in the eleventh century, there was a loosening and change from the old, early medieval order. The separation of Church from state brought this to fruition and this, in part, paved the way for the separation of the spiritual from the temporal spheres which began in other parts of Europe in the eleventh century. A typical development, both in Italy and in southern Europe generally, was the penetration of the towns by the landed aristocracy. While, north of the Alps, the nobleman built his castle outside the town, the Italian nobility found itself drawn or forced into city life. Genoa concluded treaties, the so-called *habitaculum* agreements, with its subject nobles in the surrounding countryside, in which it obliged the nobles on oath to reside in Genoa for a certain time each year, to participate in the city's military campaigns with a specified number of armed men, to marry their children to Genoese if they could honorably do so and to attend the *parlamentum* during their residence in the city. This compulsory urbanization of the landed aristocracy was widespread, although the conditions imposed upon the nobility varied very widely. In 1220, the commune of Como forced a nobleman of Bormio to reside in the city in time of war[152] bringing his family with him if he wished. Residence of noblemen in the towns became at that time a common southern European phenomenon.

In Italy these urban nobles turned to trade and in particular to maritime trade on a large scale. This meant that the Italian ports of Venice, Pisa and Genoa, eventually also the inland city of Florence, possessed colonies which they could use as a network of commercial bases. In Italy the distinction between rich merchant and nobleman participating in business disappeared. Desire for profit seized the aristocracy and drove them into colonial expansion and often war. The *contado* became the urban *territorium*. Just as the German Empire was dominated by the landed nobility, the city states controlled Italy. The power struggle, which north of the Alps expressed itself in endless territorial feuds, in Italy was fought out within the city walls from palace to palace and from tower to tower by competing patrician families. Thus the peace of the town was threatened from within.

The movement for church reform also shattered order and peace, as did the struggles of the *pataria* in which religious and social unrest were closely intertwined, and the involvement of imperial Italy in the struggle between emperor and pope. Now an attempt was also made here to enforce the town peace by means of a sworn association of the whole urban populace. Early on, the movement of sworn associations took a hold in Italy. As was the case when we were dealing with the area north of the Alps, we must distinguish between leagues under oath, created with a particular purpose, and the town communities which were based upon sworn associations. The Annals of Benevento ascribe the first commune (*prima communitas*) to the year 1015 and the *coniuratio secundo* to 1042. In the face of superior Norman power, after he had already done homage to Roger II, Duke Sergius VII of Benevento in 1134 concluded a pact with the Neapolitans, to be precise with the nobles, the *mediani* and all the inhabitants of the city of Naples. He promised them inviolability of person and property and safe passage and residence for all travellers to Naples by land or by sea whether merchants or not. He gave a pledge not to destroy the houses of Naples and not to permit the introduction of any new customs without taking the advice at least of the nobility. *Consuetudo* could here be taken to have a precise legal meaning although it could also mean a tax. He promised in no way to attempt by force or subterfuge to undermine the *societas* but on the contrary to assist it. War and peace, neutrality or alliances, were to be concluded only with the advice of the largest possible number of magnates. When Sergius died in 1137, an attempt was made with the support of the archbishop to create an aristocratic republic. But, in 1140, Roger II invaded Naples and Tancred's Great Privilege of 1190 made Naples a royal town enjoying certain advantages and privileges. The town magistrates were the *consules*, in whose election the *mediani* also played some part, but the aristocracy continued after, as before, to play the dominant role there. At their head stood the *compalazzo*, chosen by Tancred from among the Neapolitans.

However, the development of the sworn association movement was much more powerful and successful in northern Italy. After all, the *pataria* of Milan amounted to being a *coniuratio*, although in its blend of religious and political aims and in its overwhelmingly anarchical and revolutionary character, this movement stands out as an exception.

A superficial indication of the existence of a free town community is the appearance of consuls. The name was a conscious adoption of ancient tradition. The formation of consulates began towards the end of the eleventh century. Their origins lay among the advisers to the town's overlords and, very often, among episcopal advisers. The consuls appear in the last decade of the eleventh century in Pisa, Milan, Asti, Genoa and Arezzo. In 1105 in Pavia and Pistoia, in 1109 in Como, in 1115 in Lucca, 1112–1116 in Cremona, in 1117 in Bergamo, in 1120 in Bologna, Siena and Brescia and in 1120 in Bologna, Verona and Florence.

Pietro Visconti was certainly a consul at Pisa in 1094; his family played a striking rôle in the expedition of the combined fleets of Pisa, Genoa and Amalfi against Mahdiyya. Under him were lesser nobles from the *contado*. At the heart of the consulate of Pisa lay a small group of seafarers who possessed land in the *contado* as well as towers in Pisa, where they lived. They were under sworn oath to observe the *consuetudines quas habent de mari*. Side by side with the consuls in the twelfth century existed the *Consilium credentiae* or senate, elected from the same social group, and the *Parlamentum civitatis* which possessed no executive power. A writ (*breve*) of the consuls of Pisa of 1162 mentions the existence of four or five consuls, *mercatorum pisanorum*, who functioned as a commercial court and who also exercised industrial control over the craftsmen who, apparently since 1194, had organized themselves into corporate *arti*.

In Pisa's successful rival, Genoa, there was a close link between the consulate and the sworn assembly. The situation here had changed entirely since the tenth century. A policy of commercial expansion had now become the chief aim. After 1099 the commune of Genoa was organized as a *compagna*. As well as charters and writs issued by consuls and *compagna*, we can learn something about the situation in Genoa from the *Annales januenses*, written by Caffaro, who was born about 1080, and took part in Genoa's military expeditions, both as soldier and officer. He became a consul and was employed as envoy to Calixtus II and to the Emperor Frederick Barbarossa. In 1152 he presented to the consuls of Genoa his annals which he had dictated to his clerk, Macrobius. They decided to give his work to the public clerk, William de Columba, to transcribe and to include in the Cartulary of the commune. Caffaro had his continuators and his Annals provide a semi-official account of the two hundred most glorious years of Genoese history.

It is Caffaro who records that in 1099 a *compagna* was initiated at Genoa which lasted for three years and had six consuls. The creation of this *compagna* took place at a memorable moment for the three northern Italian ports. Jerusalem had been conquered and now, one after another, a Pisan, Venetian and Genoese fleet appeared off the Syrian coast, "a powerful demonstration of the west's naval power

which must have had the most profound effect on the Saracens"
(Schaube). Genoa's fleet was the last to appear because the inner
conflicts which had divided the city had first to be resolved.
Agreement on this took place in the *compagna communis*, which was
a federation of the regional *compagne*, an entity which embraced both
bishops and citizens under sworn oath. Its limited term of existence
and constant replacement remained one of the *compagna's* basic
characteristics. After 1130 the *consules de communi* were the leaders
of the *compagna* in political and military affairs; the *consules de
placitis* were a distinct group who acted as judges of first instance in
civil processes; both the criminal law and the function of an appeal
court were the province of the *consules de communi.*

The split in the consulate, between the consulate *de communi* and
the consulate *de iustitia* took place in Como between 1167 and 1172.
In the twelfth century, as opposed to four consuls *de communi*, there
were eight consuls *de placitis*, four from the city and four from the
burgus. Until 1190, in Genoa, the consuls assembled in the bishop's
palace – in many Italian towns the churches or bishops' palaces served as meeting places for assemblies administering town government.
Alongside the consuls at Como there was a further council of *con-
siliatores*, summoned only from time to time by the consuls but to
whom the members of the *compagna* were obliged to give advice on
town affairs. This procedure was later institutionalized. Every inhabitant, or member of the *populus*, had to obey summonses by bells
or by the town crier to the full assembly or *parlamentum*. The consuls
had to summon the citizens to take an oath before they could become
members of the *compagna*. Anybody who repeatedly refused the
summons was denied the right to engage in sea trade and no member
of the *compagna* dared to conclude commercial agreements with him.
The *compagna* possessed military, legal and financial prerogatives. Its
aim was military expansion, the maintenance of law and order in the
town's territories, and the creation of trading monopolies for its
members. Its aims corresponded to the preoccupations of the upper
groups in society: the office-holding patricians (*viscontile*), the landowners, the seafarers, ship-owners, merchants, new men who had
risen through trade in huge numbers and lawyers. The sworn association appears in the consular *breve* of Genoa as directed not against
the authority of the overlord but rather against inner divisions and the
formation of parties within the city. The detailed enactments, which
were intended to keep the peace in Genoa, show how difficult this was

to achieve. The carrying of weapons was customary and it easily led to armed confrontation, while internal feuds were fought out from fortified strong points. The members of the *compagna* enacted that since the use of armed fortifications was the sole privilege of the city of Genoa, no-one was allowed for the purpose of pursuing private feuds to hold fortified private towers or houses within the bishopric of Genoa or to occupy churches, church towers, town walls, town gates or fortified town wall towers. Oath-taking was also forbidden whether *conspiratio, coniuratio, rassa per sacramentum* or *fide promissa* or by *obligatio ulla*, in other words any form of agreement affecting city affairs.

Oath-taking was apparently the order of the day in the internal political life of Genoa. However strictly the consuls might have been able to control the *compagna*, it was unable to assure peace. Feuds among families and leagues of families, social conflict arising from the swift change in structure of the population and economy of the city, created financial problems for the commune. Already in the twelfth century it was engaging more and more in overseas trade in its own right. An expedient was to sell revenues to *consortia* of creditors, the *compere*, regardless of ecclesiastical prohibitions. The consulate became the prize in the struggles between the different parties and the final expedient came when councils and consuls installed a *podestà* at Genoa in 1190; this happened in many other Italian towns.

The *podestà* was an elected official chosen from some other community who was intended to maintain peace and order while acting under the control of the council. Administration of law and, above all, military command, fell under his jurisdiction. He brought with him his own collaborators and assistants. The *podestà* was often a learned jurist. The holding of the office became a profession and there were men who had held half a dozen such posts. Max Weber emphasized that this introduction of aliens to administer the law made a significant contribution to its rational codification and to the spread of Roman Law.

The Lombard communes were also organized as sworn leagues: "The burgesses were bound together in sworn associations (*iurati*). These organized the day-to-day running of the life of the town itself and bestowed upon the consuls their official power to run the community's affairs" (Dilcher).

The incoming consuls in Florence in 1138, elected to serve each town district with the help of the *sapientes*, assumed the leadership of the commune. At that time, there was a council of 100 to 150 *boni homines* who are first mentioned in 1167. Among them were, apparently, apart from the consuls who had previously held office, the organized representatives of the populace: parishes, *società della torre* – an association of families related by blood or friendship who occupied neighbouring towers – the *societates militum* and the *societas mercatorum*. The *parlamentum* met four times a year. From 1172 the Provisors exercised a supervisory authority; in 1189 the *podestà* appeared for the first time, and in 1207 it was incorporated into the framework of the constitution.

Sworn associations appear almost simultaneously in northern Italy and the northern French-Flemish-Rhenish zone. They served the same function in creating the autonomous commune – although in Italy preservation of the peace was more to the fore while, in the north, freedom from control by the overlord was the main purpose. But the essential organization, here the sworn committee and there the consulate, should be kept distinct. Rather than deriving the northern European sworn associations from those of northern Italy, or vice versa, it seems more accurate to see here a single great European movement. Gautier Dalché came to a similar conclusion[153] when he raised the question of whether the events which took place in the north-western Spanish towns of Santiago, Lugo and Sahagun in the first half of the twelfth century were independent of the communal movement of northern France. The chronology of the movements, the existence of the pilgrim route to Santiago de Compostela, and the French element in the population of these towns, would support such a supposition. But more careful study reveals that the sworn brotherhoods which sprang up in these towns, the so-called *germanitates*, are a special variant.

In contrast to the *communia* (a sworn commune) a *germanitas* seems to have formed only a stage in the emergence of an autonomous community and not something of permanent importance. It did not survive beyond the circumstances of its immediate origin. Contrary to what happened beyond the Pyrenees in the case of the communes, the word *germanitas* was never used to designate an urban community or ultimately the town itself. It was, in some respects, like the *communia*, originally a sworn association or group of men united by an oath, but it was also a sworn association that did not try to perpetuate itself or turn itself into a permanent institution.

The Italian consuls, however, certainly formed a distinguished prototype of the German town councillors. The idea that these town councils were modelled on non-German exemplars has been widely accepted, and recently the question has been asked[154] whether their origins lay in Italy, southern France or Burgundy. As far as the second possibility is concerned, it is worth mentioning that the town council first appeared in Germany when the northern Italian towns had already acquired the *podestà*. The consular system had spread early on from Italy into southern France: 1128 in Marseilles, 1131 in Arles and Béziers, 1136 in Avignon, 1141 in Montpellier, 1144 in Nice, 1148 in Narbonne. In the consular towns of France, as in Italy, there existed an assembly of all the burgesses, a council whose members were called *consiliarii* or *curiales* and, over all of them, the consuls, normally twelve in number although often fewer at first. The council was mostly filled by co-opting its own members or was nominated by the consuls. The consuls were frequently chosen by their predecessors from among the numbers of the *consularii* or from the candidates chosen by the *consularii*. A proportion of consular places was frequently reserved for the lesser nobility of the town. On the upper Rhine we find noblemen participating in the functions of the town council. In Schaffhausen, places on the council were divided between those who were knightly-born and a group of those not of knightly birth. The town council of Worms was composed of nine burgesses and six knights. The second enactment of the town law of Strasbourg laid down that the twelve *consules civitatis* should include *ministeriales* as well as citizens (*cives*). In Boppard, the town council consisted of five noble knightly councillors and twelve members from among the burgesses together with the town clerk.

If one wants to establish when the councils came into existence, one must not only examine the *consules*. If one does otherwise, as Rörig says, one ends up studying the origin of words rather than of institutions. The beginnings of the consulate in Germany lie in almost simultaneous developments in Lübeck, Utrecht, Speyer and Strasbourg around the end of the twelfth to the beginning of the thirteenth centuries. By the middle of the thirteenth century some 150 German towns had their own town councils. Early in the first decade of the thirteenth century, town councils appeared in the bishoprics of Basel and Constance but also in Zürich and the Zähringer foundations of Freiburg im Breisgau and Bern, in Colmar and Mulhouse. On the lower Rhine, town councils make a relatively late appearance in urban constitutions. Planitz named as forerunners, the leagues of *meliores* (*melioresverband*), the *Stadtschöffen* and the *Stadtsgeschworenen*.

In the towns of Flanders, Brabant and Hainault in the thirteenth century, a yearly term of office operated which is the sign of the existence of a consular system, together with co-opting by outgoing members. The yearly terms of office appeared first in Artois, in Arras in 1194 and, shortly afterwards, at Ypres in Flanders in 1209, at Ghent in 1212, Douai in 1228, Lille in 1235, Bruges in 1241 and later in Brabant and Hainault, Brussels in 1235, Louvain in 1267, Leau in 1295, Antwerp in 1300 or 1350, 's Hertogenbosch in 1336, Valenciennes in 1302, Mons in 1315. In smaller towns the echevins mostly remained in office for life. In such places, for example in the territory of Liège, sworn men took over the administration, and the yearly term of office was exceptional. Co-optation naturally meant a reduction in the power of the prince to appoint to office. A charter of Countess Matilda, granted to Ghent in 1192, states that on the death of an echevin his colleagues should present to the count the candidate whom they have nominated. In 1212 this right disappeared when Ferdinand of Portugal, count of Flanders, reserved to himself the right to name four men, one for each parish, who were in turn to choose thirteen echevins on his behalf. After 1228, in Ghent, there were three sorts of echevins, arranged in three groups, each of thirteen members. The first group were the *scabini* of the *keure*. These were the main judges and rulers of the town. The second group had only limited legal prerogatives. The third group were awaiting their turn to enter office and had only an advisory function. This régime remained in force until 1302. In Ypres after 1209 the departing echevin chose five *probi viri* who elected five echevins who in their turn elected a further eight echevins, so that the number amounted to thirteen in all. In Douai the system was even more complicated. More independent of the prince than the echevins were the *iurati* whose existence in the city in question presupposes a sworn association of the citizens. As has already been suggested, the institution of sworn members or *iurati* was not a general phenomenon in the southern Netherlands: it only appeared sporadically in Flanders and in Brabant in the course of the thirteenth century, but nowhere achieved the importance that it did in the towns around Liège. A Greater Council, composed of members from several colleges, echevins or *iurati* and eventually even other individuals, appeared sporadically in the thirteenth century and emerged in the great cities in the fourteenth.

In Cologne consuls are first mentioned in 1216. Whether this implies the existence of a town council is uncertain. At any rate, the council emerges clearly in Cologne around the middle of the century; its members changed yearly and, after 1305, it was laid down that their number should be fifteen. The outgoing members nominated their successors. Before 1318 a larger assembly of 82 members was added to this smaller council. Although not elected by it, they were summoned from among the members of the larger assembly, the *Sondergemeinde*, by its outgoing members, and confirmed by the small council. The larger council could neither meet nor institute proposals on its own initiative. It was summoned into being by the smaller council in order to be heard on more important issues. The annual turn-over in all the councils assured the patricians life-long membership of the *Schöffenkolleg* as well as the choice of the two burgomasters, who were chosen by the patrician's group, the *Richerzerche*. Thus they retained, just as they had always done, the decisive influence on urban administration.

In the east of Germany, Lübeck and Magdeburg were the pioneers in setting up the system of town councils. Among the daughter towns of Lübeck, Rostock had a council by 1218 and a council is mentioned in Schwerin, Güstrow and Parchim between 1228 and 1230. Magdeburg changed from an aldermanic to a town council type of constitution some time after 1244. The Magdeburg-Breslau law of 1261 asserted that the annually chosen council had been set up at the time that the city was founded.

Like every medieval body, the town council sought to establish an independent jurisdiction for itself. How far it achieved this depended on the success of its struggle against the town overlord. In many towns, for instance, the overlord managed to retain the sole right to impose the death penalty. The council was the highest organ of the commune and it controlled the entire administration of the town: it enacted laws, directed the town's external policies, controlled the army and taxation and, above all, administered in great detail commercial life, the town's market, its industry and its mint, although the actual right to mint remained for a long time the prerogative of the overlord. Its active economic policy always favoured its own burgesses and, in the eyes of the council, the town represented an economic unity. Nevertheless it also offered the outsider, the alien merchant who in the Middle Ages was called a 'guest' merchant, sufficient opportunities and legal rights for the town to serve as an attraction to him.

CHAPTER 5

The organization of economic life

The most important institution in the organization of foreign trade was the fair. The medieval fair offered both a comprehensive choice of wares and considerable dealings in money. The English fairs, visited by merchants from France, the Netherlands and Germany were the means of distributing English wool and cloth on the continent and of providing England with goods from western Europe and the East. We have already mentioned the fairs of Cologne – although Cologne was not primarily a fair town – and those of Flanders. In the south of France the fairs of Saint-Gilles for a time played a considerable role as the meeting-place of French merchants with those of the Mediterranean region.[155] However, all these were surpassed in importance by the attraction of the fairs of Champagne with their four fair towns, to some extent supplemented by the fairs of Lendit near Paris and Chalon in Burgundy. In Champagne, there was an almost continuous market throughout the duration of the six fairs, each of which lasted several weeks. Here goods from the Mediterranean and the East were exchanged for those of northern Europe. The fairs began in January at Lagny-sur-Marne, continued at Bar-sur-Aube in mid-Lent, moved in turn to upper Provins, to Troyes in July and August, to lower Provins in September, while in October the 'cold fair' took place at Troyes. Sales followed a special pattern according to the product – the cloth fair, the leather and fur fair, the fair for goods sold by weight, especially spices; finally the settlement of business deals. Payment was directly in cash or by promise of settlement at a further fair or by an exchange transaction or by a *lettre de foire* that is a recognizance of a debt before the bailiffs of the fair. The clerk prepared two copies of the indenture separated by a passage written in capitals and then cut the indenture into two parts.

The creditor then kept one half and the bailiffs the other half of this chirograph. If the two parts could once again be fitted together exactly, the validity of the creditor's half was proved. The town archive of Ypres possessed 7,000 such *lettres de foire* until it was destroyed by fire in 1914.

The function of the fair as a place for reckoning and settling accounts developed out of its rôle as a commodity market and, for the first time, significant international money exchange dealings began in which Italian merchants were most prominent. Certainly, swift justice was available during the fair, far-reaching security on the journeys to and from it, as well as the strictly controlled conduct of business and the practical facilities which the fair towns offered. An example was the hospital for sick merchants at Provins, founded by the counts of Champagne. The favourable central location of Champagne played its part in the success of the fairs. The counts were shrewd enough not to overburden the fairs with restrictive laws or fiscal exploitation, but about 1300 they fell into decline. It was not only the reversion of the county of Champagne to the crown of France in 1285 which harmed them and favoured those of Paris and Lendit. Nor was it solely the Flemish wars conducted by Philip IV which disturbed routes into Champagne. New forms of trade, partly developed by the fairs themselves, brought their unique position to an end. Merchants ceased to travel in person to the fair and left the transport of goods to agents, while they remained at home and conducted their business by correspondence. The Italians appointed representatives in the great textile centres of Flanders and Brabant, and from about 1300 they were using the sea route to western Europe. Eastern France thus lost its position as a stopping place on a major trade route. Bruges replaced it and became an international market centre until in its turn it was replaced by the Brabantine towns of Antwerp and Bergen op Zoom. Antwerp in the fourteenth century became important as the centre for trade between England and the Rhineland. Geneva took over the southern part of the business of the Champagne fairs although Lyons, granted a charter by the French kings in 1464, became a competitor.

In the fourteenth century the fairs of Frankfurt developed into a centre for the exchange of the goods of the whole area of the old German Empire from Lübeck to Bozen and from Aachen to Vienna. Friedberg in Hesse developed to some extent in the wake of the Frankfurt fairs.[156] The fairs of Deventer,[157] Zurzach[158] and Nördlingen[159] were of limited regional importance. Those of Bozen linked the German trade with that of Italy, those of Linz gave the Germans an outlet to the south-east. In the east the annual Naumburg fair, then that of Breslau and Brieg in Schleswig and of Poznan, Gniezno and Lublin all served wide areas. In the fifteenth century because of the changes in trade routes to the east, Leipzig became a fair town of international importance. Metz[160] and Speyer[161] became important money-exchange centres in the later Middle Ages.

The oldest type of specialization by medieval merchants was not according to the type of commodity in which they traded but according to where they did their business. Merchants trading in the same places combined to set up hanses.[162] This word, which originally meant simply a personal association, came to be used in the Middle Ages to describe the group of travelling merchants who banded together. We find the word used in this sense from the end of the twelfth century in Saint-Omer, Ghent and Bruges. Occasionally, the same association served as both hanse and guild, as in Lille, Mantes and Paris. Members of the merchants' guild of Valenciennes, called the *Caritas*, were described in the eleventh-century statutes as *hanseurs*. The term hanse was also used for the due paid by the members of such a merchant association and finally also for the special rules of the society and its individual members.

The Ghent hanse dates from the twelfth century and its aim was to limit the Rhineland trade of the other Flemish towns. The hanse of Saint-Omer similarly sought to monopolize trade to the British Isles and to the part of France south of the Somme. A larger number of towns combined to form the Flemish hanse of London, where Bruges and Ypres competed for leadership. Merchants of Flanders, Artois, Ponthieu, Vermandois, Champagne and lower Lorraine had formed the Hanse of Seventeen Towns for making common visits to the Champagne fairs; in reality the number of member towns was larger. With the decline of the fairs, this hanse accordingly lost its commercial importance.

In London, in addition to the Flemish hanse, there was the Hanse of German merchants. The oldest and most important hanse was that of the lower Rhine dominated by Tiel and Cologne. The citizens of Lübeck in 1226 complained to the emperor that the hanse would only let them into the trade with England on payment of a heavy fine – "this wrongful abuse and onerous exaction, by which the men of Cologne and Tiel and their associates are said to unite against them".[163] In 1267 Henry III allowed them to set up their own hanse, as he had already permitted the merchants of Hamburg a few months before. In 1282 the German hanse of London was founded and after 1282 one can speak of the trading establishment of the German hanse in London. The *dudesche Hanse*, which first comes to mind when thinking of the hanse, chiefly originated as a group of German merchants trading in Gotland. We shall consider its development with that of the region whose trade it dominated.

In addition to the Hanse there were associations of fellow merchants in each of the Hanseatic towns. Cologne, which always had a special position in London, in 1324 restricted its privileges there to its own merchants. The Cologne merchants trading in London maintained a separate organization in their home city in the Gaffel Windeck. Cologne also had a *fraternitas danica* (Danish fellowship) which was involved in the northern trade, and an association of merchants trading in Venice. In Lübeck, these special travellers' societies were particularly active. In 1378 the Schonen Society was set up; two years later it was followed by the Bergen Company. By the end of the fifteenth century there were some ten such societies in Lübeck, three in Hamburg, six in Rostock. One must distinguish these societies of travellers from the business associations which were being set up at the same time, often for only one business venture, but which developed into permanent companies.

In the Hanseatic zone we can distinguish between the *sendeve*, the company acting on commission and the *vera societas, vrye selschop* or *kumpanie* or *contrapositio* or *wedderlegginge*. The latter took various forms. In the first type, one merchant provided the cash while the other actually undertook the trading venture. Profit was then equally divided; occasionally the loss was met only by the merchant who had advanced the money, which provided a good chance for young merchants starting in business. The second type was more frequent: all the parties invested capital, one or two conducted the business and the profit was apportioned according to the original investment. In the third type of arrangement called *vulle mascoppei*, the parties pooled together a large part of their assets or all their business capital. This was predominantly found in inherited family businesses. All Hanseatic merchants were members of a number of such associations as a way of spreading risks.

Great firms, established on a permanent basis with their own buildings and network of branches were characteristic of southern

Germany. We shall deal with examples like the Diesbach-Watt Company and the great Ravensburg Society in the next chapter. Firms of this sort scarcely existed in the Hanse towns; the Loitz who appeared in sixteenth-century Stettin are the first northern German firm of a comparable kind.[164]

The Hanse had a number of general rules in dealing with these societies. About 1350 its Bruges trading Kontor or office excluded from the Hanse a company which had been dealing with a Hanseatic merchant who had been expelled. The company was ordered to suspend dealings within a year and a day and the Hanse forbad the formation of companies and *wedderlegginge* with Flemings. Cologne forbad its citizens to form associations with foreigners in the wine trade on penalty of imprisonment in one of the city's towers, and tried to limit the profitable middle-man trade to its own citizens by forbidding direct trading between one alien and another, although this was allowed in Bruges. As a result Cologne did not develop her fairs but tried in the thirteenth century to set up a staple by forcible methods. The archbishop confirmed this in 1259. All foreign merchants passing through Cologne had first to offer their goods for sale in the city. There was a natural basis here for such a staple, because it was in Cologne that goods had to be transferred from the ships plying the upper Rhine to those of the lower Rhine which were of a different size. In 1221 the Viennese incorporated similar staple rules into their town law. In both cities Byzantine and Venetian regulations were influential. Cologne was also preoccupied with its revenue from excise duties, because the city seldom raised direct taxes and was thus particularly dependent on the yields from these dues. An ingenious system, financed out of their proceeds, ensured that every wine barrel, or bale of goods was registered in the city and every phase of dealings in them was on record.[165]

The Hanse was maintaining the principle of individual responsibility in its economic policy at a time when otherwise the principle of collective responsibility was dominant. Under the normal custom, if for example a merchant fell into difficulties in a foreign town, reprisals were taken in his home town against the merchants of the town where he had suffered. If Hansards, however, suffered under any breach in the law, then they sought swift and sharp satisfaction. As creditors the members of the Hanse, at least in Bruges, succeeded in forcing payment of debts within three days under penalty of imprisonment or confiscation. As debtors they challenged every attempt at exercising collective responsibility against them; if there was no written contract, the debtor could clear himself by oath. The Hanse claimed freedom from salvage rights, and from the right of the lord to seize the goods of merchants who died abroad, and it strove for the lowering of all transport duties. The Hansards often had their own weighing scales, might load and unload their ships by night etc. This whole collection of privileges gave the Hanseatic merchants exceptional advantages and contributed to their success against their competitors; but it also awakened growing dislike not only among foreign merchants but also among rulers in Norway, England and elsewhere.

Just as fairs and trading companies were the basis of organization of Mediterranean trade, so the guilds were the way of organizing industry.[166] The medieval craftsman did not work for a patron but with his own raw materials for the open market. This was 'fee-work' as opposed to wage work. He acted as the retailer of his own products. The organization of work was not divided horizontally, like today, but vertically, and the different industries were sharply demarcated. Every craft guild had a monopoly of production but was also thereby limited strictly to its speciality. Herein lay the reason for the high quality of medieval craftsmanship. The craft workshops were small. In order to keep them small, the amount of productive equipment, weaving looms, furnaces, and so on, and the number of employees, journeymen and apprentices, was often deliberately restricted. In the textile and metal industries in the later Middle Ages rich guild masters or merchants set up their own distribution systems.

Craftsmen's corporations can be proved to have existed in Germany, England and France from about 1100. From the middle of the thirteenth century the guild organization was widespread throughout the towns of the Germano-Roman world, with sharp regional differences. Through the German colonization in Poland, Hungary and the Baltic it spread eastwards. The word *zunft* for guild is south German. In and around Cologne the word *fraternitas* or brotherhood was preferred and on the lower Rhine and in Flanders, *amt* or *amtbacht*, and in north Germany *innung* and *gilde*. The guilds are a complex phenomenon and the reasons for their formation are also complicated.

The sources clearly show that they grew out of a combination of voluntary associations and as the result of government and market regulations. The guilds served the function of a cartel and also had considerable military importance although they amounted to more than both these elements. Religious brotherhoods were another starting-point for the creation of guilds. The concentration of groups of craftsmen in certain streets is noticeable from early on and this often occurred for purely practical and technical reasons. It also made it easier for craftsmen of the same industry to combine together. The key feature of guild organization was the power to enforce with penalties the exclusion of craftsmen from outside the town and to limit production exclusively to guild members. The penalty already appears as a feature in the Cologne Ordinances of the Coverlet Weavers of 1149: all those who wanted to exercise their craft in the town (*infra urbis ambitum*) must belong to the guild. The guild assured the provisioning of its members and in important industrial towns also the securing of the quality of goods to maintain their distribution in the town's market. The guild frequently checked quality and often the town council had to protect the interests of the consumers against guild practices. The guild assured reasonable livelihood to every single member. At least this was its programme, which in practice was often enough modified by the profit-seeking of certain groups. The rules against regrating hindered the buying-up of raw materials by one or a few guild masters. Each guild member had the same access to the purchase of raw materials. Forestalling was not allowed; goods should come onto the market and none must by-pass it. These regulations hindered the development of large-scale industries. Nevertheless the social distinctions between the various guilds, which ranged from rich goldsmiths to poor linen weavers, remained large as they also did within the same guild. The guild was not only directed by economic considerations; religious, social and charitable obligations also bound members through common religious services, and festivals for guild patrons, for the admission of a new master, or for commemorating dead members. The guild possessed a house or at least a room, decked with the guild silver or at least with tin vessels; and lists of members were kept there. The proceedings were dominated on the one hand by sentimental and social preoccupations, namely the care of members' needs, the training of new members, the feeling of equality, the sense of respect for fellow members and for the quality of work, but sentiment and romanticism also covered narrow-mindedness and rigidity, oppression and misery, as we shall demonstrate.

The towns assumed a prominent role in the important activity of

minting and thus of the creation of a money economy and of currency, at least from the eleventh century onwards.[167] After Charlemagne's successors had abandoned his policy of centralizing mints,
the regalian right of controlling them had been assumed by abbeys
and bishops. The renaissance of commerce also depended on the use
of money, above all upon the more efficient minting of reliable money
and eventually on the minting of currency in larger denominations.
After the age-long domination of foreign trade by the silver *denarius*
(penny), a gold currency was eventually reintroduced and standard-
ized. It originated in Italy where gold coins had continued to
circulate even after Charlemagne had based his currency on silver.
The feudal lords who had mints often tried to exploit them for their
own profit. This was in part disadvantageous to economic life. In
Italy, the participation of townsmen in the episcopal government of
the cities, already described in the last chapter, also included their
participation in minting. King Lothar II confirmed the right of minting
to the church of Mantua in 945: the coinages of Mantua, Verona and
Brescia were to be of equal value. The quality of alloy used and
weight was to be regulated "according to the will and agreement of
the citizens" (*secundum libitum et conventum civium*) of the aforesaid
town. The logical conclusion of this development was that in the
twelfth century the Lombard communes took exclusive control over
the right to mint. The charter of Henry V granted to Speyer in 1111
specified that no person in control of the Speyer mint should increase
or reduce the silver content or the weight of the coin without the
permission of the citizens: "The coinage was not to be altered except
with the common consent of the citizens" (*monetam . . . nisi communi
civium consilio permutet*). Examples of this in Italy and Germany
multiply in later periods. In England this right of control by the
townspeople appeared more as an obligation laid on them by the king:
in 1100–1101 Henry I ordered all burgesses and merchants living in
the towns, both French and English, to swear to maintain his mints
and to allow no false coining. In France Philip II Augustus, in a
charter of 1195 to Saint-Quentin, commanded that the coinage be
neither decreased nor changed without the agreement of the *major*
and *jurati*. In the city museum of Cologne two leather purses dating
from 1268 survive which contain test pieces from the archiepiscopal
mint. Towns which had no mints within their walls still exercised
economic oversight over mints in the surrounding area. The towns
also took over mints as civic farmers and administrators, and finally

also assumed the right to mint themselves. E. Nau, by noting the haphazard geographical distribution and chronological development of this right in the German towns, concluded that they did not lay as much emphasis on having their own mints as had been previously believed.

Italian trading and financial institutions developed earlier and more impressively than those north of the Alps,[168] for instance the law of staple, which appeared from the eleventh century onwards. The spread of trade, commercial expeditions as far as the coast of Syria, and the creation of an entire colonial empire by the maritime cities, furthered the development of associations of merchants. The sources speak of *accomendatio, collegantia, societas maris, entica* etc. Like the loans for overseas trade, the *commenda* agreement was concluded for a single business venture. It distinguished the *socius stans* who remained at home from the *socius tractans* who undertook the business voyage. In the unilateral agreements, the Venetian *collegantia* or the actual *commenda*, only the *socius stans* invests capital, only he bears any losses and takes three-quarters of the profits. In bilateral agreements, usually called *societas maris* in Genoa, two-thirds of the capital was invested by the *socius stans* and one-third by the *socius tractans*, while profit and loss were equally apportioned. The earliest surviving texts of Venetian *collegantia* agreements go back to the eleventh century. The *comanda* was also known in various forms in Barcelona. Here ships could also be partly assigned in *commenda*. Lopez has also discovered *commenda* concluded by lesser people, and he published a Genoese example from 1198. Sixteen named people invested altogether 142 pounds worth of Genoese *denarii* in a trading venture to the harbour of Bonifacio in Corsica, and to Sardinia, that is to destinations which were not far away. The lowest investment was two pounds and the highest twenty-five pounds. Two of the investors, Embrone di Sozziglia and Master Alberto, who respectively invested six pounds and two pounds, undertook the venture. In this way a wide circle of the inhabitants of Genoa were profiting from maritime trade. It is nowhere stated that the *socius tractans* was the poorer partner. Often in successive ventures two merchants would switch rôles. There were also commercial associations for internal and overland trade. The *societas terrae* had similarities with the *commenda*. The *compagnia*, early on described as *fraterna compagnia* in Venice, soon superseded there, however, by *commenda* agreements, grew up primarily along with family firms in the Italian inland cities. One can follow its development particularly clearly in Florence. The *compagnia* was not concluded for a fixed period.

The advanced nature of Italian economic development can also be seen in the early activity of professional Christian money-changers, Cahorsins and Lombards, the latter mostly from Asti and Chieri. Their exchange stalls were to be seen in every market. Genoese bankers were accepting deposits from the twelfth century onwards, on which they were able to make assignments. It soon transpired that one needed to keep only one-third of the deposited cash in hand to maintain liquidity, and this enabled them both to make advances to customers and investments of their own. Thus deposit and giro banks came into existence. Trade at the Champagne fairs brought into existence the letter of exchange as a new financial instrument. Italian merchants, who at home utilized Genoese, Florentine or Milanese currency to buy silk or spices had at their disposal after their sales at Provins or Troyes an account in local currency which they could use to discharge their liabilities there. This was done by drawing up letters of exchange designating the different places and currency of payment before a notary. Ready-made letters of exchange also existed. The citizens of Piacenza were very skilled in this business, and in the thirteenth century almost one-half of the transactions made between Genoa and the fairs of Champagne passed through their hands. It was in Italy and at the fairs of Champagne that already in the thirteenth century Germany merchants were learning these business methods.

CHAPTER 6

The European urban landscape

The urban culture of Europe in the Middle Ages found its most splendid expression in one southern and one northern area, that is to say in northern Italy and in the area between the Seine and the Rhine.

Northern Italy, more decisively influenced than any other European region by the legacy of Roman urban life and by the reawakened spirit of ancient culture and civilization was, together with southern Italy, the area of Europe most open to Byzantine and Moslem influences. From the end of the Staufer era to 1494, it remained free from either the pressure of old feudal ties or from subjection to the power of a modern, centralized state. Led by its ruling class of mercantile town nobles and successful merchants, those urban republics which controlled the sea sought to obtain colonial possessions which would open up to them the wealth of the Orient and, in the case of Venice, monopolize it. Their shrewd and skilled financiers, who earlier than anywhere else grasped the principles of accounting and Arabic numerals, the Sienese, Lucchese and men of Asti, became the bankers to the European powers with the most widely distributed sources of revenue but also perhaps the greatest need for money – the papal curia as well as the princes of Europe. Capitalists, seeking investments, especially those of inland towns, were not only responsible for the development of industries of high quality but also, motivated by their rational commercial outlook, brought about a transformation of the countryside, both in settlement pattern and in agricultural exploitation. The industrial and exporting towns experienced a multitude of conflicts which arose both from feuds between urban nobles and rich merchants as well as between rich and poor. The availability of many literate laymen, learned in the law, in

the Italian towns, made possible a well-developed administration rely-
ing on written records and put commercial transactions on a documentary basis. The Bologna school of the great Irnerius brought
Roman law back into use. Already in the twelfth century, students
were flocking to Bologna from western and central Europe and only
the leading schools of France could offer any competition.

These trends and differing forces determined the fate and shared
the form of cities, each developing its own sharply defined individuality. At the centre of our discussions must be the great cities
of Genoa and Florence, and the smaller San Gimignano.

Genuensis ergo mercator, "A Genoese, therefore a merchant," ran
an old saying.[169] A report sent from a pilgrimage in 1065 shows that
the Genoese were already at that time engaged in full-scale commerce
on the Syrian coast. In 1098 seven distinguished Genoese concluded
an agreement with Bohemond of Antioch, to whom they offered
military help in return for thirty houses on the church square, a
fondaco and a well – all free of rent and dues. A surge of interest
brought about the Caesarea voyage, when Caesarea, still a flourishing
commercial centre, was looted in May 1101. In 1104 a naval expedition of forty galleys helped to bring about the capture of Acre. In
return Genoa's cathedral church received a site in Jerusalem, a street
in Jaffa and one-third of Arsuf, Caesarea and Acre, their revenues
and their surrounding territories up to a mile in radius as well as total
freedom from commercial dues in all their possessions. A canon of
the Genoese cathedral of San Lorenzo was chosen as viscount to
administer the newly-won territories, the first-known head of an
overseas colony in the Levant. So it went on, and Genoa gained a
series of commercial footholds along the whole Syrian coast from
Jaffa to the estuary of the Orontes.

Moslem Egypt offered still greater commercial profits than did
Syria. Here, the spices of the Far East arrived by the sea route which
made them cheaper. The notarial records of Giovanni Scriba (1155–
1164), the oldest surviving Genoese notarial acts, give us an idea of
the intensity of Geneose trade with Egypt. Commercial expeditions
were undertaken by fleets of ships. In any one year the Genoese sent
only one such combined expedition to Syria and Egypt and that took
place in September. The commercial agreements on which each
voyage was based were drawn up before notaries the previous June.
As a rule the fleet arrived in the east in October, stayed throughout
the winter until far into the new year, and was expected back home

around Midsummer. This left the merchants plenty of time to transact their business and visit various ports along the coast, as well as to travel into the interior. The commercial agreements mostly left the merchants a free hand to conduct their business beyond the sea where they wished (*ultra mare et inde quo voluerunt*). Members of the town aristocracy and Genoese consuls took part in these commercial voyages. One of the most famous was Ingo de Volta, who as a young man travelled in person to Syria, and later sent his son, when as an old man he was investing enormous sums in this kind of venture. Soliman of Salerno was another travelling merchant who had bought a house in Genoa and become a citizen, and who maintained links with former fellow-countrymen from the Norman kingdom of Sicily. Between 1156 and 1160 he travelled personally to Alexandria. We have already met poorer Genoese participating in small commercial ventures to Corsica and Sardinia.

Italian merchants were not only responsible for acting as agents in trade between their own country and the Levant. They also acted as the intermediaries in trade between the markets of Egypt and other lands, and vice-versa. The Genoese, for instance, had a flourishing trade between the Levant and the coasts of southern France. Their colony in Constantinople was important, although smaller than either that of Pisa or in particular, that of Venice. Three hundred Genoese took part in the defence of their Constantinople quarter in the attack which was made on it in 1162. We also meet them in Spain on the route to Santiago de Compostela where Andalusian oil, quicksilver from Almaden, and alum from Castile were important commodities in their trade. We also find them on the Atlantic coast of France, and they were pioneers in trading by the direct sea route from Italy to England and the Netherlands. They also visited the Champagne fairs. During Louis IX's crusade, the Genoese provided almost the only contact between the French crusaders and their homeland. With their help the king and rich magnates had goods sent from home at their disposal. The huge sums of money, raised by the king when he was abroad from Genoese financiers by letters of exchange redeemable from the royal treasury in the Temple in Paris, helped to promote trade between Genoa and France.

The neighbouring islands of Corsica and Sardinia were a cause of strife between Pisa and Genoa throughout the twelfth century. Densely forested Corsica was of immediate practical importance for ship-building, for the production of special ships' planks of a regular size and other building timber, for pitch, and for cereals, while the import of salt was essential for the island. In the event, it was Genoa which took control of Corsica, while Pisa obtained the upper hand in southern Sardinia. These possessions naturally strengthened the position of both towns in the western Mediterranean basin. But they also planted the seeds of rivalry between Pisa, Genoa and Venice over colonial possessions. We cannot follow all the changes and vicissitudes of this colonial history which often followed the ebb and flow of the crusades.

The colonies also served as bases for trade links to the inner area of central Asia, India, the East Indies and the eastern coast of Asia. From most of the Asiatic coastal towns roads led to the interior. Slowly the Italians extended their trade further eastwards along these routes. Probably about 1250 the Venetians arrived in Damascus; eventually they broke through the powerful continental land mass of Asia and penetrated as far as the fabled lands of China and Japan. In Egypt, on the other hand, the Venetians were not able to penetrate beyond Cairo and the further trade routes up the Nile remained the preserve of Moslem merchants. When the Byzantine Empire regained Constantinople in 1261 after the collapse of the short-lived Latin Empire there, Venice's possessions shrank further. Genoa profited from this and reached the high point of her might towards the end of the thirteenth century. With Pisa crushed, the kingdom of Sicily divided, the position of the Arabs in west Africa weakened, war in Spain, the French maritime trade still in its infancy and the Provençal communes in decline, Genoa profited. A certain equilibrium of power developed between Genoa and Venice. Both were exempted from customs in the Byzantine Empire. Venice, thanks to her possession of important mainland harbours and her conquest of the southern islands of the Aegean Archipelago, including Crete, dominated the Egyptian and Syrian trade. Genoa expanded in the northern part of the Aegean. Chios provided an important base for her, together with the adjacent harbour of Phocaea in Asia Minor, which were handed over to an association of Genoese state creditors, the Chios *maona*. From Chios alum, essential in the cloth industry, was despatched to the southern Netherlands. Venice came to specialize more and more in the spice trade and came to possess a monopoly in pepper. In a government maritime statute, enacted in Venice in 1233, the following wares were named as exports from

Syria: cotton, cotton yarn, wollen caps, liquorice, cane-sugar, spikenard, pepper, nutmeg, cloves, rice, sugar, castor sugar in sacks, lacquer, gum arabic, myrrh, aloe, incense, cardoman, camphor, sandalwood, galangas, gold pigment, ammoniac, wax, indigo, alum, glass, vitriol, emery, raw silk and silk goods, products of Bokhara, brazil wood, dye, cinnamon, flax, caraway, mace, aniseed, and camelhair cloth. From the beginning of the thirteenth century, Venice had spread its trading network into the region of the Black Sea and Crimea, at one time as a stage on the northern route into central Asia, at another to enter the river and transport system of southern Russia. Her main objective was the corn of southern Russia, after that furs, whale oil and suchlike. Once again Venice and Genoa confronted each other as rivals. Genoa gained Kaffa, and in 1316 planted a colony in Tana on the Don estuary. In 1325 the Venetians also appeared here. By the end of the fourteenth century, Genoa was still able to improve considerably its position in the Crimea. The export of Russian cereals by the Italian cities was so important that when Tana fell to the Tartars in 1343, not only did the price of spices rise in the Byzantine Empire and Italy, but a severe shortage of cereals and salted fish occurred.

From 1281 the Genoese were firmly established in Trabzon and in 1319 the Venetians followed them there. Cyprus, rich in goods for export like salt, sugar cane, Cyprus wine, cotton, woad, camelot, gold leaf, and brocade remained under Byzantine domination until 1193. It was often visited by Italian merchants in the fourteenth century. The Florentines also came here; Genoa, however, was the strongest power while Florence, which for a long time had remained a purely land power, successfully took up the struggle for trade with Egypt against the older rivals Venice and Genoa in the last decade of the fourteenth century. After the capture of Porto Pisano and Livorno, Florence negotiated in 1422 for concessions from the caliph of Egypt, and in 1455 regular visits by its fleets there started, but in the long run it had to bow to Venetian superiority. After 1300 we find Venetians, Genoese and Pisans in Persia especially in Tabriz. Persia then served as a stage in the penetration of India and eastern Asia, but journeys to India and eastern Asia stopped about 1350. Italian commerce with the Orient was characterized by its unfavourable balance of trade. The Italians had little to offer to the ancient civilizations that they either needed or valued.

Let us return to inland Tuscany. We can still today marvel at the picturesque appearance of a medieval Tuscan town, vividly described by Stadelmann:

Over the bare, red-brown hills a mass of gigantic stone towers stretch into the sky. Closely compressed onto a narrow plateau, these sharp-edged *colossi* stand with an almost unbelievable geometric precision. Without openings for either windows or battlements, without entrances or means of communication, one reached above another to an enormous height, dwarfing their grey surrounding walls.[170]

We have to imagine Florence in the thirteenth century as having been like this haunting San Gimignano: a dark mass of town fortresses and inhabited towers in which knightly families dwelt with their retinues, fortifying one against the other, a veritable forest of castles jostling one another along the streets. San Gimignano came into existence as the *borgo* of a castle of the bishops of Volterra.[171] About 1000 A.D. the *borgo* controlled a market and the town walls. The town derived great profit from its favourable location on trade routes and it used this to levy tolls on passing traffic. Its own carrying trade also prospered from this as did its inns, and the town had two commodities of its own to offer. One was saffron, which in the thirteenth century was taken not only to the Champagne fairs, Naples and Messina but also to North Africa and Egypt, on Pisan ships. San Gimignano's other product was wine. Industrial development, mostly in glass and cloth manufacture, was not of any great significance. An old aristocracy, the *vicedomini* of the bishop who sprang from the *familiares* and *fideles* of the bishop's *boni homines* (that is the household servants and retainers of the bishop's following) and the later consuls composed the town's upper class. These last groups derived their wealth not only from ground rents but also from trade and money-lending. The builders of the towers were merchants and money-lending families who came to adopt the way of life of a town aristocracy. The town had a balanced social structure: in the thirteenth century 28 per cent of the populace enjoyed considerable wealth; 48.3 per cent middling wealth, and 22.8 per cent had relatively little means. The nobility of feudal origin, the Cattani, Casaglia and Ruggerotti da Montagutolo took part in the political and administrative life of the commune but did not completely dominate it. In 1277 the Cattani and Ruggerotti controlled only 2.25 per cent of urban wealth. Party strife in the fourteenth century brought the decline of San Gimignano, loss of independence and annexation by Florence.

One can pursue three lines of Florentine development: the creation of Florentine territory by the city; the establishment of a great export industry with the rise of various guilds to political importance; and the transformation by the town of the agrarian economy of the surrounding area.[172] Florence, centre of ecclesiastical reform in Tuscany and base for the political activities of the Margravine Matilda, first revealed its strength in 1082 when it was able to withstand a siege by the Emperor Henry IV. The city became the main bastion of the *contado*, whose feudal aristocracy it systematically subdued and forced to reside in the town. The agreement concluded with Pisa in 1171 gave its trade an outlet to the sea. The construction of the walls, built between 1173 and 1175 outside the old Roman fortifications, which enclosed new town quarters, concluded Florence's first phase of expansion. Side by side with the nobles residing in the town, the Alberti, Buondelmonti, Firidolfi, Pazzi and others, dedicated to military service by arms, holders of the city offices of notary and podestà, there were the rich merchants who, like the nobles, inhabited fortified houses with towers without neglecting their trade or banking. Also, families like the Alberti del Giudice, Ardinghelli and Peruzzi, immigrants from the countryside, saw in the nobility their model, served as *pedites* and strove after greater political influence.

Beneath them lay the growing mass of craftsmen. In spite of family feuds which broke out in 1216 and the conflict between Guelf and Ghibelline parties, the thirteenth century brought enormous progress to Florence. Already in 1198 it headed the League of Tuscan Cities, and it took control of Poggibonsi in a victorious war against Siena in 1208, completing with this its domination of the whole surrounding countryside. In the 1220s the conflict with Pisa began which turned into sharp business rivalry and bitter hatred until, with the capture of Porto Pisano and Livorno in 1410, Florence had conquered its way to the sea. The thirteenth century witnessed a remarkable increase in the financial activities of the Florentines. With the Genoese and Lucchese, they were the bankers to the papal curia, whose need of money was enormous because of the crusade, the last battles with the Staufer and the alliance with Anjou. The Florentines were also bankers to the kings and princes of England, France and Anjou. The creation of the modern state with its expensive foreign policy, mercenary troops, paid officialdom, and subsidies to other powers all cost enormous sums of money. One needs only to remember the huge sums in bribes received by King Adolf of Nassau in which the Florentine Musciatto played a part.[173] Shortly after Genoa struck the golden *genovino* in 1252, Florence minted its golden florin which was to shape central and north European monetary and minting history for centuries.

In the thirteenth century the regime of noble predominance lost power in several stages. *Il primo popolo* formed itself into twenty companies in 1250, a politico-military organization which replaced the *societas militum* and the separate organization of the *popolani* from which nobles and great citizens were excluded, and which was supplemented by the organization of the commune.

From 1260 to 1267, Florence was Ghibelline, from 1267 onwards it was Guelf. From 1282 the *arti*, the guilds, became more and more powerful and in 1289–1293 the change in the constitution took place which made the *arti* its basis; out of the upper, middle and lower guilds a group of twenty-one guilds was endowed with political standing and from among them the highest ruling authority, the Signoria, was recruited. A Florentine could only take part in politics as member of a guild. Nobles could also enter guilds. Dante was a member of the Guild of Apothecaries, Grocers and Doctors. The actual power lay with the rich *popolo grasso*, the seven upper guilds. This constitution remained in force until the rule of the Medici (1434). What happened in Florence was by no means unusual.

The second half of the thirteenth century was full of urban unrest in Piacenza, Parma, Bologna, Milan, Siena, Pistoia and Perugia. In 1285 the revolt of Berenguer Oller took place in Barcelona and similar troubles occurred in Gerona and Lerida. In the Low Countries risings took place in Bruges, Ypres, Tournai, Huy, Saint-Trond, and Liège. In Rouen and Provins in France the troubles escalated into rebellions.[174]

Some time after 1182 the Arte dei Mercanti came into existence in Florence. Its immediate successor was the Arte di Calimala, so-called after the street in which its members had their shops. It was the most important of the commercial guilds, the guild of the great merchants and cloth finishers. Its members often possessed dyeing factories and finishing works. Most of the leading Florentine banking firms also belonged to the Calimala guild. Naturally a member of the Calimala guild could make his fortune as a banker, merchant or factory owner.

Business companies were also members of the guild. It was led by elected consuls. At the end of the thirteenth century there were about eighty business firms represented in the Calimala, with 500–800 members between them.

The guild of Cambiatores was made up chiefly of money-changers. Together with the merchants of the Calimala, they also controlled minting. The Arte di Por Santa Maria was devoted to tailoring garments, to the import of silk and the sale of silken fabrics. The Arte della Lana had as its full members wool importers and cloth manufacturers, but it also included members of the second rank such as dyers, fullers and weavers.[175]

In the thirteenth century Florence began to import and utilize English wool. Florentine merchants concluded agreements with English monastic houses which specialized in raising sheep, securing their wool by previous advances and loans. The quality of the cloth woven from English wool was so superior to all other varieties that it made the costs of transport from England and the Flemish coast to the harbours of the Tyrrhenian sea and to Florence itself worthwhile. The Florentine *lanaiolo* was thus both merchant and also director of the manufacturing process. He either produced himself or purchased raw materials through agents in their country of origin: wool in England, Flanders or France, Spain or Africa; woad in Erfurt, purple dyes from the Orient; alum from Phocaea, Volterra and Genoa. Either in person or through middlemen, who were for the most part simply agents, he controlled the whole process of production from raw material to finished product and at no stage did any change of ownership occur. The process of manufacture was very much split up and took place over a wide area: the wool was brought from the washing place on the Arno to the central workshop; from there it was taken into the country to be spun, brought back to be woven in the weavers' houses, then to the dyeing factories on the Corso dei Tintori, then to one of the fulling mills lying on one of the Arno's tributaries, back into the city to one of the great factories to be stretched, and finally back to the main factory for the final processing where it was packed, sealed by the authorities and put up for sale or for export. This amounted to relatively irrational coming and going which took time and energy. Social differentiation among the workers was created by this divided organizational process. At the lowest level, always on the borderline of subsistence, came the factory workers who mostly lived in miserable cramped quarters in the suburbs or

borghi. They were chiefly responsible for the early processing, beating, combing and carding of the wool. The situation of the weavers
and spinners was somewhat better. They at least possessed their own
tools and even engaged help. On a still higher level came the finishers
and cloth shearers who often possessed skills handed down from
previous generations. The dyers and stretchers occupied the highest
rungs of the ladder and even invested their own capital.

In addition to the four guilds of the upper group which we have
already described – Calimala, Cambiatores, Por Santa Maria and della
Lana, there were three others – for doctors combined with spice-
dealers and grocers, furriers, and finally lawyers and notaries who in
1291 numbered 65 lawyers and 575 notaries. These seven upper guilds
amounted to about ten per cent of the Florentine population.

The nobility who had been attracted into the town capitalized their
income from their landed properties. In Tuscany, and, after the
conquest of *terra firma* also among the Venetians, it was not only the
greatest citizens who possessed land. The urban middle class, in order
to satisfy its demand for wine, oil, cereals and fish, likewise possessed
properties in the country which also served as country retreats, away
from the summer heat or from epidemics in the hills or mountains or
on the plain where the air was better.

Thus, there came about the domination of the countryside by the
great communes for economic ends and in a mercantile spirit.
Townsmen took control of landed properties and the population of
the countryside was urbanized. Landed estates were exploited on a
capitalist basis and serfs were given their freedom. The law of
Bologna of 1256 ended the free sale of serfs by the commune in order
to supply the necessary working force for the city's industries.
Renewed decrees of 1282, however, show that real freedom had not
yet been achieved in the countryside. In 1289 Florence forbad the sale
of serfs when land changed hands unless the commune itself was the
purchaser. Very real interests lay behind this decree. The freeing of
the country population made them full members of the commune and
assured to landowners from the towns the most profitable exploitation
possible. This happened by means of a purely private type of legal
agreement in the form of sharecropping, the *mezzadria,* which
developed into the classical legal form of landowning in Tuscany from
the later Middle Ages onwards. The merchant who owned land tried
to rationalize its exploitation. The result was a considerable frag-
mentation of the old village settlements. The owners rounded off their

landed possessions and established a new leased manor in the middle of the newly regrouped property. In this way the *poderi* and the isolated farms of Tuscany came into existence. An entirely new structure of agrarian life resulted. Cereal production was superseded in favour of vineyards and olive groves, the latter first bearing fruit only forty to sixty years after being planted, and the cultivation of other crops which could be exploited capitalistically. Purely cereal cultivation diminished and this created a mixed type of agriculture – vines alternating with olive trees with wheat growing beneath both. This *coltura mista* also brought a better division of labour throughout the year, important for the family concerns of the country population. This is only one side of developments in the countryside. New research has revealed a variety of social and historical factors and related them to population trends – the demographic expansion in the high Middle Ages and the stagnant population from about 1300 onwards.[176]

The central and northern Italian landscape reflects the unique achievements of the population which produced it. Apart from engaging in their urban occupations, so to speak with the left hand, they completely transformed the countryside both in pattern of settlement and methods of cultivation. The enchanting Tuscan landscape with its farmhouses, olive groves and cypresses is the product of planning by the bourgeoisie and investment of their capital. So this landscape of scattered farmsteads proved to be a purely urban creation. The area of Italy most profoundly rural in its outward appearance in reality owed its inner structure to the most strongly urbanized sector of the economy (Dörrenhaus).

The southern Italian towns lagged behind the spectacular, northern Italian city republics. They were adapted to the rigidly organized Norman-Staufer-Angevin state. The largest city of southern Italy and one of the most populous of Europe was Naples. We have already mentioned its charter of privileges granted by Tancred in 1190. This assured its position of direct dependence on the king like that of Bari, Trani and Gaeta. It assured the prominence of the nobility but also favoured the rising middle class. The town commune of Naples followed the example of central Italy and organized itself under consuls who were under the direction of the *compalazzo*, nominated by the king. This régime of town liberty did not endure. The Staufer emperors revoked Tancred's charter. In other respects Frederick II made a considerable contribution to the economic and cultural development of Naples. In 1231 his *augustales* were struck here, Italy's first gold coins. In 1224 he founded a university here, primarily to specialize in the field of jurisprudence, while Salerno remained the centre for the study of medicine.[177] Under Angevin rule, Naples became more than ever the centre of a glittering court and an elegant and refined culture. It was here that the development of Italian prose began with Boccaccio. This court's demand for luxury goods stimulated both trade and industry. In the district of the *junctura civitis* the nobility had their town houses and a merchants' quarter developed with members from Genoa, Catalonia, Marseilles, Pisa, Florence and Amalfi. In 1278 Charles of Anjou began to strike the silver coin known as the *gigliato* modelled on the *gros tournois* struck in France from 1266 onwards. This silver coin set the pattern for the coinage of the Mediterranean region until the fifteenth century. The town served as the seat of the central government. The Norman tradition of keeping records, begun when William I set up the royal archive in Castel Capuano, continued under the Staufer and Angevins. By 1300 Naples had 50,000 inhabitants.

Barcelona was among the most important trading centres of the western Mediterranean. The great hall of Lonja, the old meeting place of the merchants completed in 1392, and the Atarazanas Reales, the shipyard (fourteenth and seventeenth century), enable us to envisage the commercial and maritime importance of the town in the later Middle Ages. It was always a challenge to Italian, and above all, to Genoese supremacy, but the Italian cities succeeded in eclipsing it. As the capital of Catalonia, claimed by the crown of Aragon, it had an extraordinarily favourable central location

at the head of a hierarchy of towns spread in a balanced pattern of commercial and urban centres from Perpignan to Tortosa and from Gerona to Lerida. Leaving aside some cases of competition between individuals, no conflicts occurred between Barcelona and the merchants of its province, Barcelona had no compulsory staple and there were no attempts to divert traffic artificially. Saffron and wool were exported from Catalonia by the most natural routes, either across the Pyrenees for the northern customers or by descending the Ebro. In moments of particular economic crisis, there were at most proposals for creating fairs at Barcelona where these commodities might be sold. In all this, the special importance of Barcelona stems from the presence of merchants and capital resources. The same features appear in Barcelona's dealings with adjoining coastal regions of the Mediterranean with which the city was particularly concerned, the coral of Alghero, the corn and sugar of Sicily always remained accessible. Industrial production was characterized by identical trends. While the idea of creating a powerful indigenous textile industry originated at Barcelona, the whole province took to weaving and finishing cloth, of which a great deal was exported overseas and all this without any spirit of competition between different centres of production.[178]

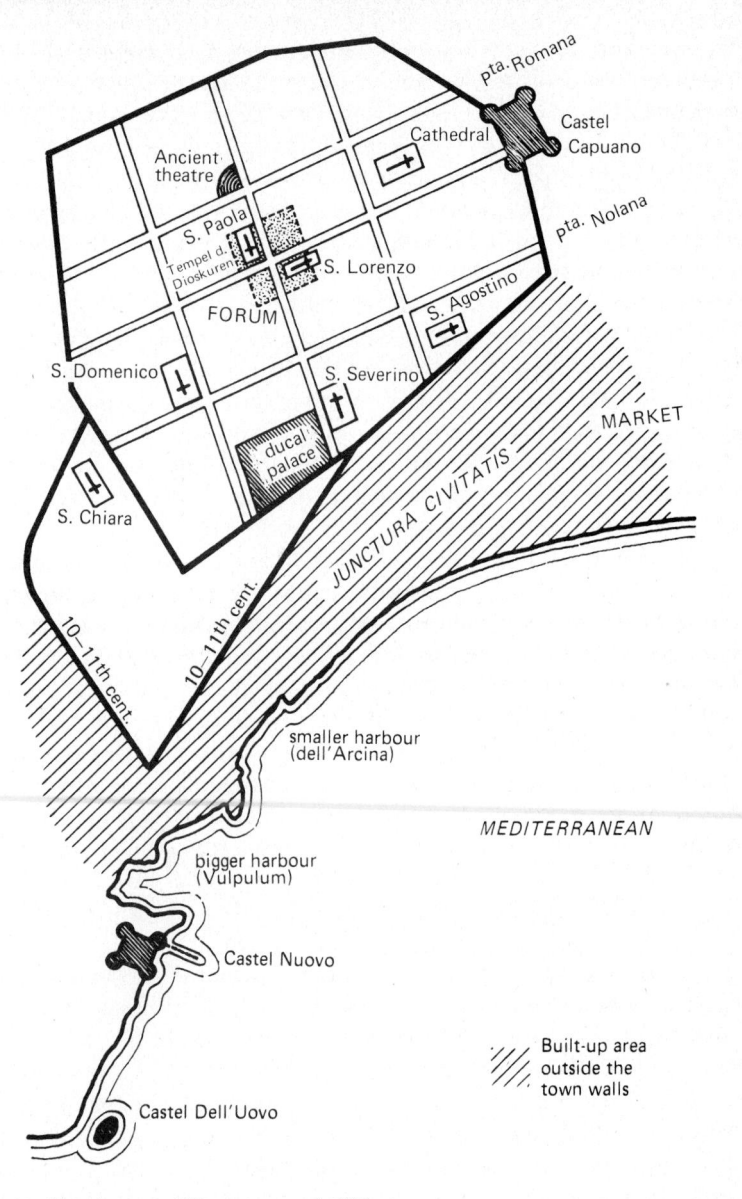

Figure 8. Sketch-map of Naples around 1300.

Participation in the wool trade of the Iberian peninsula and the creation of its own textile industry were the greatest achievements of fourteenth-century Barcelona. However, the town remained primarily a harbour. Profit from the sale of saffron, the flourishing cloth industry and the provisioning of the town with necessities, as well as the level of public income, all depended on the success of its merchants. They paid for spices from the Levant with wool from Aragon which they sold to the Venetians. Nor did they only buy spices with their Venetian ducats but alum and woad in Genoa for their home cloth industry whose product was then exchanged in Sicily for sugar. This sugar they then sold at Bruges. In the north the trade of Barcelona extended to England. Its ships went *ultramare* into the eastern Mediterranean, to Asia Minor and the Syrian harbours. Rhodes was an important harbour for them, a stage on the voyage to Alexandria. When they no longer called at the Syrian ports in the fifteenth century, they increased their trade with Egypt.

The men of southern France[179] were active in Mediterranean trade from the twelfth century onwards; Marseilles was their leading town. They moved more and more from under the shadow of the Italians. Voluminous reports describe Marseilles' trade with Syria, which did not adopt the Genoese system of annual fleets, although the *commenda* was a customary business practice here. The commodities for export were cloth from northern France and Flanders as well as from southern France and linen from Champagne and Germany. Gold thread from Genoa, Lucca and Montpellier also appears as an important commodity for export. In addition furs, tin from England, coral which was found off the coast of Provence itself, almonds from Provence and saffron doubtless from Tuscany. Alum, sugar, spices and brazil-wood from Syria were all imported.

The trade in wine and cereals was important. The import of grain was a matter of life and death for Marseilles. It came from Sicily, Sardinia, from which the Genoese were trying to exclude the merchants of Marseilles because of their Syrian trade, from the small island of Caprera, from Catalonia and from Languedoc. Wine was exported. Other merchants also travelled in ships sailing from Marseilles, men from Figeac and Orlac, Narbonne and Carcassonne, Toulouse, Cahors, Limoges, Alais, Montauban and Saint-Gilles; those of Le Puy, Aix, Nîmes and Avignon also invested in such voyages. After Marseilles, Montpellier played the most important part in the Syrian trade. Arles was one of the Rhône cities which sent its own ships for pilgrims to Syria and finally Aigues-Mortes also became important in this transport of pilgrims.

For the first time under the Latin Emperors (1204–1261), we find mention of a special quarter in Constantinople which belonged to the merchants of the south of France, although the Catalans were also included in it. It was under Venetian authority. From the beginning of the thirteenth century, Italian control of trade between southern France and North Africa decreased and the direct trade of Marseilles with the Saracens of the west underwent a surprising upsurge. Arles and Saint-Gilles also joined in this trade, but Montpellier became particularly important. Wine, Marseilles' most significant article of export, was shipped, and in addition chestnuts, beans, tallow, saffron, copper, gold, silver, coral, textiles, goods from the Levant and drugs. Skins and furs, wool, wax and almonds were Marseilles' chief imports.

It was natural that southern French merchants should also appear at the fairs of Champagne. The first to arrive, as far as we know, were those of Montpellier, then those of Marseilles. From 1224 the Catalans had a house at Provins, *domus illorum de Hispania*. In 1220 people from Marseilles and probably also Saint-Gilles and Montpellier appeared in England. A Marseilles firm was, for example, bringing alum and sugar to England. Southern French trade with Sicily expanded in spite of all Genoese attempts to stop it. Southern France was already closely linked geographically, ethnically and politically with Catalonia. Voyages between Montpellier and Catalonia are recorded from 1127. From 1219, Marseilles received trading privileges there, above all for its corn trade.

We mentioned the fairs of Saint-Gilles in the last chapter. About 1300 southern French trade began to decline because of the political situation, the development of the direct sea route between Italy and Flanders, the colonies of Italian businessmen at the papal curia at Avignon, and finally also because of the effects of plague and the activities of Barbary pirates.

The social structure of the southern and south-western French towns had much in common with those of northern Italy. Let us take Arles as an example. The agrarian economy of its hinterland – Camargue salt, manufacture of dyestuffs, cattle pastures, vineyards and olive groves – dominated trade and were dependent upon it. In the thirteenth century fifty per cent of the full citizens and members of families represented on the town council of Arles were customs farmers, mint masters, money-lenders or changers, eleven per cent were jurists, notaries or doctors, eleven per cent participated directly in trade, eleven per cent had trading interests in salt, wine, fish, cattle and wool, and all owned some land.

The biggest town of south-western France, Toulouse,[180] was almost a city state of the northern Italian type. The Albingensian Crusade brought this development to an end. The city, however, continued to control the countryside economically. Many Toulouse citizens were the owners of landed estates and indeed lords and notables in the nearby villages and market towns. The *Estimes Toulousaines*, the city's tax register, which gives us an insight into private property, confirms how typical it was for the citizens of Toulouse to own landed wealth. This was true not only of rich citizens like Messire Guilhelm de Garrigues who owned six patrician houses within Toulouse as well as great landed wealth outside the city. Small craftsmen, gardeners, and workers also might own a small house and one or two parcels of land. Fifty-eight per cent of the properties recorded in 1335 consisted of landed property, vineyards, farmhouses and lordships. Trade and particularly finance was just as important. In 1333 Toulouse had eighty money-changers. Its golden age came late, when it developed a trade in woad late in the fifteenth century which gave it international importance.

The justification for speaking of the individuality of each town is clearly shown by the case of Bordeaux.[181] Bordeaux is an Atlantic town but with the reservation that it lies far inland and that the Gironde has its estuary in the often stormy Bay of Biscay. Thus, for a long time, Bordeaux did not control all the routes that traversed the Ocean in the later Middle Ages. The Genoese and Venetians, on their sea voyages to the Netherlands and England, did not stop in Bordeaux, nor did the German and English fleets on their way to Portugal and the Holy Land. Bordeaux had no satisfactory links with the Mediterranean. Its rise, aided by its communal constitution which was in sharp contrast to the other towns of southern France, was promoted by a unique fusion of economic and political factors. Bordeaux in the later Middle Ages became the greatest wine market of Europe, comparable only with Cologne. The growth of the town was dependent from the beginning, as we have seen, on agrarian developments. Its economic progress accelerated considerably in the thirteenth century and was only disturbed temporarily by French control between 1294 and 1303. After La Rochelle (from 1224) and

Toulouse (from 1271) fell to the kings of France, Bordeaux, as the capital of the Plantagenet domains on the continent and the most important continental Atlantic harbour belonging to England, had the unprecedented opportunity to become the chief provider of wine for the English market. In the Low Countries, Bordeaux competed with the wine of Poitou, that of the area around Paris and the Rhineland, but in England it almost gained a monopoly. London was the centre of this market.

Bordeaux never developed into a city state although its distance from either its English rulers or French suzerains gave an impetus to independent administrative organization. The entire city lived more or less from wine, not only the citizens but the rest of the population, especially the vineyard workers and dockers. At the summit of the social pyramid stood the few great bourgeois families whose political strength rested upon wealth earned from the wine trade. The medieval scourge of family feuds was very evident in Bordeaux.

The most powerful economic forces were at play in the urban area between the Seine and the Rhine. A feature of this area was the existence of a close and many-sided link between the industries producing for export and more local trade. The cloth industry occupied a key-position in this.[182] The Genoese notarial registers testify to the great importance of the north-western textile industry: the French part of it comprised Champagne with the cloth towns of Châlons-sur-Marne and Provins, and the linen town of Rheims, the region of Paris including the capital itself, then Chartres, Etampes and Beauvais, furthermore Caen in Normandy and Amiens in Picardy, Saint-Quentin, Abbeville, Montreuil, Saint-Ricquier and Corbie. The Low Countries are represented by Arras, Douai, Lille, Tournai, Ghent, Ypres, Bruges, Saint-Omer and Dixmude. But cloths from Cambrai, Valenciennes, Liège as well as English cloths (*panni Anglici*) also appear. Genoa obtained these cloths via the Rhône valley and despatched them either from its harbour for export by ship or over the Alps and through Piedmont. The Italians kept part of the cloth for themselves. However, one also meets men from the northern cloth towns in considerable numbers in Genoa, especially those of Arras. A large proportion of the sales were settled at the fairs of Champagne. In the Meuse area, age-old towns were Huy, Maastricht, then Liège, Namur, Dinant and later on still Saint-Trond, Tongres, Hasselt, Roermond, Ivois-Carignan, Virton, and Luxembourg. Brabant's cloth industry began in the thirteenth century and rose to equal place with that of Flanders in the fourteenth century. Malines, Brussels and Louvain were its great centres. Ammann traced in all some 150 cloth centres, 90 of them in the Low Countries. Export was not only to the Mediterranean but also by the German Hanse to the Baltic. Cologne exported its cheaper cloth primarily to the un-demanding markets of south-eastern Europe and in the twelfth century was the collecting-point from which Maastricht and Aachen cloth was sent, some of it also destined for the Danube area. Aachen's cloth later reached Poland by way of Breslau. The Rhineland centres of Düren participated in the export of cloth while cloth from the Münstereifel region was despatched via Cologne.

Linked to the high-quality cloth producing areas of north-western Europe was the middle Rhine area, which produced a cloth of lighter quality. In the twelfth and thirteenth centuries we find German 'Greycloth' at the fairs of Champagne and in Paris. Various pieces of evidence show that at the end of the twelfth century cloth from Mainz and Cologne was to be found as far afield as Venice.[183] The distribution of cloth from the middle Rhine area reached from the North Sea and the Baltic to the Alps in the south and to Breslau and Hungary in the east. The Wetterau towns of Frankfurt, Friedberg and Wetzlar formed the core of this textile area and also the starting-point for export, followed by a group of episcopal towns on the middle Rhine, especially Speyer. In addition, small towns in the mountains of Hesse, in the Taunus, Westerwald and Eifel mountains also produced cloth.

The main centre of the metal industries lay on the Middle Meuse and in Cologne with the Bergische Land. Non-ferrous metals were used for everyday ware but also for highly artistic objects – an exquisite example is the font executed by Renier of Huy which today can be seen in Liège. In the twelfth century copper reached the Meuse valley via Cologne and Neuss from the Harz and its transit was favoured by trading privileges. The Meuse towns were also themselves engaged in the metal trade. Liège was a leading centre for the smelting of iron-ore and manufacture of metal goods. Cologne achieved as high a standing in the metal industries as it did in the textile industry where it was trading not only in woollen cloth but linen, fustian, silk and hemp. Apart from Zürich and Regensburg, the latter also renowned for its veils,[184] Cologne was the sole silk manufacturing centre north of the Alps. Its metalware – swords and harnesses among other things – developed from early medieval traditions and, like its many-sided trade in metals themselves, utilized the raw materials from the Bergland, both west and east of the Rhine as well as from north and central Germany. The manufacture of articles in precious metals also played an important role. In 1395 Cologne had 122 goldsmiths and gold beaters. The gold beaters exported abroad their gold and silver sheets, which were also used by Cologne artists to provide the gold background of paintings and the gilding of altars. Cologne was an important fur market and produced leather goods for export.

The area on the middle Meuse exported coal from a surprisingly early date. It was a pioneer in Europe, and when we find coal mentioned in Dutch customs tariffs in the middle of the thirteenth century, then this must have been brought along the Meuse from Liège. Those of Cologne's industries which used furnaces went over to coal in the fourteenth century. The Low Countries got their timber, stone and chalk from the Meuse and the Rhine.[185]

Cologne served as the link for the despatch of Baltic products to the south and for providing the north with the favourite German medieval wine, that of Alsace. The Cologne seal on a fish barrel meant best quality salted herring, while the Cologne device on a wine cask signified Alsace wine. The provision of necessities for the populous city of Cologne was very dependent upon imports. On the other hand, Cologne also acted as a corn market for the whole northern Low Countries. The Viehtafel – a municipal credit establishment – facilitated the purchase of cattle at the Cologne cattle market from the fourteenth century onwards and these animals came to be despatched over an ever-widening area.

In the twelfth and thirteenth centuries these great cities of north-western Europe were ruled and economically dominated by a mercantile patriciate. We can clarify the meaning of the newly evolved scholarly term of 'patriciate' with some examples. To begin with Cologne. The Cologne patricians in the thirteenth century termed themselves *Geschlechter*. Birth and wealth were qualifications for membership of this circle. Membership of the College of echevins (*Schöffenkolleg*), that is the High Court (*Hochgericht*), and of the association of families known as the *Richerzeche*, were essential qualifications. It was possible to rise from the ranks of the garment shearers (cloth dealers) and goldsmiths but not from any other craft. Thus a caste of around forty families, not completely exclusive but a relatively closed group, was institutionalized in the *Richerzeche*. The burgomaster with the officials of the *Richerzeche* as his councillors first appear in a guild charter of about 1180. While it is they who here were administering the guild law, in 1149 the deputy judge (*Unterrichter*), echevins and *meliores* were still exercising this right with the consent of the communal assembly. The burgomaster of Cologne, who slowly replaced the deputy judge in the leading executive position in the city community, appears linked with the *Richerzeche*, not as is elsewhere customary with the constitution of the town council.

The Cologne *Richerzeche* disappeared between 1369 and 1396 because of feuds between the great families. It had dominated the political and economic life of Cologne for two hundred years and exercised a generous cultural patronage. The last cultural achievement of the patrician families was the founding of the city's university. They owed their wealth to trade. Their commercial spirit also characterized their attitude to land. They sought to buy land because ownership of it extended their credit possibilities. The investment of business profits in land and property became a practice from an early date in Cologne. It provided a possession of stable value on the security of which, money could be raised at any time. This was an original feature of Cologne law[186] which left the debtor in possession and allowed him to recover full ownership within a year. The urban property market was very mobile and ownership very fragmented. Eighth and sixteenth parts of a house and even smaller fractions were frequent. With its *Schreinen*, which were registers of deeds of transfer of land, Cologne is the birthplace of the German registers of landed property. The surviving eighty-six *Schreinskarten* and 516 *Schreinsbücher* form the longest series of German registers of landed property. Together with investment in property including revenues from market stalls, bakeries, breweries, slaughter houses, smithies and mills the Cologne propertied class held part of their assets in liquid cash and part in the splendid furnishings of their houses. The merchant needed a store of treasure to be able to take advantage of a favourable business deal, to farm and monopolize revenues or to secure the profit from appropriating the top offices.

Many of the great Cologne families flourished for as long as five hundred years – the family of Jude between 1152 and 1674, the Lyskirchen between 1150 and 1672, each of them for half a millenium and with a succession of seventeen generations. Furthermore, as far as is now known, the Mummersloch lasted from 1167 to 1492, the family of Canus from 1142 to 1435, the Grin from 1149 to 1459, the Hardevust from 1140 to 1479, the Spiegel from 1180 to 1492, the

Quattermart from 1168 to 1441, the Gir from 1170 to 1435, the Cusinus from 1160 to 1438, the Birklin from 1150 to 1396, the Cleingedank from 1168 to 1393, the Aducht from 1150 to 1398, each flourishing for between eight and eleven generations namely more than 250 years.[187]

The Ghent patricians, the *viri hereditarii*, display similar features.[188] A few Ghent patrician houses still stand today, bearing the proud motto "Free house, free inheritance" (*Vry huys, vry erve*). An example cited by Ganshof,[189] derived from a legal dispute of about 1120, reveals an 'early patrician' and citizen of Ghent called Everwakker. He had friends among the great men of the land and was so rich and powerful that he was able to defy the counts of Flanders. His landed property was utilized for the cloth industry. A legal dispute arose concerning some two hundred hectares of marshy pasture suitable only for sheep rearing. The barrier between the early urban patriciate and the nobility was thus not an unsurmountable one in Flanders.

Medieval urban society was not lacking in its darker side, in its family feuds like that between the Weisen and Overstolzen in Cologne. Exploitation of the poor by the rich was endemic. Jehan Boinebroke of Douai is an oft-cited example from the thirteenth century. When he died in 1285, having served nine times as an echevin, he left behind a great fortune, mostly in real estate. Before it passed to his four children, the executors of his will were instructed to pay his debts and to repair any wrongs that in their judgement the deceased had committed. Many complaints were now forthcoming. These claims were written down and cover five and a half metres of parchment. Boinebroke bought his wool in England, sent it in sacks to Douai, and gave it out to the peasant women in the countryside to be spun. The yarn was then woven by craftsmen who although they were free in law were economically dependent on him. He also had his own dyeing plant. Boinebroke had thoroughly exploited his economic might, paid his workers in necessities at artificially inflated prices, while keeping low the payments for the goods which they produced for him. A rising of craftsmen and workers in Douai had already occurred. In 1280 such discontent spread from Ypres to Tournai and Douai, where Boinebroke was instrumental in putting it down.

Like the *nobiles cives Colonienses*, the Cologne patricians as they figure in royal charters, the Ghent patricians appear in control of the town in the thirteenth century. They built for themselves fortified stone houses, the Steene, first mentioned in 1212, possessed costly

horses, used seals, bought up noble properties and used the titles
domini (lords) and *sire.*

Joris can cite about forty echevinal families which composed the
ruling class in Huy in the middle of the thirteenth century. Among
these some fifteen families formed the most important group. They
were for the most part cloth merchants and also financiers, but much
more rarely, rose to riches as craftsmen. Here too they held property
for security, possessed a town house and rents from houses in the
town from the twelfth century onwards, and, from the thirteenth
century, landed property outside the town as well. Possession of
vineyards was a very favoured form of investment from the end of
the thirteenth century and shares in mills were also valued. Citizens
of Huy purchased sheep and gave them to the peasantry to rear and
the product was then divided by agreement. In his will in 1270
Etienne li Pors of Huy left his wife one hundred marks on the specific
condition that she should "trade with and make a profit on it" (*pour
marchandeir et faire son proit*), that is employ it for commercial
purposes.

As soon as we leave the north-western industrial area, the picture
changes. Metz,[190] for example, the only great city of the medieval
German Empire south-west of Cologne, had no export industry nor
was it a fair town. Its trade depended above all on the products of its
fertile surrounding area. It also became a great money-market. The
trade of Metz is a peculiar case, and the unique social structure of the
Metz patriciate makes that town even less typical. The great Metz
patrician families early on obtained landed possessions outside the
city gates which in the thirteenth and fourteenth centuries they
transformed into rural lordships. Here they had their country seats
while in the town they lived in towers. We are reminded of the
situation in Italy. The solid backing of properties in the *Pays messin*
made it possible for the Metz patriciate, whose division into five
paraiges or family associations was almost institutionalized, to
continue to dominate the city, at a time when elsewhere in the area
circumscribed by the Scheldt, Meuse and Rhine, the lordship of the
patriciate was weakening.

The imperial city of Cologne had not created any dependent
territory. The relationship between town and country on the lower
Rhine, Meuse and Scheldt took a form which was quite different from
that in Italy, Metz or in south Germany. The town's influence on the
surrounding countryside brought more intensive agriculture. Im-

provements like the utilization of land which had previously remained fallow, improved cultivation of crops which could be exploited industrially like flax, the increased amount of cattle-rearing, all emerged in the thirteenth century in the "islands of intense agricultural production" around Ghent[191] and Cologne.[192] Research is now beginning to concentrate attention on this.

In the political sphere, from the thirteenth century onwards the German towns created town leagues. Their purpose was to assure peace, also to safeguard trade and to provide protection against increasing harassment by territorial lords. In the uncertain situation of the German Interregnum, that is in the second half of the thirteenth century, a chain of town leagues from the upper Rhine to Westphalia came into existence.[193] The most famous, the Rhenish League of 1254,[194] consisted of the towns of Mainz, Worms and Oppenheim, and its initiator was the Mainz citizen and merchant Arnold Walpot, who traded abroad. The League expanded considerably after Cologne joined it and came to include towns from as far away as Bremen. Territorial lords also joined it: "A really individual and new form of land peace developed there out of the urban spirit in the special circumstances of the Interregnum" (Angermeier). This League collapsed as a political power, but its history does illustrate the political importance of the towns of western Germany. The great towns often played a role in the fourteenth century in aiding the royal and princely policies of promoting the peace of the land. This was true of the Wetterau towns of Frankfurt, Gelnhausen, Friedberg, Wetzlar, Dortmund, Soest, Osnabrück, Münster in Westphalia together with Cologne and Aachen which were included in the land peaces made between the electoral lordship of Cologne and Brabant for the territories between Meuse and Rhine from Andernach to Xanten from 1351 onwards.

In south Germany powerful town leagues appeared in the second half of the fourteenth century. The dukes of Brabant and the archbishops of Cologne included their towns in their territorial peace agreements, and this brought them into a league. In 1302 the town leagues of the middle Rhine began, incorporating the towns of different territorial states; they included Koblenz, Boppard, Oberwesel, Andernach and Bonn, later joined also by Cologne. However, in 1365, within the electoral lordship of Cologne, Andernach, Ahrweiler, Bonn, Neuss and Linz formed a league which became the core of a permanent assembly of estates.

The Flemish towns had already been obstructing the counts of Flanders in the twelfth century.[195] The influence of the *scabini Flandriae* of Bruges, Douai, Ghent, Ypres and Lille decreased in the thirteenth century while Arras and Saint-Omer had become part of the French royal domain. However, in 1208 some of the towns made an autonomous treaty with the English king John Lackland, which was binding on the whole country, without the participation of the count. In 1312 Ghent, Bruges, and Ypres remained the only major 'members' (*leden*) which held assemblies (*parlementen*) in which small towns and castle-wicks also occasionally took part (*vulle parlementen*). Finally, the 'three principal pillars' (*driex prinzipale pilare*) of Flanders, that is Ghent, Bruges and Ypres, formed a land league with the 'Franc of Bruges' (*Brugse Vriye*) – thus creating a regional communal league called the 'Four Members' (*Vier Leden*) or *quatre membres de nostre dit pays de Flandres*. The political sphere of action of the 'Members' was even wider in the fourteenth than in the thirteenth century. The defence of law and privileges was the basic corner-stone of the rights demanded by the Members' assemblies; a second demand was over the granting of taxes of which there is also early evidence in the southern Netherlands. In 1203 a *firmitas* was concluded in Liège by the assent of the clergy, citizens and knights from outside the city to the effect that taxation should be granted by the three orders, clergy, townsmen and landed nobility. It would be attractive but irrelevant here to pursue the beginnings of a state organization based on estates.[196] Herein lies the difference in the development of the political rôle of the towns between northern Italy and north-western Europe as it became crystallized in the fourteenth century – city states emerged there and a state organization based on estates here. Flanders, which had an organization by different social orders only within its city communes, could be taken as an intermediate stage but here there existed in addition to the three great towns, the Franc of Bruges as a rural, communal association. Whether communally organized or as a rural association or dominated by noble lords, the countryside always remained a political factor in north-western Europe alongside the towns.

In England, where strong social links bound all classes, the towns did not constitute a sharply differentiated element within the political organization. As the men of the city and other merchants of the shire belonged together to a merchant guild like the one which Henry II established for his city of Lincoln,[197] so we find in the county courts, landowners, clergy, representatives of towns and village communities appearing together before the itinerant justices. Royal justice began to level off the differences between the various orders of society. Autonomous towns did not exist in England.

In the fourteenth century, at the same time as north-western Europe began to consolidate a state based upon separate Orders, the German Hanse changed from being an association of merchants to being an association of towns. Both developments supply examples, independent of each other, of the importance of towns.

After the decline in Frisian trade, the Scandinavians remained the only group trading between east and west on the Baltic. After the last flourish of heathenism in 1066 Christian Gotlanders, basically independent of the Swedish crown, secured the lead.[198] The Russians gained a not insignificant place alongside them. Saxon merchants were also very interested in the Baltic trade but, having no ships of their own, were dependent on Swedish and Gotland vessels. About 1090 there came a change. The danger from the heathen Wends was over for the Danes as it was also for the Saxons. A merchant went with fewer qualms into the western Baltic, and could once again travel unmolested from the Elbe to the Schlei, to Schleswig and soon to the Trave, where the Christian Nakoniden lord controlled the castle of Old Lübeck (near Schwartau). Westphalians from Soest and Dortmund but also Cologne merchants were welcome guests in Schleswig in the twelfth century. Saxon merchants came to the castle on the Trave from the Baltic. Three events changed this situation decisively in favour of the German merchants and had the effect of turning the Baltic into a sea controlled by the German Hanse: the German colonization to the east, promoted by the Schauenburg, Ascanian and Welf dynasties, the establishment of Lübeck as a town with western urban law and technical progress in ship-building, namely the introduction of the cog.[199]

The whole Slav area, taking the Eider as the border with the kingdom of Denmark, and stretching over the considerable territory up to Schwerin, bristling with ambushes and almost entirely wasted, is now by God's grace completely changed into a single unit of settlement of the Saxons. Villages and towns have been created here and the number of churches and the service of Christ multiplied.[200]

These are the closing words of Helmold von Bosau's Chronicle of the Slavs, dating from about 1172. It is certainly true that the region was now controlled by a German authority. The double foundation of

Lübeck was part of this important process; Lübeck's inhabitants were given freedom from tolls throughout Saxony and personal freedom which, if it were secured by residence for a year and a day, could be proved by their oath alone without any documentary evidence. Throughout the duchy of Saxony they could invoke the law of their own town. This civic freedom constituted the great advantage which the towns enjoying German law had over the Slav fortress towns. Helmold also mentions the deliberate encouragement of foreign trade in Lübeck by Henry the Lion who sent embassies to the towns and kingdoms of the north, to Denmark, Sweden, Norway and Russia and offered them peace so that his city of Lübeck might receive free entry and transport throughout their domains. He concluded commercial treaties with King Cnut Ericson and Duke Birger of Sweden and also with the princes of Novgorod. He made it obligatory for the Gotlanders to call at the harbour of Lübeck. His choice of Lübeck as the seat of the bishopric of Wagria in 1160 was also favourable to the town. In contrast to Schleswig, where in the winter of 1156–1157 the fleet destined for Novgorod, at anchor in the Schlei, was plundered by King Svend Grate, the merchants from Frisia, Flanders, the lower Rhine, Westphalia and Saxony travelled from Lübeck over the Baltic without using either Slav or Scandinavian seafarers as intermediaries, and forged ahead in the areas where the goods of the north and east actually originated. They could use the same route to despatch commodities from the west in the opposite direction. The harbour at Lübeck gave the companies of merchants the possibility for the first time of building broad-hulled cogs which could carry more cargo than northern and Slav rowing boats. Lübeck could be used as a base to reach the Russian market, that is Novgorod, which still could be reached only by an indirect route. The Isle of Gotland provided a transit place which had for a long time been the centre of the older commercial networks of the Baltic. In 1161 Henry the Lion made peace between Germans and Gotlanders, which was confirmed by oaths sworn by both sides.

In Gotland the society of German merchants grew up, of "all the merchants of the Roman Empire frequenting Gotland" (*universi mercatores imperii Romani Gotlandiam frequentantes*), which included not only men of Lübeck but also Westphalian and Saxon merchants and provided the core of the 'German Hanse'. In the thirteenth century four aldermen headed the Gotland Company, chosen from among the merchants of Lübeck, Wisby, Soest and

Dortmund. They had the same authority as the later heads of the Hanseatic Kontors: they exercised legal controls over members and negotiated with foreign powers. The Company also had its own seal. It displaced, to a large extent, the earlier merchants' guilds. Indeed, it became more important than the Gotland merchants themselves were, especially in Wisby where there had been a German colony since the middle of the twelfth century which possessed a number of churches. A German town came into existence here, although when and how we do not know, with its own seal, similar to that of the main German merchant society, but bearing the inscription "seal of the Germans staying in Gotland" (*sigillum Theutonicorum in Gutlandia manentium*). We need thus to distinguish between the merchants visiting Gotland and those staying there. Wisby became a 'double' town with two councils (*Ratscollegien*) which were, however, soon amalgamated. Both Germans and Gotlanders belonged to it. Wisby developed extensively in the thirteenth century. By the middle of the century, its great wall was built and it still has the ruins of eighteen medieval churches of which the largest, St Mary of the Germans, was built between 1190 and 1225. Wisby strove to become the base for the company of merchants visiting Gotland. In Hanseatic affairs, the law was laid down from Gotland.

The Wendish Hanse towns of Lübeck, Rostock and Stralsund managed to defeat the Vikings, to free the southern and eastern coasts of the Baltic, to control lastingly the trade routes to Pomerania, Prussia, Kurland, to the Dvina and to Finland and Novgorod and also to keep this trade route open. The church and nobility of northern Germany helped them. Riga was founded in 1201 as part of Christian missionary activities but with mercantile backing. It was granted the same law as Wisby and later the law of Hamburg, itself based upon Lübeck customs. In 1213 Riga became an archiepiscopal see. In 1202 the Order of the Brotherhood of the Sword was founded to which merchants could also belong. In 1224 the older foundation of Dorpat became a bishopric. In 1230 Reval had some two hundred German merchants as well as Danish and Swedish ones. The destruction of the Order of the Brotherhood of the Sword in 1236 brought a reaction in the form of the conquest of Prussia by the Teutonic Order. The Teutonic Order was a member of the Hanse although Lithuania, which was still a heathen country, was for a long time cut off by the Prussian territory of the Teutonic Order from the eastern Baltic region. Along the water route from the Gulf of Finland by the

River Neva to the the Lake of Ladoga, then by the River Volkhov and also by sleigh from the Dvina, the Hanse merchants arrived at Novgorod, travelling first under the wing of the Gotlanders but later, after making an agreement with the city, establishing their own quarter in the St Peterhof.

Novgorod[201] was, at that time, the centre of an enormous, if loosely-knit, city state, held together only by trading links and the common obligation to pay tribute. It lay between the Baltic, the North Sea, the Urals and the Valdai Hills. As early as the eleventh century Novgorod merchants and boyars travelled far and wide over the old colonized area of the Ladoga and Onega lakes into the north Dvina basin which linked the hunting regions, where fur, fish and birds could be trapped, with central and north eastern Russia. They exploited the silver wealth of the northern Urals. Novgorod means 'New town', though where the first settlement lay is as disputable as the question of the origin of the city in general. It certainly goes back to the ninth century. The medieval town lay on both sides of the River Volkhov. On the western bank was the Sophia district; the commercial area lay on the eastern bank. The Sophia district took its name from the cathedral of St Sophia. About 1000 it was the seat of a bishopric, and from 1165 of an archbishop. It was protected by a mighty fortress, the Kremlin or *Djetinec*, which was the spiritual centre of the city republic of Novgorod. The archbishop was an important political figure and immensely wealthy. After 1158 the people's assembly, the *Wiecze*, chose the bishop from among the clergy of the city, an arrangement quite unique in Europe. Around the Kremlin lay the wide semi-circle which made up the five city districts of the Sophia side of the river, and the city wall, which stretched inland and also ran along the Volkhov. The potters' quarter or peoples' quarter was one of the five city divisions. The smiths also dwelt here in the streets around the churches dedicated to Saints Cosmas and Damian, as did the silversmiths, who were one of the more important crafts.

The streets which radiated from here, Woten Street and Tschuden or Eastern Street, ran to Narva, while the Karelian Street ran to the estuary of the Neva and a road, already in 1250 known as the Prussian Road, ran to Riga. The palaces of the boyars lay in the shadow of the castle, chiefly on the Prussian Road. The boyars were property owners and became wealthy from profits derived from selling the surpluses of the dues in kind which were owed to them, furs, wax etc. They were the 'lords' (*de Heren*), a landowning nobility

WELIKJ NOVOGORD
ODER
GROS NAVGARD

Figure 10a. View of Novgorod.

with residences in the towns. The merchants formed a middle layer beneath which lay the 'dark masses' in low German *de lude* (the people). There were also many slaves. This, roughly speaking, was the social structure in Novgorod in the fourteenth and fifteenth centuries. The Sophia and commercial sides of the Volkhov were linked by the Volkhov Bridge which is first mentioned in a chronicle entry for 1133.

The old centre of the commercial side was the Castle of the Princes, the palace built by Jaroslaw, the son of Vladimir the Holy in whose reign Kiev was christianized. Jaroslaw became ruler of Kiev in 1019. After his death in 1056 Novgorod became a sort of communal family possession of his successors, known collectively as the Jaroslawicze. It was only later that it became a principality in its own right. After the death of the last mighty Grand-Prince, Vladimir Monomach, in 1125, the assembly of the people, the *Wiecze*, managed to assume more and more legal authority. The prince was forced to give up the Palace of Jaroslaw which was fortified, and used by the *Wiecze*, which set up its chancery here and that of the *possadnik* or castellan. The Palace of Jaroslaw was situated in the market place amidst the pulsing life of the market district (the Torgovajastorona). Only a few steps away were the ships' berths while the German wharf, the Gotenhof (Gotlanders Hall) with the church of St Olaf and the Hanseatic St Peterhof, also lay in the immediate neighbourhood. From 1205–1207 the Hanseatic merchants had the right of free transit through the courtyard of the old princely palace, on which the Russians were not allowed to build, so that communication with the market and between the two centres, the Perterhof and Gotenhof, remained free. In 1156 the Company of Russians engaged in overseas trade built the Church of Good Friday (Pjatniza Church) in the market place. In 1127 their predecessors, the guild of merchants who had had a business centre in Kiev, had erected the Church of St John the Baptist. Here, the court for aliens met. A large part of the commercial side of the river was taken up by the Carpenters' Quarter. This was the famous centre of the Russian art of timber-building, for the great churches of Russia were built in wood; in Novgorod St Sophia itself was built of oak. It was burnt down in 1049 when the foundations of a stone building had probably already been laid. The commercial side also possessed the oldest quarter, the Slavno district. Routes went from here to Ladoga and into the Russian hinterland. A minor tributary of the Volkhov protected it on the land side.

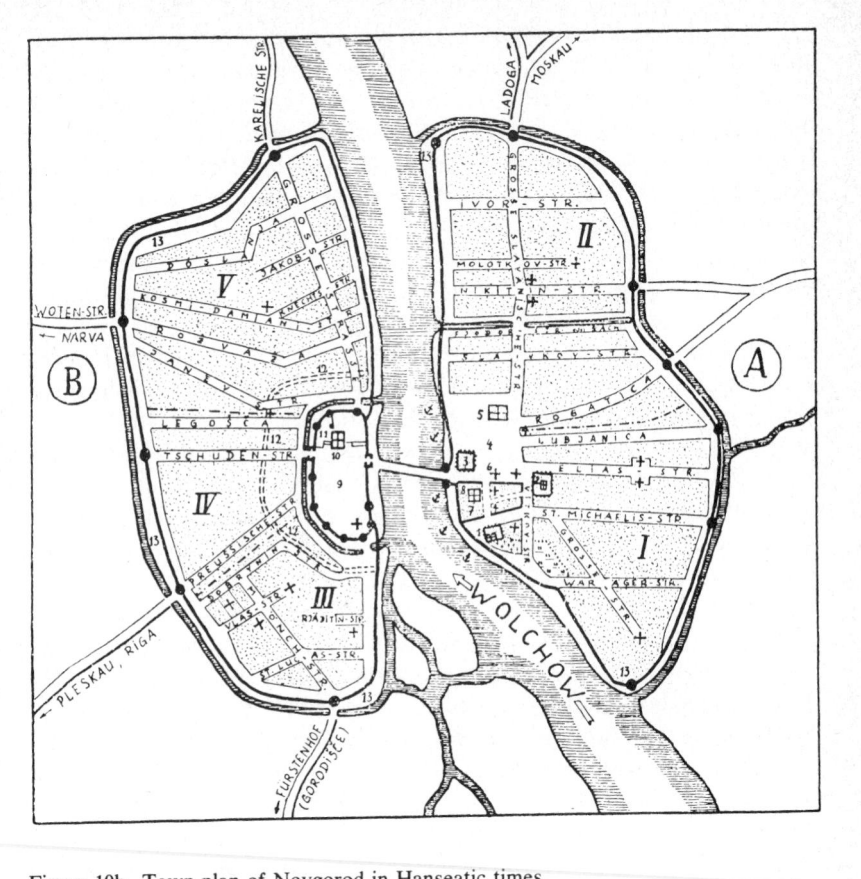

Figure 10b. Town plan of Novgorod in Hanseatic times.

Attempt at a reconstruction based upon the researches of Tolstoj, Nikitskij and on the *Russian Historical Atlas* of K.V. Kudrjasov.

Key:

A, commercial side; B, Sophia side; I, Slavno; II, Carpenters quarter; III, Peoples' or potters' quarter; IV, Environs of the castle; V, Narva town division (konec).

1, Gotenhof, with the church of St Olaf, the house belonging to the church, its meadow and site; 2, German Peterhof; 3, Pleskauer palace, possibly at that time the guild buildings of the Gotlanders; 4, Market; 5, Church of St John of the Russian merchants; 6, Church of Good Friday of the Russian long-distance merchants; 7, Prince's palace of 'Jaroslaw the Wise'; 8, Church of St Nicholas 9, Castle or Djetinec; 10, Cathedral of St Sophia; 11, Archiepiscopal palace; 12, Castle ditch; 13, Town wall or wall with towers.

The smallest administrative division of medieval Norgorod was the street. Each main street (*ulica*) had its alderman or *starosta*, its *wiecze* and its church; the street *wiecze* was responsible for choosing the priest and deacon. The streets were grouped into hundreds or *sotnie* and every two *sotnie* formed a *fifth*. The *fifths* extended into the countryside under the town's lordship. The dependent towns (*prigoroda*) included Old Ladoga with its church of St Nicholas of the Varangian merchants, Pskov, Staraya Russa and a series of smaller towns. The ten Hundreds of Novgorod were simultaneously military units and together made up the Thousand, the town's military organization under the Thousand Leader whom the German records approximate to a duke. The archbishop, the Leader of the Thousand and the Possadnik were chosen by the city *wiecze*: "the whole community of Great Novgorod, the communal 'thing'" (*de gantze gemeine Grote Nougarden, dat gemene ding*). The city *wiecze* was made up fairly arbitrarily of street associations, Hundreds and town subdivisions and in practice was dominated by merchants and boyars. It was summoned by striking the *wiecze* bell which hung in the Palace of Jaroslaw, symbol of Novgorod's independence, which Ivan III took to Moscow in 1478. The *wiecze* was the supreme organ of the town. It controlled the Council of Lords. The Possadnik, the Leader of the Thousand and their predecessors in office, and the *starostas* of the districts and hundreds all belonged to it. The prince, and after 1136 the archbishop, summoned the *wiecze*, while the prince continued to send a representative. From 1136 to 1238 Novgorod had thirty-eight princes; often "the people of Novgorod showed them where to go". "And now, prince", as the saying went, "we can no longer endure your power. Leave us and we shall find another prince." The boyars made up the Council of Lords.

The Church Ordinance of 1137 gave the church of St Sophia lucrative hunting and fishing rights. The landed wealth of the archbishop, abbeys and clergy made up 21.7 percent of the territory of Novgorod in the fourteenth and fifteenth centuries. The abbeys also played an important rôle, and they were by no means militarily insignificant because they controlled their own fortifications. At the end of the fourteenth century there were twenty-four abbeys surrounding the city's defences in three concentric circles. Suzdal and Moscow were also protected by fortified abbeys.

It was exceedingly important that Moscow did not fall to the Mongols as Kiev did in 1240. Moscow thus remained free of tax impositions by the Mongol invaders. The principality of Vladimir-Suzdal grew more and more powerful on the frontier to Novgorod's territory. The rise of the great principality of Moscow was fatal to the city republic of Novgorod. The wide area between the Baltic, Volga and Arctic Ocean was originally "a political vacuum" (Onash). This vacuum began to be filled in the second half of the thirteenth century, firstly by the principality on "both sides of the forests", Vladimir-Suzdal, and then by Moscow.

The highly-developed and widespread literacy of its population was a characteristic of Novgorod. Hundreds of late medieval legal records reflecting both business and every-day life survive written on birch bark and sometimes even in Latin script. Novgorod had features in common with the towns of the rest of Europe, for instance in the city's dual lay-out, with its Sophia side including the Kremlin and the castle, and its commercial side with its *torg*, that is the market place. Other such elements were the domination of the city by the archbishop, the relation of the clergy to laity in the city's administration, and the function of the town as a centre of trade and industry. The phenomenon of merchants' churches is also one which is common to the whole of northern Europe. The importance of the clergy is true of other Russian towns as well – of Kiev, Vladimir-Suzdal and Moscow. It is even more significant here than in central Europe. The element which was unique in these Russian towns, and only possible in the vastness and emptiness of Russia, was the town's lordship over a huge area and its use of merchants and trading links to make its control felt throughout its extent. Each capital with its Kremlin, churches, and abbeys formed the symbol and core of this whole domain, whether of Vladimir-Suzdal or Moscow.

Before its conquest by Moscow, Novgorod experienced a breath of western freedom. In the Hanseatic period it was Russia's gateway to the west. It was not only western commodities like Flemish cloth and white Lüneburg salt that came into Russia through Novgorod. Western cultural influences came in by the same routes.[202] The bronze doors of the cathedral of St Sophia, itself influenced by the Romanesque style of the west, were cast at Magdeburg in 1152–1156 and brought to Novgorod in the twelfth century (?). We do not know how they came to the city but they exercised a considerable influence on the native craftsmen in stone and wood.

It is important to establish what direct access to Novgorod meant to the Hanse. The trade of the city itself was very much concerned with the so-called 'Lower Region', that is the river area of the upper Volga and the new principality of Vladimir-Suzdal and ultimately of Moscow. Novgorod, with a population of more than 20,000 in its hey-day, was dependent on the import of grain. This could be obtained from the fertile region of Suzdal. The Lower Region also lay on the route to the Orient, especially when the alternative way to Byzantium was blocked by invading Mongols and Tartars. Active trade by the Russians themselves in the Baltic declined and almost disappeared as the result of Hanseatic economic activity.

Novgorod for the Hanse meant access to northern Russia's rich fur market, which provided all qualities of fur from costly sables to squirrel. Fur in the Middle Ages was a symbol or rank and there was a huge demand for it. The second most important trading commodity was wax, which came to Novgorod from Nijni-Novgorod and Karelia and from Smolensk and the Lithuanian forests as far as Polotsk. Silk from Baghdad, Chinese silk, spices and other Oriental goods also could be bought in the market of Novgorod.

From early on in their commercial activity in Russia the Hanseatic merchants travelled far beyond Novgorod. In the thirteenth century they regularly appeared in Smolensk and Witebsk. In 1229 at Riga the Hanse concluded a treaty with the prince of Smolensk; it was also trading with the princes of Polotsk and Witebsk. The evidence of the treaties mentions, among others, three Gotlanders, three Lübeck merchants, two from Soest, two from Münster, two from Groningen, two from Dortmund, one from Bremen and three from Riga. This does not mean that merchants from all these towns actually came to Smolensk; it is unlikely that those from Groningen did so but it does show that they were interested in the trade with Russia and that their business ventures took them as far as Riga. Riga merchants also went to Suzdal and sent back home 'Bulgar' goods, that is wares of the Volga Bulgars. They certainly reached the very frontiers of the Mongol Empire. After the beginning of the fourteenth century the Hanse discontinued journeys beyond Novgorod and Polotsk. There were a number of reasons for this: one was the intolerance and reaction to anything western which developed in Russia. Western cloth ceased to be in demand. Europe's balance of trade with Russia was also passive. The rise in power of the Grand Principality of Moscow also had a disturbing effect.

The *Schragen*, as the Ordinances of the Novgorod Kontor were called, give us a clear picture of the life of the Hanseatic merchants there. The earliest ot these records dates from the middle of the thirteenth century. The centre of the Hanse's organization in Novgorod was the stone church of St Peter. The church, a merchants' church in the true sense of the word, was apparently exceedingly spacious and had a sort of vaulted cloister. The merchants used this as a warehouse and archive; in it stood the St Peter's chest, containing both parchment charters and the treasure belonging to the Kontor. Even the weights and scales were stored there overnight. Each evening a merchant spent the night there to keep watch. When the season came for the merchants to leave, the key of the church was given into the custody of a Russian dignitary to be kept in a sealed box. Trade and business were forbidden in the church itself. No Russian was allowed to enter. The idea was to prevent others from seeing the stores of goods kept by the German merchants and thus having a detrimental effect on prices. Two merchants were given control of the church by the alderman. They were responsible for its finances and upkeep. The money came from a tax on turnover which has already been mentioned; 0.25 per cent was raised from winter arrivals. Those who came in the summer paid less. There were other forms of revenue too. The result was that if a merchant fell ill or into financial difficulties he could be helped with a payment from the chest. Surplus money was then taken by the merchants travelling back to Gotland in the winter and deposited in the German church of St Mary, where there was another special chest belonging to the merchants travelling to Novgorod and using the St Peter's church there. The church of St Peter also had its own cemetery, the right to fell timber, and its own meadows in Ladoga for the merchants' horses. Their clerical needs were also taken care of, and the itinerant priest accompanying the merchants as their clerk was a familiar sight in the Baltic area.

At almost the same time as the beginning of the Russian trade, the Hanse moved into the northern market, especially concentrating on the fair at Schonen which at that time belonged to Denmark. In the herring season from August to October, Danish fishermen brought their catches here to be salted with Lüneburg salt brought by Lübeck merchants. This provided the first possibility of fully utilizing the rich catches of herring. In this way Lübeck came to dominate Schonen. It had also been trading in Norway from the end of the twelfth century: in Bergen cod, stockfish, fish oil, butter and skins were to be had, while the Hansards brought rye, flour and malt. Norway became dependent on the import of cereals by the Hanse and this dependence occasionally proved oppressive, although it did increase the demand for fish and the number of fishermen active in the Lofotens.

The Hanse was better integrated into Swedish commercial life than into that of Norway, where in Bergen the Hansards occupied the 'German Bridge'. The Hanse had some part in the founding of Stockholm in 1252, and Lübeck merchants as financiers and German miners from the Harz mountains were engaged in the exploitation of the copper mines of Falun. The Hanse was represented on the town councils of the Swedish towns. In 1345 it was laid down that councils should consist of Swedes and Germans in equal numbers. The Swedish economy never became as restrictingly dependent on the Hanse as Norway's did since Sweden did have her own flourishing agriculture.

From the thirteenth century onwards, German merchants were coming into the North Sea and reaching England and the Low Countries. To reach the latter, they chiefly used the overland route. Here, the Hanse encountered developed urban economies and the older trading networks of Cologne and Bremen. In England the Hanse had a large number of competitors: in 1277, for instance, Italians were exporting 29 per cent of English wool, the French 21 per cent, the men of Holland 20 per cent and the Germans 11 per cent. The London and Bruges Kontors joined those of Bergen and Novgorod. Between these outer Kontors stretched the great commercial network which put the Baltic area on a new basis "harnessed to the western economic and cultural zone" (A. von Brandt). The Hanse was made up of those towns whose merchants in the Kontors enjoyed Hanseatic privileges in foreign trade – an imprecise definition.

The character of the Hanse as a separate organization with its own rules brought a great deal of strife. In the great struggle with England in the fifteenth century, the Hanse claimed to be a *societas, collegium* and *universitas*, directly contrary to the assertions of the English royal council. It defined itself as a permanent league (*firma confederatio*) of towns. In the middle of the fourteenth century the towns had spectacularly brought about the subordination of the foreign Kontors, first of all at Bruges. Already at the end of the thirteenth century Lübeck began to assume the leading rôle in the Hanse. In 1293 it brought about an agreement of Rhineland, Westphalian, Saxon and Prussian towns to make the legal route from Novgorod use Lübeck instead of Wisby as the stipulated port of call. In 1299, in

Lübeck, the Wendish and Westphalian towns agreed to abolish the seal of the Merchants' Gotland Company and to replace it with the seal of the towns trading there – a first step to the Hanse of towns. However, the decisive break-through came only between 1347 and 1356. In 1347 the *ghemenen koplude uten Romeschen rike van Alemannien* ("society of all the merchants of the Roman Empire of Germany") separated in Bruges into three divisions: the Wendish-Saxon towns, the Westphalian and Prussian towns, and those of the Gotland-Swedish-Livland axis. These divisions were still not elements of town leagues, but divisions of the Hanse of German merchants in Flanders, a Hanse which was already divided according to the towns of origin of the merchants. Then in Bruges in 1356, the fully empowered delegates to a special meeting brought about the subordination of the Kontor there to the towns. The transition from merchants' Hanse to town Hanse remained fluid. Particularly in Westphalia, the character of the Hanse as an association of merchants survived for a long time. The Hanse served as a link between economic regions with very different structures. In the Hanseatic zone, manufacture of industrial goods by the towns themselves played a secondary rôle, apart from the exceptional case of beer – Trave beer, Hamburg and Wismar beer and the brass ware of Brunswick. Thanks to its superior trade routes Brunswick had taken over the copper export of the mining town of Goslar.

The upper Rhine, Zuider Zee and Ijssel formed the western boundaries of the Hanse. The towns on the Ijssel and Zuider Zee[203] – Deventer, Zwolle and Kampen – were closely connected with Westphalia and the lower Rhine, especially with Cologne. Because of their Bergen and Baltic maritime trade they came to develop their specifically Hanseatic rôle. They were the heirs of the Frisian traders. Groningen was the first to appear in the Baltic. We meet its merchants in Riga; Harderwijk, Kampen, Zutphen, Stavoren, Elburg, Deventer and Zwolle all sent traders to the fairs at Schonen. Zwolle and Kampen are known to have joined in the Gotland trade in the late thirteenth century. Groningen and Stavoren were trading in England even earlier than in the Baltic. The counts of Holland sought to transfer the trade of these towns with Flanders to Dordrecht. Kampen took the lead in the maritime trade of the eastern Netherlands and its profits from the carrying trade, a northern Dutch speciality, were more important than those from fishing. On the lower Rhine, Cologne and Emmerich were the oldest Hanse towns; Wesel and

Duisburg became important in the fifteenth century. The Cologne Confederation of November 1367, which was the preliminary to the great Hanseatic victory over Denmark at Stralsund in 1370, was joined by the towns of Holland and Zealand, which were not really part of the Hanse. Cologne participated in this war but it kept out of the war with England, for which it was excluded from the Hanse in 1471. The result of this was the collapse of its circle of the Hanse. From 1418 the Westphalian part of the Bruges Kontor was represented not by Dortmund but by Cologne. About 1500 this Cologne part finally developed into four sections: the Westphalian towns under Münster and Paderborn, those of Cleves under Wesel, of Guelders under Nijmegen and those of the Zuider Zee under Deventer.

The Hanseatic commercial zone merged with that of the southern Netherlands Meuse and Rhineland in the lower Rhine area, and Cologne's commercial interests spread much further south than those of the other Hanseatic towns. It thus formed a border area of the Hanseatic zone. The core of the Hanse lay in the Wendish group of towns dominated by Lübeck and to a lesser degree by Kiel and Hamburg, and from 1358 Bremen, Wismar, Rostock, Stralsund and Lüneburg which belonged to the Wendish as well as the Saxon group of towns. The Hanse's control of the eastern salt trade until the fourteenth century rested on Lübeck's links with Lüneburg's salt mines. Using the Stecknitz canal route, which linked Lübeck with Hamburg and was the greatest water construction undertaken by the Hanse, Lüneburg salt ships could reach Lübeck. Lüneburg's attempt to link the Elbe and Baltic at Wismar was only partly successful – mainly as a route for importing the vast quantities of wood needed in the salt mines.

Brunswick competed with Magdeburg for the control of the Saxon towns within the Hanse. As a stopping place between Rhine and Elbe, Brunswick had a history going back to the early Middle Ages and also acted as a trading link between England and Denmark. It developed a textile industry of some importance and, as we have mentioned, a brass industry. The Brunswick Cupmakers Guild is an example of great differences in wealth within a single industrial corporation: manufacturers, masters and apprentices were all members. Magdeburg, chiefly engaged in the export of cereals and salt, was the member which linked the Hanse to the more southerly towns and to those of Brandenburg. Among the latter Berlin, created a town in 1230, played some part. About 1300 Berlin merchants were bringing

Berlin rye and oak planks to the Hamburg market and trading them for cloth there brought by Ghent merchants.

The corn surpluses of the whole of the hinterland of the Elbe played an important part in the rise of Lübeck and Hamburg but also of the towns of Mecklenburg, Pomerania, Brandenburg and Prussia. The towns of Danzig, Elbing, Braunsberg, Königsberg, Chelmno and Torun, which until 1466 were under the control of the Grand Master of the Teutonic Order, because of the weighty nature of their export goods, timber and corn, were interested in the roundabout route through the Sound and Kattegat to the prejucice of the route via Lübeck and Hamburg. This tension between the Wendish and Prussian-Livonian towns often brought friction. The far distant towns of Krakow and Breslau joined the Prussian section of the Hanse. The traditional activity of their merchants in the west in Flanders, the importance to the Hanse of the Slovakian copper going down the Vistula, and the predominance of German inhabitants in these towns determined their allegiance to the Hanse. In Krakow only Germans could become citizens. It was the strengthening of the Polish element and increasing links with the east via Leipzig and Nürnberg which weakened trade on the Vistula and thereby the Hanseatic character of Krakow. In the last thirty years of the fifteenth century it left the Hanse. Breslau grew in the late thirteenth century into a great commercial city which had a compulsory staple from 1274, possessed flourishing industries with thirty guilds. It also possessed in Silesia and its industrial towns a surrounding territory which made it a commercial centre of the first rank.

In central Germany, Duderstadt, Erfurt, Göttingen, Halle, Merseburg, Mühlhausen, Naumburg, Nordhausen, Northeim, Osterode and Uslar were all members of the Hanse. Erfurt, at the juncture of important routes and in the middle of a fertile area which specialized in the production of woad, was the most important of this group of towns. Its trade in woad is known to date from the twelfth century.

The social structures within the Hanseatic towns varied considerably. The trading group dominated in the ports. The Hamburg list of oathtakers of 1376, drawn up when the council made all townsmen swear a new oath after the suppression of a craftsmen's revolt, reveals the following picture.[204] Of the 1,175 people who appeared on the list, 178, that is 15.1 per cent, were independent merchants trading to foreign countries, eighty-four to Flanders, thirty-five to England, forty to Lübeck together with nineteen cloth shearers. Then came retailers comprising twenty-one grocers and ten shopkeepers, that is 2.7 per cent; 457 brewers amounting to 38.8 per cent, including 126 who were brewing for export to Amsterdam and fifty-five who were sending their beer to Frisia. 43.3 per cent were in crafts other than brewing. In all there were 37.5 per cent independent merchants; 19.2 per cent small brewers for local consumption and 43.3 per cent craftsmen. Of the craftsmen the coopers also served the export industry and in the troubles of 1376 they took the side of the merchants. We must also include the tin workers among the trading craftsmen. In the same way the goldsmiths' craft must be linked with the jewellers, the butchers with the cattle dealers, and the tanners and shoemakers with the leather trade. Economically there was no sharp distinction between trade and craft, and it remained possible to switch from one to the other; the class of the wealthy included craftsmen. An institution comparable to the Cologne *Richerzeche* or the *Paraiges* of Metz was lacking here. According to the findings of Reincke for Hamburg and those of von Brandt for Lübeck,[205] there was a relatively equal distribution of wealth among the citizens at the end of the fourteenth century. This worsened in the second half of the fifteenth century but never reached the state of crisis such as at Augsburg. A recent study[206] of social divisions among the population of Reval, which emphasizes the differences between the various levels of society more sharply, also includes inhabitants who were not citizens. Reval lived primarily from foreign trade and there was no great division in status within the merchant class as such. The distinction rather lay between merchants and craftsmen. The crafts, with their predominantly German masters, were not of great significance. The middle class consisted in the main of different branches of the guilds or *Ämtern*, as they were called here. Among these were the barbers, sailors, grocers or shopkeepers, Estonian hemp-spinners, the so-called *Püstemaker*, namely the belt-makers, who also kept shops. The lower group included the brewery workers who were employed by those citizens who possessed the right to brew, stone masons, carpenters, cobblers, tailors' cutters, slaughterers, who were distinguished from the bone-carvers, the merchants' house-servants, the industrial workers in the export businesses, navigators, porters used for transporting salt and beer, loaders, packers, sack-binders and 'pounders' who were important in the salt industry because the Bay salt arrived in large rough pieces which had to be broken up before it could be sent on its way, and other specialist trades like the workers engaged in packing Russian and Livonian flax into barrels, as well as many others.

These social distinctions were reflected in different styles of houses. In contrast to the spacious town houses of merchants and craftsmen which, in addition to a room for the family, often included a guest room because of the lack of other accommodation, they also had offices, warehouse space and a workshop, the dwellings for servants and apprentices, on the other hand, were really wretched places. Because their houses were mostly tall but housed between five or six, or even as many as nine, families, living conditions were very cramped. Some lived in cellars, others in attics or partitioned off quarters.

A prerequisite for membership of the Hanse was that the town should be ruled by patricians. Brunswick, which was entirely patrician-controlled in its territorial policy as well as city affairs, witnessed a bloody revolt in 1374. Patrician rule ended and an elected council took its place, to be filled by representatives from nineteen corporations, fourteen privileged guilds and an assembly, for those who belonged to no guild, made up of men from the five town districts. Under this system the cupmakers came to hold one-third of all the seats on the council. Because of this revolution Brunswick was expelled from the Hanse for five years.

Thus, in the later Middle Ages the Hanseatic towns were controlled by a mercantile upper class, closed to the lower orders, and one which was linked not only within the town but which frequently had connections with others of the same class throughout the Hanseatic region.

The towns which belonged to the margrave of Meissen and the Pleissenland did not belong to the Hanse. The special feature of the Saxon towns lay in the importance of mining in the area, which led to a new wave of town foundations after 1400, after the founding of towns in the rest of Germany had ceased. Freiberg was the principal mining town in this region; the mining colony there began about 1170 and by the thirteenth and fourteenth centuries Freiberg's commercial links had spread throughout central Europe.[207]

South Germany was full of lively towns: Bodensee and north Swabia with Constance, Ulm and Augsburg; Bavaria with the ancient city of Regensburg and newly-founded München; inner Swabia with Esslingen, and finally Nürnberg, at this time already a large and flourishing city.

South Germany was the land of imperial cities in the strict sense of the word, namely towns on imperial soil "whose true and only lord is the king, that is the Emperor" (Sydow).[208] We must distinguish them from the Free Cities. To the latter category in the fourteenth century belonged Mainz, Worms, Speyer, Cologne, Strasbourg, Basel and Regensburg which were in the process of throwing off the control by their territorial rulers. The imperial towns achieved this freedom by the central authority's surrender of all local control. Only in south Germany do we find towns which were approaching being city states. The limited extent of the real territorial power of the emperor in the southern part of the Empire has been shown in a comparative study of the territorial policies of Zürich and Lübeck.[209] The consistent factor in Lübeck's territorial policy was to protect its transport network, while Zürich aimed at and achieved both financial and economic exploitation and real domination of its surrounding territory. This sprang not only from its enjoyment of the protection of the Swiss Confederation even though, in the long run, Zürich and Bern display a quite different type of political power from the German imperial towns. Nevertheless Nürnberg, Schwäbisch-Hall, Ulm, Strasbourg, Rottweil and Überlingen held considerable areas of land. Ulm's territory extended to about fifteen square miles and formed an upper and lower lordship administered by a total of thirteen higher officials and their deputies and thirty communes. Rich hospital foundations often played an important rôle in the build-up of these territories and this was the case in Überlingen, Ravensburg, Memmingen, Biberach, Reutlingen, Schwäbisch-Gmund, and Esslingen.[210]

Finally, south Germany was the land of the town leagues[211] and of the great business firms. In these respects it remained clearly distinct from the north Rhine-Westphalian region with its regional peaces arranged and controlled by great lords, its territorial leagues and its leagues of princes, in which a more or less important lord, archbishop, duke and great city like Cologne called the tune while the smaller towns and lesser lords only joined in. South Germany had a quite different political structure: a number of great, middling and often quite small imperial towns, and also numerous nobles who were not able to found territorial lordships and appear as free imperial knights. Only leagued together could these imperial towns and imperial knights exercise any political power. In the second half of the fourteenth century they created extensive leagues: in 1371 and 1373 the Emperor Charles IV demanded heavy subsidies from the Swabian imperial towns and in 1373–1374 extended his demands by requiring Nördlingen, Donauwörth, Dinkelsbühl and Bopfingen to pledge themselves to Bavaria. This was the motive behind the Swabian league formed in 1376 between Ulm, Constance, Überlingen, Ravensburg, Lindau, St Gall, Wangen, Buchhorn, Reutlingen, Rottweil, Memmingen, Biberach, Isny and Leutkirch. Half the members of this league were towns around Lake Constance which had already been forming leagues together, of varying composition, since 1312. The League of 1376 was outlawed and the emperor himself took up arms against it without success. The League tightened its hold on the area around it. Its increase in power suited the Swabian lords and knights. The knights for their part created societies which were hostile to the towns. When in 1380 the League of the Lion, particularly hostile to towns, began a feud with the town of Frankfurt, that place joined with Mainz, Worms, Speyer, Strasbourg and Pfedersheim in 1381, as well as with a group of imperial towns of Alsace. In the same year, the Swabian and Rhineland town leagues united in a military association. Regensburg joined the Swabian League in 1381 and Nürnberg in 1384. In 1382 a series of Saxon towns created a Saxon League. Count-palatine of the Rhine Rupert II defeated the Rhineland levies in 1388 following a decisive defeat inflicted a few months earlier by Count Eberhard of Württemberg on the army of the League at Döffingen, south-west of Stuttgart. The Swabian League collapsed and the towns adhered one after another to the land peace of Eger. Only the towns around Lake Constance maintained their close league. In general the political activity of town leagues on a larger scale was henceforth ended.

In economic activity the Lake of Constance and northern Swabia belonged to the textile region of the Rhineland. The production of linen took first priority here, and this was replaced in the course of the fourteenth century by the weaving of fustians. Constance, with a mercantile community going back to the eleventh century, was sending linen to Genoa at the beginning of the thirteenth century. In 1224 a man from Lindau was selling his linen cloths from Germany (*tele de Alemannia*) in Genoa. In 1214 Ravensburg merchants were buying silk there, in 1262 St Gall merchants bought pepper there and sold south German linen. Ammann has provided a variety of types of evidence to trace the appearance of south German linen throughout the Mediterranean where, by way of Marseilles, Genoa and Venice, it made its way to Asia and North Africa. It reached the north-west partly by way of the Frankfurt fairs and partly in the foreign trade dealings of the linen towns themselves, in both cases to Cologne, Bruges, Antwerp and England. It went over the Baltic to Reval, to the north-east to Poland and south-east to Hungary. Here too we meet the two streams of trade and industry.

Trade was organized by great business firms which were typical of south Germany.[212] In 1909 the director of the Baden archive, Karl Obser, found, in a room in the castle and earlier Cistercian cloister of Salem in a chest of drawers, a packet labelled "useless business things"; they were the business records of the great Ravensburg Company. The grandson of Alexius Hilleson, who had audited the accounts of the company at its dissolution, had taken them with him into the cloister when he became a monk. Aloys Schulte searched through them and, using supplementary evidence, made them available to scholars. At the end of the fourteenth century the Humpis of Ravensburg, the Muntprat of Constance, and the Mötteli who came from Buchhorn had combined to found the Company. Their aim was to end their competition and losses by inaugurating a common business, and also to reduce the number of agents which they needed. The Company's capital was made up of the shares of members, who had to be citizens of imperial towns and not subordinated to foreign interests. The Company's centre was Ravensburg, but with authorized agents in Constance, St Gall and Memmingen. There were also branches in Venice, Milan, Genoa, Geneva, Lyons, Avignon, Barcelona, Zaragoza, Valencia, Bruges and later in Antwerp and finally in Nürnberg, Cologne and Vienna. Their main articles of export were south German linen and fustians and they imported among other things sugar from Spain and especially saffron. The variety of wares in which the firm traded far and wide was very great, and it remained in existence until 1530, still bound, in its initiatives and aims, by the old medieval traditions.

Hektor Ammann made a special study of the Diesbach-Watt Company founded in the first third of the fifteenth century by Nicholas von Diesbach in Bern and by the Watt brothers in St Gall. Its trading network reached Zaragoza, Valencia and Barcelona in the west, and Prague, Krakow, Warsaw, Poznan and Danzig in the east. Its main export commodity was again linen, and it imported saffron, furs and wax. The Meuting Company which had branches in London, Vienna and Venice has been known for a long time, as has the Imhof

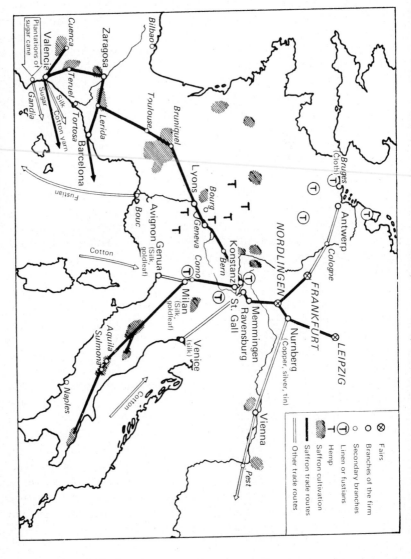

Figure 11. The Great Ravensburg Company.

Company from Nürnberg which had agents in Messina, Venice, Lisbon, Lyons, Leipzig and Antwerp. Both dated from the middle of the fifteenth century.

However, in Nürnberg von Stromer has discovered important older companies which date from the last quarter of the fourteenth century and which were moving into the mining areas of the Carpathians and the main economic nerve centres of Hungary: those of the Flexdorfer-Kegler-Zenner and of the Ammann-Kamerer-Grau-Seiler. Their commercial interests spanned central Europe from the ore deposits of the Carpathians along the Vistula from Krakow to Danzig, from the ports on the sea coast down the Scheldt, Meuse and Rhine to Liège, Dinant, Cologne, Frankfurt and Strasbourg, and Basel, or overland to Eger and Prague, or to the Lake of Constance towns, over the Alps into Lombardy or by way of Freiburg to the fair at Geneva. Both firms worked in close co-operation and were related to the other important Nürnberg families, the Stromer and Eisvogel among others. Their transporting of copper over the Baltic through the Sound to Flanders in 1399 in their own and in chartered vessels brought a loud outcry from the Hanse. Nor was the Hanse happy with Nürnberg's intervention in the silver trade of Livonia. The breach of the Hanseatic blockade of Flanders of 1358–1360 by the Nürnberg firm of Eisvogel was apparently part of the same business policy. It is a foretaste of the competition by which the Fuggers were later to challenge the Hanse. These great firms had a strong financial basis and a mastery of bookkeeping and the techniques of exchange. About 1405 they created a monopoly for themselves in the Carpathians in precious metals. That is to say they obtained a totally dominant position in the trade in precious metals.

This brings us to the economic centre of which one immediately thinks when one speaks of the rise of south Germany in the fourteenth century: Nürnberg.[213] The imperial castle of the Salians rising above the banks of the Pegnitz on a steep block of sandstone in spite of lying within a barren and forested surrounding area and a considerable distance from the great central European river network, was otherwise favourably situated for land transport. It lacked either an ancient church or market as a focal point, although Fürth at the confluence of the Pegnitz and Regnitz had both. However, Nürnberg rose in the thirteenth and fourteenth centuries to a transit centre of European importance and an industrial centre because of its favourable situation on land routes. The thrifty character of its inhabitants brought industrial development early on. It owed its early rise to the Staufer, who created Nürnberg as an urban centre for a great principality in the centre of eastern Germany, and granted it privileges. One can watch the rise of Nürnberg through these customs privileges. In 1332 Ludwig of Bavaria granted it a general confirmation of its customs privileges in the sixty-nine towns where it held them and listed them in a definite geographical order. It may be that not all of them are included in this 1332 list. There were further agreements which protected the Nürnberg merchants by granting them rights of safe and free passage. Ammann writes

Already in 1881, Willhelm Roscher had compared the system of customs' agreements of 1332 with the Hanseatic network in his *System der Volkswirtschaft*, and in 1901 Inama-Sternegg in his *Deutsche Wirtschaftsgeschichte* judged Ludwig of Bavaria's charter as perhaps the greatest act of commercial policy of the Empire. One can thus see that the importance of the Nürnberg system of toll privileges was recognized early on. However, to my mind, one has to take the achievement, as far as the Empire is concerned, back much earlier, to the period of the Staufer. The overall success of this commercial policy is the achievement of a town which through centuries had carried through a tough and successful policy in spite of the enormous difficulties of a system based on commerce from Hungary to Flanders and from Poland to the western border of the Empire. To define it even more precisely it was the achievement of the Nürnberg mercantile aristocracy to hold town policy tightly in its grasp so that in business dealings and commercial agreements from the thirteenth to the fifteenth centuries we meet, again and again, the same names.

One encounters therein the whole process of Nürnberg's social and constitutional life. The guilds never achieved any political importance here; the craftsmen's revolt in 1348 brought no changes. In the fourteenth and fifteenth centuries there was some mobility within the mercantile upper class, but rise from the ranks of the craftsmen to the town council was hardly possible. In 1521 patricians confined membership of the town council to a strictly limited number of families.

The metal industries dominated the industrial sector in medieval Nürnberg. The proximity of extensive mining areas and convenient passage to the copper and silver mines of Bohemia made this achievement possible. Professor Hermann Heimpel pointed out, at the 900th anniversary of the town's foundation, on 10 June 1950, that

In the fifteenth century, in Denmark and England one shot with Nürnberg crossbows, dressed English soldiers in Nürnberg armour; the smiths of Europe wrought with Nürnberg metal sheets; in far-off lands knights rode with Nürnberg spurs and pilgrims made their way to Rome with land maps drawn with Nürnberg compasses; while the ladies gazed in mirrors manufactured in Nürnberg.

The skill of its craftsmen combined with technical inventiveness and business enterprise to create this achivement. About 1300 the domestic system of production was introduced into the Nürnberg metal industry. Hektor Ammann also revealed the importance of the city's textile industry; the early appearance of the paper industry is well known. Nürnberg was not only the focal point of widespread foreign links but also a central point in the political and economic spheres. The Nürnberg suburbs of Wöhrd and Gostenhof, indeed a whole chain of outlying industrial districts, strengthened and enlarged the metal and cloth industries of the city itself.

CHAPTER 7

The end of the Middle Ages

The wealth of surviving materials for the later Middle Ages gives us the chance of making statistical calculations, and these are necessary if we are to estimate the achievement of the medieval towns and their relationship with the countryside around them. Medieval statistics were mostly not drawn up out of a deliberate desire to provide information; most had quite concrete and practical purposes. It is rarely possible to provide a continuous series of statistics and the result is that the size of town populations, for instance, which can be reckoned only with great difficulty, can be estimated for only one particular point in time. We never know whether we are dealing with a typical year or not.

In comparison either with the towns of Antiquity or with those of our own day, medieval towns were small.[214] We can certainly say which were the large, middle and small ones in the Middle Ages, but the scale is quite different. By medieval standards, a town with more than 10,000 inhabitants was a large town; the leading towns in the Middle Ages are those with a population bigger than 20,000. Towns of middle size are those with between 2,000 and 10,000 people, and small towns include those with between 500 and 2,000 inhabitants. Anything with under 500 inhabitants must be classified as a mini-town.

Since information provided by literary sources is often very unreliable, we have to rely primarily on official lists, lists of houses, hearth registers, lists of townsmen obliged to bear arms, taxation records and material of this sort. In any case they only give the number of town houses or households, and we then have to find the correct multiplier to calculate the number of inhabitants. Hearth lists are of more use here than lists of houses. One can generally reckon four to five people per household. The reverse calculation of the number of houses based upon the size of the population is much more difficult; one has to take into account the increase in renting out which took place in the larger towns at the end of the Middle Ages. The number of plots of land built on also provides a possible basis for calculating the size of the town, but such calculations give questionable results because the density of building was very variable. The lists of townspeople on which we depend generally only include fully recognized townsmen, and we have to take into account those groups of people in the town in question which the lists do not include, like beggars who were too poor to pay taxes. The great difficulty of finding any evidence about the lower classes means that there is a very uncertain element in many estimates. We must also not forget the privileged classes who often paid no taxes, nobles, clergy and members of universities, and include them in our estimates, if we want to come anywhere near a true population figure for a town.

Another, seldom used, method of calculating population is based upon demand for necessities. The difficulty of this approach arises with the realization that part of the imported necessities was re-exported rather than used for home consumption so that one can rely on this approach only under special conditions. These might include a siege, economic blockade or suchlike and, even then, we must bear in mind that in times of war the population of the countryside sought protection within the town walls and that the number of people was also augmented by soldiers etc.

So this method is only useful as a rough calculation. A check is possible by comparing the results from various pieces of information which the town provides with results based upon the area covered by the town at that time and such cross-checks can preserve us from the gravest miscalculations. In spite of this, it has been a matter of dispute for a long time whether the population of Paris at the beginning of the fourteenth century numbered 80,000 or 210,000 inhabitants.[215] The possibility of there having been only 80,000 is based upon comparison with the rest of the northern French towns, which were not radically different in size from Paris – Amiens had 20–30,000 inhabitants, Rheims, 14,000. If one takes into account the ground area of Paris, the fact remains that there would have been room for a population of 210,000 only if they had lived in high buildings. One is still left with the need to explain the figure of 210,000, which is based upon hearth tax numbers. Was it a clerical error or did the number include districts outside the city? One must also reckon with fraudulent manipulation of the figures. In 1247, for example, the echevins of Ypres requested the pope to create more churches and canons because the city had 200,000 people to serve but the canons of the church of St Martin, who believed that their position was being threatened, informed the pope that Ypres had only 40,000 people,[216] which probably came nearer the mark.

Cologne was the most populous city of the medieval German Empire with a population numbering 40,000 inhabitants in its hey-day in the thirteenth and fourteenth centuries. This population lived within the walls built in 1180, which covered an area of 400 hectares. In the neighbouring southern Low Countries there were whole groups of exceedingly populous large towns: Tournai in the fourteenth century had 40–50,000 people. The second circle of walls around Ghent, dating from the thirteenth century, enclosed 644 hectares, and by the fourteenth century Ghent's population had reached 60,000. Bruges covered some 430 hectares with 50,000 inhabitants; Louvain 410 hectares and 45,000 people; Brussels 449 hectares and 30,000 people, while Antwerp grew from a population of 5,000 in 1347 to 20,000 in 1440. The next rise in Antwerp's population was the consequence of changes in the early modern period. Liège, Aachen and Maastricht also belonged to the category of large medieval towns: Maastricht in the fourteenth century had 10,000 souls. In the northern Low Countries, only Utrecht rose to a total number of 20,000 people. The oldest trading centres on the Ijssel, Deventer, Zwolle, and Kampen, had 12–14,000 inhabitants each. The next large town to the south-west of Cologne was Metz with 25,000 people in 1325; it was the only large town on the Moselle. Trier, with scarcely 10,000 inhabitants in the late fourteenth century, was far from belonging to the category of great towns. Strasbourg in the fifteenth century had some 18,000 inhabitants.[217] The fair towns of Frankfurt,[218] Ulm and Augsburg each had about 10,000 people around 1400. Augsburg in the fifteenth century must have been Swabia's largest and most populous town. Basel which, with Geneva, was among Switzerland's most populous towns, had 8,800 people in 1495. Nürnberg belongs to the category of leading towns because, according to the *Grobenbuch* of 1430, it had a population of 22,800. Würzburg was another of the large towns. Erfurt's population in 1493 was about 18,500. Goslar, Soest and Münster's population rose slightly to above 10,000 each. Breslau in the fifteenth century had 20,000 people. Calculations for Rostock, Brunswick and Lüneburg lie somewhere between 10,000 and 18,000 inhabitants each.

In the north, Lübeck led with 25,000 inhabitants in about 1400, and Bremen had at least 20,000. The total for Hamburg in the middle of the fifteenth century wavers between 16,000 and 18,000. The varying density in housing presents difficult problems. In Hamburg, the number of rented properties was high, while in Danzig the number of houses occupied by one family is in dispute;[219] it seems that the population at that date was 30,000, which brings it into the category of great towns as a centre for foreign trade and industrial production for export. Paris and London showed that having the status of a capital city played a part, especially London, which had a population of around 30,000 and was the cosmopolitan centre of the later Middle Ages.

Among the important middle-sized towns were Trier, Mainz, Wesel, Osnabrück, Emden, Kassel, Görlitz, Nördlingen, Constance, and Schaffhausen. In the class of small but economically important towns were Düren, Essen, Marburg, Friedberg, and Butzbach in Hesse. However, ninety to ninety-five per cent of all medieval towns were small centres with populations of less than 2,000. These smallest towns and mini-towns sprang up chiefly in territorially fragmented areas, where each lord founded his own town, which then had no further possibility for growth. Privileged market towns of this sort dominated by their castles were not really towns in the economic sense. Schönecken in the Eifel and Blankenberg on the Sieg are examples. The largest of the small towns could not, however, be self-sufficient like the villages and in any case, it has almost become a cliché that villages too might be market-orientated in the Middle Ages. Hektor Ammann has shown that they were more than this, and he provided a whole series of examples from the region of Switzerland[220] – Baden with 1,500 inhabitants about 1550, Rheinfelden with 220–250 households, if we add its suburbs, including 150 craftsmen and 10–20 merchants, Aarau with 1,300 inhabitants. These active small towns also took part in the medieval economic expansion; they imported the necessities of daily life as well as rarer luxury goods. Their craftsmanship could be widely disseminated through the practice of wandering apprentices; their catchment area for immigrants became considerable and their populations socially differentiated. Considerable fortunes were amassed in them.

Many Italian towns had high populations,[221] and the density of housing was much greater in the south. The population per hectare was 56 for Brussels, 81 for Bruges, 89 for Strasbourg, 100 for Ghent, 138 for Toulouse, 142 for Nürnberg, 158 for Rostock, 180 for Paris, 210 for Lübeck, 322 for Béziers, 500 for Toulon and 545 for Genoa.[222]

Professor Jacques Heers has described in detail the densely built up nature of Genoa with its narrow streets and lack of great squares, small gardens, high stone houses, the palaces in which town nobles lived and informally rented out the ground floor to craftsmen. The fortifications of 1155 contained only fifty-three hectares, those of 1346, 110 hectares. Heers has estimated that the fifteenth-century walls contained 84,000 people; if you include Genoa's suburbs there were 97,500; and the total population within the city's boundaries was 117,000, without taking clergy into account. By 1338 Venice had 90,000 inhabitants, by 1320 Verona had 30,000, Padua in the same year had 33,000 and Pavia already had 30,000 in 1250. Bonvicinus de Ripa, in his pioneer work, *De magnalibus urbis Mediolani*, written in 1288, provides a great deal of statistical evidence for Milan. He maintained that every prosperous household had its own well and that there were 6,000 wells in Milan. He enumerated 12,500 houses, 200 churches and chapels with 480 altars, 120 bell towers with 200 bells. The *contado* had fifty important *borghi*, among them Monza, 150 villages had a castle controlled by Milan, and the whole *contado* contained 2,050 churches. The city of Milan had ten hospitals, the oldest and richest of them being San Stefano nel Brolo with 500 beds. Bonvesin attributes to Milan a population of 200,000 with 500,000 people in the whole *contado*. These last global figures seem exaggerated, but one must reckon with a population of at least 100,000 for Milan in 1288. Florence about 1300 had 95,000, Lucca, Siena and Pisa 20,000 each, San Gimignano 13,000, Bologna about 1370 had 40,000, Orvieto 11,000 in 1292, Rome 35,000 around 1200, Naples 50,000 around 1300, Palermo 44,000 and Messina 27,000.

Barcelona was the largest town in Christian Spain with 35,000 inhabitants about the end of the fourteenth century. One hundred years earlier the total was estimated at 24,000.

The proportion of townspeople to the overall population in the fifteenth century was twenty to twenty-five per cent. This meant that a considerable process of urbanization had already taken place, a process which was especially advanced in the southern Low Countries. In Brabant, where the hearth-lists provide useful material,[223] in

1437 almost one-third of the total population, or 32.8 percent, lived in towns.

The population curve altered in the fourteenth century. The frequency of abandoned settlements in the countryside, the pause in the colonization movement eastwards of the peasantry, the abandonment of new town foundations and the arrested growth of many existing towns even to the extent of a considerable decline in urban populations are all indisputable signs of this negative trend. The plague was neither the original nor the sole cause of the crisis.[224] In many individual cases the decline in population can be shown to have set in before the Black Death of 1348. With the high medieval mortality rate, only a small fall-back in births sufficed to bring a population reduction. Here we find a phenomenon which reflects human vitality and which requires biological investigation and proof. The plague accentuated the existing negative tendencies. There were famines on top of plague, notably that of 1315–1317 which affected the whole of northern Europe and may have contributed to the high death rate in the first great plague of 1348 by weakening the population.[225]

Whether or not one is dealing with a general and century-long crisis in the later Middle Ages is a matter for dispute.[226] The situation varied from one economic region to another. One must contrast signs of depression in Flanders and Provence with indications of progress in other regions, in south Germany,[227] especially in Nürnberg, as well as in the Saar and Moselle regions and in Holland and England. In France non-economic factors were at work, notably the Hundred Years' War. The chronology of the crises varied. In Barcelona its high-point was between 1431 and 1443 and was caused as much by the military ventures of King Alfonso as by the economic stagnation in Genoa. The meagre nature of the statistical work which has been done still makes a closer definition of 'up and down' tendencies impossible. The question, in any case, cannot be solely answered by studying the towns. Thus, a conclusive answer to the question of whether there was a cyclical or a structural crisis, and whether the change in the agrarian economy was decisive, still cannot be given.

In north-western Europe, the late-medieval economic crisis expressed itself in the sharp rise and decline of different regions, in bitter competition for markets, and in the powerful reaction of the towns to advances in rural industries. Within the towns considerable social tensions accompanied the creation of an urban proletariat from displaced master-craftsmen and from apprentices who had lost all hope of ever becoming masters. There were sharp distinctions of wealth and ossification and stagnation in the economic sector.

Industry found itself more dependent on trade. The great distance between places of production and markets meant permanent uncertainty and risk. The cloth industry, for instance, was dependent on the supplies of wool and of alum and dyes. The discovery of alum mines at Tolfa within papal territory, which took the bottom out of the market for the alum of Asia Minor, was celebrated as a victory over the Turk. In the sphere of cloth export from north-western Europe, the fourteenth century was the age of Brabant. Its cloth dominated the Frankfurt fairs and those of south Germany. In northern Germany, Flemish cloth, on which the Hanse tenaciously maintained its hold, still played the major role. In the Mediterranean region, Flemish and Brabantine cloth suffered a set-back. In Toulouse, for example, its proportion of the market fell from 72 percent in 1379 to 61 percent in 1399, to 1.5 percent in 1437; but it then increased again to 10 percent about 1450.[228] In the fifteenth century, Holland became a great cloth centre; England also took a great step forward and its increased production meant a reduction in its wool exports which deeply affected the cloth industry of Flanders until it found an alternative source of supply in Spanish wool. The Dutch bought a high proportion of their wool at the Calais staple, and they created the companies of the *Calaisvairders* and organized credit for purchases. Their cloth first appeared on the markets of Bruges and Antwerp, then in Delft and Bergen op Zoom, and went eastwards to Leipzig, Breslau, Bohemia and Poland.

While Southampton was still controlled by the Italians, cosmopolitan London provided the meeting-place for Hanseatic merchants, and bankers from Florence, Milan and Lucca. Bristol serves as the example of the rise of an English town through its own economic enterprise. Situated on the Rivers Avon and Frome, it brought wares from inland, wool from Buckinghamshire for its own industry, iron and coal from the Forest of Dean, cloth from Coventry to which it supplied woad, cloth from Ludlow, and alabaster statues from Nottingham which were exported as far as Portugal. Ireland provided fish, butter, bacon, smoked meat, copper, hides and good Irish linen. In the fifteenth century Bristol's harbours were enlarged and it conquered the overseas markets. Its ships went to Spain and Lisbon. From the beginning of the fifteenth century the English were reaching Iceland, especially the east-coast vessels of Cromer or Newcastle. People from Bristol followed them. As the Hanse had once done in Bergen, they created a regular exchange of salt and fish for their own corn, butter, beer, wine, Irish linen and Breton, Flemish and English cloth.[229]

Holland and England won for themselves an expanding economic zone in the North Sea. The Hanse still held onto its position there, however. Admittedly, in 1494 the Novgorod Kontor practically ceased to exist and the Bruges Kontor suffered as part of the general economic decline of the town. Much too late, in 1520, the Hanse moved to Antwerp, which had already taken Bruges' place in 1495. But this damage was at least economically balanced by western links which were now created. The growing demand for salt led to regular trips to La Rochelle and finally to Setubal and Lisbon.

The greatest volume of Mediterranean trade was concentrated in its western basin, especially as the result of the Genoese creation of a direct route through the Straits of Gibraltar, along which it transported the bulk products of the Low Countries. Venice held onto its traditional Orient trade in pepper. However, it was as trapped in the Adriatic as the Hanse was in the Baltic. The Genoese had to make a stop on their western route in the great ports of the Ibernian peninsula. Thus the rise of newly-reconquered Andalusia, the towns of Seville and Cadiz, and also of Lisbon had already started before the great discoveries began.[230] The rise of Castile was comparable to the rise of England in the north. For France, which was held back by the Hundred Years' War, recovery began in Normandy.[231] All the fleets of the north sought the Bay salt on the French Atlantic coast. Marseilles suffered from Catalonian policies; the port of Aigues-Mortes finally came under Genoese control after that of the Venetians and of the factors of Jacques Coeur.

Credit was essential for the smooth conduct of trade and production. Its use was a natural part of the chain of transactions from the purchase of raw materials to the sale of the finished article to the consumer.[232] Industrial production for export was largely based on credit, either in the form of supplying craftsmen in their homes or of collective purchases by the guild. Credit linked one merchant with another. Creditworthiness was an essential prerequisite for a merchant's success. Interest was a natural accompaniment to it. Here we are faced with the teaching of the Church, and the Church had to come to terms with the prevailing situation. The doctrine that the existence of risk justified profit must be attributed to the scholastic theologians of the later Middle Ages. They began an extension of the theory of interest. The public sector also intervened in credit transactions: the favourite urban form of borrowing was the sale of rents.

A striking feature of the last part of the fourteenth century was the amount of social unrest. In Cologne in 1369–1370 the weavers brought about the overthrow of patrician control, and in 1396, after an embittered family feud between the Greifen and Freunden, they brought about a change in the constitution. The *Richerzeche* disappeared and the *Verbundbrief* formed the basis of the constitution until the imperial towns disappeared altogether as a concept. In the last years of the fifteenth century, unresolved differences brought about a renewed outbreak of trouble in the rising of 1482. In 1513 another insurrection led to the *Transfixbrief* which enlarged the clauses of the *Verbundbrief*. All the towns producing textiles for export suffered revolts by weavers in the fourteenth century: Constance and Augsburg in the south, Stendal in north Germany, and other towns from Flanders to Florence. There was unrest in the Hanseatic area, in the *Knochenhauer* (butchers) Revolt in Lübeck, in Danzig, Brunswick, in Nürnberg, Liège and Metz. The cliché 'guild wars' does not sufficiently explain this phenomenon. Its antecedents are more complex. The movements led by the Parisian merchant, Étienne Marcel and the Jacquerie in France reflected the political crisis of a land at war as well as its serious social problems. Steinbach and Maschke have rightly warned against misunderstanding these movements. They were not the beginning of modern democracy. The political equality of corporations and not of individuals was in question. The work of Steinbach and Herborn for Cologne shows how quickly a closed society of the privileged reformed itself after 1396. Van Werveke has shown the same for Ghent.[233] Here too, while the guilds were successful in controlling some or the majority of seats on the town council, they did not really rule the towns. In Ulm, Esslingen and other Swabian towns, the office of town mayor was still always held by a patrician although the constitution permitted a craftsman to be chosen. The cause lies in the operation of the principle of indispensability already recognized by Weber and more fully marked out by Maschke.

In many towns in which the guilds took control, in Strasbourg, Constance, Basel, and Augsburg, the patricians cut themselves off and formed an exclusive group. The result was that they declined in numbers. Urban society was organized according to occupation, and status symbols consisted in ways of dressing and in invitations to festivals and dances which were limited to chosen people. The dress permitted to each class was laid down by the town council.[234] Patricians met in drinking societies. Their control of the town continued unweakened in trading towns without large export industries, for instance in Metz. Genoa too recognized only *nobili* and *populari* but no distinction between the *popolo grasso* and *popolo minuto* which was such a marked feature of Florentine society. Genoa also had the *albergo* which served as a social meeting place of the *nobili* and which corresponded to the German *Trinkstube* and from the fourteenth century there was also a popular equivalent to the *alberghi* of the nobility.

In central Europe egoism and conservation dominated guild life. The many apprentices with no hope of ever becoming masters also became an element likely to cause unrest and rebellion. They formed bands, and wandering apprentices became an ever-increasing phenomenon. The master craftsmen also combined, often on a regional basis in common cause against their apprentices. For example, in 1352 the bakers of Mainz, Worms, Speyer, Oppenheim, Frankfurt, Bingen, Bacharach and Boppard formed a super-guild to prevent an apprentice who had been dismissed by his master in one town from being able to find lodging and work elsewhere. The inter-town guild also turned against married apprentices: if the wife of a baker's apprentice came to market and sold flour and cereal, no master in any of the eight towns might employ her husband.[235] The practice of masters and their apprentices living together in the same house became less frequent. Solidarity among the apprentices themselves increased and had its outward manifestation in the uniform which they wore. The masters continued their opposition nevertheless. In 1442, for example, the furriers of Bavaria and Austria met to deny their apprentices every corporative right. In Strasbourg in 1404 forty-eight apprentice furriers from Bohemia and the Tyrol combined to form a separate brotherhood; in this very capital intensive business the chance of ever becoming a master was particularly remote. The master-craftsmen maintained that the urban authorities alone were empowered to settle conflicts between masters and apprentices. In 1465 this association of masters broadened when it acquired further links in Franconia, Swabia and the Rhineland. Unrest, strikes, and strife between master and apprentice filled the whole of the four-teenth and fifteenth centuries.

In Florence in 1378 disturbances turned into the revolt of the *ciompi* or woolcarders. This rising was of great interest to Renais-sance historical writers and has been also to modern neo-Marxist researchers,[236] although it has been correctly interpreted by neither group. This was no 'proletarian revolution' with social revolutionary aims. In the July revolt, which resulted in a new political regime, people from all classes of Florentine society took part including patrician leaders from famous families like the Strozzi, Alberti and Medici; members of the industrial and mercantile middle classes and a great mass of wage earners. The revolt took its name from the woolcarders or *ciompi*, but every class of worker from the lower orders was represented – cloth dyers, fullers, finishers and small entrepreneurs who were not members of the Arte della Lana but their subordinate employees, namely *sottoposti*. Character-istically, three new guilds were formed to include them and these were added to the seven upper guilds and the fourteen lower ones. The aims and wishes of the *sottoposti* and *ciompi* were very mixed. Disappointment of the *ciompi* with the new conservative regime brought a further outbreak of trouble in August which produced no clear programme. As Brucker says:

It was a characteristic Florentine *imbroglio*, neither very bloody nor very destructive and as strongly influenced by personal hatreds and loyalties as by any spirit or sense of class. The historical significance of the Ciompi episode was its utilization by the Florentine patriciate to justify the increasingly[237] narrow social base of politics and the progressive exclusion of the lower classes from office.

In 1382 "order was restored".

At the same time the craftsmen of Ghent, supported by those of Bruges and Ypres, rose against the count, but he, with his allies the French knights, defeated them at West-Roosebeke in 1382. The overwhelmingly political character of the Ghent revolts in the four-teenth century is unmistakeable. In Liège the patricians were ex-cluded from the town council. The corps of craftsmen who now wielded power had already begun to exclude apprentices and aliens. The entry fee for becoming a master was increased. This was a widespread development. The rule of the patricians was replaced by control by small artisan entrepreneurs. A proletariat grew up below them in the fifteenth century.

The town's monopoly over industrial production came more and more under attack. In the fourteenth century the towns still managed to keep this challenge in check. The Ghent militia, for instance, invaded the countryside and destroyed weaving equipment in the villages. In the fifteenth century the Flemish towns complained to their ruler, the duke of Burgundy, that their monopoly was being destroyed. Nevertheless, in Ghent and Ypres half the population continued to live from the cloth industry and in Bruges one-third of it. The guilds were not organized to arrest the decline. Indeed they tried, in the face of opposition even by traders, to protect their craftsmen from the worst consequences of the market crisis by imposing minimum wages for work. This, however, only lessened the adaptability of the major towns in the face of competition and acted in favour of small towns and villages. They had already achieved specialization in the manufacture of luxury and semi-luxury cloth as a way of solving their economic problems, as the example of 's Hertogenbosch and Antwerp shows. They had switched their main interest from the troubled large-scale export industry with its proletarian work force to the new types of fine textiles catering for the demand of the middle classes. In a penetrating analysis of the situation in the Netherlands, van Houtte[238] has shown that this switch meant a sharp decline for the small towns while the big cities took advantage of increased specialization within the industry. The relatively greater prosperity of the major towns is revealed through statistics of poverty. The Brabantine accounts also provide evidence here. While the number of poor in Antwerp decreased between 1437 and 1480 from 13.5 percent to 10.5 percent, the proportion in Louvain increased from 7.6 percent to 18.3 percent, in Brussels between 1437 and 1496 from 10.5 percent to 17.1 percent. In smaller towns the number of poor rose as high as 36 percent. These poor came from declining industries or were made up of unskilled workers and immigrants from the countryside.

The time of most severe misery for the mass of workers coincided with the high-point of bourgeois luxury in the Low Countries. The most splendid buildings were erected by the prosperous upper class. In the meantine, the gulf between the moneyed aristocracy and the proletarian masses widened. The urban magistracy was no longer able to cope with the problems arising from poverty and the government had to intervene. In the fifteenth century, princes like Philip the Good intervened actively, if not systematically, against begging.

Poverty also had a place in the medieval social hierarchy: it gave the rich the possibility of doing acts of charity. The rich man was dependent on the intercession of the poor so that the poor man had prayers to offer in return for alms. The poor also formed their own associations. In 1454 a Brotherhood of Beggars was formed in Zülpich and was joined by cripples, the blind and other poor people. It raised fees from members and cared for the sick. The fierce struggle against the poor and beggars is an expression of early modern feeling and a product of the situation in early modern times. The beggar was still integrated into medieval society. Even if the lower classes in the Middle Ages were politically without rights and economically weak, frequent movement into the upper classes took place. Possibilities of saving and thereby advancement existed, especially for servants and apprentices. In Basel servants and craftsmen's assistants accounted for 17 percent of the population and 29 percent of all those who had to pay taxes. In general they formed what was the upper working class while among the wage earners, merchants' apprentices formed a lower middle class. Beneath the apprentices and servants were the day workers, unskilled workers, single women and, beneath them again, the beggars.

Two groups stood apart in medieval urban society. They were the Jews and the clergy. At first the position of the Jews was not bad,[239] for in the early Middle Ages they were indispensable as traders and, as such, enjoyed royal protection, customs' privileges and freedom from dues on sales. There were Jewish communities in many of the German imperial towns. The slave trade and dealings in Oriental goods were their speciality in foreign trade. In the latter, they encountered competition early on from the Italian maritime cities. In 952 the Venetians forbad anyone to take Jewish merchants on their ships. About the same time Jewish communities appeared in Mainz, Augsburg, Worms, Regensburg and Prague. Mainz was their base for trading ventures into eastern Europe and Prague and Krakow were important places on this route. Cologne had a synagogue in 1010 and Worms had one before 1034. In 1084 Jews emigrated from Mainz to Speyer as part of a deliberate settlement programme organized by Bishop Rüdiger who granted them privileges.[240] These privileges and the charter granted by the Emperor Henry IV in 1090 to Worms and Speyer created the legal status of the Jews in the Rhineland towns. They were allowed to travel freely and without payment of dues throughout the Empire and to conduct trade and both buy and sell without paying tolls. These privileges laid down that in dealing in second hand goods they should enjoy the same special protection from loss while handling goods that had been stolen as did the pawnbrokers in pawnshops: the stolen goods were to be restored to the owner only on repayment of the purchase price. Heathen slaves might not be withdrawn from their service and baptised but they were not permitted to buy Christian slaves. They could possess property in both town and countryside and also enjoy the services of Christian day labourers. A Jewish *Schreinsbuch* (register of property transactions) survive for Cologne. The slave trade died out with the increased christianization of the Slav lands. In the Rhineland a series of frightful outrages against the Jews followed in the wake of the First Crusade. Attracted by the wealth of the Jewish communities fanatical groups plundered Jews all along the Rhine, in Speyer, Worms, Mainz, Cologne and Trier, and Archbishop Hermann of Cologne had the Jews removed to seven localities for protection. Nevertheless, many of them were slaughtered or committed suicide.

The overwhelmingly religious motivation behind this persecution is revealed by the fact that, once baptised, they married into and became fused with the native urban population. Thus, in Cologne the son of a converted Jew appears on the list of those attesting a commercial treaty between Cologne and Verdun in 1178. His brother married the daughter of the founder of one of the great Cologne patrician families of Lyskirchen. Another patrician family called Jude was also probably Jewish in origin. The Jews paid a collective tax which constituted an important element in royal revenue. The famous *Matrikel* (list of regalian revenue) of 1241, shows that at that time the greatest concentration of Jewish communities was on the middle Rhine. In Cologne in 1178 they had forty-eight houses. By 1325 the number had risen to seventy. In 1266 Archbishop Engelbert II renewed the Jews' privileges, which were not being observed, throughout the diocese of Cologne; he had them engraved on limestone tablets.[241] In 1321 Archbishop Henry II of Cologne maintained that the city had accepted Jews who had resided for ten years into full citizenship and into the town's protection. Lena Dasberg's theories about the decline in status of the Jews in the eleventh century is in need of wholesale revision, but in the fourteenth century a quite decisive worsening of the standing of the Jews took place. The formation of the guilds had the effect of excluding them from industry, for a non-Christian could not be a member of a medieval guild. In trade, where they had been totally indispensable, they were increasingly restricted to money-dealings, especially pawnbroking, which certainly had the effect of making them the object of hatred. Evidence of their money-dealings in the first half of the fourteenth century is especially abundant when credit expanded and was used not only by the upper class but also by the mass of the people on a scale which was unprecedented. In 1957 a hoard of coins worth about 241 guilders, dating from between 1338 and 1349, was found in the Jewish quarter of Limburg; certainly buried for fear of persecution.[242] Persecution of Jews began about this time in France, Alsace and on the middle Rhine, and its main aim was robbery. The plague of 1348 brought a wave of attacks on Jews in the Rhineland towns from Basel to Cologne which can once again be documented from a series of hoards which were hidden by the persecuted Jews. The Cologne Debt Ordinance of 1390 provides some instances of enormous Jewish wealth. After the Black Death the Jews quickly returned to economic activity, but in general the position remained frought with crisis for them. They were excluded from many towns, from Cologne in 1424, from Speyer in 1435. Many moved eastwards, others into the countryside, especially into the small villages belonging to the lesser nobility. The famous old Jewish cemetery at the small town of Beilstein on the Moselle is evidence of this development. In the fifteenth century there were eighteen Jewish communities in the imperial towns, the largest being in Worms, Frankfurt and Nürnberg. Their part in credit operations should not, however, be exaggerated. In the Rhineland it was often the business of Lombards and Cahorsins. A town of the size of Liège, in 1138, apart from one named Jewish doctor, had no Jewish community. The Liège people kept credit business to themselves and in 1303 managed also to have the Lombards expelled.

As for the clergy, who were falling considerably in number,[243] tension mounted in the later Middle Ages over the quantity of property in the towns falling into the 'dead hand' of the church by mortmain, and against their exemption from taxation, which varied from town to town. There was also dislike of clerical activity in the economy, where clerics used their freedom from dues to exploit the urban market. Canons and abbeys in general misused their privilege, of bringing goods for their own consumption duty-free into the towns, to sell the surplus of corn and especially of wine from their country estates on the town market. The guilds had to wage war against the abbeys, particularly in the textile industry. The religious houses remained great economic powers. As such they were closely linked with the urban economy, not only for the sale of their surpluses on the urban market but also because of the demand which they created. Hector Ammann investigated the demand created by the abbeys on the urban market and, using accounts, revealed the network of economic links between the Swiss and south German abbeys and the inner structure of their distribution links and the area for which they provided. The result was to reveal the great variety of foreign goods which were in use.[244] The problem of the relationship between town and Church does not consist only in their economic links. The relationship between the urban community and this separate corporate body and the attempts by townspeople, using their council, to control the presentation of clergy to parishes remain unexplored questions. The urban upper class and citizens exercised charitable functions which had originally been the sphere of church and cloister: the setting-up of hospitals is part of this story.

The tension and strife between town and clergy in the later Middle Ages are in no way a reflection of hostility to the Church. On the contrary, the later Middle Ages was an age of devotion: it is stamped by a piety which, on the one hand inclined to mass manifestations, to emotion with elements of hysteria, and on the other hand to a warmer inner religion and simplicity.[245] The increase in the number of chantries, processions, brotherhoods, pilgrimages and the profusion of devotional and edifying literature, the creation of mystery plays, the overvaluing of relics, all reveal the quantity and quality of late medieval piety. At the beginning of the Reformation, Hamburg had ninety-nine brotherhoods, most of which had come into existence since 1450. The foundation of many chantries brought an increase in the numbers of minor clergy. In the church of St Elizabeth in Breslau there were 120 clergy serving forty-seven altars. The market church in Goslar, apart from its rector, had fifteen chaplains and altar boys. These altar boys often had to live from a part of the chantry endowment and there were vast social distinctions within the ranks of the clergy. We have the least precise information about the education and sources of livelihood of the poor clergy. The general standard of clerical education was not too bad; the chance of their having some education in the fifteenth century was better than earlier on. The number of schools and universities had increased and printing also helped. The expectations of the laity, however, also grew. Patricians, who in their youth had attended university, expected more from preaching and instruction in the faith. Prebends for preachers were founded and town councils were concerned to have able preachers but also exercised some oversight over the clergy.

Intensity and depth of religious feeling characterized the religious movements of the later Middle Ages and the new style of piety called the *devotio moderna*. A feature of religious life in the towns of the day was the Beguine movement.[246] The Beguines and Beghards were people dedicated to a religious life who lived as laymen and laywomen and did not belong to a regular religious community. They neither took a monastic vow nor did they recognize the rule of any order accepted by the Church. Grundmann[247] connected the origins of the Beguine movement with the religious movement among women in the thirteenth century; already in the twelfth century there was insufficient room in nunneries for all the women who felt a religious vocation. Nor could the Franciscan and Dominican nunneries accept all into a religious life in the sense of the *vita apostolica*. The foundation of new houses corresponded to the financial means available. Jacques de Vitry, regular canon of Liège, obtained permission from Honorius III for the pious women in the bishopric of Liège to live together and to strengthen themselves by mutual admonition. This was how the Beguine movement began. In 1215 the movement still had a heretical flavour but it lost this and spread far and wide. In the first half of the thirteenth century there were Beguines in Cologne, Strasbourg, Frankfurt and Mainz. The tendency to individual self-expression was as strong at this time as the movement to form convents. Under pressure from their ecclesiastical opponents the number of Beguines living freely in the community declined, while in the fifteenth century the convents alone remained active and the inclination to bind oneself to the rule of an Order prevailed. There were two types of Beguine house: in western Germany, northern France and the Walloon lands there was a sort of communal house. In Holland itself, especially in the south, a type of organization based on small houses grouped together round a church and administered by their own confessor was the rule. Here there were often separate houses for the rich, and communal dwellings for the poor, Beguines.

In the later Middle Ages the urban bourgeoisie broke the educational monopoly of the clergy and created a bourgeois lay culture. Merchants had become literate in the thirteenth century and had used their knowledge to rationalize their businesses which they now based around the Kontor, the *skrivekamere* ("writing office").[248] In the transitional period, when merchants could not find sufficient help, a system of registers of debt was created in the Hanse towns; these were not a list of the debts of the town itself but a record of the debts of private individuals. These were kept in Lübeck, Hamburg and Riga.[249] The total number of entries in the Riga debt register is 1,909, more than half of them entered in the first eight years down to 1294. Fragments of mercantile book-keeping can be found from as far back as the thirteenth century in Germany.[250] In the fourteenth century individual written accounts were the general rule. The towns themselves had already set up chanceries long before, and kept their archive in the town hall as well as the civic library.

Schools were set up for the sons of the mercantile upper class who were intended to follow in their fathers' footsteps into the business. This system of schools breached the monopoly which the Church had exercised. The Church still held that God should be served before Mammon and a medieval merchant was less than delighted if his son returned from school, that is the clerical school, the abbey school or the cathedral school having been taught that a merchant's profession was scarcely pleasing to God. Pressure to set up schools which corresponded to the needs of the urban upper class had already begun in Flanders in the twelfth century and they wanted schools which they themselves controlled. In 1262 the Lübeck city council created the Latin St James's School. By a lucky chance wax tablets dating from 1370 showing the pupils' working have survived.[251] Many of these tablets contained only formulae for conducting business correspondence, and this was what the pupils were regularly learning. In one example a Lübeck merchant despatched thirty-one tuns of wine to a business friend; in another, a merchant sought advice from a visiting friend as to whether he should travel in person to Thuringia and Frankfurt to trade in herrings and stockfish. In this way the pupil at St James's School learnt what he would later be using in his own writing office. In case he should perhaps also become a member of the town council, the school made provision here too: the wax tablets gave formulae for political correspondence. If he should become town clerk, this was also provided for because he received instruction in the writing-styles which were in use in the town chancery. All these appeared on the wax tablets. This educational provision represented a break-through by the merchants. There was also in Italy a breach of the educational monopoly of the clergy by industrialists.

Here literacy had never completely disappeared among the lay populace and such merchant schools were created on an even more imposing scale. They were known as the *abacus* after the reckoning boards which they employed. The will of a Venetian doctor of 1420 recommended to his sons that after completing their private education they should go "to the abacus in order to be taught how to conduct business" (*ad abacum ut discant ad facere mercantias*).

In 1338 Florence had six such schools with 1,000–1,200 pupils. In 1486 the Arte della Lana, Genoa's cloth guild, set up schools for the sons of craftsmen. School books of arithmetic appeared from the thirteenth century. In the fourteenth and fifteenth centuries the vernacular replaced Latin, and the theoretical study of numbers was replaced by working out practical examples. Exercises were also set, for example, a Florentine dealer comes to buy wool in Genoa and cloth in Pisa and resells them in Florence. The difference in money, weights and measures had then to be worked out.[252] In Italy, there is the unique and huge archive of a merchant, Francesco Datini, who died in Prato in 1410. It included 574 books of accounts (*libri contabili*) and 153,000 other business records.

Attendance at university by members of the bourgeoisie increased continually in the later Middle Ages. It is, time and again, surprising to find that sons of townsmen from middle and small German towns attended far-off universities, then a considerable strain on the parental purse. The famous universities of Italy and France were especially favoured – Bologna, Padua, and Perugia contained highly esteemed 'German Nations', as also did Paris and Orleans. The pressure for education corresponded to the size and economic power of a town. One can scarcely scan the matriculation lists of an ancient university without finding someone from Cologne, whether in Krakow or Orleans. The medieval universities were predominantly urban institutions. This is true of almost all the Italian universities and in Cologne, Erfurt, Basel, Rostock, Greifswald, Lüneburg and Breslau, the universities were either founded, equipped and maintained by the town or by the citizens and local lord. Cologne was the first German city to create a university. It had earlier possessed famous abbey and church schools, namely the Dominican foundation where Thomas Aquinas had sat at the feet of Albertus Magnus. The University of Cologne was not, however, created by merging these separate institutions. It was a new foundation by the town council. The council was its patron and it was the *consules, scabini, cives et commune civitatis Coloniensis* who received the charter of privilege to found the University from Urban VI on 21 May 1388.

Printing was a town invention. It spread quickly from Mainz to all the important towns. In Nürnberg printing and publishing became separate and the Nürnberg publisher, Koberger, won international renown. The Frankfurt fair was also a book fair and it was from Cologne that printing reached England. The son of a Siegburg weaver and humanist, John Lair or John Siberch, founded Cambridge University Press, which still exists today. Cologne was the greatest printing centre of the north-west as Lübeck was for the Baltic area. Strasbourg was an important printing centre as well as a centre of humanism. Then the towns became the focus of the new movements of humanism, Renaissance and Reformation. Once again they were indisputably the great spiritual centres of Europe. In them, a type of historical writing flourished whose development was closely linked with the development of the urban community. Frequently, it was an official historical writing which grew up in the council chamber.[253]

The cultural motivation of the bourgeoisie expressed itself in town planning and building, both of secular and religious public buildings, and in the houses of the bourgeoisie themselves. The urban bourgeoisie had learnt well how to deal with such assignments, to combine beauty with utility in building. The greatest responsibility of each bourgeois was the town's defences. The defensive strength of town walls was still unbroken in the fifteenth century; the small town of Neuss, for example, withstood Charles the Bold.

A visitor entered a medieval town through the town gate, often a double gate, which was both a fortress and a decorative symbol. Crooked Gothic alleys gave him surprising glimpses of groups of houses or great buildings and led to the town hall and to the churches whose towers had already stood out from afar. He could refresh himself at the town fountain and try to puzzle out the figures and reliefs carved upon it; he could follow a pretty wrought iron shield into a tavern. He looked for a friend's house not under house numbers but under the sign of the Coloured Ox, the Whale or the Moor. When he came to the market he could observe how the many-sided building programme in the town had been master minded. In a small town both council and law court were in the same building and the town weights were kept here and marriages and feasts were celebrated in it too. In larger towns, there were special buildings or combined complexes consisting of town hall, market hall, cloth hall, and a hall for dances and marriages. We would have to take another trip around Europe to appreciate the wealth and variety of medieval urban architecture although there were many common features within the variable social structure and differing economic conditions. Even today, after all the revolutions, destruction by war and changes in style, we can still observe the great contrast between northern and southern urban cultures. We only have to contrast the imposing stone piazza of an ancient Tuscan town and the severe façades of their town houses with the painted gables of the timber houses in the crowded alleys of an old German town.

Notes

[1]Carl Haase (350); Edith Ennen (231); Karlheinz Blaschke (86). From the geographical standpoint: Peter Schöller (743); Rudolf Klöpper (459) and also André Joris (428).

[2]Discovery of the stone-age urban settlements at Tell-es-Sultan near Jericho and those of Catal Hüyük in the western Anatolian plateau near Konya have pushed back our knowledge of urban development to the seventh millenium B.C: Hartmut Schmökel (738); Kathleen Kenyon (443); James Mellaart (573).

[3]Fritz Dörrenhaus (184 and 185).

[4]Sir Mortimer Wheeler (918); Fritz M. Heichelheim (365 and 366).

[5]Paul Sander (707).

[6]A.H.M. Jones (421, 422, 423); Friedrich Vittinghoff (873).

[7]Hermann Aubin (51, 53, 49); Harald v. Petrikovits (633); Germania Romana (315); Otto Doppelfeld (194 and 195); Fritz Fremersdorf (286, 285 and 287); Charlotte Fischer (269); W. Schleiermacher (720); A.W. Byvanck (132); J.E. Bogaers (91). What Aubin did for *Germania inferior* was achieved for *Belgica secunda* by Pirenne's pupil Fernand Vercauteren (851); his most recent appraisal of the problem is in (849). For Trier above all Josef Steinhausen (791 and 836) and the report of the Trier Landesmuseum (407). For the Saarland and Lorraine: (300) and E. Ennen (227). For England: Sheppard Frere (289).

[8]Joachim Werner (902); Jacques Moreau (599 and 598); Werner Krämer (472); Klaus Fehn (264).

[9]Erich Swoboda (813).

[10]For Jerome's problematical evidence, see Leo Weisgerber (895).

[11]*Idem* (893) and the relevant articles in (894).

[12]Rolf Hachmann, Georg Kossack, Hans Kuhn (352).

[13]Gerold Walser, Thomas Pekary (883).

[14]Joseph Bidez (82), pp. 175ff.

[15]P.A. Février (265).

[16]Herbert Nesselhauf (606), pp. 93ff.

[17]Erich Gose (329).

[18]Eduard Hegel (363); Hans Eiden (213).

[19]The volumes edited by Paul Egon Hübinger provide a very good study of the question: (281, 483, 62). There is a volume of collected studies by Aubin which covers the subject in (50). The works of Vercauteren which we have cited above as well as the

collected articles of Karl Friederich Stroheker (805) should be mentioned. On the Arab question, see Maurice Lombard (533). For Pirenne add (555) and Jan Dhondt (171).

[20]Stroheker (805).

[21]Ernst Levy (523 and 524) and Fr. Wieacker (922).

[22]J. Gustav Droysen (202), p. 12.

[23]Knut Borchardt (98), p. 357.

[24]Eduard Hlawitschka (390).

[25]Ernesto Sestan (762); Gina Fasoli (257).

[26]Ferdinand Lot (540).

[27]Gerhard Dilcher (178).

[28]Gian Piero Bognetti (94).

[29]Cincio Violante (869).

[30]Heinrich Felix Schmid (736).

[31]Dietrich Claude (147).

[32]In addition to the work of Vercauteren which we have cited above and the relevant articles in the collected papers (143), see A. Dupont (205); Heinrich Büttner (130), Paul Albert Février (265).

[33]Joachim Werner (905).

[34]François Louis Ganshof (304).

[35]Karl Friedrich Stroheker (804 and 805).

[36]Adriaan Verhulst (856).

[37]*Gregorii episcopi Turonensis* (331), Vol. 1, p. 174.

[38]Dietrich Claude (148).

[39]Charles Higounet (386).

[40]Joachim Werner (901 and 904).

[41]E. Ennen, articles in: (143) and (234).

[42]Willi Weyres (916 and 917).

[43]Heinrich Büttner (125).

[44]Anton Doll (187).

[45]Heinrich Büttner (128, 122).

[46]See the relevant chapter in Klaus Fehn (264) and the detailed work of Jürgen Findeisen (268).

[47]Jean Hubert (400) and Eugen Ewig (249).

[48]H.R. Lyon (541), Martin Biddle (81) and the additional material in (1069).

[49]Franz Irsigler (406).

[50]Jean Durliat (207).

[51]For further information, see E. Ennen (226) pp. 270ff.

[52]Dietrich Claude (149 and 145).

[53]Carlrichard Brühl (114 and 113).

[54]Jan Dhondt (168 and 172); Franz Petri (631); Herbert Jankuhn (408 and 410); summary (579).

[55]Wilhelm Holmquist (253); Agneta Lundström (548).

[56]H. Sweet (812); Richard Hennig (373).

[57]Hans Planitz (649).

[58]*Rimberti vita Anskarii* (686), par. 26.

[59]Hans Planitz (651).

[60]Max Pappenheim (619 and 620); Jacob Somner (767).

[61] A.C.F. Koch (462); Franz Petri (629); Francine Deisser-Nagels (159).

[62] Werner Haarnagel (349).

[63] *Idem*, (348 and 347).

[64] Félix Rousseau (700).

[65] Georges Despy (164).

[66] Rafael v. Uslar (842).

[67] Heinrich Büttner (121); Gerhard Baaken (56).

[68] Joachim Werner (903).

[69] Gregory of Tours (331), IX, 12.

[70] N. Wand (884) and additionally in (1069).

[71] Edmund E. Stengel (792).

[72] In (808).

[73] Reinhard Schindler (719).

[74] *Rimberti vita Anskarii* (686), 16.

[75] François Louis Ganshof (309). See also Michael Mitterauer (585).

[76] Peter Schöller (559); Hertha Borchers (99); Heinrich Büttner (127); Edith Ennen (227); most recently the additional work by Schlesinger in (1069).

[77] Traute Endemann (217).

[78] Manfred Hellmann (372); Herbert Ludat (543); Aleksander Gieysztor (318 and 317); Witold Hensel (374).

[79] G. Jacob (71).

[80] Witold Hensel (375), with a French summary.

[81] E. Fügedi (299), György Székely (816, 818, 819).

[81a] A.E. Herteig (997).

[82] Walter Janssen (412).

[83] Paul Johansen (416).

[84] H.R. Loyn (541); Helen Maud Cam (135); Mary D. Lobel (528); Addyman, Biddle (1069).

[85] Cl. Cahen (134).

[86] Evariste Lévi-Provençal (521).

[87] Claudio Sanchez-Albornoz (705), II, pp. 33ff; José Maria Lacarra (493); José Maria Font Ruis (280).

[88] For Europe, Georges Duby (203); for Germany, Gunther Franz's *German agrarian history* (1,283 and 546); for the history of technology, Lynn White Jr. (920); for the history of forestry, Charles Higounet (387).

[89] Luise von Winterfeld (931).

[90] *Elenchus fontium* (216), *textes belges*, no. 9, par. 19.

[91] *Ibid*, no. 21.

[92] *Vita Meinwerci* (870), par. 96, 97 and 98.

[93] Heinz Stoob (799).

[94] Walter Schlesinger (725).

[95] Richard Laufner (507); see also *Elenchus fontium* (216), German text, no. 39.

[96] Henri Laurent (508); Hektor Amman (16, 10 and 9).

[97] Still essential are Adolf Schaube (711) and the synthesis by Y. Renouard (681).

[98] Gino Luzzatto (552).

[99] Vito Vitale (871).

[100] Robert Lopez (536).

[101]Philippe Wolff (940).

[102]Henri Pirenne (643); Hans Planitz (654); Fritz Rörig (689); see also the bibliography in Rörig (780).

[103]Marianne Schalles-Fischer (710) and, for the whole question of the sites of royal palaces, Carlrichard Brühl (114 and 113).

[104]Karl Bosl (107).

[105]Walter Schlesinger (728).

[106]Aloys Schulte (750); Pietro Vaccari (845); Carlo Guido Mor (597).

[107]Heinrich Sproemberg (773).

[108]H. van Werveke, A.E. Verhulst (908); François Louis Ganshof (305 and 308).

[109]Richard Laufner, Hans Eichler (506).

[110]E. Ennen (232).

[111]François Louis Ganshof (310 and 307); E. Ennen (224).

[112]Charles Verlinden (860).

[113]Erich Maschke and Jürgen Sydow (776).

[114]Karlheinz Blaschke (85 and 84).

[115]J. Schepers (714).

[116]F. Metz (580).

[117]Walter Schlesinger (732); Max Pfütze (638); Hans van Werveke (907); Gerhard Köbler (464).

[118]Heinrich Büttner (130).

[119]Jan Dhondt (167); Paul Bonenfant (96).

[120]Walter Schlesinger (733).

[121]Heinz Stoob (797); Walter Schlesinger (721 and 731).

[122]Walter Schlesinger (727).

[123]Gina Fasoli (258).

[124]E. Ennen (235).

[125]Charles Higounet (385).

[126]H. Ammann has been responsible for showing this in a series of articles. See the bibliography in his *Festschrift* (63).

[127]I hope to have covered a large proportion of the older literature in (222). The most important new publications include: Bernhard Diestelkamp (176 and 175); Wolfgang Hess (384); Karl Kroeschell (475); Emil Schaus (712 and 713) and the collected papers in (525).

[128]Walter Schlesinger (729).

[129]Hans Planitz's synthesis published in three large studies between the years 1940 and 1944 (651, 647 and 655) has been reviewed by me in (219) where I described them as an oversimplification. I similarly dealt with Planitz's posthumous work (654) in the *Rhein. VjBll.* (228) and further in (224). Diverging, also one sided, conceptions of the development of town communes appear in Franz Steinbach (150) and Karl Kroeschell (475 and 474). For the Italian situation, which I have discussed in (224), see also Gerhard Dilcher (178). F.L. Ganshof, Heinrich Büttner and Walter Schlesinger have taken up various standpoints and contributed a great deal of new information in various articles.

[130]*Alpertus Mettensis* (7); J.F. Niermeyer (610); J.B. Akkerman (4 and 3).

[131]A. Joris (427).

[132]R.C. van Caenegem (133).

[133]Heinrich v. Loesch (531).

[134]Wilhelm Ebel (209).

[135]*Idem*, (208).

[136]Robert von Keller (440).

[137]Walter Schlesinger (727).

[138]Albert Vermeesch (861).

[139]Toni Diederich (174).

[140]Heinz F. Friedrichs (291); Knut Schulz (754 and 755); Tadeusz Roslanowski (699).

[141]R. v. Keller provides a collection of sources which is still essential (440).

[142]E. Ennen (224), p. 244.

[143]Wilhelm Ebel (210).

[144]I remain convinced that the market settlement of Freiburg took the form of a *coniuratio*, of which the Zähringer lord was a member. Schlesinger also considers this possible: (284).

[145]F.L. Ganshof (306).

[146]R. Latouche (502).

[147]Cited in (669).

[148]H. Stoob (798), p. 51.

[149]Max Weber (887).

[150]Gino Luzzatto (552).

[151]Vito Vitale (871).

[152]Cl. Campiche (136), p. 321.

[153]J. Gautier Dalché (313).

[154]Horst Rabe (666).

[155]H. Ammann (14).

[156]*Idem*, (28).

[157]Z.W. Sneller (766).

[158]H. Ammann (27).

[159]*Idem* (26).

[160]Jean Schneider (742 and 741).

[161]E. Maschke (566).

[162]Philippe Dollinger (190); Heinrich Sproemberg (772); Hans van Werveke (914).

[163]*Elenchus fontium* (216), German text, no. 134, par. 8.

[164]J. Papritz (621).

[165]Ernst Pitz (645).

[166]Wolfgang Zorn (951) and, in addition to the works cited there, see also H. v. Loesch (532).

[167]E. Nau (604 and 605).

[168]R. Lopez and J.W. Raymond (539) and the works cited there.

[169]Apart from the older work by Schaube (711); A. Doren (199) see also A. Sapori (708); Robert S. Lopez (537 and 538); Jacques Heers (359).

[170]R. Stadelmann (774), p. 141.

[171]Enrico Fiumi (275).

[172]Yves Renouard (679); G. Schneider (740); A.E. Sayous (709).

[173]W. Kienast (449). For the relations between Germany and Lombardy, see Aloys Schulte (748).

[174]P. Wolff (937).

[175]A. Doren (198, 200, 201).

[176]P.J. Jones (424); D. Herlihy (379).

[177]E. Maschke (570).

[178]C. Carrère (139), p. 951.

[179]P.A. Février (265); *Histoire du commerce de Marseille* (389).

[180]P. Wolff (939 and 938).

[181]Yves Renouard (678).

[182]H. Ammann (10, 16, 20, 25, 31).

[183]Schaube (711), p. 449, n.4.

[184]Hermann Heimpel (368).

[185]Bruno Kuske (489, 490, 491).

[186]Hans Planitz (653); Konrad Beyerle (77); Hans Planitz (652).

[187]*Idem* (648).

[188]F. Blockmans (87).

[189]F.L. Ganshof (303).

[190]Jean Schneider (742).

[191]A. Verhulst (855).

[192]Wilhelm Abel (1).

[193]Heinz Angermeier (45); Gerhard Pfeiffer (637).

[194]Julius Weizsäcker (896); Erich Bielfeldt (83); H.J. Rieckenberg (682).

[195]W. Prevenier (663); B. Lyon (554).

[196]Jan Dhondt (166).

[197]W. Stubbs (807), p. 166.

[198]Wilhelm Koppe (468).

[199]Paul Heinsius (370).

[200]Helmold von Bosau (372a), pp. 380ff.

[201]Konrad Onasch (616); B. Widera (921); A.V. Arcichowski (47); Paul Johansen (418); Carsten Goehrke (323).

[202]V.N. Lazarev (509).

[203]Franz Petri (630).

[204]Heinrich Reincke (672).

[205]A.V. Brandt (109).

[206]Heinz von d. Mühlen (600).

[207]Manfred Unger (839).

[208]Jürgen Sydow (815).

[209]E. Raiser (667).

[210](769).

[211]Karl Siegfried Bader (58); Jörg Füchtner and the works cited there (298); H. Ammann (9).

[212]Akoys Schulte (749); H. Ammann (17); W.v. Stromer (806).

[213](64); H. Ammann (33); Hermann Heimpel (367); (614).

[214]Roger Mols (594); H. Ammann (37).

[215]P. Dollinger (189).

[216]J. Demey (162).

[217]P. Dollinger (192).

[218]Dietrich Andernacht (119).

[219]Hugo Weczerka (888).

[220]H. Ammann (11, 41, 8 and 32).

[221]K.J. Beloch (65).

[222]Jacques Heers (359).

[223]J. Cuvelier (156); J.A. van Houtte (399).

[224]This view is stressed in particular by Friedrich Lütge (546a).

[225]H. van Werveke (910).

[226]Ernst Pitz (646); see further literature cited there.

[227]Bernhard Kirchgässner (451).

[228]M. Mollat, P. Johansen, M. Postan and others (591).

[229]E.M. Carus-Wilson (928).

[230](144).

[231]M. Mollat (590).

[232]B. Kuske (486); Raymond de Roover (697, 698, 696).

[233](841); Erich Maschke (569 and 567); (840); F. Steinbach (787); H. van Werveke (909); F. Vercauteren (852); Mollat-Wolff (1021).

[234]L.C. Eisenbart (214).

[235](445), no. 308, pp. 411ff.

[236]Ernst Werner (900).

[237]Gene A. Brucker (112).

[238]J.A. van Houtte (399).

[239]Hermann Kellenbenz (438); Lea Dasberg (157).

[240]*Elenchus Fontium* (216), no. 47, pp. 75ff.

[241]*Regesten Eb. Köln* (670), III, no. 1913.

[242]Peter Berghaus (69).

[243]Karl Frölich (295); Siegfried Reicke (671); (769); Dietrich Kurze (485).

[244]H. Ammann (23 and 30).

[245]Willy Andreas (44); Friedrich Wilhelm Oediger (615); Bernd Möller (587).

[246]E.G. Neumann (607); Günter Peters (626); Otto Nübel (613) and the older works cited there.

[247]Herbert Grundmann (340 and 341).

[248]Fritz Rörig (693); Henri Pirenne (641); E. Ennen (230).

[249]Erich von Lehe (512).

[250]See the published medieval merchants' books listed in Ludwig Beutin (73), pp. 19ff. Also Gustav Korlén (470); F. Tremel (835); Othmar Pickl (639); Chiaudano Mario (558); A.v. Brandt (110); C. Wehmer (892; see also *Hans. Gesch. Bll.*, 83, 1965, p. 129); Federigo Melis (572).

[251]J. Warncke (885).

[252]Amintore Fanfani (255); Armando Sapori (708), bibliography, p. 5.

[253]J. Bernhard Menke (575); Heinrich Schmidt (737).

Bibliography

Introductory remarks

A whole series of research groups are preoccupied with urban history. The *Commission Internationale pour l'Histoire des Villes* is a branch of the international historical commission. It has three scholarly aims. 1. It provides a bibliography of urban development, organized on a regional basis. So far, there has appeared the *International bibliography of urban history, Denmark, Finland, Norway, Sweden*, Univ. of Stockholm, Swedish Institute for Urban History, 1960; Charles Gross, *A bibliography of British municipal history*, 2nd ed., 1966; Paul Guyer, *Bibliographie der Städtegeschichte der Schweiz*, 1960; Phil. Dollinger, Phil. Wolff, Simonne Guenée, *Bibliographie d'histoire des villes de France*, 1967; Erich Keyser, *Bibliographie zur Städtegeschichte Deutschlands*, 1969. 2. It is responsible for a source work intended to reproduce the most important documents for the early history of medieval towns down to around 1250. The volume containing the sources for Belgium, Germany, the Netherlands, and Scandinavia has already appeared under the title: *Elenchus fontium historiae urbanae, quem edendum curaverunt*, C. van de Kieft et J.F. Niermeyer, Leiden 1967. For Germany we are still reliant on Friedrich Keutgen, *Urkunden zur städtischen Verfassungsgeschichte*, Berlin 1899, reprinted, Aalen 1965. There is a good synthesis for the Mediterranean region: Robert S. Lopez and Irving W. Raymond, *Medieval trade in the Mediterranean world*. Illustrative documents, translated with introductions and notes, New York and London 1955. 3. It is to publish an atlas containing typical town plans on the scale 1:2500. This enterprise is still at the planning stage with regional studies being prepared for the Netherlands, Rhineland and Westphalia. The volume of *Historic towns* has appeared. Maps and plans of towns and cities in the British Isles, with historical commentaries, from earliest times to circa 1800, Oxford-London 1969ff.

The *Cahiers Bruxellois* provide reports of annual conferences and bibliographies.

The *Société Jean Bodin* provides a global view of problems in urban history. Notable publications appear in the *Recueils de la Société Jean Bodin*: vol. V *La Foire* (1953); vol. VI *La ville. Institutions administratives et judiciaires* (1954). Vol. VII *La ville. Institutions économiques et sociales* (1955). Vol. VIII *La ville. Le droit privé.* (1957).

The centre *Pro Civitate* under the direction of Fernand Vercauteren has so far produced Vol. VII *Finances et comptabilités urbaines du XIIIᵉ au XVIᵉ siècle.* Colloque international Blankenberge, 1962, 1964. No. 13. *L'impôt dans le cadre de la Ville et de l'État.* Colloque international Spa, 1964, 1966. *Les libertés urbaines et rurales du XIᵉ au XIVᵉ siècle.* Colloque international Spa, 1966, 1968.

The medieval research group in Spoleto has published: *La Citta nell'alto medioevo.* Settimane di studio del centro italiano di studi sull' alto medioevo VI, 1959. *Moneta e scambi nell' alto medioevo.* Settimane . . . VIII, 1961.

The Reichenau research group has frequently included urban history amongst its projects. Already published are: *Studien zu den Anfängen des europäischen Städtewesens.* Reichenau-Vorträge 1955–1956 (Vorträge und Forschungen IV) 1958. *Untersuchungen zur gesellschaftlichen Struktur der mittelalterlichen Städte in Europa.* Reichenau-Vorträge 1963–1964 (Vorträge und Forschungen XI) 1966.

Since 1956 W. Schlesinger and E. Ennen have been responsible for the research group studying history of German urban development (*Arbeitskreis für landschaftliche deutsche Städteforschung*). Its conference reports appear in the journal *Westfälische Forschungen. Mitteilungen des Provinzialinstituts für westfälische Landes- und Volkskunde* and these provide short summaries on the state of research: Archäologische Methoden und Quellen zur Stadtkernforschung und ihr Verhältnis zu den historischen Quellen und Methoden (*Westfäl. F.* 13) 1960. Das Marktproblem im Mittelalter (*Westfäl. F.* 15) 1962. Die Frage der Kontinuität in den Städten an Mosel und Rhein im Frühmittelalter (*Westfäl. F.* 16) 1963. Diskussion um die frühen Gründungsstädte in Deutschland (*Westf. F.* 17) 1964. Territorien und Städtewesen (*Westfäl. F.* 19) 1966. Landes- und stadtgeschichtliche Grundfragen im Raum von Maas, Mosel, Saar und Mittelrhein (*Westf. F.* 22) 1969/70.

The *Arbeitskreis für süd-westdeutsche Stadtgeschichtsforschung* under the direction of Erich Maschke and Jürgen Sydow has produced the following reports: Gesellschaftliche Unterschichten in den südwestdeutschen Städten (Veröffentlichungen der Kommission für geschichtliche Landeskunde in Baden-Württemberg 41) 1967. Stadterweiterung und Vorstadt (Veröffentlichungen ... 51) 1969.

The proceedings of a colloquium in Paris on Polish towns were published in: *Les origines des villes polonaises.* École pratique des Hautes Etudes. Sixième section. Congrès et Colloques II. Paris, La Haye 1960.

An important aid to the study of German urban history was the *Deutsche Städtebuch*, founded and edited by Erich Keyser until his death in 1968. Organized regionally, it produces articles of all the present-day German towns in alphabetical order. The journal, *Blätter für deutsche Landesgeschichte*, publishes a collective report on new publications on German towns while the *Hansische Geschichtsblätter* provides comprehensive reports on new publications for all the Hanseatic towns, not only the German ones.

The following list, which appeared in the 1972 edition, was designed not so much as a bibliography but as a selection of the literature which has been consulted. It includes above all the older classic works which are still valuable today. The works listed suffice to provide a comprehensive view, and also provide voluminous bibliographies for further study.

Alphabetical list – bibliography of the first, 1972, edition

1 William Abel, Geschichte der deutschen Landwirtschaft vom frühen Mittelalter bis zum 19. Jahrhundert, Stuttgart 1962; [2]1967 = Deutsche Agrargeschichte, (ed.) Günther Franz, vol. 2.
2 Joseph Ahlhaus, Civitas und Diözese, in: Aus Politik und Geschichte. Gedächtnisschrift für Georg v. Below, Berlin 1928.
3 J.B. Akkerman, De vroeg-middeleeuwse emporia, in: Tijdschrift voor Rechtsgeschiedenis 35, 1967.
4 J.B. Akkerman, Het koopmansgilde van Tiel omstreeks het jaar 1000, in: Tijdschrift voor Rechtsgeschiedenis 30, 1962.
5 W. Jappe Alberts, De middeleeuwse stad, Bussum [2]1968 = Fibulareeks 6.

6 Günther Albrecht, Das Münzwesen im niederlothringischen und friesischen Raum vom 10. bis beginnenden 12. Jahrhundert, in: Numismatische Studien 6, 1959.

7 Alpertus Mettensis, De diversitate temporum, A. Hulshof, Amsterdam 1916.

8 Hector Ammann, Alt-Aarau, Aarau ²1944.

9 Hector Ammann, Die Anfänge der Leinenindustrie des Bodenseegebietes und der Ostschweiz, in: Alemannisches Jahrbuch 1, 1953.

10 Hector Ammann, Die Anfänge des Aktivhandels und der Tucheinfuhr aus Nordwesteuropa nach dem Mittelmeergebiet, in: Studi in onore di Armando Sapori, 2 vols., Milano 1957.

11 Hector Ammann, Die Stadt Baden in der mittelalterlichen Wirtschaft, in: Argovia 63, 1951.

12 Hector Ammann, Die Bevölkerung von Stadt und Landschaft Basel am Ausgang des Mittelalters, in: Basler Zeitschrift für Geschichte 49, 1950.

13 Hector Ammann, Die Deutschen auf den Messen von Chalon, in: Deutsches Archiv für Landes- und Volksforschung 5, 1941.

14 Hector Ammann, Die Deutschen in Saint-Gilles im 12. Jahrhundert, in: Festschrift Hermann Aubin zum 80. Geburtstag, (ed.) Hermann Kellenbenz, Erich Maschke, Wolfgang Zorn, vol. 1, Wiesbaden 1965.

15 Hector Ammann, Deutschland und die Messen der Champagne, in: Deutsches Archiv für Landes- und Volksforschung 3, 1939.

16 Hector Ammann, Deutschland und die Tuchindustrie Nordwesteuropas im Mittelalter, in: Hans. Geschbill. 72, 1954.

17 Hector Ammann, Die Diesbach-Watt-Gesellschaft, St. Gallen 1928.

18 Hector Ammann, Freiburg als Wirtschaftsplatz im Mittelalter, in: Fribourg–Freiburg 1157–1957, Fribourg 1957.

19 Hector Ammann, Die Froburger und ihre Städtegründungen, in: Festschrift Hans Nabholz zum 60. Geburtstag, Zürich 1934.

20 Hector Ammann, Huy an der Maas in der mittelalterlichen Wirtschaft, in: Städtewesen und Bürgertrum als geschichtliche Kräfte. Gedächtnisschrift Fritz Rörig, (ed.) Ahasver v. Brandt and W. Koppe, Lübeck 1953.

21 Hector Ammann, Die Judengeschäfte im Konstanzer Ammann-Gerichtsbuch, in: Schriften d. Vereins f. Gesch. des Bodensees 71, 1952.

22 Hector Ammann, Die schweizerische Kleinstadt, in: Festschrift für W. Merz, Aarau 1928.

23 Hector Ammann, Klöster in der städtischen Wirtschaft des ausgehenden Mittelalters, in: Festgabe Otto Mittler, (ed.) Georg Bauer and Heinrich Meng, Aarau 1960 = Argovia 72.

24 Hector Ammann, Vom Lebensraum der mittelalterlichen Stadt. Eine Untersuchung an schwäbischen Beispielen, in: Berichte zur deutschen Landeskunde 31, 1963.

25 Hector Ammann, Maastricht in der mittelalterlichen Wirtschaft, in: Mélanges Félix Rousseau. Etudes sur l'histoire du Pays Mosan au Moyen Age, Bruxelles 1958.

26 Hector Ammann, Die Nördlinger Messe im Mittelalter, in: Aus Verfassungs- und Landesgeschichte. Festschrift zum 70. Geburtstag von Theodor Mayer, (ed.) Friends and Pupils, vol. 2, Lindau, Konstanz 1955.

27 Hector Ammann, Die Zurzacher Messen im Mittelalter, Aarau 1923 = Taschenbuch der Aargauer Historischen Gesellschaft.
28 Hector Ammann, Die Friedberger Messen, in: RhVjbll. 15/16, 1950/51.
29 Hector Ammann, Der hessische Raum in der mittelalterlichen Wirtschaft, in: Hess. Jb. f. Landesgesch. 8, 1958.
30 Hector Ammann, Das Kloster Salem in der Wirtschaft des ausgehenden Mittelalters, in: Zschr. f. Gesch. d. Oberrheins 110, 1962.
31 Hector Ammann, Sankt Trauten (= St. Trond), in: VSWG 54, 1967.
32 Hector Ammann, Über das waadtländische Städtewesen und über landschaftliches Städtewesen im allgemeinen, in: Schweizerische Zschr. f. Gesch. 4, 1954.
33 Hector Ammann, Die wirtschaftliche Stellung der Reichsstadt Nürnberg im Spätmittelalter, Nürnberg 1970 = Nürnberger Forschungen vol. 13.
34 Hector Ammann, Die französische Südostwanderung im Rahmen der mittelalterlichen französischen Wanderungen, in: Festgabe Harold Steinacker, München 1957.
35 Hector Ammann, Die Talschaftshauptorte der Innerschweiz in der mittelalterlichen Wirtschaft, in: Geschichtsfreund 102, 1949.
36 Hector Ammann, Untersuchungen über die Wirtschaftsstellung Zürichs im ausgehenden Mittelalter, in: Zschr. f. Schweizerische Gesch. 29, 1949; 30, 1950; and in: Schweizerische Zschr. f. Gesch. 2, 1952.
37 Hector Ammann, Wie groß war die mittelalterliche Stadt?, in: Studium Generale 9, 1956.
38 Hector Ammann, Mittelalterliche Wirtschaft im Alltag. Quellen zur Geschichte von Gewerbe, Industrie und Handel des 14. und 15. Jhds. aus den Notariatsregistern von Freiburg i. Ue., vol. 1, Aarau 1942/44, 1950, 1955.
39 Hector Ammann, Wirtschaft und Lebensraum einer aargauischen Kleinstadt (Brugg) im Mittelalter, in: Beiträge zur Kulturgeschichte. Festschrift Reinhold Bosch zum 60. Geburtstag, Aarau 1947.
40 Hector Ammann, Schaffhauser Wirtschaft im Mittelalter, Thayngen 1949.
41 Hector Ammann, Wirtschaft und Lebensraum der mittelalterlichen Kleinstadt, vol. 1, Rheinfelden 1950.
42 Hector Ammann, Von der Wirtschaftsgeltung des Elsaß im Mittelalter, in: Alemannisches Jahrbuch 3, 1955.
43 Die Amtleutebücher der kölnischen Sondergemeinden, (ed.) Thea Buyken and Hermann Conrad, Weimar 1936 = Publikationen d. Ges. f. Rhein. Geschichtskunde 45.
(119) Dietrich Andernacht, Otto Stamm, (ed.), see under Bürgerbücher der Reichsstadt . . . (No. 119).
44 Willy Andreas, Deutschland vor der Reformation. Eine Zeitenwende, Stuttgart, Berlin 1932; [2]1934; [5]1948; [6]1959.
45 Heinz Angermeier, Königtum und Landfriede im deutschen Spätmittelalter, München 1966.
46 Annali di Caffaro, (ed.) Luigi Tom. Belgrano and Ces. Imperiale, Rome 1901, 1923 = Fonti per la storia d'Italia. Scrittores sec. 12 e 13.
47 A.V. Arcichowski, La ville de Nowgorod le Grand du XIe au XVe siècle, in: XIe Congrès International des Sciences Historiques. Stockholm 1960. Communications.

48 Gustav Aubin, Arno Kunze, Leinenergzeugung und Leinenabsatz im östlichen
    Mitteldeutschland zur Zeit der Zunftkämpfe, Stuttgart 1940.
49 Hermann Aubin, Die wirtschaftliche Entwicklung des römischen Deutschlands,
    in: HZ 141, 1929; also in: *idem.*, Grundlagen und Perspektiven . . .
50 Hermann Aubin, Grundlagen und Perspektiven geschichtlicher Kulturraum-
    forschung und Kulturmorphologie, Bonn 1965.
51 Hermann Aubin, Küsten- und Binnenkultur im Altertum. Ein Beitrag zur
    Wirtschaftsgeschichte Galliens und Germaniens, in: SchmJb. 49, 1925; also in:
    idem., Grundlagen und Perspektiven . . .
52 Hermann Aubin, Maß und Bedeutung der römisch-germanischen Kulturzus-
    ammenhänge im Rheinland, in: Berichte der Römisch-germanischen Kom-
    mission 13, 1921; also in: *idem.*, Vom Altertum zum Mittelalter, München 1949;
    also in: *idem.*, Grundlagen und Perspektiven . . .
53 Hermann Aubin, Der Rheinhandel in römischer Zeit, in: Bonner Jahrbücher 130,
    1926; also in: *idem.*, Grundlagen und Perspektiven . . .
54 Hermann Aubin, Stufen und Triebkräfte der abenländischen Wirtschaftsent-
    wicklung im frühen Mittelalter, in: VSWG 42, 1955; also in: *idem.*, Grundlagen
    und Perspektiven . . .
55 Hermann Aubin, Zum Übergang von der Römerzeit zum Mittelalter auf deut-
    schem Boden. Siedlungsgeschichtliche Erörterungen über das Städteproblem,
    in: Historische Aufsätze Aloys Schulte zum 70. Geburtstag gewidmet, Düs-
    seldorf 1927; also in: *idem.*, Grundlagen und Perspektiven . . .
56 Gerhard Baaken, Königtum, Burgen und Königsfreie, Konstanz, Stuttgart
    1961 = Vorträge und Forschungen vol. 6.
57 Friedrich Bachmann, Die alte deutsche Stadt. Ein Bilderatlas der Städtean-
    sichten bis zum Ende des 30jährigen Krieges, 3 vols., Leipzig 1941–1949. vol. 4,
    (ed.) Max Schefold, Stuttgart 1961.
58 Karl Siegfried Bader, Der deutsche Südwesten in seiner territorialstaatlichen
    Entwicklung, Stuttgart 1950.
59 Walter Bader, Die christliche Archäologie in Deutschland nach den jüngsten
    Entdeckungen an Rhein und Mosel, in: AnnNdrh. 144/145, 1946/47.
60 Joh. Bärmann, Die Städtegründungen Heinrichs des Löwen und die Stadtver-
    fassung des 12. Jahrhunderts, Köln 1961 = Forschungen zur deutschen Rechts-
    geschichte vol. 1.
61 Adolphus Ballard, British Charters 1042–1216, Cambridge 1913.
62 Bedeutung und Rolle des Islam beim Übergang vom Altertum zum Mittelalter,
    (ed.) Paul Egon Hübinger, Darmstadt 1968 = Wege der Forschung vol. 202.
63 Beiträge zur Wirtschafts- und Stadtgeschichte. Festschrift für Hector Ammann,
    (ed.) Hermann Aubin, Edith Ennen and others, Wiesbaden 1965.
64 Beiträge zur Wirtschaftsgeschichte Nürnbergs, (ed.) Stadtarchiv Nürnberg, 2
    vols., Nürnberg 1967.
(46) Luigi Tom. Belgrano, Ces. Imperiale, (ed.), see under Annali di Caffaro . . . (No.
    46)
65 Karl Julius Beloch, Bevölkerungsgeschichte Italiens, 3 vols., Berlin, Leipzig
    1937–1961. vol. II ²1965.
66 Georg v. Below, Probleme der Wirtschaftsgeschichte, Tübingen ²1926.
67 F. Benoit, P.A. Février, J. Formigé, H. Rolland, Villes épiscopales de Province

(Aix, Arles, Fréjus, Marseille et Riez) de l'époque galloromaine au moyen-âge, Paris 1954.

68 Maurice Beresford, New towns of the Middle Ages: town plantation in England, Wales and Gascony, London 1967.

69 Peter Berghaus, Der mittelalterliche Goldschatzfund aus Limburg/Lahn, in: Nassauische Annalen 72, 1961.

70 Peter Berghaus, Der Kölner Pfennig in Westfalen. Zwei neue westfälische Schatzfunde les 12. und 13. Jhds., in: Dona numismatica. Walter Hävernick zum 23. Januar 1965 dargebracht, (ed.) Peter Berghaus and others, Hamburg 1965.

71 Arabische Berichte von Gesandten an germanische Fürstenhöfe aus dem 9. und 10. Jahrhundert, (ed.) G. Jacob, Berlin 1927.

72 Chanoine Paul Bertin, Une commune flamande-artésienne: Aire-sur-la-Lys des origines au XVIᵉ siècle, Arras 1946.

73 Ludwig Beutin, Einführung in die Wirtschaftsgeschichte, Köln, Graz 1958.

74 Franz Beyerle, Das mittelalterliche Konstanz. Verkehrslage und wirtschaftliche Entwicklung, in: Syntagma Friburgense. Historische Studien. Hermann Aubin Dargebracht zum 70. Geburtstag, Lindau, Konstanz 1956.

75 Franz Beyerle, Zur Typenfrage in der Stadtverfassung, in: ZRG Germ. Abt. 50, 1930.

76 Franz Beyerle, Zur Wehrverfassung des Hochmittelalters, in: Festschrift Ernst Mayer zum 70. Geburtstag, Weimar 1932.

77 Konrad Beyerle, Die Anfänge des Kölner Schreinswesens, in: ZRG Germ. Abt. 51, 1931.

78 Konrad Beyerle, Die Entstehung der Stadtgemeinde Köln, in: ZRG Germ. Abt. 31, 1910.

79 Bibliographie zur Städtegeschichte Deutschlands, (ed.) Erich Keyser, Köln, Wien 1969 = Veröffentlichung d. internat. Komm. f. Städtegeschichte.

80 International bibliography of urban history. Denmark, Finland, Norway, Sweden, Stockholm: Swedish Institute for Urban History, 1960.

81 Martin Biddle, Archaeology and the history of British towns, in: Antiquity 42, 1968.

82 Joseph Bidez, Julian der Abtrünnige, München 1947.

83 Erich Bielfeldt, Der rheinische Bund von 1254. Ein erster Versuch einer Reichsreform, Berlin 1937.

84 Karlheinz Blaschke, Nikolaikirchen und Stadtentstehung im pommerschen Raum, in: Greifswald-Stralsunder Jahrbuch 9, 1970/71.

85 Karlheinz Blaschke, Nikolauspatrozinien und städtische Frühgeschichte, in: ZRG Kan. Abt. 84, 1967.

86 Karlheinz Blaschke, Qualität, Quantität und Raumfunktion der Stadt vom Mittelalter bis zur Gegenwart, in: Jahrbuch für Regionalgeschichte 3, 1968.

87 Fr. Blockmans, Het Gentsche stadspatriciaat tot omstreeks 1302, Antwerpen, 's Gravenhage 1938.

88 W. Blockmans, I. de Meyer, J. Mertens, C. Pauwelyn, W. Vanderpyren, Studien betreffende de sociale strukturen te Brugge, Kortrijk en Gent in de 14ᵉ en 15ᵉ eeuw, Heule 1971 = Anciens Pays et Assemblées d'Etats 54 = Studia Hist. Gandensia 139.

89 Kurt Böhner, Die fränkischen Altertümer des Trierer Landes, Berlin 1958 =

Germanische Denkmäler der Völkerwanderungszeit. Ser. B: Die Fränkischen Altertümer des Rheinlandes vol. 1.

90 Kurt Böhner, Die Frage der Kontinuität zwischen Altertum und Mittelalter im Spiegel der fränkischen Funde des Rheinlandes, in: Trierer Zeitschrift 19, 1950.

91 J.E. Bogaers, Civitas en stad van de Bataven en Canninefaten, Nijmegen, Utrecht 1960.

92 Gian Piero Bognetti, Arimannie nella città di Milano, in: Rendiconti. Istituto lombardo di scienze e lettere. Classe di lettere e scienze morali e storiche 3rd Ser. 72, 1938/39; also in: *idem.*, L'età longobarda . . .

93 Gian Piero Bognetti, L'età longobarda, 4 vols., Milano 1966–1968.

94 Gian Piero Bognetti, S. Maria foris portas di Castelseprio e la storia religiosa dei Longobardi, in: Gian Piero Bognetti, Gino Chierici, Alberto de Capitani d'Arzago, Santa Maria di Castelseprio, Milano 1948; also in: L'età longobarda . . . II (No. 93).

95 Luigi Bonazzi, Storia di Perugia, 2 vols., Perugia 1875–79. Reprinted: Città di Castello 1959–60.

96 Paul Bonenfant, La fondation de "villes neuves" en Brabant au moyen-âge, in: VSWG 49, 1962.

97 Paul Bonenfant, L'origine des villes brabançonnes et la "route" de Bruges à Cologne, in: Revue belge de phil. et d'hist. 31, 1953.

98 Knut Borchardt, Grundriß der deutschen Wirtschaftsgeschichte, in: Kompendium der Volkswirtschaftslehre, (ed.) Werner Ehrlicher, Ingeborg Esenwein-Rothe and others, vol. 1, Göttingen 1967.

99 Hertha Borchers, Beiträge zur rheinischen Wirtschaftsgeschichte, in: Hess. Jb. f. Landesgesch. 4, 1954.

100 Hertha Borchers, Untersuchungen zur Geschichte des Marktwesens im Bodenseeraum, in: Zschr. f. Gesch. d. Oberrheins 104, 1956.

101 Hugo Borger, Die Ausgrabungen an St. Quirin zu Neuß in den Jahren 1959–1964, in: Beiträge zur Archäologie des Mittelalters, Köln, Graz 1968 = Rheinische Ausgrabungen 1 = suppl. Bonner Jahrbücher vol. 28.

102 Hugo Borger, Friedrich Wilhelm Oediger, Beiträge zur Frühgeschichte des Xantener Viktorstifts, Köln, Graz 1969 = Rheinische Ausgrabungen 6.

103 Hugo Borger, Bemerkungen zu den "Wachstumsstufen" einiger mittelalterlicher Städte im Rheinland, in: Landschaft und Geschichte. Festschrift für Franz Petri, (ed.) Georg Droege, Peter Schöller and others, Bonn 1970.

104 Hugo Borger, Xanten. Entstehung und Geschichte der mittelalterlichen Stadt, in: Beiträge zur Gesch. d. Kreises Dinslaken am Niederrhein suppl. 2, Xanten 1960.

105 Otto Borst, Esslingen am Neckar, Esslingen ²1967.

106 Karl Bosl, Frühgeschichte und Typus der Reichsstadt in Franken und Oberschwaben mit besonderer Berücksichtigung Rothenburgs o. d. T., Nördlingens und Dinkelsbühls, in: Esslinger Studien (Jb. f. Gesch. d. oberdt. Reichsstädte) 14, 1968.

(355) Karl Bosl, (ed.), see under Handbuch der Geschichte der böhmischen Länder (No. 355).

107 Karl Bosl, Die Sozialstruktur der mittelalterlichen Residenz- und Fernhandelsstadt Regensburg, München 1966 = Abh. d. Bayerischen Akad. d. Wiss., Phil.-hist. Kl.

new ser. 63.

108 Ahasver v. Brandt, Rezension zu Carl Wehmer, Mainzer Probedrucke in der Type des sog. Astronomischen Kalenders für 1448, München 1948, in: Hans. Geschbll. 83, 1965.

109 Ahasver v. Brandt, Die gesellschaftliche Struktur des spätmittelalterlichen Lübeck, in: Untersuchungen zur gesellschaftlichen Struktur der mittelalterlichen Städte in Europa. Reichenau-Vorträge 1963–1964, Konstanz, Stuttgart 1966 = Vorträge und Forschungen vol. 11.

110 Ahasver v. Brandt, Ein Stück kaufmännischer Buchführung aus dem letzten Viertel des 13. Jhds., in: Zschr. d. Ver. f. Lübeck. Gesch. u. Altertumskunde 44, 1964.

(356) Leo Brandt, (ed.), see under Die Deutsche Hanse ... (No. 356).

111 Wolfgang Braunfels, Mittelalterliche Stadtbaukunst in der Toskana, Berlin 1953.

112 Gene A. Brucker, The ciompi revolution, in: Florentine Studies, (ed.) Nicolai Rubinstein, London ^{2}1968.

113 Carlrichard Brühl, Fodrum, gistum, servitium regis. Studien zu den wirtschaftlichen Grundlagen des Königtums im Frankenreich und in den fränkischen Nachfolgestaaten Deutschland, Frankreich und Italien vom 6. bis zur Mitte des 14. Jahrhunderts, 2 vols., Köln, Graz 1968 = Kölner historische Abhandlungen vol. 14.

114 Carlrichard Brühl, Königspfalz und Bischofsstadt in fränkischer Zeit, in: RhVjbll. 23, 1958.

115 Otto Brunner, Europäisches und russisches Bürgertum, in: VSWG 40, 1953.

116 Otto Brunner, Hamburg und Wien. Versuch einer sozialgeschichtlichen Konfrontation, 1200–1800, in: Festschrift Hermann Aubin zum 80. Geburtstag, (ed.) Otto Brunner, Wiesbaden 1965.

117 Otto Brunner, Neue Wege der Sozialgeschichte. Vorträge und Aufsätze, Göttingen 1956.

118 Friedrich Bruns, Hugo Weczerka, Hansische Handelsstraßen. Atlas, Köln 1962 = Quellen und Darstellungen zur Hansischen Geschichte new ser. XIII, 1.

119 Bürgerbücher der Reichsstadt Frankfurt 1311–1400, (ed.) Dietrich Andernacht and Otto Stamm, Frankfurt 1955.

120 Heinrich Büttner, Die Anfänge der Stadt Kreuznach und der Grafen von Sponheim, in: Zschr. f. Gesch. d. Oberrheins 100, 1952.

121 Heinrich Büttner, Zur Burgenbauordnung Heinrichs I., in: Bll. f. dt. Landesgesch. 92, 1956.

122 Heinrich Büttner, Frühes fränkisches Christentum am Mittelrhein, in: AMrhKG 3, 1951.

123 Heinrich Büttner, Das Diplom Heinrichs III. für Fulda von 1049 und die Anfänge der Stadt Fulda, in: Archiv für Diplomatik 4, 1958.

124 Heinrich Büttner, Freiburg und das Kölner Recht, in: Schau-ins-Land 72, 1954.

125 Heinrich Büttner, Das fränkische Mainz. Ein Beitrag zum Kontinuitätsproblem und zur fränkischen mittelalterlichen Stadtgeschichte, in: Aus Verfassungs- und Landesgeschichte. Festschrift zum 70. Geburtstag von Theodor Mayer, (ed.) Friends and Pupils, vol. 2, Lindau, Konstanz 1955.

126 Heinrich Büttner, Markt und Stadt zwischen Waadtland und Bodensee bis zum Anfang des 12. Jahrhunderts, in: Schweizerische Zschr. f. Gesch. 11, 1961.

127 Heinrich Büttner, Die Bremer Markturkunden von 888 und 965 und die ottonische Marktrechtsentwicklung, in: Bremisches Jahrbuch 50, 1965.

128 Heinrich Büttner, Zur Stadtentwicklung von Worms im Früh- und Hochmittelalter, in: Aus Geschichte und Landeskunde. Forschungen und Darstellungen. Franz Steinbach zum 65. Geburtstag gewidmet von Freunden und Schülern, Bonn 1960.

129 Heinrich Büttner, Zum Städtewesen der Zähringer und Staufer am Oberrhein während des 12. Jahrhunderts, in: Zschr. f. Gesch. d. Oberrheins 105, 1957.

130 Heinrich Büttner, Studien zum frühmittelalterlichen Städtewesen in Frankreich, vornehmlich im Loire- und Rhônegebiet, in: Studien zu den Anfängen des europäischen Städtewesens. Reichenau-Vorträge 1955–1956, Lindau, Konstanz 1958 = Vorträge und Forschungen vol. 4.

131 Alexander Bugge, Altschwedische Gilden, in: VSWG 11, 1913.

(43) Thea Buyken, Hermann Conrad, (ed.), see under Die Amtleutebücher . . . (No. 43).

132 A.W. Byvanck, Nederland in den Romeinschen tijd, Leiden 1943.

133 R.C. van Caenegem, La preuve dans le droit du moyen-âge occidental, Gent 1965 = Studia Hist. Gandensia 23.

134 Claude Cahen, Zur Geschichte der städtischen Gesellschaft im islamischen Orient des Mittelalters, in: Saeculum 9, 1958.

135 Helen Maud Cam, The origin of the Borough of Cambridge. Proceedings of the Cambridgeshire Antiquarian Society, 1935.

136 Claude Campiche, Die Kommunalverfassung von Como im 12. und 13. Jahrhundert, Zürich 1929 = Schweizer Studien zur Geschichtswissenschaft XV, 2.

137 Bart. Capasso, Monumenta ad Neapolitani ducatus historiam pertinentia, 2 vols., Napoli 1881–92.

138 E. Carpentier, Autour de la peste noire: Famines et épidémies au XIVe siècle, in: Annales. Economies, sociétés, civilisations 17, 1962.

139 Claude Carrère, Barcelone, centre économique à l'époque des difficultés 1380–1462, 2 vols., Paris 1967 = EPHE VIe sec. Sér. Civilisations et sociétes 5.

140 J.L. Charles, La ville de Saint-Trond au moyen-âge. Des origines à la fin du XIVe siècle, Paris 1965 = Bibliothèque de la Faculté de Philosophie et Lettres de l'Université de Liège, No. 173.

141 Luigi Chiapelli, La formazione storica del commune cittadino in Italia, in: Archivio storico italiano 84, 1926; 85, 1927; 86, 1928; 88, 1930.

142 E. Christiani, Nobilità e popolo nel commune di Pisa dalle origini del podestoriato alla signoria dei Donoratico, Napoli 1962.

143 La città nell'alto medioevo, Spoleto 1959 = Settimane di studio del centro Ital. di studi sull'alto medioevo 6.

144 Città, mercanti e dottrine nell' economia europea. Dal IV al XVIII secolo. Saggi in memoria di Gino Luzzatto, (ed.) Amintore Fanfani, Milano 1964.

145 Dietrich Claude, Zu Fragen frühfränkischer Verfassungsgeschichte, in: ZRG Germ. Abt. 83, 1966.

146 Dietrich Claude, Die byzantinische Stadt im 6. Jahrhundert, München 1969.

147 Dietrich Claude, Studien zu Reccopolis, in: Madrider Mitteilungen 6, 1965.

148 Dietrich Claude, Topographie und Verfassung der Städte Bourges und Poitiers bis in das 11. Jhd., Lübeck, Hamburg 1960 = Historische Studien 380.

149 Dietrich Claude, Untersuchungen zum frühfränkischen Comitat, in: ZRG Germ. Abt. 81, 1964.

150 Collectanea Franz Steinbach, (ed.) Franz Petri and Georg Droege, Bonn 1967.

151 Hermann Conrad, Stadtgemeinde und Stadtfrieden in Koblenz während des 13. und 14. Jahrhunderts, in: ZRG Germ. Abt. 58, 1938.

152 Emile Coornaert, Le commerce de la Lorraine vue d'Anvers à la fin du XVᵉ et au XVIᵉ siècle, in: Annales de l'Est 1, 1950.

153 Emile Coornaert, Les ghildes médiévales, in: Revue hist. 199, 1948.

154 Jan Craeybeckx, Un grand commerce d'importation: les vins de France aux anciens Pays-Bas (XIIIᵉ–XVIᵉ siècles), Paris 1958.

155 René Crozet, Villes d'entre Loire et Gironde, Paris 1949.

156 Joseph Cuvelier, Les dénombrements de foyers en Brabant (XIVᵉ–XVIᵉ siècle), Bruxelles 1912–1913.

157 Lea Dasberg, Untersuchungen über die Entwertung des Judenstatus im 11. Jhd., Paris 1965.

158 Jos. Déer, Aachen und die Herrschersitze der Arpaden, in: MIÖG 79, 1971.

159 Francine Deisser-Nagels, Valenciennes, ville Carolingienne, in: Le Moyen Age 68, 1962.

(669) H. François Delaborde, Ch. Petit-Dutaillis, (ed.) see under Recueil des actes . . . (No. 669).

160 Karl E. Demandt, Das Fritzlarer Patriziat im Mittelalter, in: Zschr. d. Ver. f. hess. Gesch. u. Altertumskunde 68, 1957.

161 Karl E. Demandt, Quellen zur Rechtsgeschichte der Stadt Fritzlar im Mittelalter, Marburg 1939 = Veröffentlichungen d. Hist. Komm. für Hessen und Waldeck 13,3 = Quellen zur Rechtsgeschichte der hessischen Städte vol. 3.

162 J. Demey, Proeve tot raming van de bevolking en de weefgetouwen te Jeper van de XIII tot de XVII eeuw, in: Revue belge de phil. et d'hist. 28, 1950.

163 Guillaume Des Marez, Etudes inédites, Bruxelles 1936.

164 Georges Despy, Villes et campagnes aux IXᵉ et Xᵉ siècles: L'exemple du pays mosan, in: Revue du Nord 50, 1968.

165 Luc Devliegher, De huizen te Brugge, 2 vols., Tielt o. J. (1968).

166 Jan Dhondt, Les assemblées d'Etats en Belgique avant 1795, in: Standen en Landen 33, 1965.

167 Jan Dhondt, Développement urbain et initiative comtal, in: Revue du Nord 30, 1948.

168 Jan Dhondt, L'essor urbain entre Meuse et Mer du nord à l'époque mérovingienne, in: Studi in onore di Armando Sapori, vol. 1, Milano 1957.

169 Jan Dhondt, Une mentalité du XIIᵉ siècle: Galbert de Bruges, in: Revue du Nord 39, 1957.

170 Jan Dhondt, Het ontstaan van Oudenaarde, in: Handelingen van de Geschied- en Oudheidkundig Kring van Oudenaarde 10, 1952.

171 Jan Dhondt, Henri Pirenne: historien des institutions urbaines, in: Annali della Fondazione italiana per la storia amministrativa 3, 1966.

172 Jan Dhondt, Les problèmes de Quentovic, in: Studi in onore di Amintore Fanfani, vol. 1, Milano 1962.

173 Jan Dhondt, De vroege topographie van Brugge, in: Handelingen d. Maatschappij v. Geschiedenis en Oudheidkunde te Gent, new ser. 11, 1957.

174 Toni Diederich, Das älteste Kölner Stadtsiegel, in: Aus kölnischer und rheinischer Geschichte. Festgabe Arnold Güttsches zum 65. Geburtstag gewidmet, (ed.) Hans Blum, Köln 1969 = Veröffentlichungen des Kölnischen Geschichtsvereins 29.

175 Bernhard Diestelkamp, Welfische Stadtgründungen und Stadtrechte des 12. Jahrhunderts, in: ZRG Germ. Abt. 81, 1964.

176 Bernhard Diestelkamp, Die Städteprivilegien Herzog Ottos d. Kindes, ersten Herzogs von Braunschweig-Lüneburg (1204–1252), Hildesheim 1961 = Quellen und Darstellungen zur Geschichte Niedersachsens vol. 59.

177 Gerhard Dilcher, Bischof und Stadtverfassung in Oberitalien, in: ZRG Germ. Abt. 81, 1964.

178 Gerhard Dilcher, Die Entstehung der lombardischen Stadtkommune. Aalen 1967 = Untersuchungen zur deutschen Staats- und Rechtsgeschichte new ser. vol. 7.

179 Diskussion um die frühen Gründungsstädte in Deutschland. Fragen und Ergebnisse des fünften Kolloquiums des Arbeitskreises für landschaftliche deutsche Städteforschung 1963 in Freiburg/Br., (ed.) Peter Schöller, in: Westfälische Forschungen 17, 1964.

180 Renée Doehaerd, Etudes anversoises, 3 vols., Paris 1962–63.

181 Renée Doehaerd, Le Haut Moyen Age occidental. Economies et sociétés, Paris 1971 = Nouvelle Clio 14. English translation, The early Middle Ages in the West – Economy and Society, vol. 13 in this series, Amsterdam 1978.

182 Renée Doehaerd, Notes sur l'histoire d'un ancien impôt. Le tonlieu d'Arras, Arras 1946. Extrait du Bulletin de l'Académie d'Arras 1943/44; 1945/46.

183 Renée Doehaerd, Les relations commerciales entre Gênes, la Belgique et l'Outremont d'après les archives notariales génoises 1400–1440, Bruxelles 1952 = Institut historique belge de Rome. Etudes d'histoire économique et sociale, Vol. 5.

184 Fritz Dörrenhaus, Urbanität und gentile Lebensform. Der europäische Dualismus mediterraner und indoeuropäischer Verhaltensweisen, entwickelt aus einer Diskussion um den Tiroler Einzelhof, Wiesbaden 1971 = Erdkundliches Wissen 25.

185 Fritz Dörrenhaus, Wo der Norden dem Süden begegnet: Südtirol. Ein geographischer Vergleich, Bozen 1959.

186 Anton Doll, Historisch-archäologische Fragen der Speyerer Stadtentwicklung im Mittelalter, in: Pfälzer Heimat 11, 1960.

187 Anton Doll, Zur Frühgeschichte der Stadt Speyer, in: Mitteilungen des Hist. Vereins der Pfalz 52, 1954.

188 Phil. Dollinger, Phil. Wolff, Simonne Guenée, Bibliographie d'histoire des Villes de France, Paris 1967 = Publ. de la Commission internationale pour l'histoire des villes.

189 Phil. Dollinger, Le chiffre de la population de Paris au XIVᵉ siècle 210 000 ou 80 000 habitants? in: Revue hist. 216, 1956.

190 Phil. Dollinger, La Hanse (XIIᵉ–XVIIᵉ siècles), Paris 1964. Deutsch: Die Hanse, Stuttgart 1966 = Kröners Taschenausgabe vol. 371. English translation, London 1970.

191 Phil. Dollinger, Le patriciat des villes du Rhin supérieur et ses dissensions

internes dans la première moitié du XIVe siècle, in: Schweizerische Zschr. f. Gesch. 3, 1953.

192 Phil. Dollinger, Le premier recensement et le chiffre de population de Strasbourg en 1444, in: Revue d'Alsace 94, 1955.

193 Otto Doppelfeld, Römisches und fränkisches Glas in Köln, Köln 1966 = Schriftenreihe der archäologischen Gesellschaft Köln No. 13.

194 Otto Doppelfeld, Quellen zur Geschichte Kölns in römischer und fränkischer Zeit, Köln 1958 = Ausgewählte Quellen zur Kölner Stadtgeschichte vol. 1.

195 Otto Doppelfeld, Heinz Held, Der Rhein und die Römer, Köln 1970.

196 Alfons Dopsch, Beiträge zur Sozial- und Wirtschaftsgeschichte. Gesammelte Aufsätze 2. Reihe, Wien 1938.

197 Alfons Dopsch, Wirtschaftliche und soziale Grundlagen der europäischen Kulturentwicklung von Cäsar bis auf Karl den Großen, Wien ²1923–24.

(759) Alfons Dopsch, Ausgewählte Urkunden zur Verfassungsgeschichte ... see under Ernst Frh. v. Schwind (No. 759).

198 Alfred Doren, Entwicklung und Organisation der Florentiner Zünfte im 13. und 14. Jahrhundert, Leipzig 1897.

199 Alfred Doren, Italienische Wirtschaftsgeschichte, Jena 1934.

200 Alfred Doren, Die Florentiner Wollentuchindustrie vom 14. bis zum 16. Jahrhundert, Stuttgart 1901.

201 Alfred Doren, Das Florentiner Zunftwesen vom 14. bis zum 16. Jahrhundert, Stuttgart, Berlin 1908.

202 Joh. Gustav Droysen, Historik, (ed.) Rudolf Hübner, München ⁴1960.

203 Georges Duby, L'économie rurale et la vie des campagnes dans l'occident mévléval, Paris 1962.

204 Düren, (ed.) August Schoop, Bonn 1920 = Quellen zur Rechts- und Wirtschaftsgeschichte der rheinischen Städte 1 = Publikationen d. Ges. f. Rhein. Geschichtskunde 29.

205 A. Dupont, Les cités de la Narbonnaise première depuis les invasions germaniques jusqu'à l'apparition du consulat, Nîmes 1942.

206 Eugenio Dupré-Theseider, Roma dal comune del popolo alla Signoria pontifica 1252–1377, Bologna 1952 = Storia di Roma 11.

207 Jean Durliat, La vigne et le vin dans la région parisienne au début du IXe siècle d'après le Polyptique d'Irminon, in: Le Moyen Age 74, 1968.

208 Wilhelm Ebel, Der Bürgereid als Geltungsgrund und Gestaltungsprinzip des deutschen mittelalterlichen Stadtrechts, Weimar 1958.

209 Wilhelm Ebel, Bursprake, Echteding, Eddag in den niederdeutschen Stadtrechten, in: Festschrift für Hans Niedermeyer zum 70. Geburtstag, Göttingen 1953 = Göttinger rechtswissenschaftliche Studien vol. 10.

210 Wilhelm Ebel, Über die rechtsschöpferische Leistung des mittelalterlichen deutschen Bürgertums, in: Untersuchungen zur gesellschaftlichen Struktur der mittelalterlichen Städte in Europa. Reichenau-Vorträge 1963–1964, Konstanz, Stuttgart 1966 = Vorträge und Forschungen vol. 11.

211 Wilhelm Ebel, Lübisches Recht im Ostseeraum, Köln und Opladen 1967 = Arbeitsgemeinschaft für Forschung des Landes Nordrhein-Westfalen, Geisteswissenschaften No. 143.

212 Rudolf Egger, Die Stadt auf dem Magdalensberg, ein Großhandelsplatz. Die

ältesten Aufzeichnungen des Metallwarenhandels auf dem Boden Österreichs, Graz, Wien, Köln, 1961 = Österreichische Akad. d. Wiss. Phil.-hist. Kl. Denkschriften 79.

213 Hans Eiden, Zur Siedlungs- und Kulturgeschichte der Frühzeit, in: Zwischen Rhein und Mosel. Der Kreis St. Goar, (ed.) Franz-Josef Heyen, Boppard 1966.

214 Liselotte Constanze Eisenbart, Kleiderordnungen der deutschen Städte zwischen 1350 und 1700, Göttingen 1962.

215 Peter Eitel, Die oberschwäbischen Reichsstädte im Zeitalter der Zunftherrschaft. Untersuchungen zu ihrer politischen und sozialen Struktur unter besonderer Berücksichtigung der Städte Lindau, Memmingen, Ravensburg und Überlingen, Stuttgart 1970 = Schriften zur südwestdeutschen Landeskunde vol. 8.

216 Elenchus fontium historiae urbanae, quem edendum curaverunt C. van de Kieft et J.F. Niermeyer, vol. 1, Leiden 1967.

217 Traute Endemann, Markturkunde und Markt in Frankreich und Burgund vom 9. bis 11. Jhd., Konstanz, Stuttgart 1964.

218 Franz Engel, Stadtgeschichtsforschung mit archäologischen Methoden, ihre Probleme und Möglichkeiten, in: Bll. f. dt. Landesgesch. 88, 1951.

219 Edith Ennen, Neuere Arbeiten zur Geschichte des nordwesteuropäischen Städtewesens im Mittelalter, in: VSWG 38, 1, 1949.

220 Edith Ennen, Die Bedeutung der Kirche für den Wiederaufbau der in der Völkerwanderungszeit zerstörten Städte, in: Kölner Untersuchungen, ed. Walther Zimmermann, Ratingen 1950 = Die Kunstdenkmäler des Landesteiles Nordrhein, suppl. 2.

221 Edith Ennen, Einige Bemerkungen zur frühmittelalterlichen Geschichte Bonns, in: RhVjbll. 15/16, 1950/51.

222 Edith Ennen, Burg, Stadt und Territorialstaat in ihren wechselseitigen Beziehungen, in: RhVjbll. 12, 1942.

223 Edith Ennen, Die Entwicklung des Städtewesens an Rhein und Mosel vom 6. bis 9. Jahrhundert, in: La città nell'alto medioevo, Spoleto 1959 = Settimane di studio del centro ital. di studi sull' alto medioevo 6.

224 Edith Ennen, Frühgeschichte der europäischen Stadt, Bonn 1953.

225 Edith Ennen, Dietrich Höroldt, Kleine Geschichte der Stadt Bonn, Bonn 1966.

226 Edith Ennen, Ein geschichtliches Ortsverzeichnis des Rheinlandes. Exkurs: Veräußerungen grundherrlichen Streubesitzes im 13. Jhd., in: RhVjbll. 9, 1939.

227 Edith Ennen, Stadtgeschichtliche Probleme im Saar-Mosel-Raum, in: Landschaft und Geschichte. Festschrift Franz Petri, (ed.) Georg Droege and Peter Schöller, Bonn 1970.

228 Edith Ennen, Rezension zu Hans Planitz, Die deutsche Stadt im Mittelalter. Von der Römerzeit bis zu den Zunftkämpfen, Graz, Köln 1954, in: RhVjbll. 19, 1954.

229 Edith Ennen, Die europäische Stadt des Mittelalters als Forschungsaufgabe unserer Zeit, in: RhVjbll. 11, 1941.

230 Edith Ennen, Stadt und Schule in ihrem wechselseitigen Verhältnis vornehmlich im Mittelalter, in: RhVjbll. 22, 1957.

231 Edith Ennen, Die Stadt zwischen Mittelalter und Gegenwart, in: RhVjbll. 30, 1965; also in: 775a.

232 Edith Ennen, Stadt und Wallfahrt, in: Festschrift Matthias Zender, (1972).

233 Edith Ennen, Die Stadtwerdung Bonns im Spiegel der Terminologie, in: Bonner Geschichtsblätter 4, 1950.

234 Edith Ennen, Das Städtewesen Nordwestdeutschlands von der fränkischen bis zur salischen Zeit, in: Das erste Jahrtausend. Düsseldorf 1964; also in: Die Stadt des Mittelalters, ed. Carl Haase, Darmstadt 1969 = Wege der Forschung, vol. 243.

235 Edith Ennen, Ein Teilungsvertrag des Trierer Simeonsstiftes, der Herren von Berg, von Linster und des Ritters von Südlingen, in: RhVjbll. 21, 1956.

236 Edith Ennen, Zur Typologie des Stadt-Land-Verhältnisses im Mittelalter, in: Studium Generale 16, 1963.

237 Entwicklungsgesetze der Stadt. Vorträge und Berichte, Köln, Opladen 1963.

238 Martin Erbstösser, Ernst Werner, Ideologische Probleme des mittelalterlichen Plebejertums. Die freigeistige Häresie und ihre sozialen Wurzeln, Berlin 1960 = Forschungen zur mittelalterlichen Geschichte vol. 7.

239 Adalbert Erler, Bürgerrecht und Steuerpflicht im mittelalterlichen Städtewesen mit besonderer Untersuchung des Steuereides, Frankfurt a. M. 1939; [2]1963.

240 Georges Espinas, Documents relatifs à la draperie de Valenciennes au moyen-âge (1283–1403), Paris, Lille 1931 = Documents et travaux publ. par la Société d'Histoire du Droit des Pays Flamands, Picards et Wallons vol. 1.

241 Georges Espinas, Les origines du capitalisme. III: Deux fondations de villes dans l'Artois et la Flandre française. Saint-Omer. Lannoy-du-Nord, Lille 1946 = Bibliothèque de la Société d'Histoire du Droit des Pays Flamands, Picards et Wallons 16.

242 Georges Espinas, Le privilège de St. Omer de 1127, in: Revue du Nord 29, 1947.

243 Georges Espinas, Charles Verlinden, J. Buntinx, Privilèges et chartes de franchises de Flandre. vol. 1, Bruxelles 1959. vol. 2, Bruxelles 1961.

244 Georges Espinas, Recueil de documents relatifs à l'histoire du droit municipal en France des origines à la Révolution, vols. 1–3, Paris 1934–1943.

245 Georges Espinas, La vie urbaine de Douai au moyen-âge, Paris 1913.

246 Eugen Ewig, Die ältesten Mainzer Bischofsgräber, die Bischofsliste und die Theonestlegende, in: Universitas. Dienst an Wahrheit und Leben. Festschrift für Bischof Albert Stohr, (ed.) Ludwig Lenhart, vol. 2, Mainz 1960.

247 Eugen Ewig, Civitas, Gau und Territorium in den Trierischen Mosellanden, in: RhVjbll. 17, 1952.

248 Eugen Ewig, Die Civitas Ubiorum, die Francia Rinensis und das Land Ribuarien, in: RhVjbll. 19, 1954.

249 Eugen Ewig, Kirche und civitas in der Merowingerzeit, in: Le chiese nei regni dell'Europa occidentale e i loro rapporti con Roma sino all'800, Spoleto 1960 = Settimane di studio del centro ital. di studi sull'alto medioevo 7.

250 Eugen Ewig, Der Mittelrhein im Merowingerreich, in: Nassauische Annalen 82, 1971.

251 Eugen Ewig, Résidence et capitale pendant le haut Moyen Age, in: Revue hist. 230, 1963.

252 Eugen Ewig, Trier im Merowingerreich. Civitas, Stadt, Bistum, Trier 1954.

253 Excavations at Helgö, (ed.) Wilhelm Holmquist, vol. 1: Report for 1954–1956, Stockholm 1961; vol. 2: Report for 1957–1959, Stockholm 1964.

254 M.L. Fanchamps, Etude sur les tonlieux de la Meuse Moyenne du VIIIe au milieu du XIVe siècle, in: Le Moyen Age 70, 1964.

255 Amintore Fanfani, La préparation intellectuelle et professionelle à l'activité économique en Italie du XIVe au XVIe siècle, in: Le Moyen Age 57, 1951.

256 Gina Fasoli, Dalla Civitas al Comune nell'Italia settentrionale. Lezioni tenute
    alla Facoltà di Magistero dell'Università di Bologna, Bologna 1969.

257 Gina Fasoli, Che cosa sappiamo delle città italiane nell'alto medioevo? in:
    VSWG 47, 1960.

258 Gina Fasoli, Ricerche sui borghi franchi dell'alta Italia, in: Rivista di storia del
    diritto italiano XV, 1942.

259 R. Feenstra, Het stadrecht van Maastricht van 1220, in: Vereeniging tot uitgaaf
    der bronnen van het oud-vaderlandsche recht, Verslagen en mededelingen 11,
    1958.

260 Otto Feger, Auf dem Weg vom Markt zur Stadt, in: Zschr. f. Gesch. d.
    Oberrheins 106, 1958.

261 Otto Feger, Kleine Geschichte der Stadt Konstanz, Konstanz 1957.

262 Otto Feger, Konstanzer Stadtrechtsquellen. vol. I: Das Rote Buch, Konstanz
    1949. vol. IV: Die Statutensammlung des Stadtschreibers Jörb Vögeli, Konstanz
    1951. vol. VII: Vom Richtebrief zum Roten Buch, Konstanz 1955.

263 Otto Feger, Peter Rüster, Das Konstanzer Wirtschafts- und Gewerberecht z. Z.
    der Reformation, Konstanz 1961 = Konstanzer Geschichts- und Rechtsquellen.
    New ser. of Konstanzer Stadtrechtsquellen vol. 11.

264 Klaus Fehn, Die zentralörtlichen Funktionen früher Zentren in Altbayern,
    Wiesbaden 1970.

(63) Festschrift für Hector Ammann, see under Beiträge zur Wirtschafts- und
    Stadtgeschichte (No. 63).

265 Paul Albert Février, Le développement urbain en Provence de l'époque romaine
    à la fin du XIVe siècle, Paris 1964 = Bibliothèque des Écoles françaises
    d'Athènes et de Rome No. 202.

266 Zdeněk Fiala, Die Anfänge Prags. Eine Quellenanalyse zur Ortsterminologie bis
    zum Jahre 1235, Wiesbaden 1967 = Gießener Abhandlungen zur Agrar- und
    Wirtschaftsforschung des europäischen Ostens 40.

267 Finances et comptabilités urbaines du XIIIe au XVIe siècle. Colloque inter-
    national Blankenberge 6–9. IX. 1962, Bruxelles 1964 = Pro Civitate. Collection
    Histoire in-8⁰, No. 7.

268 Jürgen Findeisen, Spuren römerzeitlicher Siedlungsvorgänge im Dorf- und
    Stadtbild Süddeutschlands und seiner Nachbargebiete, Bonn 1970 (phil. Diss.).

269 Charlotte Fischer, Die Terra-Sigillata-Manufaktur von Sinzig a. Rhein, Köln,
    Graz 1969 = Rheinische Ausgrabungen 5.

270 Herbert Fischer, Burgbezirk und Stadtgebiet im deutschen Süden, Wien 1956.

271 Herbert Fischer, Die Siedlungsverlegung im Zeitalter der Stadtbildung. Unter
    bes. Berücksichtigung des österreichischen Raumes, Wien 1952 = Wiener
    rechtsgeschichtliche Arbeiten 1.

272 Joachim Fischer, Frankfurt und die Bürgerunruhen in Mainz (1332–1462), Mainz
    1938 = Beiträge zur Geschichte der Stadt Mainz vol. 15.

273 Enrico Fiumi, Demografia, movimento urbanistico e classi sociali in Prato
    dall'età comunale ai tempi moderni, Firenze 1968 = Biblioteca storica toscana
    14.

274 Enrico Fiumi, Sui rapporti economici tra città e contado nell'età comunale, in:
    Archivio storico italiano 114, 1956.

275 Enrico Fiumi, Storia economica e sociale di S. Gimigniano, Firenze 1961.
276 Klaus Flink, Geschichte der Burg, der Stadt und des Amtes Rheinbach, Bonn
     1965 = Rheinisches Archiv 59.
277 Claude Fohlen, Histoire de Besançon. Des origines à la fin du XVIe siècle, 2
     vols., Paris 1964–65.
278 La foire, Bruxelles 1953 = Recueils de la Société Jean Bodin vol. V.
279 José Maria Font Rius, Cartas de población y Franquicia de Cataluna, 2 vols.,
     Madrid, Barcelona 1969.
280 José Maria Font Rius, Origines del Regimen municipale de Cataluna, in: Anuario
     de historia del derecho Español 16, 1945; 17, 1946.
281 Zur Frage der Periodengrenze zwischen Altertum und Mittelalter, (ed.) Paul
     Egon Hübinger, Darmstadt 1959 = Wege der Forschung vol. 51.
282 Die Frage der Kontinuität in den Städten an Mosel und Rhein im Früh-
     mittelalter. Referate und Aussprachen auf der vierten Arbeitstagung des Kreises
     für landschaftliche deutsche Städteforschung 1962 in Trier, (ed.) Richard Lauf-
     ner, in: Westfälische Forschungen 16, 1963.
282a Günther Franz, (ed.), Deutsche Agrargeschichte, 5 vols. Stuttgart 1962 ff. (see
     under No. 1, 283, 546).
283 Günther Franz, Geschichte des deutschen Bauernstandes vom frühen Mittelalter
     bis zum 19. Jahrhundert, Stuttgart 1970 = Deutsche Agrargeschichte, (ed.) Gün-
     ther Franz, vol. 4.
284 Freiburg im Mittelalter. Vorträge zum Stadtjubiläum 1970, (ed.) Wolfgang
     Müller, Bühl/Baden 1970 = Veröffentlichungen des Alemannischen Instituts
     Freiburg/Br. 29.
285 Fritz Fremersdorf, Neue Beiträge zur Topographie des römischen Köln, in:
     Röm.-germ. Forschungen 18, 1950.
286 Fritz Fremersdorf, Die Denkmäler des römischen Köln. vol. I: Neuerwerbungen
     des römisch-germanischen Museums während der Jahre 1923–1927, Köln 1928,
     ²1964. vol. II: Urkunden zur Kölner Stadtgeschichte aus römischer Zeit, Köln
     1950, ²1963.
287 Fritz Fremersdorf, Die römischen Inschriften Kölns als Quellen der Stadt-
     geschichte, in: Jb. d. Köln. Geschichtsvereins 25, 1950.
288 Ferdinand Frensdorff, Das Stadtrecht von Wisby, in: Hans. Geschbll. 22, 1916.
289 Sheppard Frere, Britannia: A History of Roman Britain, London 1967 = History
     of the Provinces of the Roman Empire, ed. by Donald Duddle vol. 1.
290 Heinz F. Friederichs, Entstehung und Frühgeschichte des ältesten Friedberger
     Patriziats, in: Wetterauer Geschichtsblätter 10, 1961.
291 Heinz F. Friederichs, Herkunft und ständische Zuordnung des Patriziats der
     wetterauischen Reichsstädte bis zum Ende des Staufertums, in: Hess. Jb. f.
     Landesgesch. 9, 1959.
292 Birgitta Fritz, Helgö und die Vorgeschichte der Skandinavischen Stadt, in:
     Antikvariskt Arkiv 38, 1970 (Stockholm).
293 Konrad Fritze, Am Wendepunkt der Hanse. Untersuchungen zur Wirtschafts-
     und Sozialgeschichte Wendischer Hansestädte in der ersten Hälfte des 15. Jhds.,
     Berlin 1967 = Veröffentlichungen d. Hist. Inst. d. Ernst-Moritz-Arndt-Uni-
     versität Greifswald vol. 3.

232 BIBLIOGRAPHY

294 Karl Frölich, Kaufmannsgilde und Stadtverfassung im Mittelalter, in: Festschrift Alfred Schultze zum 70. Geburtstag, (ed.) Walth. Merk, Weimar 1934.

295 Karl Frölich, Kirche und städtisches Verfassungsleben im Mittelalter, in: ZRG Kan. Abt. 22, 1933.

296 Karl Frölich, Das Stadtbild von Goslar im Mittelalter, Gießen 1949 = Beiträge zur Geschichte der Stadt Goslar No. 11.

297 Karl Frölich, Zur Verfassungstopographie der deutschen Städte des Mittelalters, in: ZRG Germ. Abt. 58, 1938.

298 Jörg Füchtner, Die Bündnisse der Bodenseestädte bis zum Jahre 1390, Göttingen 1970 = Veröffentlichungen des Max-Planck-Instituts für Geschichte 8.

299 E. Fügedi, Die Entstehung des Städtewesens in Ungarn, in: Alba Regia, Annales Musei Stephani Regis 10, 1969.

300 Führer zu vor- und frühgeschichtlichen Denkmälern. vol. 5: Saarland, Mainz 1966.

301 Josianne Gaier-Lhoest, L'Evolution topographique de la ville de Dinant au moyen-âge, Bruxelles 1964 = Pro Civitate. Collection Histoire. Ser. in-8⁰ No. 4.

302 Giuseppe Galasso, Il commercio amalfitano nel periodo normanno, in: Studi in onore di Riccardo Filangieri, vol. 1, Napoli 1959.

303 François Louis Ganshof, Bemerkungen zu einer flandrischen Gerichtsurkunde, in: Festschrift Percy Ernst Schramm zu seinem 70. Geburtstag, (ed.) Peter Classen and Peter Scheibert, vol. 2, Wiesbaden 1964.

304 François Louis Ganshof, Les bureaux du tonlieu de Marseille et de Fos. Contributions à l'histoire des institutions financières de la monarchie franque, in: Etudes historiques à la mémoire de Noël Didier, Paris 1960.

305 François Louis Ganshof, Le Comté de Flandre, la ville de Bruges, Paris 1962.

306 François Louis Ganshof, Einwohnergenossenschaft und Graf in den flandrischen Städten während des 12. Jhds., in: ZRG Germ. Abt. 74, 1957.

307 François Louis Ganshof, Etude sur le développement des villes entre Loire et Rhin au Moyen Age, Paris 1943. Translation of no. 310.

308 François Louis Ganshof, Iets over Brugge gedurende de preconstitutioneele periode van haar geschiedenis, in: Nederl. Historiebladen 1, 1938.

309 François Louis Ganshof, Note sur l'inquisitio de theloneis Raffelstettensis, in: Le Moyen Age 72, 1966.

310 François Louis Ganshof, Over Stadsontwikkeling tusschen Loire en Rijn gedurende de Middeleeuwen, Antwerpen 1941 = Verhandelingen v. d. Koninkl. Vlaamse Acad. v. Wetensch., Letteren en Schone Kunsten v. Belgie. Kl. d. Letteren vol. 3, No. 1.

311 Julian Garcia Sainz de Baranda, La ciudad de Burgos y su concejo en la Edad Media, 2 vols. Burgos 1967.

312 Fritz Gause, Die Geschichte der Stadt Königsberg in Preußen, 2 vols., Köln, Graz 1965 and 1968 = Ostmitteleuropa in Vergangenheit und Gegenwart 10, 1 and 10, 2.

313 J. Gautier Dalché, Les mouvements urbains dans le nord-ouest de l'Espagne au XII³ siècle. Influences éntrangères ou phénomènes originaux?, in: Cuadernos de Historia. Anexos de la revista Hispania (Madrid) 2, 1968.

(780) Gedächtnisschrift Fritz Rörig, see under Städtewesen und Bürgertum...(No. 780).

314 Dietrich Gerhard, Regionalismus und ständisches Wesen als ein Grundthema europäischer Geschichte, in: HZ 174, 1952.

315 Germania Romana. vol. I: Römerstädte in Deutschland, Heidelberg 1960 = Gymnasium suppl. 1. vol. II: Kunst und Kunstgewerbe in römischen Deutschland, Heidelberg 1965 = Gymnasium suppl. 5. vol. III: Römisches Leben auf germanischem Boden, Heidelberg 1970 = Gymnasium suppl. 7.

316 Rafael Gibert, El Derecho municipal de León y Castilla, in: Anuario de historia del derecho Español 31, 1961.

317 Aleksander Gieysztor, Aux origines de la ville slave: ville de Grands, ville d'Etat au IXe–XIe siècle, in: Cahiers bruxellois 12, 1967.

318 Aleksander Gieysztor, Le origini delle città nella Polonia médiévale, in: Studi in onore di Armando Sapori, 2 vols., Milano 1957.

319 Aleksander Gieysztor, Les structures économiques en pays slaves à l'aube du moyen-âge jusqu'au XIe siécle et l'échange monétaire, in: Moneta e scambi nell'alto medioevo, Spoleto 1961 = Settimane di studio del centro ital. di studi sull'alto medioevo 8.

320 Karl Glöckner, Die Lage des Marktes im Stadtgrundriß, in: Nassauische Annalen 65, 1954.

321 Philippe Godding, La bourgeoisie foraine de Bruxelles du XIVe au XVIe siècle, in: Cahiers bruxellois 7, 1962.

322 Philippe Godding, Le droit foncier à Bruxelles au moyen-âge, Bruxelles 1960 = Etudes d'histoire et d'ethnologie juridiques 1.

323 Carsten Goehrke, Die Sozialstruktur des mittelalterlichen Nowgorod, in: Untersuchungen zur gesellschaftlichen Struktur der mittelalterlichen Städte in Europa. Reichenau-Vorträge 1963–1964, Konstanz, Stuttgart 1966 = Vorträge und Forschungen vol 11.

324 Otto Gonnenwein, Das Stapel- und Niederlagsrecht, Weimar 1939.

325 Theodor Goerlitz, Verfassung, Verwaltung und Recht der Stadt Breslau, Würzburg 1962 = Quellen und Darstellungen zur schlesischen Geschichte vol. 7.

326 Hans Goetting, Die Anfänge der Stadt Gandersheim. Wik, mercatus und forum als Stufen der frühstädtischen Entwicklung, in: Bll. f. dt. Landesgesch. 89, 1952.

327 Walter Goetz, Die Entstehung der italienischen Kommunen im frühen Mittelalter, München 1944 = Sbb. d. Bayerischen Akad. d. Wiss., Phil.-hist. Kl. vol. 44, No. 1.

328 Julio González, Repartimento de Sevilla. Estudio y edición 2 vols., Madrid 1951.

329 Erich Gose, Katalog der frühchristlichen Inschriften in Trier, Berlin 1958 = Trierer Grabungen und Forschungen vol. 3.

330 Roger Grand, Les paix d'Aurillac, Paris 1945.

331 Gregor v. Tours, Gregorii episcopi Turonensis Historiarum libri decem, (ed.) Rudolf Buchner, 2 vols., Darmstadt 1959 = Ausgewählte Quellen zur deutschen Geschichte des Mittelalters. Freiherr vom Stein-Gedächtnisausgabe vols., 2 and 3.

332 Philip Grierson, Commerce in the Dark Ages: a critique of the evidence, London 1959 = Transactions of the Royal Historical Society, 5th Ser., vol. 9.

333 Philip Grierson, Carolingian Europe and the Arabs: The Myth of the Mancus, in: Revue belge de phil. et d'hist. 32, 1954.

334 Paul Grimm, Archäologische Beiträge zur Lage ottonischer Marktsiedlungen in

den Bezirken Halle und Magdeburg, in: Jahresschrift für mitteldeutsche Vorgeschichte 41/42, 1958.

335 Paul Grimm, Zum Stand der archäologischen Erforschung der Stadtentwicklung in der Deutschen Demokratischen Republik, in: Visbysymposiet für historika vetenskapen 1963.

336 Paul Grimm, Zum Verhältnis von Burg und Stadt nach archäologischen Beobachtungen in Mittel- und Ostdeutschland, in: Omagiu lui K. Daicoviciu cu prilejul implinerii a 60 de ani, Academia rep. pop. Romine 1960.

337 Charles Gross, A bibliography of British municipal history. Including gilds and parliamentary representation, London ²1966.

338 Wilhelm Grotelüschen, Die Städte am Nordostrande der Eifel, Bonn, Köln 1933 = Beiträge zur Landeskunde der Rheinlande 2nd ser., vol. 1.

339 Klaus-Detlev Grothusen, Entstehung und Geschichte Zagrebs bis zum Ausgang des 14. Jahrhunderts, Wiesbaden 1967 = Osteuropastudien der Hochschulen des Landes Hessen. ser. 1 = Gießener Abhandlungen zur Agrar- und Wirtschaftsforschung des europäischen Ostens vol. 37.

340 Herbert Grundmann, Religiöse Bewegungen im Mittelalter, Darmstadt ²1961.

341 Herbert Grundmann, Zur Geschichte der Beginen im 13. Jhd., in: Archiv f. Kulturgeschichte 21, 1931.

342 Hans Güldner, Unsere Stadt – Tragödie einer Spätkultur, Pinneberg b. Hamburg 1968.

343 Karl Gutkas, St. Pölten. Werden und Wesen einer österreichischen Stadt, St. Pölten 1964.

344 Paul Guyer, Bibliographie der Städtegeschichte der Schweiz, Zürich 1960 = Schweizerische Zeitschrift für Geschichte suppl. 11.

345 J.C. de Haan, De Italiaansche stadscommune van consulaat tot signorie, in: Tijdschr. v. Geschiedenis 54, 1939.

346 J.C. de Haan, De wording van de Italiaansche stadscommune in de Middeleeuwen, in: Tijdschr. v. Geschiedenis 51, 1936.

347 Werner Haarnagel, Die Ergebnisse der Grabung Feddersen Wierde, in: Germania 41, 1963.

348 Werner Haarnagel, Die Grabung Feddersen Wierde und ihre Bedeutung für die Erkenntnisse der bäuerlichen Besiedlung im Küstengebiet . . . , in: Zeitschrift für Agrarsoziologie 2, 1963.

349 Werner Haarnagel, Die frühgeschichtliche Handels-Siedlung Emden und ihre Entwicklung bis ins Mittelalter, in: Friesisches Jahrbuch 1955.

350 Carl Haase, Die Entstehung der westfälischen Städte, Münster ²1965.

(775a) Carl Haase, (ed.) see under Die Stadt des Mittelalters . . . (No. 775a).

351 Waldemar Haberey, Die römischen Wasserleitungen nach Köln, Düsseldorf 1971.

352 Rolf Hachmann, Georg Kossack, Hans Kuhn, Völker zwischen Germanen und Kelten, Neumünster 1962.

353 Walter Hävernick, Der Kölner Pfennig im 12. und 13. Jahrhundert, Stuttgart 1930 = VSWG suppl. 18.

354 Ernst Hamm, Die Städtegründungen der Herzöge von Zähringen in Südwestdeutschland, Freiburg/Br. 1932 = Veröffentlichungen des Alemannischen Instituts Freiburg/Br. 1.

355 Handbuch der Geschichte der böhmischen Länder, (ed.) Karl Bosl, Stuttgart 1967.

356 Die Deutsche Hanse als Mittler zwischen Ost und West, (ed.) Leo Brandt, Köln, Opladen 1963 = Wissenschaftliche Abhandlungen d. Arbeitsgemeinschaft f. Forschungen d. Landes Nordrhein-Westfalen 27.

357 J. Hansen, Stadterweiterung, Stadtbefestigung, Stadtfreiheit im Mittelalter, in: Mitteilungen des Rheinischen Vereins f. Denkmalpflege und Heimatschutz 5, 1911.

358 Das Hauptstadtproblem in der Geschichte. Festgabe zum 90. Geburtstag Friedrich Meineckes, Tübingen 1952 = Jahrbuch für Geschichte des deutschen Ostens vol. 1.

359 Jacques Heers, Gênes au XVe siècle, Paris 1961 = EPHE VIe sec. Sér. Affaires et gens d'affaires 24.

360 Jacques Heers, L'occident aux XIVe et XVe siècles. Aspects économiques et sociaux, Paris 1963 = Nouvelle Clio 23.

361 Jacques Heers, Urbanisme et structure sociale à Gênes au moyen-âge, in: Studi in onore di Amintore Fanfani, vol. 1, Milano 1962.

362 Eduard Hegel, Die Entstehung des mittelalterlichen Pfarrsystems der Stadt Köln, in: Kölner Untersuchungen, (ed.) Walther Zimmermann, Ratingen 1950 = Die Kunstdenkmäler im Landesteil Nordrhein, suppl. 2.

363 Eduard Hegel, Die rheinische Kirche in römischer und frühfränkischer Zeit, in: Das erste Jahrtausend. Kultur und Kunst im Werdenden Abendland an Rhein und Ruhr. Text vol. I, (ed.) Kurt Böhner, Victor H. Elbern and others, Düsseldorf ^{2}1963.

364 Eduard Hegel, Kölner Kirchen und die Stadtzerstörungen von 350 und 881, in: Kölner Untersuchungen, (ed.) Walther Zimmermann, Ratingen 1950 = Die Kunstdenkmäler im Landesteil Nordrhein, suppl. 2.

365 Fritz M. Heichelheim, An Ancient Economic History from the Palaeolithic Age to the Migrations of the Germanic, Slavic and Arabic Nations, 2 vols., Leyden 1958–1964.

366 Fritz M. Heichelheim, Römische Sozial- und Wirtschaftsgeschichte. Von der Königszeit bis Byzanz, in: Historia Mundi IV, 1956.

367 Hermann Heimpel, Nürnberg und das Reich des Mittelalters, in: Zschr. f. bayer. Landesgesch. 16, 1951.

368 Hermann Heimpel, Seide aus Regensburg, in: MIÖG 62, 1954.

369 Hermann Heimpel, Auf neuen Wegen der Wirtschaftsgeschichte, in: Vergangenheit und Gegenwart 32, 1933.

370 Paul Heinsius, Das Schiff der hansischen Frühzeit, Köln, Graz, 1956.

371 Pierre Héliot, Sur les résidences princières bâties en France du Xe au XIIe siècle, in: Le Moyen Age 61, 1955.

372 Manfred Hellmann, Grundfragen slavischer Verfassungsgeschichte des frühen Mittelalters, in: Jbb. für Gesch. Osteuropas new ser. 2, 1954.

372a Helmoldi presbyteri Bozoviensis Chronica Slavorum, Berlin 1963 = Ausgewählte Quellen zur deutschen Geschichte des Mittelalters 19.

373 Richard Hennig, Terrae incognitae. Eine Zusammenstellung und kritische Bewertung der wichtigsten vorcolumbischen Entdeckungsreisen an Hand der darüber vorliegenden Originalberichte, vol. 2, Leiden ^{2}1950; vol. 3, Leiden ^{2}1953.

374 Witold Hensel, Anfänge der Städte bei den Ost- und Westslaven, Bautzen 1967.

375 Witold Hensel, Poznań w zaranin dziejów, Wrocław (Breslau) 1968.

376 Stanislaus Herbst, Les études polonaises d'histoire urbaine, in: Cahiers bruxellois 12, 1967.

377 David Herlihy, Pisa in the Early Renaissance. A Study of Urban Growth, New Haven, Yale 1958.

378 David Herlihy, Medieval and Renaissance Pistoria. The social history of an Italian town, 1200–1430, New Haven, London 1967.

379 David Herlihy, Santa Maria Impruneta: a rural commune in the late Middle Ages, in: Florentine Studies, (ed.) Nicolai Rubenstein, London ²1968.

380 Erich Herzog, Die ottonische Stadt. Die Anfänge der mittelalterlichen Stadtbaukunst in Deutschland, Berlin 1964.

381 Wolfgang Heß, Geldwirtschaft am Mittelrhein in karolingischer Zeit, in: Bll. f. dt. Landesgesch. 98, 1962.

382 Wolfgang Heß, Hersfeld, Fulda und Erfurt als frühe Handelsneiderlassungen, in: Festschrift für Harald Keller zum 60. Geburtstag, (ed.) Hans Martin Frhr. von Erffa and Elisabeth Herget, Darmstadt 1963.

383 Wolfgang Heß, Der Hersfelder Marktplatz. Ursprung und Bedeutung der Ebenheit für die Entwicklung der Stadt, in: Hess Jb. f. Landesgesch. 4, 1954.

384 Wolfgang Heß, Hessische Städtegründungen des Landgrafen von Thüringen, Marburg 1966.

385 Charles Higounet, Cisterciens et bastides, in: Le Moyen Age 56, 1950.

386 Charles Higounet, Bordeaux pendant le haut moyen-âge, Bordeaux 1963 = Histoire de Bordeaux 2.

387 Charles Higounet, Les forêts de l'Europe occidentale du Ve au XIe siècle, in: Agricoltura e mondo rurale in occidente nell'alto medioevo, Spoleto 1966 = Settimane di studio del centro ital. di studi sull'alto medioevo 13.

388 Rudolf Hillebrecht, Stadtentwicklung – wozu und wohin?, in: Bild der Wissenschaft April 1967.

389 Histoire du commerce de Marseille, 5 vols., Paris 1949 ff. vol. I (ed.) Raoul Busquet and Régime Pernoud, Paris 1949, vol. II (ed.) Edouard Baratier and Félix Reynaud, Paris 1952. vol. III (ed.) Raymond Collier and Joseph Billioud, Paris 1951. vol. IV (ed.) Louis Bergasse and Gaston Rambert, Paris 1954. vol. V (ed.) R. Paris (Index), Paris 1956.

390 Eduard Hlawitschka, Franken, Alamannen, Bayern und Burgunder in Oberitalien. Zum Verständnis der fränkischen Königsherrschaft in Italien (774–962), Freiburg 1960 = Forschungen zur oberrheinischen Landesgeschichte vol. 8.

391 Hans Hoederath. Forensis ecclesia, in: ZRG Kan. Abt. 67, 1950.

392 Albert K. Hömberg, Zur Erforschung des westfälischen Städtewesens im Hochmittelalter, in: Westfälische Forschungen 14, 1961.

(253) Wilhelm Holmquist. (ed.) see under Excavations at Helgö . . . (No. 253).

393 Wilhelm Holmquist, Die Metallwerkstätten auf Helgö, in: Kölner Jahrbuch f. Vor- und Frühgesch. 9, 1967/68.

394 J.H. Holwerda, Dorestad en onze vroegste middeleeuwen, Leiden 1929.

395 J.H. Holwerda, Aus Holland, in: Berichte der Römisch-germanischen Kommission 16, 1925/26.

396 J.A. van Houtte, Die Beziehungen zwischen Köln und den Niederlanden vom Hochmittelalter bis zum Beginn des Industriezeitalters, Köln 1969 = Kölner Vorträge zur Sozial- und Wirtschaftsgeschichte vol. 1.

397 J.A. van Houtte, Die Handelsbeziehungen zwischen Köln und den südlichen Niederlanden bis zum Ausgang des 15. Jahrhunderts, in: Jb. d. Köln. Geschichtsvereins 23, 1941.

398 J.A. van Houtte, Het ontstaan van de grote international markt van Antwerpen op het einde der Middleeeuwen, in: Econ. en Sociaal Tijdschrift 8, 1954.

399 J.A. van Houtte, Die Städte der Niederlande im Übergang vom Mittelalter zur Neuzeit, in: RhVjbll. 27, 1962.

400 Jean Hubert, Evolution de la topographie et de l'aspect des villes de Gaule du Ve au Xe sc., in: La città nell'alto medioevo, Spoleto 1959 = Settimane di studio del centro ital. di studi sull'alto medioevo 6.

(62) Paul Egon Hübinger, (ed.) see under Bedeutung und Rolle des Islam . . . (No. 62).

(281) Paul Egon Hübinger, (ed.) see under Zur Frage der Periodengrenze . . . (No. 281). 281).

(483) Paul Egon Hübinger, (ed.) see under Kulturbruch oder Kulturkontinuität . . . (No. 483).

401 Paul Egon Hübinger, Spätantike und Frühes Mittelalter, in: Deutsche Vierteljahrsschrift f. Literaturwissenschaft u. Geistesgeschichte 26, 1952.

402 Arnold Hugh, Martin Jones, The Later Roman Empire. 284–602, Norman/Oklahoma 1964.

403 Lajos Huszár, Der Umlauf der Kölner Denare im mittelalterlichen Ungarn, in: Dona numismatica. Walter Hävernick zum 23. Januar 1965 dargebracht, (ed.) Peter Berghaus and others, Hamburg 1965.

404 Ces. Imperiale, Codice diplomatico della Repubblica di Genova, 2 vols., Roma 1936–38.

405 L'impôt dans le cadre de la ville et de l'état. Colloque international Spa 1964, Bruxelles 1966 = Pro Civitate. Collection Histoire in-8^0, No. 13.

406 Franz Irsigler, Untersuchungen zur Geschichte des frühfränkischen Adels, Bonn 1969 = Rheinisches Archiv 70.

(71) G. Jacob, (ed.) see under Arabische Berichte . . . (No. 71).

407 Jahresberichte des Landesmuseums und des Landesdienstes für Vor- und Frühgeschichte im Regierungsbezirk Trier und im Kreis Birkenfeld 1945–1958, in: Trierer Zeitschrift 24–26, 1956–1958.

408 Herbert Jankuhn, Haithabu, ein Handelsplatz der Wikingerzeit, Neumünster ^{4}1965.

409 Herbert Jankuhn, Probleme des rheinischen Handels nach Skandinavien im frühen Mittelalter, in: RhVjbll 15/16, 1950/51.

410 Herbert Jankuhn, Die frühmittelalterlichen Seehandelsplätze im Nord- und Ostseeraum, in: Studien zu den Anfängen des europäischen Städtewesens. Reichenau-Vorträge 1955–1956, Lindau, Konstanz 1958 = Vorträge and Forschungen vol. 4.

411 Herbert Jankuhn, Die Slawen in Mitteleuropa im Spiegel neuer archäologischer Forschungsergebnisse, in: Bll. f. dt. Landesgesch. 106, 1970.

412 Walter Janssen, Mittelalterliche deutsche Keramik in Norwegen und ihre Bedeutung für die Handelsgeschichte, in: Studien zur europäischen Vor- und Frühgeschichte, (ed.) Martin Claus, Neumünster 1968.

413 Konrad Jazdzewski, Gdansk wczesnós redniowieczny w swietle wykopalisk (Das frühmittelalterliche Danzig im Lichte der Ausgrabungen), Gdansk 1961.

414 Horst Jecht, Studien zur gesellschaftlichen Struktur der mittelalterlichen Städte, in: VSWG 19, 1926.

415 W. Jecht, Neue Untersuchungen zur Gründungsgeschichte der Stadt Görlitz und zur Entstehung des Städtewesens in der Oberlausitz, in: Neues Laus. Magazin 95, 1919.

416 Paul Johansen, Die Kaufmannskirche im Ostseegebiet, in: Studien zu den Anfängen des europäischen Städtewesens. Reichenau-Vorträge 1955–1956, Lindau, Konstanz 1958 = Vorträge und Forschungen vol. 4.

417 Paul Johansen, Nordische Mission, Revals Gründung und die Schwedensiedlung in Estland, Stockholm 1951 = Kungl. Vitterhets Historie och Antikvitets Akademiens Handlingar Del 74.

418 Paul Johansen, Nowgorod und die Hanse, in: Städtewesen und Bürgertum als geschichtliche Kräfte. Gedächtnisschrift Fritz Rörig, (eds.) Ahasver v. Brandt and W. Koppe, Lübeck 1953.

419 Paul Johansen, Umrisse und Aufgaben der hansischen Siedlungsgeschichte und Kartographie, in: Hans. Geschbll. 73, 1955.

420 Oscar Albert Johansen, Der deutsche Kaufmann in der Wiek in Norwegen im späteren Mittelalter, in: Hans. Geschbll. 53, 1928.

421 A.H.M. Jones, The cities of the eastern Roman provinces, Oxford [2]1971.

422 A.H.M. Jones, The cities of the Roman Empire. Political, administrative and judicial institutions, in: La ville. vol. I: Institutions administratives et judiciaires, Bruxelles 1954 = Recueils de la Société Jean Bodin vol. VI.

423 A.H.M. Jones, The Economic Life of the Towns of the Roman Empire, IN: La ville. vol. II: Institutions économiques et sociales, Bruxelles 1955 = Recueils de la Société Jean Bodin vol. VII.

424 P.J. Jones, From Manor to Mezzadria: a Tuscan case-study in the medieval origins of modern agrarian society, in: Florentine Studies, (ed.) Nicolai Rubinstein, London [2]1968.

425 Karl Jordan, Die Städtepolitik Heinrichs des Löwen. Eine Forschungsbilanz, in: Hans. Geschbll. 78, 1960.

426 André Joris, Der Handel der Maasstädte im Mittelalter, in: Hans. Geschbll. 79, 1961.

427 André Joris, Huy et sa charte de franchise 1066, Bruxelles 1966 = Pro Civitate. Collection Histoire. Ser. in-4⁰, No. 3.

428 André Joris, La notion de "ville", in: Les catégories en histoire, (ed.) Chaim Perelman, Bruxelles 1969.

429 André Joris, Un problème d'histoire mosane: la prospérité de Huy aux environs de 1300, in: Le Moyen Age 58, 1952.

430 André Joris, Quelques problèmes relatifs au patriciat hutois du XIe au XIIIe siècle, in: Annales du Congrès de la Fédération hist. et archéol. de Belgique 36, 1955.

431 André Joris, La ville de Huy au moyen âge, des origines à la fin du XIVe siècle,

Paris 1959 = Bibliothèque de la Faculté de Philosophie et Lettres de l'Université de Liège, No. 152.

432 Paul Kaegbein, (ed.) see under Fritz Rörig, Wirtschaftskräfte im Mittelalter ... (No. 694).

433 Jiři Kejř, Les privilèges des villes de Bohème depuis les origines jusqu'aux guerres hussites (1419), in: Les libertés urbaines et rurales. Pro civitate, Collection Histoire 19, 1968.

434 Jiři Kejř, Zwei Studien über die Anfänge der Städteverfassung in den böhmischen Ländern, in: Historica 16, 1969 (Prag. Akademie).

435 Hermann Kellenbenz, Der Aufstieg Kölns zur mittelalterlichen Handelsmetropole, Köln 1967 = Ges. f. Rhein. Geschichtskunde, Vorträge No. 17.

436 Hermann Kellenbenz, Bürgertum und Wirtschaft in der Reichsstadt Regensburg, in: Bll. f. dt. Landesgesch. 98, 1962.

437 Hermann Kellenbenz, Der italienische Großkaufmann und die Renaissance, in: VSWG 45, 1958.

438 Hermann Kellenbenz, Die Juden in der Wirtschaftsgeschichte des rheinischen Raumes, in: Monumenta Judaica. 2000 Jahre Geschichte und Kultur der Juden am Rhein, Köln 1963.

439 Hermann Kellenbenz, Bäuerliche Unternehmer im Bereich der Nord- und Ostsee vom Hochmittelalter bis zum Ausgang der neueren Zeit, in: VSWG 49, 1962.

440 Robert v. Keller, Freiheitsgarantien für Person und Eigentum im Mittelalter, Heidelberg 1933 = Deutschrechtliche Beiträge vol. XIV No. 1.

441 Theodor Konrad Kempf, Die altchristliche Bischofsstadt Trier, in: Rheinischer Verein f. Denkmalpflege und Heimatschutz year, 1952.

442 Gottfried Kentenich, Geschichte der Stadt Trier von ihrer Gründung bis zur Gegenwart, Trier 1915.

443 Kathleen Kenyon, Archäologie im Heiligen Land, Neukirchen-Vluyn 1967.

444 Friedrich Keutgen, Ämter und Zünfte. Zur Entstehung des Zunftwesens, Jena 1903. Reprinted Aalen 1965.

445 Friedrich Keutgen, Urkunden zur städtischen Verfassungsgeschichte, Berlin 1899. Reprinted Aalen 1965.

446 Erich Keyser, Die Ausbreitung der Pest in den deutschen Städten, in: Ergebnisse und Probleme moderner geographischer Forschung. Hans Mortensen zu seinem 60. Geburtstag, Bremen 1954 = Raumforschung und Landesplanung. Abhandlungen 28.

447 Erich Keyser, Die polnischen Ausgrabungen in Alt-Danzig, in: Zschr. f. Ostforschung 12, 1963.

(79) Erich Keyser, (ed.) see under Bibliographie zur Städtegeschichte Deutschlands (No. 79).

(799) Erich Keyser, (ed.) see under Deutsches Städtebuch (No. 779).

448 Erich Keyser, Städtegründungen und Städtebau in Nordwestdeutschland, 2 vols., Remagen 1958.

(216) C. van de Kieft, J.F. Niermeyer, (ed.) see under Elenchus fontium ... (No. 216).

449 Walther Kienast, Rezension zu Vincenz Samanek, Studien zur Geschichte König Adolfs, Wien 1930, in: Hz 143, 1931.

450 Bernhard Kirchgässner, Währungspolitik, Stadthaushalt und soziale Fragen

südwestdeutscher Reichsstädte im Spätmittelalter, in: Esslinger Studien (Jb. f. Gesch. d. oberdt. Reichsstädte) 11, 1965.

451 Bernhard Kirchgässner, Wirtschaft und Bevölkerung der Reichsstadt Eßlingen im Spätmittelalter, in: Esslinger Studien 9, 1964.

(825) Karl-Heinz Kirchoff, (ed.), see under Territorien und Städtewesen (No. 825).

452 Erich Kittel, Die städtischen Siegel und Wappen und der Landesherr im Mittelalter, in: Festschrift zum hundertjährigen Bestehen des Herold zu Berlin 1869–1969, Berlin 1969.

453 Ernst Klebel, Die Städte und Märkte des baierischen Stammesgebietes in der Siedlungsgeschichte, in: Zschr. f. bayer. Landesgesch. 12, 1939/40.

454 Herbert Klein, Beiträge zur Geschichte der Stadt Salzburg im Mittelalter, in: Mitteilungen d. Ges. f. Salzburger Landeskunde 107, 1967.

455 Arthur Kleinclausz, Histoire de Lyon. I. Des origines à 1595, Lyon 1939.

456 Paul Kletler, Nordwesteuropas Verkehr, Handel und Gewerbe im Frühen Mittelalter, Wien 1924 = Deutsche Kulturhistorische ser. 2.

457 Friedrich v. Klocke, Patriziat und Stadtadel im alten Soest, Lübeck 1927 = Pfingstbll. d. Hans. Geschver. 18.

458 Friedrich v. Klocke, Das Patriziatsproblem und die Werler Erbsälzer, Münster 1965 = Veröffentlichungen der Hist. Komm. Westfalens 22 = Geschichtliche Arbeiten zur westfälischen Landesforschung, No. 7.

459 Rudolf Klöpper, Der geographische Stadtbegriff, in: Geographisches Taschenbuch, (ed.) Emil Meynen, Stuttgart 1956/57.

460 Rudolf Klöpper, Rheinische Städte. Entwicklung und heutige Stellung, in: Beiträge zur Rheinkunde 15, 1963.

461 John Knaepen, Les anciennes foires internationales de Visé (IXe–XIIIe siècles), in: Bulletin de l'Institut archéol, liégeois 129, 1966.

(670) Richard Knipping, (ed.), see under Die Regesten der Erzbischöfe von Köln ... (No. 670).

(778) Herbert Knittler, (ed.), see under Die Städte Oberösterreichs (No. 778).

462 A.C.F. Koch, Die Anfänge der Stadt Deventer, in: Westfälische Forschungen 10, 1957.

463 A.C.F. Koch, Brugge's topografische ontwikkeling tot in de 12e eeuw, in: Handelingen van het Genootschap "Société d'Emulation" te Brugge 94, 1962.

464 Gerhard Köbler, Zur Entstehung des mittelalterlichen Stadtrechtes, in: ZRG Germ. Abt. 86, 1969.

465 Richard Koebner, Die Anfänge des Gemeinwesens der Stadt Köln, Bonn 1922.

466 Richard Koebner, Zur ältesten Geschichte des nordholländischen Städtewesens, in: VSWG 18, 1925.

466a Köln, das Reich und Europa. Abhandlungen über weiträumige Verflechtungen der Stadt Köln in Politik, Recht und Wirtschaft im Mittelalter, Köln 1971 = Mitt. aus dem Stadtarchiv Köln 60.

(775) René König (ed.) and others, see under Die Stadt als Lebensform (No. 775).

467 Rudolf Kötzschke, Markgraf Dietrich von Meißen als Förderer des Städtebaues, in: Neues Archiv f. Sächs. Gesch. u. Altertumskunde 45, 1924.

468 Wilhelm Koppe, Schleswig und die Schleswiger, in: 780.

468a Wilhelm Koppe, Lübeck-Stockholmer Handelsgeschichte im 14. Jhd., Neumünster 1933 = Abh. z. Handels- u. Seegesch, new ser. 2.

469 Wilhelm Koppe, Das Stockholmer Testament eines deutschen Kaufgesellen, in: Zschr. d. Ver. f. Lübeck. Gesch. u. Altertumskunde 34, 1954.

470 Gustav Korlén, Kieler Bruchstücke kaufmännischer Buchführung aus dem Ende des 13. Jhds., in: Niederdeutsche Mitteilungen des Germ. Seminars zu Lund 5, 1949.

471 Gustav Korlén, Norddeutsche Stadtrechte. I. Das Stader Stadtrecht vom Jahre 1279. II. Das mittelniederdeutsche Stadtrecht von Lübeck nach seinen ältesten Formen, Lund, Kopenhagen 1950/51.

472 Werner Krämer, Manching, ein vindelikisches oppidum an der Donau, in: Neue Ausgrabungen in Deutschland, Berlin 1958.

473 Karl Kroeschell, Rodungssiedlung und Stadtgründung. Ländliches und städtisches Hagenrecht, in: Bll. f. dt. Landesgesch. 91, 1954.

474 Karl Kroeschell, Stadtgründung und Weichbildrecht in Westfalen, Münster 1960 = Schriften d. Hist. Komm. Westfalens 3.

475 Karl Kroeschell, Weichbild. Untersuchungen zur Struktur und Entstehung der mittelalterlichen Stadtgemeinde in Westfalen, Köln, Graz 1960 = Forschungen zur deutschen Rechtsgeschichte vol. 3.

476 Erik Kroman, (ed.), Danmarks gamle købstadlovgivning, vol. 2, Kopenhagen 1952.

477 Bruno Krüger, Die Kietzsiedlungen im nördlichen Mitteleuropa. Beiträge der Archäologie zu ihrer Altersbestimmung, Berlin 1962.

478 H. C. Krueger, Genoese merchants. Their association and investments, 1155 to 1230, in: Studi in onore di Amintore Fanfani, vol. 1, Milano 1962.

479 Winfried Küchler, Das Bannmeilenrecht. Ein Beitrag der mittelalterlichen Ostsiedlung zur wirtschaftlichen und rechtlichen Verschränkung von Stadt und Land, Würzburg 1964 = Marburger Ostforschungen 24.

480 Hans Kuhn, Renzension von Paul Heinsius, Das Schiff der hansischen Frühzeit, Köln, Graz 1956, in: Hans. Geschbll. 75, 1957.

481 Walter Kuhn, Die Entstehung der deutschrechtlichen Stadt Płock, in: Zschr. f. Ostforschung 13, 1964.

482 Walter Kuhn, Die Stadtdörfer der mittelalterlichen Ostsiedlung, in: Zschr. f. Ostforschung 20, 1971.

483 Kulturbruch oder Kulturkontinuität im Übergang von der Antike zum Mittelalter, (ed.) Paul Egon Hübinger, Darmstadt 1967 = Wege der Forschung vol. 201.

484 Godefroid Kurth, La cité de Liège au moyen-âge, 3 vols., Bruxelles 1910.

485 Dietrich Kurze, Pfarrerwahlen im Mittelalter, Köln, Graz 1966.

486 Bruno Kuske, Die Entstehung der Kreditwirtschaft und des Kapitalverkehrs, in: Die Kreditwirtschaft, vol. 1, Leipzig 1927 = Kölner Vorträge vols. 1 and 2; also in *idem*, Köln, der Rhein und das Reich. Beiträge aus fünf Jahrzehnten wirtschaftsgeschichtlicher Forschung, Köln, Graz, 1956.

487 Bruno Kuske, Die Handelsbeziehungen zwischen Köln und Italien im späten Mittelalter, in: Westdt. Zschr. 27, 1910.

488 Bruno Kuski, "Köln". Zur Geltung der Stadt, ihrer Waren und Maßstäbe in älterer Zeit, in: Jb. d. Köln. Geschichtsvereins 17, 1935.

489 Bruno Kuske, Die wirtschaftlichen Leistungen des Maasraumes im 12. und 13. Jahrhundert, in: Zwischen Rhein und Maas, Köln 1942.

490 Bruno Kuske, Quellen zur Geschichte des Kölner Handels und Verkehrs im

Mittelalter, 4 vols., Bonn 1917–1934 = Publikationen d. Ges. f. Rhein. Geschichtskunde 33.

491 Bruno Kuske, Die Wirtschaft der Stadt in älterer Zeit, in: Köln, (ed.) by the city of Cologne, Köln 1948.

492 José Maria Lacarra, Es desarollo de las ciudades de Navarra y Aragón en la Edad Medià, in: Pireneos 6, 1950.

493 José Maria Lacarra, Documentos para el estudio de la reconquista y repoblación del valle del Ebro, Zaragoza 1946–48 = Estudios de Edad Media de la Corona de Aragón vols 2 and 3.

494 José Maria Lacarra, Estella – San Sebastián. Fueros derivados de Jaca 1. Fueros de Navarra 1, Pamplona 1969.

495 José Maria Lacarra, Para el estudio del Municipio Navarro medieval, in: Principe de Viana 2, 1941.

496 Hertha Ladenbauer-Orel, Die Burganlage in der Restsiedlung des frühmittelalterlichen Wien, in: Deutsche Akad. d. Wiss. zu Berlin. Schriften d. Sektion f. Vor- und Frühgesch. 25, 1969.

497 Georges de Lagarde, La naissance de l'esprit laigue au déclin du moyen-âge. II. Secteur social de la scolastique, Louvain, Paris 1958. IV. Guillaume d'Ockham défense de l'Empire, Louvain, Paris 1962.

498 Henning Landgraf, Bevölkerung und Wirtschaft Kiels im 15. Jahrhundert, Neumünster 1959 = Quellen und Forschungen zur Geschichte Schleswig-Holsteins vol. 39.

499 Götz Landwehr, Die Verpfändung der deutschen Reichsstädte im Mittelalter, Köln, Graz 1967 = Forschungen zur deutschen Rechtsgeschichte vol. 5.

500 Gioacchino Lanza Tomasi, Le ville di Palermo, Palermo 1966.

501 Joseph Lappe, Wirtschaftsgeschichte der Städte des Kreises Lippstadt. 1. vol. Zur Geschichte der Sondergemeinde in den westfälischen Städten, in: VSWG 10, 1912.

502 Robert Latouche, La commune de Mans (1970), in: Mélanges d'histoire du moyen-âge dédiées à la mémoire de Louis Halphen, Paris 1951.

503 Robert Latouche, Histoire de Nice, 2 vols., Nice 1951–1955.

504 Friedrich Lau, Entwicklung der kommunalen Verfassung und Verwaltung der Stadt Köln bis zum Jahre 1396, Bonn 1898 = Preisschriften der Mevissenstiftung 1.

505 Friedrich Lau, Siegburg, Bonn 1907 = Quellen zur Rechts- und Wirtschaftsgeschichte der rheinischen Städte. Bergische Städte 1.

(282) Richard Laufner, (ed.), see under Die Frage der Kontinuität . . . (No. 282).

506 Richard Laufner, Hans Eichler, Hauptmarkt und Marktkreuz in Trier, Trier 1958.

507 Richard Laufner, Der älteste Koblenzer Zolltarif, in: Landeskundliche Vierteljahrsbll. 10, 1964.

(579) R[ichard] Laufner, Jürgen Sydow, suppl., see under Archäologische Methoden . . . (No. 579).

508 Henri Laurent, Un grand commerce d'exportation au moyen-âge. La draperie des Pays Bas en France et dans les pays méditerranéens, Paris 1935.

509 Viktor Nikitich Lazarev. L'art de la Russie médiévale et l'occident XIe–XVe siècles, in: XIIIe Congrès international des sciences historiques, Moscow 1970.

510 Lech Leciejewicz, Die Anfänge und die älteste Entwicklung der westpommerschen Ostseestädte, in: Archäologia Polona 3, 1960.

511 Erich v. Lehe, Die Märkte Hamburgs von den Anfängen bis in die Neuzeit, Wiesbaden 1966 = VSWG suppl. 50.

512 Erich v. Lehe, Die Schuldbücher von Lübeck, Riga und Hamburg, in: Städtewesen und Bürgertum als geschichtliche Kräfte. Gedächtnisschrift Fritz Rörig, (eds.), Ahasver v. Brandt and W. Koppe, Lübeck 1953.

513 Erich v. Lehe, Stade als Wikort der Frühzeit, in: Stader Jahrbuch 1948.

514 Karl Lehmann, Altnordische und hanseatische Handelsgesellschaften, in: Zschr. f. d. gesamte Handelsrecht 62, 1908.

515 François Lehoux, Le Bourg Saint-Germain-des-Prés depuis ses origines jusqu'à la fin de la Guerre de Cent Ans, Paris 1951.

516 Georges Lesage, Marseille angevine. Recherches sur son évolution administrative, économique et urbaine de la victoire de Charles d'Anjou à l'arrivée de Jeanne Ire (1264–1348), Paris 1950 = Bibliothèque des Ecoles françaises d'Athènes et de Rome No. 168.

517 Jean Lestocquoy, Abbayes et origines des villes, in: Revue d'hist. de l'Eglise de France 8, 1947.

518 Jean Lestocquoy, Etudes d'histoire urbaine. Villes et abbayes. Arras au moyenâge, Arras 1966.

519 Jean Lestocquoy, Aux origines de la bourgeoisie: Les villes de Flandre et d'Italie sous le gouvernement des patriciens. XIe–XVe siècles, Paris 1952.

520 Jean Lestocquoy, Patriciens du moyen-âge. Les dynasties bourgeoisies d'Arras du XIe au XVe siècle, Arras 1945 = Mém. de la Comm. dép des Mon. hist. du Pas-de-Calais vol. 5, No. 1.

521 Evariste Lévi-Provençal, Histoire de l'Espagne musulmane, vol. 3, Paris 1953.

522 Wilhelm Levison, Die Bonner Urkunden des frühen Mittelalters, in: Bonner Jahrbücher 136/37, 1932.

523 Ernst Levy, Weströmisches Vulgarrecht. Das Obligationenrecht, Weimar 1956.

524 Ernst Levy, Römishces Vulgarrecht und Kaiserrecht, Milano 1959.

525 Les libertés urbaines et rurales du XIe au XIVe siècle. Colloque international Spa 5–8 IX. 1966, Bruxelles 1968 = Pro Civitate. Collection Histoire in-8^0, No. 19.

526 Felix Liebermann, Die Gesetze der Angelsachsen, 3 vols., Halle 1903–1916. Reprinted Aalen 1960.

527 Folke Lindberg, Das Studium der Städtegeschichte in den skandinavischen Ländern, in: Cahiers bruxellois 12, 1967.

528 Mary D. Lobel, The Borough of Burg St. Edmund's, Oxford 1935.

529 Mary D. Lobel, Some Oxford Borough Customs, in: Miscellanea Mediaevalia in memoriam Jan Frederik Niermeyer, Groningen 1967.

(833) Mary D. Lobel, W.H. Johns, (ed.) see under Historic Towns ... (No. 833).

530 Heinrich v. Loesch, Die Grundlagen der ältesten Kölner Gemeindeverfassung, in: ZRG Germ. Abt. 53, 1932.

531 Heinrich v. Loesch, Die Kölner Kaufmannsgilde im 12. Jahrhundert, in: Westdt. Zschr. Ergänzungsheft 12, 1904.

532 Heinrich v. Loesch, Die Kölner Zunfturkunden nebst anderen Kölner Gewerbeurkunden bis zum Jahre 1500, 2 vols., Bonn 1907.

533 Maurice Lombard, L'évolution urbaine au moyen-âge, in: Annales. Economies, sociétés, civilisations 12, 1957.

534 Maurice Lombard, Un problème cartographié: le bois dans la médievale musulmane VIIe–XIe sc., in: Annales. Economies, sociétés, civilisations 14, 1959.

535 Maurice Lombard, La route de la Meuse et les relations lointaines des pays mosans entre le VIIIᵉ et le XIᵉ siècle, in: L'art mosan, (ed.) Pierre Francastel, Paris 1953.

536 Ropert S. Lopez, Aux origines du capitalisme Génois, in: Ann. d'hist. écon. et sociale 9, 1937.

537 Ropert S. Lopez, Le marchand génois, in: Annales. Economies, sociétés, civilisations 13, 1958.

538 Ropert S. Lopez, Storia delle colonie genovesi nel Mediterraneo, Bologna 1938.

539 Robert S. Lopez and Irving W. Raymond, Medieval trade in the Mediterranean world. Illustrate Documents, translated with introductions and notes, New York, London 1955.

540 Ferdinand Lot, Recherches sur la population et la superficie des cités remontant à la période gallo-romaine, 3 vols., Paris 1945–1953.

541 Henry Royston Loyn, Anglo-Saxon England and the Norman Conquest, London 1962.

542 Herbert Ludat, Die Bezeichnung für Stadt im Slawischen, in: Syntagma Friburgense. Historische Studien. Hermann Aubin dargebracht zum 70. Geburtstag, Lindau, Konstanz 1956.

543 Herbert Ludat, Frühformen des Städtewesens in Osteuropa, in: Studien zu den Anfängen des europäischen Städtewesens. Reichenau-Vorträge 1955–1956, Lindau, Konstanz 1958 = Vorträge und Forschungen no. 4.

544 Herbert Ludat, Die ostdeutschen Kietze, Bernburg 1936.

545 Herbert Ludat, Vorstufen und Entstehung des Städtewesens in Osteuropa, Köln-Braunsfeld 1955.

546 Friedrich Lütge, Geschichte der deutschen Agrarverfassung vom frühen Mittelalter bis zum 19. Jahrhundert, Stuttgart 1963 = Deutsche Agrargeschichte, (ed.) Günther Franz, vol. 3.

546a Friedrich Lütge, Deutsche Sozial- und Wirtschaftsgeschichte, 1952, Berlin, Göttingen, Heidelberg ³1966.

547 Friedrich Lütge, Strukturwandlung im ostdeutschen und osteuropäischen Fernhandel des 14. bis 16. Jahrhunderts, München 1964 = Sbb. d. Bayerischen Akad. d. Wiss., Phil.-hist. Kl. vol. 64, No. 1.

548 Agneta Lundström, Helgö als frühmittelalterlicher Handelsplatz in Mittelschweden, in: Frühmittelalterliche Studien 2, 1968.

549 Gustav Luntowski, Bemerkungen zu einigen Fragen der Sozial- und Verfassungsgeschichte der Städte Dortmund und Lüneburg, in: Beiträge z. Gesch. Dortmunds u. d. Graftschaft Mark 65, 1969.

550 Gustav Luntowski, Dortmunder Kaufleute in England im 13. und 14. Jahrhundert. Ein Quellennachweis, in: Beiträge z. Gesch. Dortmunds u. d. Graftschaft Mark 66, 1970.

551 Gino Luzzatto, Les activités économiques du patriciat vénétien (Xᵉ–XIVᵉ siècles), in: Ann. d'hist. écon. et sociale 9, 1937.

552 Gino Luzzatto, Storia economica di Venezia dall' XI al XVI secolo, Venezia 1961.

553 J. Lyna, Het onstaan der steden in de Massvallei. Synthetische studie, in: Miscellanea Jan Gessler, vol. 2, 's Gravenhage 1948.

554 Bryce Lyon, Medieval Constitutionalism: a Balance of Power, in: Album Helen

Maud Cam, 2 vols., Louvain 1960–1961 = Studies presented to the internat. Comm. for the History of Representative and Parliamentary Institutions 23.

555 Bryce Lyon, L'oeuvre de Henri Pirenne après vingt-cinq ans, in: Le Moyen Age 66, 1960.

556 Karl Maleczynski, Die ältesten Märkte in Polen und ihr Verhältnis zu den Städten vor der Kolonisierung nach dem deutschen Recht, Breslau 1930.

557 Joseph Maréchal, La colonie espagnole de Bruges du XIVe au XVIe siècle, in: Revue du Nord 35, 1953.

558 Chiaudano Mario, Le livre rouge de la Compagnie florentine de Jacopo Girolami . . . 1332–1337, Torino 1963.

559 Das Marktproblem im Mittelalter. Referate und Aussprachen auf der dritten arbeitstagung des Kreises für Stadtgeschichte 1960 in Konstanz, (ed.) Peter Schöller, in: Westfälische Forschungen 15, 1962.

560 Mina Martens, Le censier ducal de Bruxelles de 1321, Bruxelles 1958

561 Mina Martens, Les survivances domaniales du castrum carolingien de Bruxelles à la fin du moyen-âge, in: Le Moyen Age 69, 1963.

562 Lauro Martines, The Social World of the Florentine Humanists 1390–1460, London 1963.

563 Erich Maschke, Das Berufsbewußtsein des mittelalterlichen Fernkaufmanns, in: Miscellanea Medievalia, (ed.) Paul Wilpert and Willehad Eckert, vol. 3: Beiträge zum Berufsbewußtsein, Berlin 1964.

564 Erich Maschke, Continuité sociale et histoire urbaine médiévale, in: Annales. Economies, sociétés, civilisations 15, 1960.

(769) Erich Maschke, Jürgen Sydow, (eds.), siehe unter Spital und Stadt . . . (No. 769).

(776) Erich Maschke, Jürgen Sydow, (eds.), siehe unter Stadterweiterung und Vorstadt . . . (No. 776).

565 Erich Maschke, Deutsche Stadtgeschichtsforschung auf der Grundlage des historischen Materialismus, in: Esslinger Studien (Jb. f. Gesch. d. oberdt. Reichsstädte) 12/13, 1966/67.

566 Erich Maschke, Die Stellung der Reichsstadt Speyer in der mittelalterlichen Wirtschaft Deutschlands, in: VSWG 54, 1967.

567 Erich Maschke, Die Unterschichten der mittelalterlichen Städte Deutschlands, in: Gesellschaftliche Unterschichten in den südwestdeutschen Städten, (eds.) Erich Maschke and Jürgen Sydow, Stuttgart 1967 = Veröffentlichungen d. Komm. f. gesch. Landeskunde in Baden-Württemberg ser. B Forschungen vol. 41.

(840) Erich Maschke, Jürgen Sydow, (eds.), see under Gesellschaftliche Unterschichten . . . (No. 840).

568 Erich Maschke, Die Verbreitung des Speyerer Stadtrechts mit besonderer Berücksichtigung von Neustadt an der Haardt, in: *idem* and Geo. Friedrich Böhn, Beiträge zum Recht der Stadt Neustadt a. d. Haardt, Speyer 1962 = Veröffentlichungen zur Geschichte von Stadt und Kreis Neustadt a. d. Weinstraße 2.

569 Erich Maschke, Verfassung und soziale Kräfte in der deutschen Stadt des späten Mittelalters, vornehmlich in Oberdeutschland, in: VSWG 46, 1959.

570 Erich Maschke, Die Wirtschaftspolitik Kaiser Friedrichs II. im Königreich Sizilien, in: VSWG 53, 1966.

571 Mélanges M.N. Tichomirow. Problèmes sociopolit. de l'histoire de la Russie et des pays slaves (in Russian), Moscow 1963.

572 Federigo Melis, Aspetti della vita economica medievale. Studi nell' archivio Datini di Prato, Siena 1962.

573 James Mellaart, Catal Hüyük, Stadt aus der Steinzeit, Bergisch Gladbach 1967.

574 Guido Mengozzi, La città italiana nell'alto medioevo. Il periodo longobardo-franco, Firenze ²1931.

575 Johannes Bernhard Menke, Geschichtsschreibung und Politik in deutschen Städten des Spätmittelalters, in: Jb. d. Köln. Geschichtsvereins 33, 1958; 34/35, 1959/60.

576 Margarete Merores, Gaëta im frühen Mittelalter. (8–12. Jhd.), Gotha 1911.

577 Margarete Merores, Der große Rat von Venedig und die sog. Serrata vom Jahre 1297, in: VSWG 21, 1928.

578 Friedrich Merzbacher, Die Bischofsstadt, Köln, Opladen 1961 = Arbeitsgemeinschaft f. Forschung d. Landes Nordrhein-Westfalen. Geisteswiss. No. 93.

579 Archäologische Methoden und Quellen zur Stadtkernforschung und ihr Verhältnis zu den historischen Quellen und Methoden. Protokoll der Tagung des Arbeitskreises für Stadtforschung der Arbeitsgemeinschaft Hist. Komm. und landesgesch. Institute Deutschlands in Hamburg 1959, (ed.) Richard Laufner and Jürgen Sydow, in: Westfälische Forschungen 13, 1960.

580 Friedrich Metz, Die Tiroler Stadt, in: Land und Leute. Gesammelte Beiträge zur deutschen Landes- und Volksforschung, (ed.) Emil Meynen and Ruthardt Oehme, Stuttgart 1961.

581 Gunnar Mickwitz, Die Kartellfunktionen der Zünfte und ihre Bedeutung bei der Entstehung des Zunftwesens, Helsingfors, Leipzig 1936.

582 Alexander Mitscherlich, Die Unwirtlichkeit unserer Städte. Anstiftung zum Unfrieden, Frankfurt a. M. ⁷1969.

583 Heinrich Mitteis, Über den Rechtsgrund des Satzes "Stadtluft macht frei", in: Festschrift Edmund E. Stengel zum 70. Geburtstag, Münster, Köln 1952.

584 Michael Mitterauer, Jahrmärkte in Nachfolge antiker Zentralorte, in: MIÖG 75, 1967.

585 Michael Mitterauer, Zollfreiheit und Marktbereich, in: Forschungen zur Landeskunde von Niederösterreich 19, 1969.

586 Sergio Mochi-Onory, Vescovi e Città, Bologna 1933.

587 Bernd Möller, Frömmigkeit in Deutschland um 1500, in: Archiv für Reformationsgeschichte 56, 1965.

588 Sibyl Moholy-Nagy, Die Stadt als Schicksal, München 1968.

589 Michel Mollat, Les affaires de Jacques Coeur, 2 vols., Paris 1952–1953.

590 Michel Mollat, Le commerce de la Haute Normandie au XVᵉ sc. et au début du XVIᵉ sc., Paris 1953.

591 M. Mollat, P. Johansen, M. Postan, A. Sapori, Ch. Verlinden, L'économie européenne aux deux derniers siècles du moyen-âge, in: X. Congresso internaz. Sc. Stor. Rom 1955. Relazioni Vol. VI.

592 Michel Mollat, Rouen, avant-port de Paris à la fin du moyen-âge, in: Bull. Soc. Etudes hist., géo. et scientifiques régions parisiennes 71, 1951.

593 Karl Mollay, Das Ofener Stadtrecht, Eine deutschsprachige Rechtssammlung des 15. Jhds. aus Ungarn, Weimar 1959 = Monumenta hist. Budapestiensia 1.

594 Roger Mols, Introduction à la démographie historique des villes d'Europe du XIVe au XVIIIe siècle, 3 vols., Louvain 1954–1956 = Université de Louvain. Recueil de travaux d'histoire et de philogie. 4e ser. No. 1, 2, 3.

595 Moneta et scambi nell'alto medioevo, Spoleto 1961 = Settimane di studio del centro ital. di studi sull'alto medioevo 8.

596 Carlo Guido Mor, Moneta publica civitatis Mantuae, in: Studi in onore di Gino Luzzatto, Milano 1949.

597 Carlo Guido Mor, Pavia Capitale, in: Atti del 4⁰ Congresso internazionale di studi sull'alto medioevo Pavia 1967, Spoleto 1969.

598 Jacques Moreau, Die Kelten im Saarland, in: Saarbrücker Hefte 11, 1960.

599 Jacques Moreau, Die Welt der Kelten. Große Kulturen der Frühzeit, Stuttgart 1958.

600 Heinz v. d. Mühlen, Versuch einer soziologischen Erfassung der Bevölkerung Revals im Spätmittelalter, in: Hans. Geschbll. 75, 1957.

(284) Wolfgang Müller, (ed.), see under Freiburg im Mittelalter . . . (No. 284).

601 Lewis Mumford, Die Stadt. Geschichte und Ausblick, Köln, Berlin 1961.

602 Hans Nabholz, Die Anfänge der hochmittelalterlichen Stadt und ihrer Verfassung als Frage der Forschungsmethode betrachtet, in: Bericht über die konstituierende Versammlung des Verbandes österreichischer Geschichtsvereine vom 21–24. September 1949, (ed.) Hanns Leo Mikoletzky, Wien 1950.

603 Emilio Nasalli Rocca, Palazzi e torri gentilizie nei quartieri delle città italiani medioevali. L'esempia di Piacenza, in: Contributi dell'Istituto di storia medioevale vol. 1, Milano 1968.

604 Elis. Nau, Stadt und Münze im frühen und hohen Mittelalter, in: Esslinger Studien 10, 1964.

605 Elis. Nau, Stadt und Münze im späten Mittelalter und beginnender Neuzeit, in: Bll. f. dt. Landesgesch. 100, 1964.

606 Herbert Nesselhauf, Die spätrömische Verwaltung der gallisch-germanischen Länder, Berlin 1938 = Abh. d. Preußischen Akad. d. Wiss., Phil.-hist. Kl. 2.

607 Eva Gertrud Neumann, Rheinisches Beginen- und Begardenwesen, in: Mainzer Abhandlungen z. mittleren und neueren Gesch. 4, 1960.

608 David M. Nicholas, The population of 14th century Ghent, in: Handelingen d. Maatschappij v. Geschiedenis en Oudheidkunde te Gent new ser. 24, 1970.

609 Ernst Nickel, Der Alte Markt in Magdeburg, Berlin 1964 = Ergebnisse d. archäolog. Stadtkernforschung in Magdeburg vol. 1 = Deutsche Akad. d. Wiss. zu Berlin. Schriften d. Sektion f. Vor- und Frühgeschichte vol. 18.

610 J.F. Niermeyer, Schreef Alpertus van Metz over verscheidenheid van tijden of van zeden?, in: Jan Gessler, Miscellanea, vol. 2, 's Gravenhage 1948.

611 John T. Noonan, The scholastic analysis of usury, Cambridge/Mass. 1957.

612 Claus Nordmann, Oberdeutschland und die deutsche Hanse, Lübeck 1939 = Pfingstbll. d. Hans. Geschver. 26.

613 Otto Nübel, Mittelalterliche Beginen- und Sozialsiedlungen in den Niederlanden. Ein Beitrag zur Vorgeschichte der Fuggerei, Tübingen 1970 = Studien zur Fuggergeschichte 23.

614 Nürnberg – Geschichte einer europäischen Stadt, (ed.) Gerhard Pfeiffer, München 1971.

615 Friedrich Wilh. Oediger, Über die Bildung der Geistlichen im späten Mittelalter, Leiden, Köln 1953.

(670) Friedrich Wilhelm Oediger, (ed.), see under Die Regesten der Erzbischöfe von Köln . . . (No. 670).

616 Konrad Onasch, Gross-Nowgorod. Aufstieg und Niedergang einer russischen Stadtrepublik, Wien, München, Leipzig 1969.

617 Les origines des villes polonaises, Paris 1960 = EPHE VIe sec. Sér. Congrès et colloques 2.

618 Madeleine Oursel-Quarré, Les origines de la commune de Dijon, Dijon o. J. (1947).

619 Max Pappenheim, Die altdänischen Schutzgilden, Breslau 1885.

620 Max Pappenheim, Ein altnorwegisches Schutzgildestatut, Breslau 1888.

621 Johannes Papritz, Das Handelshaus der Loitz zu Stettin, Danzig und Lüneburg, in: Baltische Studien new ser. 44, 1957.

622 Hans Patze, Recht und Verfassung Thüringischer Städte, Weimar 1955 = Thüringische Archivstudien vol. 6.

623 I. Peri, Città e campagna in Sicilia, in: Atti della Accad. di Scienze, Lettere e Arti di Palermo ser. 4 vol. 13, 1953.

624 Charles Edmond Perrin, Catalogue des chartes de franchises de la Lorraine. Antérieures à 1350, Metz 1924. Aus: Annuaire d'hist. et d'archéol. lorr. vol. 33, 1924.

625 Charles Edmond Perrin, Chartes, franchises et rapports de droit en Lorraine, in: Le Moyen Age 42, 1946.

626 Günter Peters, Norddeutsches Beginen- und Begardenwesen im Mittelalterer, in: Niedersächs. Jb. f. Landesgesch. 41/42, 1969/70.

627 Charles Petit-Dutaillis, Les communes françaises au XIIe sc. Charte de Commune et chartes de franchises, in: Revue hist. de droit français et étranger 23, 1944.

628 Charles Petit-Dutaillis, Les communes françaises, caractères et évolution des origines au XVIIIe siècle, Paris 1947. English translation, The French Communes in the Middle Ages, vol. 6 of this series, Amsterdam 1977.

629 Franz Petri, Die Anfänge des mittelalterlichen Städtewesens in den Niederlanden und dem angrenzenden Frankreich, in: Studien zu den Anfängen des europäischen Städtewesens. Reichenau-Vorträge 1955–1956, Lindau, Konstanz 1958 = Vorträge und Forschungen vol. 4.

(150) Franz Petri, Georg Droege, (eds.), see under Collectanea Franz Steinbach (No. 150).

630 Franz Petri, Die Stellung der Südersee- und Ijsselstädte im flandrisch-hansischen Raum, in: Hans. Geschbll. 79, 1961.

631 Franz Petri, Merovingerzeitliche Voraussetzungen für die Entwicklung des Städtewesens zwischen Maas und Rhein, in: Bonner Jahrbücher 158, 1958.

632 Harald v. Petrikovits, Rezension zu Sheppard Frere, Britannia: A History of Roman Britain, London 1967, in: Bonner Jahrbücher 170, 1970.

633 Harald v. Petrikovits, Das römische Rheinland. Archäologische Forschungen seit 1945, Köln, Opladen 1960.

634 Hans Conrad Peyer, Zur Getriedepolitik oberitalienischer Städte im 13. Jahrhundert, Wien 1950 = Veröffentlichungen d. Instituts f. Österreichische Geschichtsforschung 12.

635 Hans Conrad Peyer, Stadt und Stadtpatron im mittelalterlichen Italien, Zürich

1955 = Wirtschaft, Gesellschaft, Staat. Züricher Studien zur allgemeinen Geschichte 13.

636 Hans Conrad Peyer, Żürich im Früh- und Hochmittelalter, in: Zürich von der Urzeit zum Mittelalter, Zürich 1971.

637 Gerhard Pfeiffer, Die Bündnis- und Landfreidenspolitik der Territorien zwischen Weser und Rhein im späten Mittelalter, in: Der Raum Westfalen, vol. II, 1, (eds.) Hermann Aubin and Franz Petri, Münster 1955.

(614) Gerhard Pfeiffer, (ed.) see under Nürnberg... (No. 614).

638 Max Pfütze, Burg und Stadt in der deutschen Literatur des Mittelalters, Halle 1958.

639 Othmar Pickl, Das älteste Geschäftsbuch Österreichs. Die Gewölberegister der Wiener Neustädter Firma Alexius Funck (1516–ca. 1538), Graz 1966 = Forschungen zur geschichtlichen Landeskunde der Steiermark 23.

640 Stanislaw Piekarczyk, Studien zur Geschichte der polnischen Städte im 13–14. Jahrhundert, Warsaw 1955.

641 Henri Pirenne, L'instruction des marchands au moyen-âge, in: Annales. Economies, sociétés, civilisations 1, 1929.

642 Henri Pirenne, Mahomet et Charlemagne, Paris 1937. German ed. by Paul Egon Hübinger, Geburt des Abendlandes. Untergang der Antike am Mittelmeer und Aufstieg des germanischen Mittelalters, Amsterdam 1940.

643 Henri Pirenne, Les villes et les institutions urbaines, 2 vols., Paris ⁴1939.

644 Ernst Pitz, Die Entstehung der Ratsherrschaft in Nürnberg im 13. und 14. Jhd., München 1956 = Schriftenreihe zur bayerischen Landesgeschichte No. 55.

645 Ernst Pitz, Schrift- und Aktenwesen der städtischen Verwaltung im Spätmittelalter, Köln 1959 = Mitteilungen aus dem Stadtarchiv Köln No. 45.

646 Ernst Pitz, Die Wirtschaftskrise des Spätmittelalters, in: VSWG 52, 1965.

647 Hans Planitz, Frühgeschichte der deutschen Stadt, in: ZRG Germ. Abt. 63, 1943.

648 Hans Planitz, Zur Geschichte des städtischen Meliorats, in: ZRG Germ. Abt. 67, 1950.

649 Hans Planitz, Handelsverkehr und Kaufmannsrecht im fränkischen Reich, in: Festschrift Ernst Heymann zum 70. Geburtstag, 2 vols. Weimar 1940.

650 Hans Planitz, Die Handfeste von Huy von 1066, der älteste städtische Freiheitsbrief im deutschen Reich, in: Rheinische Kulturgeschichte in Querschnitten aus Mittelalter und Neuzeit, (ed.) Gerhard Kallen, vol. III: Zwischen Rhein und Maas, Köln 1942.

651 Hans Planitz, Kaufmannsgilde und städtische Eidgenossenschaft in niederfränkischen Städten im 11. und 12. Jahrhundert, in: ZRG Germ. Abt. 60, 1940.

652 Hans Planitz, Konstitutivakt und Eintragung in den Kölner Schreinsurkunden des 12. und 13. Jhds., in: Festschrift Alfred Schultze zum 70. Geburtstag, (ed.) Walther Merk, Weimar 1934.

653 Hans Planitz, Das Kölner Recht und seine Verbreitung in der späteren Kaiserzeit, Weimar 1935. Auch in: ZRG Germ. Abt. 55, 1935.

654 Hans Planitz, Die deutsche Stadt im Mittelalter von der Römerzeit bis zu den Zunftkämpfen, Graz, Köln 1954.

655 Hans Planitz, Die deutsche Stadtgemeinde, in: ZRG Germ. Abt. 64, 1944.

656 Hans Planitz, Studien zur Rechtsgeschichte des städtischen Patriziats, in: MIÖG 58, 1950.

657 Henri Plotelle, La reconstruction d'une ville d'après un incendie urbain au moyen-âge, in: Album J. Balon, Namur 1968.

658 G. de Poerck, La draperie médiévale en Flandre et en Artois, Bruges 1951 = Rijksuniversiteit te Gent. Werken . . . No. 110.

659 Marcel Poëte, Une vie de cité, Paris, dès sa naissance à nos jours, Paris 1924.

660 Austin Lane Poole, Medieval England, Oxford 1958.

661 M.M. Postan, Die wirtschaftlichen Grundlagen der mittelalterlichen Gesellschaft, in: Jahrbücher f. Nationalökonomie u. Statistik 166, 1954.

662 Eileen Power, Medieval English wool trade, London 1941.

663 W. Prevenier, De Leden en de Staaten van Vlaanderen (1384–1405), Bruxelles 1961 = Verhandelingen v. d. Koninkl. Vlaamse Acad. v. Wetensch., Letteren en Schone Kunsten v. Belgie. Kl. d. Letteren vol. 23, No. 43.

664 C.W. Prévité-Orton, The Italien Cities till c. 1200, in: The Cambridge Medieval History vol. 5, Cambridge 1926.

665 Joseph Prinz, Mimigernaford – Münster. Die Entstehungsgeschichte einer Stadt, Münster 1960 = Geschichtl. Arbeiten zur westfäl. Landesforschung 4 = Veröffentlichungen d. Hist. Komm. Westfalens 22.

666 Horst Rabe, Der Rat der niederschwäbischen Reichsstädte, Köln, Graz 1966 = Forschungen zur deutschen Rechtsgeschichte vol. 4. Jur. Diss. Tübingen 1963.

667 Elis. Raiser, Städtische Territorialpolitik im Mittelalter, Lübeck, Hamburg 1969.

668 Virginia Rau, Subsidios para o Estudo das Feirias medievas portuguesas, Lissabon 1943.

669 Recueil des actes de Philippe Auguste Roi de France, (ed.) H. François Delaborde and Ch. Petit-Dutaillis, 2 vols., Paris 1916, 1943.

670 Die Regesten der Erzbischöfe von Köln im Mittelalter. vol. I: 313–1099, (ed.) Freidrich Wilhelm Oediger, Bonn 1954–1961. vols. II (1100–1205), III, 1 (1205–1261), III, 2 (1261–1304) (ed.) Richard Knipping, Bonn 1901–1913. vol. IV (1304–1332), (ed.) W. Kisky, Bonn 1915 = Publikationen d. Ges. f. Rhein. Geschichtskunde 21.

671 Siegfried Reicke, Das deutsche Spital und sein Recht, Stuttgart 1932.

672 Heinrich Reincke, Bevölkerungsprobleme der Hansestädte, in: Hans. Geschbll. 70, 1951.

673 Heinrich Reincke, Forschungen und Skizzen zur Geschichte Hamburgs, Hamburg 1951.

674 Heinrich Reincke, Kölner, Soester, Lübecker und Hamburger Reckt in ihren gegenseitigen Beziehungen, in: Hans. Geschbll. 69, 1950.

675 Heinrich Reincke, Über Städtegründung. Betrachtungen und Phantasien, in: Hans. Geschbll. 75, 1957.

676 Wilhelm Reinecke, Geschichte der Stadt Cambrai bis zur Erteilung der Lex Godefridi (1227), Marburg 1896.

677 Wilhelm Reinecke, Lüneburg als Hansestadt, Lüneburg ²1940.

678 Yves Renouard, Bordeaux sous les rois d'Angleterre, Bordeaux 1965 = Histoire de Bordeaux 3.

679 Yves Renouard, Histoire de Florence, Paris ²1967.

680 Yves Renouard, Les hommes d'affaires italiens au moyen-âge, Paris 1949.

681 Yves Renouard, Les villes d'Italie de la fin du Xe siècle au début du XIVe siècle, new ed. Rh. Braunstein, vol. 1, Paris 1969.

682 Hans Jürgen Rieckenberg, Arnold Walpot, der Initiator des Rheinischen Bundes von 1254, in: Deutsches Archiv 16, 1960.

683 Siegfried Rietschel, Das Burggrafenamt und die hohe Gerichtsbarkeit in den deutschen Bischofsstädten während des frühen Mittelalters, Leipzig 1905.

684 Siegfried Rietschel, Die civitas auf deutschem Boden bis zum Ausgang der Karolingerzeit, Leipzig 1894.

685 Siegfried Rietschel, Markt und Stadt in ihrem rechtlichen Verhältnis, Leipzig 1897.

686 Rimberti vita Anskarii, (ed.) Georg Waitz, Hannover 1884 = MGH SS rer. Germ. in usum scholarum . . . 55.

687 Michel Roblin, Cités ou citadelles? Les enceintes romaines du Bas-Empire d'après l'exemple de Paris, in: Revue des Etudes anciennes 53, 1951.

688 Michel Roblin, Le terroir de Paris aux époques gallo-romaine et franque, Paris 1951.

689 Fritz Rörig, Hansische Beiträge zur deutschen Wirtschaftsgeschichte, Breslau 1928 = Schriften der Baltischen Kommission zu Kiel vol. 9 = Veröffentlichungen d. Schleswig-Holsteinischen Universitätsgesellschaft No. 12.

690 Fritz Rörig, Heinrich der Löwe und die Gründung Lübecks. Grundsätzliche Erörterung zur städtischen Ostseesiedlung, in: Deutsches Archiv 1, 1937.

691 Fritz Rörig, Magdeburgs Entstehung und die ältere Handelsgeschichte, in: Miscellanea Academica Berolinensia. Gesammelte Abhandlungen zur Feier des 250 jährigen Bestehens der Deutschen Akad. d. Wiss. zu Berlin, vol. II, 1, Berlin 1950.

692 Fritz Rörig, Das Meer und das europäische Mittelalter, in: Zschr. d. Vereins f. Hamburgische Geschichte 41, 1951.

693 Fritz Rörig, Mittelalter und Schriftlichkeit, in: Die Welt als Geschichte 13, 1953.

694 Fritz Rörig, Wirtschaftskräfte im Mittelalter. Abhandlungen zur Stadt- und Hansegeschichte, (ed.) Paul Kaegbein, Weimar 1959. 2 ed. Wien, Köln, Graz 1971.

695 Barbara Rohwer, Der friesische Handel im frühen Mittelalter, Kiel 1937. Phil. Thesis Kiel 1935.

696 Raymond de Roover, Banking and Credit in Medieval Bruges, Cambridge (Mass.) 1948.

697 Raymond de Roover, L'évolution de la lettre de change, Paris 1953 = EPHE VIᵉ sec. Sér. Affaires et gens d'affaires 4.

698 Raymond de Roover, The Rise and Decline of the Medici Bank (1397–1494), Cambridge (Mass.) 1963.

699 Tadeusz Rosłanowski, Recherches sur la vie urbaine et en particulier sur le patriciat dans les villes de la moyenne Rhénanie septentrionale, Warsaw 1964.

700 Félix Rousseau, La Meuse et le pays Mosan en Belgique, Namur 1930.

(809) Nicolai Rubenstein, (ed.), see under Florentine Studies . . . (No. 809).

701 Giuseppe Russo, Napoli come città, Napoli 1966.

702 Et. Sabbe, Quelques types des marchands des IXᵉ et Xᵉ siècles, in: Revue belge de phil. et d'hist. 13, 1934.

703 Henryk Samsonowicz, Untersuchungen über das Danziger Bürgerkapital in der zweiten Hälfte des 15. Jahrhunderts, Weimar 1969 = Abhandlungen zur Handels- und Sozialgeschichte 8.

704 Claudio Sanchez-Albornoz, Una ciudad de la España cristiana hace mil anos. Estampas de la vida en León. Prólogo sobre el habla de la época por Ramón Menéndez Pidal, Madrid 1966 (Reprint of a work first published in 1926.)

705 Claudio Sanchez-Albornoz, España. Un enigma historico, 2 vols., Buenos Aires no date.

706 Claudio Sanchez-Albornoz, Ruina y extincion del municipio romano en España et instituciones que le reemplazan, Buenos Aires 1943.

707 Paul Sander, Geschichte des deutschen Städtewesens, Bonn, Leipzig 1922.

708 Armando Sapori, Le marchand italien au moyen-âge, Paris 1952 = EPHE VIe sec. Ser. Affaires et gens d'affaires 1.

709 A.E. Sayous, Les opérations des banquiers italiens en Italie et aux foires de la Champagne pendant le XIIIe siècle, in: Revue hist. 170, 1932.

710 Marianne Schalles-Fischer, Pfalz und Fiskus Frankfurt, Göttingen 1969 = Veröffentlichungen des Max-Planck-Instituts für Geschichte 20.

711 Adolf Schaube, Handelsgeschichte der romanischen Völker des Mittelmeergebietes bis zum Ende der Kreuzzüge, München, Berlin 1906.

712 Emil Schaus, Stadtrechtsorte und Flecken im Regierungsbezirk Koblenz, in: Rhein. Heimatpflege 7, 1935; 8, 1936; 9, 1937.

713 Emil Schaus, Stadtrechtsorte und Flecken im Regierungsbezirk Trier und im Landkreis Birkenfeld, Trier 1958.

714 Jos. Schepers, Mittelmeerländische Einflüsse in der Bau- und Wohnkultur des westlichen Mitteleuropas, in: Europäische Kulturverflechtungen im Bereich der volkstümlichen Überlieferung. Festschrift zum 65. Geburtstag Bruno Schiers, (ed.) Gerhard Heilfurth and Hinrich Siuts, Göttingen 1967 = Veröffentlichungen des Instituts für mitteleuropäische Volksforschung an der Philipps-Universitat Marburg/L. vol. 5.

715 Luigi Schiaparelli, I Diplomi di Ugo e di Lotario, di Berengario e di Adalberto, Roma 1924.

716 Karl Schib, Der Schaffhauser Adel im Mittelalter, in: Zschr. f. Schweizerische Gesch. 18, 1938.

717 Karl Schib, Geschichte der Stadt Schaffhausen, Thayngen-Schaffhausen 1945.

718 Reinhard Schindler, Ausgrabungen in Alt-Hamburg. Neue Ergebnisse zur Frühgeschichte der Hansestadt, Hamburg 1957.

719 Reinhard Schindler, Hamburgs Frühzeit im Lichte der Ausgrabungen, in: Zschr. d. Vereins f. Hamburgische Geschichte 43, 1956.

720 Wilhelm Schleiermacher, Die spätesten Spuren der antiken Besiedlung im Raum von Speyer, Worms, Mainz, Frankfurt und Ladenburg, in: Bonner Jahrbücher 162, 1962.

721 Walter Schlesinger, Die Anfänge der Stadt Chemnitz, Weimar 1952.

722 Walter Schlesinger, Beiträge zur deutschen Verfassungsgeschichte des Mittelalters, 2 vols., Göttingen 1963.

723 Walter Schlesinger, Beobachtungen zur Geschichte und Gestalt der Aachener Pfalz in der Zeit Karls des Großen, in: Studien zur europäischen Vor- und Frühgeschichte, (ed.) Martin Claus, Werner Haarnagel, Klaus Raddatz, Neumünster 1968.

724 Walter Schlesinger, Burg und Stadt, in: Aus Verfassungs- und Landesgeschichte. Festschrift für Theodor Mayer, vol. 1, Lindau, Konstanz 1954. Also in: idem., Beiträge zur deutschen Verfassungsgeschichte . . ., vol. 2.

725 Walter Schlesinger, Forum, Villa fori, Jus fori. Einige Bemerkungen zu den Marktgründungsurkunden des 12. Jhds. aus Mitteldeutschland, in: Aus Geschichte und Landeskunde. Forschungen und Darstellungen Franz Steinbach zum 65. Geburtstag gewidmet, Bonn 1960. Also in *idem.*, Mitteldeutsche Beiträge zur deutschen Verfassungsgeschichte des Mittelalters, Göttingen 1961.

726 Walter Schlesinger, Städtische Frühformen zwischen Rhein und Elbe, in: Studien zu den Anfängen des europäischen Städtewesens, Lindau, Konstanz 1958 = Vorträge und Forschungen vol. 4. Also in *idem.*, Beiträge zur deutschen Verfassungsgeschichte ..., vol. 2.

727 Walter Schlesinger, Zur Frühgeschichte des norddeutschen Städtewesens, in: Lüneburger Blätter 17, 1966.

728 Walter Schlesinger, Zur Geschichte der Magdeburger Königspfalz, in: Bll. f. dt. Landesgesch. 104, 1968.

729 Walter Schlesinger, Herrschaft und Gefolgschaft in der germanisch-deutschen Verfassungsgeschichte, in: Hz 176, 1953. Also in *idem.*, Beiträge zur deutschen Verfassungsgeschichte ..., vol. 1.

730 Walter Schlesinger, Pfalz und Stadt Ulm bis zur Stauferzeit, in: Ulm und Oberschwaben, Zschr. f. Gesch. u. Kunst 38, 1967.

731 Walter Schlesinger, Pfalzen und Königshöfe in Württembergisch Franken und angrenzenden Gebieten, in: Jahrb. d. Hist. Ver. f. Württ. Franken 53, 1969.

732 Walter Schlesinger, Stadt und Burg im Lichte der Wortgeschichte, in: Studium Generale 16, 1963.

733 Walter Schlesinger, Das älteste Freiburger Stadtrecht, in: ZRG Germ. Abt. 83, 1966.

734 Walter Schlesinger, Über mitteleuropäische Städtelandschaften der Frühzeit, in: Bll. f. dt. Landesgesch. 93, 1957. Also in *idem.*, Beiträge zur deutschen Verfassungsgeschichte ..., vol. 2.

735 Heinrich Felix Schmid, Dalmatinische Stadtbücher, in: Kosow Zbornik–Mélanges Kos, Laibach 1953 = Zgodovinski Časopis – Historical Review – 6/7, 1952/53.

736 Heinrich Felix Schmid, Das Weiterleben und die Wiederbelebung antiker Institutionen im mittelalterlichen Städtewesen, in: Annali di storia del diritto 1, 1957.

737 Heinrich Schmidt, Die deutschen Städtechroniken als Spiegel des bürgerlichen Selbstverständnisses im Spätmittelalter, Göttingen 1958.

738 Hartmut Schmökel, Die Ausgrabungen in Vorderasien seit 1945, in: Die Welt als Geschichte 21, 1961; 22, 1962.

739 Gustav Schmoller, Deutsches Städtewesen in älterer Zeit, Bonn, Leipzig 1922.

740 Georg Schneider, Die finanziellen Beziehungen der florentinischen Bankiers zur Kirche von 1285–1304, Leipzig 1899 = Staats- und Sozialwissenschaftliche Forschungen, (ed.) Gustav Schmoller, vol. 17 No. 1.

741 Jean Schneider, Les marchands siennois et la Lorraine au XIIIe siècle, in: Studi in onore di Armando Sapori, 2 vols., Milano 1957.

742 Jean Schneider, La ville de Metz au XIIIe et XIVe siècles, Nancy 1950.

743 Peter Schöller, Aufgaben und Probleme der Stadtgeographie, in: Erdkunde 7, 1953.

(179) Peter Schöller, (ed.), see under Diskussion um die frühen Gründungsstädte ... (No. 179).

(559) Peter Schöller, (ed.), see under Das Marktproblem im Mittelalter ... (No. 559).

744 Peter Schöller, Die deutschen Städte, Wiesbaden 1967 = Erdkundliches Wissen 17.

(204) August Schoop, (ed.), see under Düren ... (No. 204).

745 Gertrud Schubard-Fikentscher, Die Verbreitung der deutschen Stadtrechte in Osteuropa, Weimar 1942 = Forschungen zum Deutschen Recht IV, 3.

746 Adolf Schück, Die deutsche Einwanderung in das mittelalterliche Schweden und ihre kommerziellen und sozialen Folgen, in: Hans. Geschbll. 55, 1930.

747 Konrad Schünemann, Die Entstehung des Städtewesens in Südosteuropa, Breslau no date (1929) = Südosteuropäische Bibliothek 1 = Veröffentlichungen der Arbeitsgemeinschaft für Südosteuropaforschung an der Universität Berlin 1.

748 Aloys Schulte, Geschichte des mittelalterlichen Handels und Verkehrs zwischen Westdeutschland und Italien mit Ausschluß Venedigs, 2 vols., Leipzig 1900.

749 Aloys Schulte, Geschichte der Großen Ravensburger Handelsgesellschaft 1380–1530, 3 vols., Stuttgart 1923, Reprinted Wiesbaden 1964 = Deutsche Handelsakten des Mittelalters und der Neuzeit vol. 1–3.

750 Aloys Schulte, Pavia und Regensburg, in: Hist. Jahrb. d. Görresgesellsch. 52, 1932.

751 Aloys Schulte, Regensburg und seine Eigenart in der deutschen Geschichte, in: Volkstum und Kulturpolitik. Eine Sammlung von Aufsätzen gewidmet Georg Schreiber zum 50. Geburtstag, (ed.) H. Konen and J.P. Steffens, Köln 1932.

752 Werner Schultheiss, Geschichte des Nürnberger Ortsrechtes. Historische Einleitung zur Ausgabe 1956 des "Nürnberger Ortsrechtes", Nürnberg 1957.

753 Joh. Schultze, Die Stadtviertel. Ein städtegeschichtliches Problem, in: Bll. f. dt. Landesgesch. 92, 1956.

754 Knut Schulz, Ministerialität und Bürgertum in Trier, Bonn 1968 = Rheinisches Archiv 66.

755 Knut Schulz, Die Ministerialität als Problem der Stadtgeschichte, in: RhVjbll. 32, 1968.

756 Herbert Schwarzwälder, Bremen im Mittelalter. Gestaltwandel einer "gewachsenen" Stadt in ganzheitlicher Sicht, in: Stadium Generale 16, 1963.

757 Herbert Schwarzwälder, Entstehung und Anfänge der Stadt Bremen. Bremen 1955 = Veröffentlichungen aus dem Staatsarchiv der Freien Hansestadt Bremen No. 24.

758 Wilhelm Schwer, Stand und Ständeordnung im Weltbild des Mittelalters. Die geistes- und gesellschaftsgeschichtlichen Grundlagen der berufsständischen Idee, Paderborn 1934 = Veröffentlichungen d. Sekt. f. Sozial- und Wirtschaftswiss. Görresges. z. Pflege d. Wiss. i. kath. Deutschland 7.

759 Ernst Frh. v. Schwind, Alfons Dopsch, Ausgewählte Urkunden zur Verfassungsgeschichte der deutsch-österreichischen Erblande im Mittelalter, Innsbruck 1895. Reprinted Aalen 1968.

760 Giandomenico Serra, Contributo alla storia dei derivati di "Burgus" Borgale Borgaria Borgoro, in: Filologia Romanza 5, 1958.

761 J. Serra Vilaró, Historia de Cardona, Tarragona 1966.

762 Ernesto Sestan, La città comunale italiana dei secoli XI–XIII nellè sue note caratteristiche rispetto al movimento comunale europeo, in: Miscellanea historiae ecclesiasticae. XIe congrès international des sciences historiques Stock-

holm 1960, Louvain 1961 = Bibliothèque de la Revue d'Hist. Ecclésiastique No. 38.

763 Wilhelm Silberschmidt, Die Bedeutung der Gilde, insbesondere der Handelsgilde für die Entstehung der italienischen Städtefreiheit, in: ZRG Germ. Abt. 51, 1931.

764 Luigi Simeoni, La liberazione dei servi a Bologna nel 1256–1257, in: Archivio storico italiano 109, 1952.

765 Lucien Sittler, La decapole alsacienne des origines à la fin du moyen-âge, Strasbourg, Paris 1955.

766 Z.W. Sneller, Deventer, die Stadt der Jahrmärkte, Lübeck 1936 = Pfingstbll. d. Hans. Geschver. 25.

767 Jacob Sommer, Westfälisches Gildewesen mit Ausschluß der geistlichen Bruderschaften und Gewerbegilden, in: Archiv f. Kulturgeschichte 7, 1909.

768 T. de Souza Soares, Apontamentos para o estudo da origem das instituiceos municipais portuguesas, Lisbon 1936.

769 Spital und Stadt. Protokoll der zweiten Arbeitstagung des Arbeitskreises für südwestdeutsche Stadtgeschichtsforschung, (ed.) Erich Maschke and Jürgen Sydow, Tübingen 1963.

770 Rolf Sprandel, Das Eisengewerbe im Mittelalter, Stuttgart 1968.

771 Rolf Sprandel, Die Handwerker in den nordwestdeutschen Städten des Spätmittelalters, in: Hans. Geschbll. 86, 1968.

772 Heinrich Sproemberg, Die Hanse in europäischer Sicht, in: Annales de la Société Royale d'Archéol. de Bruxelles 50, 1961.

773 Heinrich Sproemberg, Residenz und Territorium im niederländischen Raum, in: *idem*, Beiträge zur belgisch-niederländischen Geschichte, Berlin 1959 = Forschungen zur mittelalterlichen Geschichte No. 3.

773a Heinrich Sproemberg, Mittelalter und demokratische Geschichtsschreibung. Ausgewählte Abhandlungen, ed. Manfred Unger. Berlin 1971 = Forschungen zur mittelalterlichen Geschichte 18.

774 R. Stadelmann, Persönlichkeit und Staat in der Renaissance, in: Die Welt als Geschichte 5, 1939.

775 Die Stadt als Lebensform, (ed.) René König and others, Berlin 1970 = Forschung und Information 6.

775a Die Stadt des Mittelalters I, Begriff, Entstehung und Ausbreitung, (ed.) Carl Haase, Darmstadt 1969 = Wege der Forschung 243.

776 Stadterweiterung und Vorstadt, (ed.) Erich Maschke and Jürgen Sydow, Stuttgart 1969 = Veröffentlichungen d. Komm. f. gesch. Landeskunde in Baden-Württemberg ser. B Forschungen No. 51.

777 Die Städte Mitteleuropas im 12. und 13. Jahrhundert, (ed.) Fernand Vercauteren, Richard Laufner, Wilhelm Rausch, Linz 1963 = Beiträge zur Geschichte der Städte Mitteleuropas 1.

778 Die Städte Oberösterreichs, (ed.) Herbert Knittler, Wien 1968; Die Städte des Burgellandes, (ed.) H. Knittler, Wien 1970 = Österreichisches Städtebuch, (ed.) Alfred Hoffmann, Nos. 1, 2.

779 Deutsches Städtebuch. Handbuch städtischer, Geschichte, (ed.) Erich Keyser, 10 vols., Stuttgart 1339 ff.
   Vol. I Nordostdeutschland, Stuttgart 1939
   Vol. II Mitteldeutschland, Stuttgart 1941

Vol. III, 1 Niedersachsen and Bremen, Stuttgart 1952
Vol. III, 2 Westfalen, Stuttgart 1954
Vol. III, 3 Landschaftsverband Rheinland, Stuttgart 1956
Vol. IV, 1 Land Hessen, Stuttgart 1957
Vol. IV, 2 Land Baden-Württemberg, part on Baden, Stuttgart 1959, part on Württemberg, Stuttgart 1962
Vol. IV, 3 Land Rheinland-Pfalz und Saarland, Stuttgart 1964
Vol. V, 1 Bayerisches Städtebuch, (ed.) Erich Keyser and Heinz Stoob, Stuttgart 1971 (part 1).

780 Städtewesen und Bürgertum als geschichtliche Kräfte. Gedächtnisschrift Fritz Rörig, (ed.) Ahasver v. Brandt and W. Koppe, Lübeck 1953.
781 Walter Stein, Handels- und Verkehrsgeschichte der deutschen Kaiserzeit, Berlin 1922. Reprint Darmstadt 1967.
782 Franz Steinbach, Rheinische Anfänge des deutschen Städtewesens, in: Jb. d. Köln. Geschichtsvereins 25, 1950; also in: *idem.*, Collectanea ...
(150) Franz Steinbach, see under Collectanea ... (No. 150).
784 Franz Steinbach, Geburtsstand, Berufsstand und Leistungsgemeinschaft, in: RhVjbll. 14, 1949; also in: *idem*, Collectanea ...
785 Franz Steinbach, Zur ältesten Geschichte von Bonn, in: Rhein. Heimatbll. 2, 1925; also in: *idem*, Collectanea ...
786 Franz Steinbach und Erich Becker, Geschichtliche Grundlagen der kommunalen Selbstverwaltung in Deutschland, Bonn 1932 = Rheinisches Archiv No. 20.
787 Franz Steinbach, Zur Sozialgeschichte der Stadt Köln im Mittelalter, in: Spiegel der Geschichte, Festgabe für Max Braubach, Münster 1964; also in: *idem*, Collectanea ...
788 Franz Steinbach, Stadtgemeinde und Landgemeinde. Studien zur Geschichte des Bürgertums I, in: RhVjbll. 13, 1948; also in: *idem*, Collectanea ...
789 Franz Steinbach, Ursprungsbedingungen der Stadt Euskirchen, in: 650 Jahre Stadt Euskirchen. 1302–1952. Festschrift zum Stadtjubiläum. Euskirchen 1952; also in: *idem*, Collectanea ...
790 Josef Steinhausen, Die Hochschulen im römischen Trier, in: Rheinischer Verein f. Denkmalpflege und Heimatschutz year 1952.
791 Josef Steinhausen, Archäologische Siedlungskunde des Trierer Landes, Trier 1936.
792 Edmund E. Stengel, Die fränkische Wurzel der mittelalterlichen Stadt in hessischer Sicht, in: Städtewesen und Bürgertum als geschichtliche Kräfte. Gedächtnisschrift Fritz Rörig, (ed.) Ahasver v. Brandt and W. Koppe, Lübeck 1953.
793 Frank Merry Stenton, Anglo-Saxon England, Oxford [2]1947.
794 Carl Stephenson, Borough and Town. A Study of Urban Origins in England, Cambridge/Mass. 1933.
795 Heinz Stoob, Die Ausbreitung der abendländischen Stadt im östlichen Mitteleuropa, in: Zschr. f. Ostforschung 10, 1961.
796 Heinz Stoob, Westfälische Beiträge zum Verhältnis von Landesherrschaft und Städtewesen, in: Westfälische Forschungen 21, 1968.
797 Heinz Stoob, Formen und Wandel staufischen Verhaltens zum Städtewesen, in: *idem.*, Forschungen zum Städtewesen in Europa, vol. 1, Köln, Wien 1970.

798 Heinz Stoob, Forschungen zum Städtewesen in Europa. vol. 1: Räume, Formen und Schichten der mitteleuropäischen Städte. Eine Aufsatzfolge, Köln, Wien 1970.

799 Heinz Stoob, Über Zeitstufen der Marktsiedlung im 10. und 11. Jhd. auf sächsischem Boden, in: *idem*, Forschungen zum Städtewesen ... vol. 1.

800 Hans Strahm, Der zähringische Gründungsplan der Stadt Bern, in: Festgabe Richard Feller zum 70. Geburtstag, Bern 1948 = Archiv des hist. Ver. d. Kantons Bern vol. 39, No. 2.

801 Hans Strahm, Die Berner Handfeste, Bern 1953.

802 Hans Strahm, Mittelalterliche Stadtfreiheit, in: Schweizer Beiträge zur allgem. Gesch. 5, 1947.

803 Raphael Straus, Die Judengemeinde Regensburg im ausgehenden Mittelalter, Heidelberg 1932 = Heidelberger Abhandlungen zur mittleren und neueren Geschichte 61.

804 Karl Friedrich Stroheker, Der senatorische Adel im spätantiken Gallien, Tübingen 1948.

805 Karl Friedrich Stroheker, Germanentum und Spätantike, Zürich, Stuttgart 1965.

806 Wolfgang v. Stromer, Oberdeutsche Hochfinanz 1350–1450, Wiesbaden 1970 = VSWG Suppl. 55–57.

807 William Stubbs, Select Charters ... of English Constitutional History, Oxford [8]1905.

808 Studien zu den Anfängen des europäischen Städtewesens. Reichenau-Vorträge 1955–1956, Lindau, Konstanz 1958 = Vorträge und Forschungen vol. 4.

809 Florentine Studies: Politics and society in Renaissance Florence, (ed.) Nicolai Rubinstein, London [2]1968.

810 Bernhard E.J. Stüdeli, Minoritenniederlassungen und mittelalterliche Stadt, Werl 1969 = Franziskanische Forschungen 21.

811 J. de Sturler, Les relations politiques et les échanges commerciaux entre le duché de Brabant et l'Angleterre au moyen-âge, Paris 1936.

812 Henry Sweet, King Alfred's Orosius, London 1883.

813 Erich Swoboda, Carnuntum. Seine Geschichte und seine Denkmäler, Graz, Köln [4]1964.

814 Jürgen Sydow, Der Regensburger Markt im Früh- und Hochmittelalter, in: Histor. Jb. 80, 1961.

815 Jürgen Sydow, Zur verfassungsgeschichtlichen Stellung von Reichsstadt, freier Stadt und Territorialstadt im 13. und 14. Jhd., in: Les libertés urbaines et rurales du XIe au XIVe siècle. Colloque international Spa 1966, Bruxelles 1968 = Pro Civitate. Collection Histoire in-8[0], No. 19.

816 György Székely, Le développement des bourgs hongrois à l'époque du féodalisme florissant et tardif, in: Annales Universitatis Scientiarum Budapestiensis, Sectio Hist. vol. 5, Budapest 1963.

817 György Székely, Le développement de la magistrature de la ville de Buda au XIVe siècle, in: Folia diplomatica 1, Brünn 1971.

818 György Székely, A pannóniai települések kontinuitásának kérdéx és a hazai városfejlödés kezdetei. Summary: *idem*, Die Frage der Kontinuität der Siedlungen in Pannonien und die Anfänge der Städteentwicklung in Ungarn, in: Tanulmányok Budapest Múltjából, Budapest 1957.

819 György Székely, Le sort des agglomérations pannoniennes au début du moyen-âge et les origines de l'urbanisme en Hongrie, in: Annales Universitatis Scientiarum Budapestiensis, Sectio Hist. vol. 3, Budapest 1961.

820 György Székely, Wallons et italiens en Europe centrale aux XIᵉ–XVIᵉ scs., in: Annales Universitatis Scientiarum Budapestiensis, Sectio Hist. vol. 6, Budapest 1964.

821 Giov. Tabacco, I liberti del re nell'Italia carolingia e postcarolingia, Spoleto 1966 = Bibl. degli Studi medioevali 2.

822 G.L. Fr. Tafel, G.M. Thomas, Urkunden zur älteren Handels- und Staatsgeschichte der Republik Venedig mit bes. Beziehung auf Byzanz und die Levante. Vom 9. bis zum Ausgang des 15. Jhds., 3 vols., Wien 1856–57, Reprint Amsterdam 1964 = Fontes rerum Austriacarum. Österreichische Geschichtsquellen. 2. Abt. Diplomataria et Acta vols. 12–14.

823 James Tait, The Mevieval English Borough. Studies on its Origins and Constitutional History, Manchester 1936.

824 Coenrad Liebrecht Temminck-Groll, Middeleeuwse stenen huizen te Utrecht en hun relatie met die van andere Noordwesteuropese steden, 's Gravenhage 1963.

825 Territorien und Städtewesen. Referate und Aussprachen auf der sechsten Tagung des Arbeitskreises für landschaftliche deutsche Städteforschung 1965 in Münster/W., (ed.) Karl-Heinz Kirchhoff, in: Westfälische Forschungen 19, 1966.

826 Hans Thieme, Die Funktion der Regalien im Mittelalter, in: ZRG Germ. Abt. 62, 1942.

827 Sylvia Lettice Thrupp, The merchant class of medieval London 1300–1500, Chicago 1948.

(571) M.N. Tichomirow, see under Mélanges M.N. Tichomirow (No. 571).

828 Fritz Timme, Die wirtschaftlichen und verfassungsgeschichtlichen Anfänge der Stadt Braunschweig, Leipzig 1931.

829 Fritz Timme, Ursprung und Aufstieg der Städte Niedersachsens, Hannover: Landeszentrale für Heimatdienst in Niedersachsen 1956 = Schriftenreihe der Landeszentrale für Heimatdienst in Niedersachsen ser. B No. 2.

830 Fritz Timme, Ostsachsens früher Verkehr und die Entstehung alter Handelsplätze, in: Braunschweig. Heimat 36, 1950.

(866) Nikolaj Todorov, (ed.), see under La ville balkanique . . . (No. 866).

831 Amelio Tagliaferri, L'economia veronese secondo gli estimi dal 1409 bis 1635, Milano 1966 = Bibl. del Rivista Econ. e Storia 17.

832 Pietro Torelli, Un comune cittadino in territorio ad economia agricola, 2 vols., Mantua 1930 and 1952.

833 Historic Towns. Maps and Plans of Towns and Cities in the British Isles, with Historical commentaries from earliest times to circa 1800, (ed.) M.D. Lobel and W.H. Johns, Oxford, London 1969.

834 J.P. Trabut-Cuissac, Bastides ou forteresses? Les bastides de l'Aquitaine anglaise et les intentions de leurs fondateurs, in: Le Moyen Age 60, 1954.

835 Ferdinand Tremel, Das Handelsbuch des Judenburger Kaufmanns Clemens Körbler 1526–1548, Graz 1960 = Beiträge zur Forschung steirischer Geschichtsquellen No. 47 (new ser. No. 15).

836 Trier. Ein Zentrum abendländischer Kultur, Neuß 1952 = Rheinischer Verein f. Denkmalpflege und Heimatschutz year 1952.

837 Kas. Tymieniecki, Organisation des frühmittelalterlichen Handwerks und die Genesis der polnischen Städte, in: Studia Wczesnosred 3, 1955.

838 Friedrich Uhlhorn, Beobachtungen über die Ausdehnung des sogenannten Frankfurter Stadtrechtskreises, in: Hess. Jb. f. Landesgesch. 5, 1955.

839 Manfred Unger, Stadtgemeinde und Bergwesen Freibergs im Mittelalter, Weimar 1963 = Abhandlungen zur Handels- und Sozialgeschichte No. 5.

840 Gesellschaftliche Unterschichten in den südwestdeutschen Städen, (ed.) Erich Maschke and Jürgen Sydow, Stuttgart 1967 = Veröffentlichungen d. Komm. f. gesch. Landeskunde in Baden-Württemberg ser. B Forschungen No. 41.

841 Untersuchungen zur gesellschaftlichen Struktur der mittelalterlichen Städte in Europa. Reichenau-Vorträge 1963–1964, Konstanz, Stuttgart 1966 = Vorträge und Forschungen No. 11.

842 Rafael v. Uslar, Studien zu frühgeschichtlichen Befestigungen zwischen Nordsee und Alpen, Köln, Graz 1964.

843 Rafael v. Uslar, Turris, Curtis und Arx im Mainz des frühen Mittelalters, in: Kölner Jahrbuch f. Vor- und Frühgesch. 9, 1967/68.

844 R. van Uytven, Die Bedeutung des Kölner Weinmarktes im 15. Jhd., in: RhVjbll. 30, 1965.

845 Pietro Vaccari, Pavia nell'alto medioevo e nell'età comunale, Pavia 1956.

846 Luis Garcia de Valdevellano y Arcimis, Sobre los burgos y los burgueses de la España Medieval, Madrid 1960.

847 Jules Vannérus, Trois villes d'origine romaine dans l'ancien Pays de Luxembourg-Chiny: Arlon, Bitbourg et Yvois, in: Bulletin. (Academie Royale de Belgique) Classe des lettres et des sciences morales et politiques 5th Ser. 21, 1935.

848 Helmut Veitshans, Die Judensiedlungen der schwäbischen Reichsstädte und der württembergischen Landstädte im Mittelalter, Stuttgart 1970.

849 Fernand Vercauteren, Die spätantike Civitas im frühen Mittelalter, in: Bll. f. dt. Landesgesch. 98, 1962.

850 Fernand Vercauteren, Conceptions et méthodes de l'histoire urbaine méviévale, in: Cahiers bruxellois 12, 1967.

851 Fernand Vercauteren, Etude sur les civitates de la Belgique seconde, Bruxelles 1934 = Académie Royale de Belgique. Classe des lettres et des sciences morales et politiques. Mémoires. 2nd Ser. vol. 33.

852 Fernand Vercauteren, Luttes sociales à Liège, Bruxelles ²1946.

853 Fernand Vercauteren, Note critique sur un diplôme du roi de France Charles le Simple du 20 décembre 911, in: Miscellanea medievalia in memoriam Jan Frederik Niermeyer, Groningen 1967.

(777) Fernand Vercauteren, Richard Laufner, Wilhelm Rausch, (ed.), see under Die Städte Mitteleuropas... (No. 777).

854 Giovanni de Vergottini, Origini e sviluppo storico della comitatinanza I, Siena 1929.

855 Adriaan Verhulst, Bronnen en problemen betr. de Vlaamse Landbouw in de late middeleeuwen, Gent 1964 = Studia Hist. Gandensia 17.

856 Adriaan Verhulst, Der Handel im Merowingerreich. Gesamtdarstellung nach schriftlichen Quellen, Gent 1970 = Studia Hist. Gandensia 125.

857 Adriaan Verhulst, Les origines et l'histoire ancienne de la ville de Bruges (IXᵉ–XIIᵉ siècle), in: Le Moyen Age 66, 1960.

858 Charles Verlinden, L'esclavage dans l'Europe méditerranéene, Bruges 1955.
859 Charles Verlinden, Problèmes d'histoire économique franque. I. Le Franc Samo, in: Revue belge de phil. et d'hist. 12.3–4, 1933.
860 Charles Verlinden, Traite et esclavage dans la vallée de la Meuse, in: Mélanges Félix Rousseau. Etudes sur l'histoire du Pays Mosan au Moyen Age, Bruxelles 1958.
861 Albert Vermeesch, Essai sur les origines et la signification de la Commune dans le nord de la France (XIᵉ et XIIᵉ siècles), Heule 1966.
862 Sergij Vilfan, Rechtsgeschichte der Slowenen bis zum Jahre 1941, Graz 1968.
863 La ville. vol. I: Institutions administratives et judiciaires, Bruxelles 1954 = Rècueils de la Société Jean Bodin vol. VI.
864 La ville. Vol. II: Institutions économiques et sociales, Bruxelles 1955 = Recueils de la Société Jean Bodin vol. VII.
865 La ville. Vol. III: Le droit privée, Bruxelles 1957 = Recueils de la Société Jean Bodin vol. VIII.
866 La ville balkanique XVᵉ–XIXᵉ siècles, (ed.) Nikolaj Todorov, Sofia 1970.
867 Cincio Violante La Pataria milanese e la riforma ecclesiastica I. Le premesse (1045–1057), Roma 1955.
868 Cincio Violante, Les prêts sur gage foncier dans la vie économique et sociale de Milan au XIᵉ sc., in: Cahiers de civil. méd. 5, 1962.
869 Cincio Violante, La società Milanese nell'età precomunale, Bari 1953.
870 Vita Meinwerci episcopi Patherbrunnensis, (ed.) Franz Tenckhoff, Hannover 1921 = MGH SS rer. Germ. in usum scholarum . . . 59.
871 Vito Vitale, Breviario della storia di Genova, 2 vols., Genua 1955.
872 Friedrich Vittinghoff, Römische Stadtrechtsformen der Kaiserzeit, in: ZRG Germ. Abt. 68, 1951.
873 Friedrich Vittinghoff, Zur verfassung der spätantiken Stadt, in: Studien zu den Anfängen des europäischen Städtewesens. Reichenau-Vorträge 1955–1956, Lindau, Konstanz 1958 = Vorträge und Forschungen vol. 4.
874 Hans-Jochen Vogel, Städte im Wandel, Stuttgart, Berlin, Köln, Mainz 1971.
875 Walter Vogel, Handelsverkehr, Städtewesen und Staatenbildung in Nordeuropa im frühen Mittelalter, in: Zschr. d. Gesellschaft f. Erdkunde year 1931.
876 Walter Vogel, Ein seefahrender Kaufmann um 1100, in: Hans. Geschbll. 18, 1912.
877 Walter Vogel, Wik-Orte und Wikinger. Eine Studie zu den Anfängen des germanischen Städtewesens, in: Hans. Geschbll. 60, 1935.
878 Gisela Vollmer, Die Stadtentstehung am unteren Niederrhein. Eine Untersuchung zum Privileg der Reeser Kaufleute von 1142, Bonn 1952 = Rheinisches Archiv 41.
879 Gioacchino Volpe, Questioni fondamentali sull'origine dei comuni italiani, in: Medioevo italiano, Firenze ²1961.
880 A. van de Vyver, Charles Verlinden, L'auteur et la portée du "conflictus ovi et lini", in: Revue belge de phil. et d'hist. 12.1–2, 1933.
881 Friedrich Ludwig Wagner, Stadt Bacharach und Samtgemeinde der Viertäler, in: Jahrbuch f. Gesch. u. Kunst d. Mittelrheins u. seiner Nachbargebiete 6/7, 1954/55.
882 Georg Waitz, Deutsche Verfassungsgeschichte, 8 vols., Kiel 1860–78.

883 Gerold Walser, Thomas Pekary, Die Krise des Römischen Reiches, Berlin 1962.

884 N. Wand, Die Ausgrabungen auf dem Büraberg bei Fritzlar. Vorbericht, in: Fundberichte aus Hessen 9/10, 1969/70.

885 Joh. Warncke, Mittelalterliche Schulgeräte im Museum zu Lübeck, in: Zschr. f. Gesch. d. Erziehung und d. Unterrichts 2, 1912.

886 Charl. Warnke, Die Anfänge des Fernhandels in Polen, Würzburg 1964 = Marburger Ostforschungen 22.

887 Max Weber, Die Stadt, in: Archiv f. Sozialwissenschaft und Sozialpolitik 47, 1921. Also in: *idem*, Wirtschaft und Gesellschaft, vol. 2, Tübingen 1947 = Grundriß der Sozialökonomik 3.

888 Hugo Weczerka, Bevölkerungszahlen der Hansestädte (insbesondere Danzigs), nach H. Samsonowicz, in: Hans. Geschbll. 82, 1964.

889 Herman van der Wee, The growth of the Antwerp market and the European economy (14th–16th centuries), 3 vols., The Hague 1963.

890 H. van de Weerd, L'origine de la ville de Tongres, in: Musée belge No. 33, 1929.

891 H. van de Weerd, Tongeren van de vierde tot de twaalfde eeuw: geschiedkundig onderzoek, in: Limburg 29, 1950; 30, 1951.

892 Carl Wehmer, Mainzer Probedrucke in der Type des sog. Astronomischen Kalenders für 1448. Ein Beitrag zur Gutenbergforschung, München 1948.

893 Leo Weisgerber, Die Namen der Ubier, Köln, Opladen 1968.

894 Leo Weisgerber, Rhenania Germano-Celtica. Gesammelte Abhandlungen, (ed.) Joh. Knobloch and Rud. Schützeichel, Bonn 1969.

895 Leo Weisgerber, Die Sprache der Festlandkelten, in: Berichte der Römisch-Germanischen Kommission 20, 1931. Now also in: *idem*, Rhenania Germano-Celtica...

896 Julius Weizsäcker, Der rheinische Bund von 1254, Tübingen 1879.

897 Wilhelm Weizsäcker, Wien und Brünn in der Stadtrechtsgeschichte, in: ZRG Germ. Abt. 70, 1953.

898 Karl Weller, Die staufischen Städtegründungen in Schwaben, in: Württ. Vierteljahrshefte new ser. 36, 1930.

899 Reinhard Wenskus, Probleme einer kartographischen Darstellung der Ausbreitung deutscher Stadtrechte in den Städten des Ostens, in: Bll. f. dt. Landesgesch. 91, 1954.

900 Ernst Werner, Der Florentiner Frühkapitalismus in marxistischer Sicht, in: Studi medievali 3rd Ser. 1, 1960.

901 Joachim Werner, Zur Ausfuhr koptischen Bronzegeschirrs, in: VSWG 43, 1956.

902 Joachim Werner, Die Bedeutung des Städtewesens für die Kulturentwicklung des frühen Keltentums, in: Die Welt als Geschichte 5, 1939.

903 Joachim Werner, Zu den alemannischen Burgen des 4. und 5. Jhds., in: Speculum Historiae. Geschichte im Spiegel von Geschichtsschreibung und Geschichtsdeutung, (ed.) Clemens Bauer, Laetitia Boehm, Max Müller (Joh. Spörl aus Anlaß seines 60. Geburtstages), Freiburg, München 1965.

904 Joachim Werner, Fernhandel und Naturalwirtschaft, in: Moneta e scambi nell'alto medioevo, Spoleto 1961 = Settimane di studio del centro ital. di studi sull'alto medioevo 8.

905 Joachim Werner, Waage und Geld in der Merowingerzeit, München 1954 = Sbb. d. Bayerischen Akad. d. Wiss., Phil.-hist. Kl. vol. 54, No. 1.

906 Hans van Werveke, La banlieue primitive des villes flamandes, in: Etudes d'histoire dédiées à la mémoire de Henri Pirenne, Bruxelles 1937.

907 Hans van Werveke, "Burgus", versterking of nederzetting?, Bruxelles 1965 = Verhandelingen v. d. Koninkl. Vlaamse Acad. v. Wetensch. Letteren en Schone Kunsten v. Belgie. Kl. d. Letteren vol. 27, No. 59.

908 Hans van Werveke, A.E. Verhulst, Castrum en Oudburg te Gent. Bijdragen tot de oudste Geschiedenis van de Vlaamse Steden, in: Handelingen d. Maatschappij v. Geschiedenis en Oudheidkunde te Gent new ser. 14, 1960.

909 Hans van Werveke, Gand. Esquisse d'histoire sociale, Bruxelles 1946.

910 Hans van Werveke, De middeleeuwse hongersnood, Bruxelles 1967 = Mededelingen v. d. Koninkl. Vlaamse Acad. v. Wetensch., Letteren en Schone Kunsten v. Belgie. Kl. d. Letteren vol. 29, No. 3.

911 Hans van Werveke, Jacques van Artevelde, Bruxelles 1948 = Notre Passé ser. I, 2.

912 Hans van Werveke, Miscellanea medievalia. Gent 1968.

913 Hans van Werveke, De economische politiek van Filips van de Elzas (1157–68 tot 1191), Bruxelles 1952 = Mededelingen v. d. Koninkl. Vlaamse Acad. v. Wetensch., Letteren en Schone Kunsten v. Belgie. Kl. d. Letteren vol. 14.

914 Hans van Werveke, Das Wesen der flandrischen Hansen, in: Hans. Geschbll. 76, 1958; also in: idem, Miscellanea medievalia.

915 Westfalen, Hanse, Ostseeraum, Münster 1955 = Veröffentlichungen d. Provinzialinstituts f. westfälische Landes- und Volkskunde 7.

916 Willi Weyres, Die Domgrabung XVI. Die frühchristlichen Bischofskirchen und Baptisterien, in: Kölner Domblatt 30, 1969.

917 Willi Weyres, Die Domgrabung XVII. Die Baptisterien östlich des Domchores, in: Kölner Domblatt 31/32, 1970.

918 Sir Mortimer Wheeler, Der Fernhandel des römischen Reiches in Europa, Afrika und Asien, München, Wien 1965.

919 Sir Mortimer Wheeler, Rome beyond the Imperial Frontiers, London 1955.

920 Lynn White jr., Medieval technology and social change, Oxford 1962. German: Die mittelalterliche Technik und der Wandel der Gellschaft, München 1968.

921 B. Widera, Die Frühgeschichte Nowgorods im Lichte der neuesten sowjetischen Archäologie, in: Ethnographisch-archäologische Zschr. 1, 1960.

922 Fr. Wieacker, Recht und Gesellschaft in der Spätantike, Stuttgart 1964.

923 Fritz Wiegand, Über hansische Beziehungen Erfurts, in: Hansische Studien, Heinrich Sproemberg zum 70. Geburtstag, (ed.) Gerhard Heitz and Manfred Unger, Berlin 1961 = Forschungen zur mittelalterlichen Geschichte vol. 8.

924 Fritz Wiegand, Erfurt. Eine Monographie, Rudolstadt 1964.

925 Helene Wieruszowski, Die Zusammensetzung des gallischen und fränkischen Episkopats bis zum Vertrag von Verdun (843) mit besonderer Berücksichtigung der Nationalität und des Standes, in: Bonner Jahrbücher 127, 1922.

926 Hans Wilkens, Zur Geschichte des niederländischen Handels im Mittelalter, in: Hans. Geschbll. 14, 1908.

927 Gwynn Alfred Williams, Medieval London: from commune to capital, London 1963 = University of London Historical Studies 11.

928 E.M. Carus Wilson, The overseas trade of Bristol, London 1954.

929 Luise v. Winterfeld, Geschichte der freien Reichs- und Hansestadt Dortmund, Dortmund ⁴1963.

930 Luise v. Winterfeld, Gottesfrieden und deutsche Stadtverfassung, in: Hans. Geschbll. 52, 1927.

931 Luise v. Winterfeld, Handel, Kapital und Patriziat in Köln bis 1400, Lübeck 1925 = Pfingstbll. d. Hans. Geschver. 16.

932 Luise v. Winterfeld, Nochmals Gottesfrieden und deutsche Stadtverfassung, in: ZRG Germ. Abt. 54, 1934.

933 Luise v. Winterfeld, Das Dortmunder Patriziat bis 1400, in: Mitteilungen d. westdt. Ges. f. Familienkunde 4, 1925.

934 Luise v. Winterfeld, Neue Untersuchungen über die Anfänge des Gemeinwesens der Stadt Köln, in: VSWG 18, 1925.

935 Luise v. Winterfeld, Versuch über die Entstehung des Marktes und den Ursprung der Ratsverfassung in Lübeck, in: Zschr. d. Ver. f. Lübeck. Gesch. u. Altertumskunde 25, 1929.

936 Phil. Wolff, Commerces et marchands de Toulouse (vers 1350–vers 1450) Paris 1954.

937 Phil. Wolff, L'épisode de Berenguer. Oller à Barcelone en 1285. Essai d'interprétation sociale, in: Anuario de estudios medievales 1968.

938 Phil. Wolff, Les "Estimes" Toulousaines des XIVe et XVe siècles, Toulouse 1956.

939 Phil. Wolff, Histoire de Toulouse, Toulouse 1958.

940 Phil. Wolff, Quidam homo nomine Roberto negociatore, in: Le Moyen Age 69, 1963.

941 Phil. Wolff, Les luttes sociales dans les villes du Midi français XIIIe-XVe siècles, in: Annales. Economies, sociétés, civilisations 2, 1947.

942 Phil. Wolff, Réflexions sur l'histoire méviévale de Montauban, in: Actes du Congrès d. Soc. Savantes Montauban 1954, Montauban 1956.

943 Phil. Wolff, De Rome à Toulouse: aux origines de la Banque Toulousaine, in: Studi in onore di Amintore Fanfani, vol. 3, Milano 1962.

944 Gerhard Wunder, Georg Lenckner, Die Bürgerschaft der Reichsstadt Hall von 1395–1600, Stuttgart, Köln, 1956 = Württembergische Geschichtsquellen vol. 25.

945 Carlos Wyffels, Hanse, grands marchands et patriciens de St. Omer, St. Omer 1962 = Mém. de la Soc. acad. des antiquaires de la Morinie vol. 38.

946 Carlos Wyffels, De oorsprong der ambachten in Vlaanderen en Brabant, Bruxelles 1951 = Verhandelingen v. d. Koninkl. Vlaamse Acad. v. Wetensch., Letteren en Schone Kunsten v. Belgie. Kl. d. Letteren vol. 13, No. 13.

947 Charles Robert Young, The English borough and royal administration 1130–1307, Durham, London 1961.

948 Mireille Zarb, Histoire d'une autonomie communale. Les privilèges de la ville de Marseille au Xe siècle à la Revolution, Paris 1961.

949 Wolfgang Zorn, Augsburg. Geschichte einer deutschen Stadt, Augsburg o. J. (1955).

950 Wolfgang Zorn, Die politische und soziale Bedeutung des Reichsstadtbürgertums im Spätmittelalter, in: Zschr. f. bayer. Landesgesch. 24, 1961.

951 Wolfgang Zorn, Zünfte, in: HDSW 12, 1965.

952 Adolf Zycha, Über den Ursprung der Städte in Böhmen und die Städtepolitik der Premysliden, in: Mitteilungen d. Ver. f. Gesch. d. Deutschen in Böhmen 52, 1914; 53, 1915.

Additional bibliography up to 1974, prepared for the second German edition

Continuing interest in urban history has led to the setting up of new research institutes, such as the Institute for the Comparative History of Towns, recently established in Münster in Westphalia and at present under the direction of Heinz Stoob. Its most important publication is the German urban atlas, of which the first volume appeared in 1973. In Bonn the *Rheinische Städteatlas* is the product of a co-operative undertaking between the *Institut für geschichtliche Landeskunde* of the Rhineland and the department of Historical Geography in the University of Bonn and the Rhineland *Landschaftsverband*. Two further volumes are in preparation. In 1969 Wilhelm Rausch founded the Austrian urban history group and organized conferences in Linz (1971), Villach (1973) and Vienna (1974). He also edits the series *Beiträge zur Geschichte der Städte Mitteleuropas*. The urban history groups mentioned above continue their activities and details can be found in the bibliography. I should like to draw attention in particular to vols. XV–XVI (1970–1971) of the *Cahiers Bruxellois* which contain reports of the conferences of the International Commission for Urban History held in Salzburg (1969), Moscow (1970) and Barcelona (1971) and which have produced a total of twelve regional bibliographies. The commission is also responsible for the *Guide international pour l'histoire urbaine*. Since 1971 Jürgen Sydow has been responsible for a bibliographical report on the latest publications on German town history in the *Blätter für deutsche Landesgeschichte*. The only progress on the *Deutsches Städtebuch* since the first edition of this work has been the second part of the Bavarian town section. For Austria a third volume on the towns of the Vorarlberg has appeared.

Because of considerations of space, volumes containing collected studies on towns are mentioned only under their general titles. Choice of titles was a thorny problem and I decided to choose above all those which provide introductions to further literature.

(1043) W. Jappe Alberts, (ed.), see under De stadsrekeningen van Arnhem...(No. 1043).

(1044) W. Jappe Alberts, (ed.), see under De stadsrekeningen van Deventer...(No. 1044).

   953 H. Hellmuth Andersen, P.I. Crabb, H.J. Madsen, Århus Søndervold. En byark-

aeologisk undersøgelse. Summary: Århus Süderwall – Eine Stadtkernunter-
suchung, Aarhus 1972 = Jysk Arkaeologisk Selskabs Skrifter 9.

954 Hans Andersson, Urbanisierte Ortschaften und lateinische Terminologie. Studien zur Geschichte des nordeuropäischen Städtewesens vor 1350, Göteborg
1971 = Acta regiae societatis scientiarum et litterarum Gothoborgensis.
Humaniora 6.

955 1221–1971. Ansbach – 750 Jahre Stadt. Ein Festbuch, ed. by the town council.
Ansbach 1971.

956 Günter Bandmann, Die vorgotische Kirche als Himmelsstadt, in: Frühmittelalterliche Studien 6, 1972.

957 Július Bartl, Bratislavsky obchod v stredoveku. Zbornik Filozifickej faculty
Univ. Komenskèho (Bratislava). (Der Handel Preßburgs im Mittelalter), in:
Historica 21, 1970/71.

958 Jean Baumel, Histoire d'une seigneurie du midi de la France (Montpellier au
Moyen Age), parts 1–3, Montpellier 1969–1973.

959 Beiträge zur Stadt- und Regionalgeschichte Ost- und Nordeuropas, Herbert
Ludat zum 60. Geburtstag, (ed.) Klaus Zernack, Wiesbaden 1971 = Osteuropastudien der Hochschulen des Landes Hessen, Ser. 1 = Gießener Abhandlungen
zur Agrar- und Wirtschaftsforschung des europäischen Ostens 55.

960 Bergen. Handelszentrum des beginnenden Spätmittelalters. Referate und Dis-
kussionen des Hansischen Symposions in Bergen, (ed.) Hansischer Geschichts-
verein, revised by Klaus Friedland, Köln 1971 = Quellen und Darstellungen zur
Hansischen Geschichte new ser. 17.

961 Brigitte Berthold, Evamaria Engel, Adolf Laube, Die Stellung des Bürgertums in
der deutschen Feudalgesellschaft bis zur Mitte des 16. Jahrhunderts, in: Zschr.
f. Geschichtswissenschaft 21, 1973, No. 2.

(1046) Werner Besch, (ed.), see under Die Stadt in der europäischen
Geschichte . . . (No. 1046).

962 Karlheinz Blaschke, Studien zur Frühgeschichte des Städtewesens in Sachsen,
in: Festschrift für Walter Schlesinger, (ed.) Helmut Beumann, vol. 1, Köln,
Wien 1973 = Mitteldeutsche Forschungen No. 74/I.

963 Hans Bögli, Aventicum. Zum Stand der Forschung, in: Bonner Jahrbücher 172,
1972.

964 Kurt Böhner, Vom Römerkastell zu Hof, Burg und Stadt, in: 1750 Jahre Alzey.
Festschrift, (ed.) Friedrich Karl Becker, Johannes Bärmann, Kurt Böhner,
Heinrich Steitz, Alzey 1973.

965 J.E. Bogaers, Civitates und Civitas-Hauptorte in der nördlichen Germania
inferior, in: Bonner Jahrbücher 172, 1972.

966 Jürgen Bohmbach, Die Sozialstruktur Braunschweigs um 1400, Braunschweig
1973.

967 Otto Borst, Die Esslinger Pliensaubrücke. Kommunale Verkehrs- und Wirtschaftspolitik vom frühen Mittelalter bis zur Gegenwart, Esslingen 1971 =
Esslinger Studien Schriftenreihe 3.

(1049) Karl Bosl, (ed.), see under Die mittelalterliche Stadt in Bayern . . . (No. 1049).

968 William Marvin Bowsky, The Finance of the Commune of Siena 1287–1355,
Oxford 1970.

969 Ahasver v. Brandt, Mittelalterliche Bürgertestamente. Neuerschlossene Quellen

zur Geschichte der materiellen und geistigen Kultur, Heidelberg 1973 = Sbb. d. Heidelberger Akad. d. Wiss., Phil.-hist. Kl. year 1973, No. 3.

(987) Anton Ph. Brück, (ed.), see under Geschichte der Stadt Mainz . . . (No. 987).

970 J. Charlier, La peste à Bruxelles de 1667 à 1669 et ses conséquences démographiques, Bruxelles 1969 = Pro Civitate. Collection Histoire in-8⁰, No. 20.

971 Raymond Chevallier, Cité et territoire. Solutions romaines aux problèmes de l'organisation de l'espace. Problématique 1948–1973, in: Aufstieg und Niedergang der römischen Welt. Geschichte und Kultur Roms im Spiegel der neueren Forschung, (ed.) Hildegard Temporini, vol. II/1, Berlin, New York 1974.

972 Les constructions civiles d'intérêt public dans les villes au Moyen Age et sous l'Ancien Régime et leur financement. Colloque international Spa 5–8 IX. 1968, Bruxelles 1971 = Pro Civitate. Collection Histoire in-8⁰, No. 26.

973 Karl Czok, Die Stadt. Ihre Stellung in der deutschen Geschichte, Leipzig, Jena, Berlin 1969.

974 Alain Derville, Les draperies flamandes et artésiennes vers 1250–1350, in: Revue du Nord 54, 1972.

975 Alain Derville, Le problème des origines de Lille, in: Economies et Sociétés au Moyen Age. Mélanges offerts à Edouard Perroy, Paris 1973 = Publications de la Sorbonne. Ser. "Etudes" vol. 5.

976 Georges Despy, A propos du droit urbain de Louvain au XIIIᵉ siècle. L'exemple de la ville de Wavre, in: Mélanges offerts à G. Jacquemyns, Bruxelles 1968.

977 Bernhard Diestelkamp, Gibt es eine Freiburger Gründungsurkunde aus dem Jahre 1120? Ein Beitrag zur vergleichenden Städtegeschichte des Mittelalters sowie zur Diplomatik hochmittelalterlicher Städteprivilegien, Berlin 1973.

978 Philippe Dollinger, Le premier statut municipal de Strasbourg (XIIᵉ siècle), in: L'Annuaire de la Société des Amis du Vieux-Strasbourg 1972/73.

979 Otto Doppelfeld, Das Fortleben der Stadt Köln vom 5.–8. Jhd. n. Chr., in: Early Medieval Studies 1, Stockholm 1970 = Antikvariskt arkiv 38.

980 Ch.-E. Dufourcq, J. Gautier Dalché, Economies, sociétés et institutions de l'Espagne chrétienne du Moyen Age, in: Le Moyen Age 79, 1973.

981 Raimund Eirich, Memmingens Wirtschaft und Patriziat von 1347–1551. Eine wirtschafts- und sozialgeschichtliche Untersuchung über das Memminger Patriziat während der Zunftverfassung, Weißenhorn 1971.

982 August Engel, Alfred Bruns, Geschichte der Stadt Eversberg, Eversberg 1972.

(1054) Edith Ennen, (ed.), see under Rheinischer Städteatlas . . . (No. 1054).

983 Siegfried Epperlein, Die Anfänge des frühmittelalterlichen Städtewesens in Polen im Lichte der erzählenden Quellen, in: Jahrbuch für Wirtschaftsgeschichte 1970.

984 Arnold Esch, Anhaltspunkte für ein Budget Giangaleazzo Viscontis (1397), in: VSWG 60, 1973.

985 Etudes sur l'histoire de la pauvreté (Moyen Age – XVIᵉ siècle), (ed.) Michel Mollat, 2 vols., Paris 1974 = Publications de la Sorbonne. Ser. "Etudes" vol. 8.

(987) Ludwig Falck, (ed.), see under Geschichte der Stadt Mainz . . . (No. 987).

986 Gina Fasoli, Francesca Bocchi, La città medievale italiana, Firenze 1973.

(1046) Klaus Fehn, (ed.), see under Die Stadt in der europäischen Geschichte . . . (No. 1046).

(1054) Klaus Fehn, (ed.), see under Rheinischer Städteatlas . . . (No. 1054).

(960) Klaus Friedland, (ed.), see under Bergen. Handelszentrum des beginnenden Spätmittelalters . . . (No. 960).

(1047) Klaus Friedland, (ed.), see under Stadt und Land in der Geschichte des Ostseeraumes . . . (No. 1047).

987 Geschichte der Stadt Mainz, (ed.) Anton Ph. Brück and Ludwig Falck.
   Vol. II: Ludwig Falck, Mainz im frühen und hohen Mittelalter (Mitte 5. Jh. bis 1244), Düsseldorf 1972.
   Vol. III: *Idem*, Mainz in seiner Blütezeit als freie Stadt (1244–1328), Düsseldorf 1973.
   Vol. V: Anton Ph. Brück, Mainz vom Verlust der Stadtfreiheit bis zum Ende des Dreißigjährigen Krieges (1462–1648), Düsseldorf 1972.

988 Helmut Gilliam, Die Bedeutung des Kölner Krieges für die Stadt Neuß, Neuß 1968 = Schriftenreihe des Stadtarchivs Neuß 5.

989 Frantisek Graus, Struktur und Geschichte. Drei Volksaufstände im mittelalterlichen Prag, Sigmaringen 1971 = Vorträge und Forschungen. part 7.

990 Guide international pour l'histoire urbaine, vol. 1: Belgien – Deutschland – Italien – Frankreich – Niederlande – Spanien, Paris.

(775a, 1050, 1051) Carl Haase, (ed.), see under Die Stadt des Mittelalters . . . (No. 775a, 1050, 1051).

991 Thomas Hall, Stockholms förutsättningar och uppkomst. En studie i medeltida urbanism (with summary in German: Die Anfänge Stockholms. Eine Studie mittelalterlichen Städtewesens), Stockholm 1972.

992 Ursula Hauschild, Studien zu Löhnen und Preisen in Rostock im Spätmittelalter, Köln, Wien 1973 = Quellen und Darstellungen zur Hanischen Geschichte new ser. 19.

993 Karl Heinemeyer, Die Gründung der Stadt Münden. Ein Beitrag zur Geschichte des hessisch-sächsischen Grenzgebietes im hohen Mittelalter, in: Hess. Jb. f. Landesgesch. 23, 1973.

994 Witold Hensel, Zentrumbildung und Handel im osteuropäischen Raum vor der Wikingerzeit, in: Early Medieval Studies 1, Stockholm 1970 = Antikvariskt arkiv 38.

995 Wolfgang Herborn, Die politische Führungsschicht der Stadt Köln im Spätmittelalter, Bonn 1977 = Rheinisches Archiv 100.

996 Wolfgang Herborn, Zur Rekonstruktion und Edition der Kölner Bürgermeisterliste bis zum Ende des Ancien Régime, in: RhVjbll. 36, 1972.

997 Asbjörn E. Herteig, Bergen Kongershavn og handelssete, Oslo 1969.

998 François J. Himly, Atlas des villes médiévales d'Alsace, Strasbourg 1970 = Publications de la Fédération des Sociétés d'Histoire et d'Archéologie d'Alsace vol. VI.

(1046) Dietrich Höroldt, (ed.) see under Die Stadt in der europäischen Geschichte . . . (No. 1046).

999 Franz Irsigler, Ein großbürgerlicher Kölner Haushalt am Ende des 14. Jahrhunderts, in: Festschrift Matthias Zender. Studien zu Volkskultur, Sprache und Landesgeschichte, (ed.) Edith Ennen and Günter Wiegelmann, vol. 2, Bonn 1972.

(1046) Franz Irsigler, (ed.), see under Die Stadt in der europäischen Geschichte . . . (No. 1046).

1000 Franz Irsigler, Die wirtschaftliche Stellung der Stadt Köln im 14. und 15.

Jahrhundert. Strukturanalyse einer spätmittelalterlichen Exportgewerbe- und Fernhandelsstadt, Bonner Habil.-Schrift.

1001 Herbert Jankuhn, Spätantike und merowingische Grundlagen für die frühmittelalterliche nordeuropäische Stadtbildung, in: Early Medieval Studies 1, Stockholm 1970 = Antikvariskt arkiv 38.

(1069) Herbert Jankuhn, (ed.) see under Vor- und Frühformen der europäischen Stadt . . . (No. 1069).

1002 Karl Jordan, Zu den Gotland-Urkunden Heinrichs des Löwen, in: Hans. Geschbll. 91, 1973.

(1064) W. Kaemmerer, (ed.) see under Urkundenbuch der Stadt Düren . . . (No. 1064).

1003 Rainer Kallmann, Das Privatrecht der Stadt Göttingen im Mittelalter, Göttingen 1972 = Göttinger Studien zur Rechtsgeschichte vol. 5.

1004 Jiři Kejř, Die Entstehung der Stadtverfassung von Tabor, in: Festschrift für Hermann Heimpel zum 70. Geburtstag, (ed.) Max-Planck-Institut für Geschichte, vol. 2, Göttingen 1972 = Veröffentlichungen des Max-Planck-Instituts für Geschichte 36/II.

1005 Jiři Kejř, Wogastisburk-Burgum?, in: Československý časopis historický 21, 1973.

(1073) Hermann Kellenbenz, (ed.), see under Wirtschaftsgeschichte der Stadt Köln . . . (No. 1073).

1006 Hagen Keller, Der Gerichtsort in oberitalienischen und toskanischen Städten. Untersuchungen zur Stellung der Stadt im Herrschaftssystem des Regnum Italicum vom 9. bis 11. Jahrhundert, in: Quellen und Forschungen aus italienischen Archiven und Bibliotheken 49, 1969.

1006a Hagen Keller, Spätantike und Frühmittelalter im Gebiet zwischen Genfer See und Hochrhein, in: Frühmittelalterliche Studien 7, 1973.

1007 Hagen Keller, Die soziale und politische Verfassung Mailands in den Anfängen des kommunalen Lebens, in: HZ 211, 1970.

1008 Hans-Jörg Kellner, Die Römer in Bayern, München ^{2}1972.

1008a Erich Keyser and Heinz Stoob, (ed.), Bayerisches Städtebuch, Pt. 2, Stuttgart, Berlin, Köln, Mainz 1974 = Deutsches Städtebuch vol. V, Bayern Pt. 2.

1009 Erich Kittel, Stadtburgen und Burgstädte, in: Westfalen 51, 1973.

1010 Alfons Kolling, Schwarzenacker an der Blies, in: Bonner Jahrbücher 172, 1972.

1011 Andreàs Kubinyi, Die Anfänge Ofens, Berlin, Gießen 1972.

1012 Kjell Kumlien, Der Historiker und das Birkaproblem, in: Early Medieval Studies 1, Stockholm 1970 = Antikvariskt arkiv 38.

1012a Helmut Lahrkamp, Münsters wirtschaftliche Führungsschichten, in: Quellen und Forschungen z. Gesch. d. Stadt Münster new ser. 9, 1970.

1013 Michail P. Lesnikov, Die Handelsbücher des hansischen Kaufmanns Veckinchusen, Berlin 1973 = Forschungen zur mittelalterlichen Geschichte vol. 19.

1014 Jürgen Lindenberg, Stadt und Kirche im spätmittelalterlichen Hildesheim, Hildesheim 1963 = Quellen und Darstellungen zur Geschichte Niedersachsens vol. 61.

1015 Wolfgang Maier, Stadt und Reichsfreiheit. Entstehung und Aufstieg der elsässischen Hohenstaufenstädte, Zürich 1972.

(1019) Erich Maschke, (ed.), see under Städtische Mittelschichten . . . (No. 1019).

(1048) Erich Maschke, (ed.), see under Stadt und Ministerialität . . . (No. 1048).

1016 Horst Matzerath, Von der Stadt zur Gemeinde. Zur Entwicklung des rechtlichen Stadtberiffs im 19. und 20. Jahrhundert, in: Archiv für Kommunalwissenschaften 13, 1974.

1017 Helmut Maurer, Konstanz als ottonischer Bischofssitz. Zum Selbstverständnis geistlichen Fürstentums im 10. Jahrhundert, Göttingen 1973 = Studien zur Germania Sacra 12 = Veröffentlichungen des Max-Planck-Instituts für Geschichte 39.

(1063) Erich Meuthen, (ed.), see under Aachener Urkunden ... (No. 1063).

(1044) G.M. De Meyer, (ed.), see under De stadsrekeningen van Deventer ... (No. 1044).

1018 Jean Meyer and others, Histoire de Rennes, Toulouse 1972.

1019 Städtische Mittelschichten. Protokoll der VIII. Arbeitstagung des Arbeitskreises für südwestdeutsche Stadtgeschichtsforschung Biberach 14–16. November 1969, (ed.) Erich Maschke and Jürgen Sydow, Stuttgart 1972 = Veröffentlichungen d. Komm. f. gesch. Landeskunde in Baden-Württemberg ser. B Forschungen vol. 69.

1020 Michael Mitterauer, Das Problem der zentralen Orte als sozial- und wirtschaftshistorische Forschungsaufgabe, in: VSWG 58, 1971.

1021 Michel Mollat, Philippe Wolff, Ongles bleus. Jacques et Ciompi. Les révolutions populaires en Europe aux XIVe et XVe siècles, Paris 1970.

1022 Helga Mosbacher, Kammerhandwerk, Ministerialität und Bürgertum in Straßburg. Studien zur Zusammensetzung und Entwicklung des Patriziats im 13. Jahrhundert, in: Zschr. f. Gesch. d. Oberrheins 119, 1971.

(1054) Martin Müller, (ed.), see under Rheinischer Städteatlas ... (No. 1054).

1023 Alfred Neumann, Vindobona. Die römische Vergangenheit Wiens. Geschichte, Erforschung, Funde, Wien, Köln, Graz 1972.

1024 David Nicholas, Town and countryside: social, economic and political tensions in fourteenth-century Flanders, Bruges 1971 = Rijksuniversiteit te Gent. Werken uitg. door de Fac. van de Letteren en Wijsbegeerte 152.

1025 J.F. Niermeyer, Judaeorum sequaces. Joodse kooplieden en christelijke kooplieden. Bijdrage tot de ontstaansgeschiedenis van de Lotharingse burgerij (elfde eeuw), Amsterdam 1967 = Mededelingen d. Koninkl. Nederlandse Akad. v. Wetenschappen. Afd. Letterkunde new ser. 30, 6.

1026 Hildegard Nordhoff-Behne, Gerichtsbarkeit und Strafrechtspflege in der Reichsstadt Schwäbisch Hall seit dem 15. Jahrhundert, Schwäbisch Hall 1971 = Forschungen aus Württembergisch Franken 3.

1027 Gundolf Precht, Baugeschichtliche Untersuchungen zum römischen Praetorium in Köln, Köln 1973 = Rheinische Ausgrabungen vol. 14.

1028 Pierre Racine, Cité et Seigneur: Plaisance au Xe siècle, in: Economies et Sociétés au Moyen Age. Mélanges offerts à Edouard Perroy, Paris 1973 = Publications de la Sorbonne. Ser. "Etudes" vol. 5.

(1052) Wilhelm Rausch, (ed.), see under Stadt und Stadtherr ... (No. 1052).

(1045) R.A.D. Renting, (ed.), see under De stadsrekeningen van Doesburg ... (No. 1045).

1029 Hans Friedrich Rothert, Die Anfänge der Städte Oldenburg, Neustadt und Heiligenhafen, Neumünster 1971 = Quellen und Forschungen zur Geschichte Schleswig-Holsteins 59.

1030 Hans Friedrich Rothert, Stadtrechtsverleihungen an holsteinische Städte im 13. Jahrhundert, in: Aus Reichsgeschichte und Nordischer Geschichte, (ed.) Horst Fuhrmann, Hans Eberhard Mayer, Klaus Wriedt, Stuttgart 1972 = Kieler Historische Studien vol. 16.

1031 Hans Sauer, Hansestädte und Landesfürsten. Die wendischen Hansestädte in der Auseinandersetzung mit den Fürstenhäusern Oldenburg und Mecklenburg während der 2. Hälfte des 15. Jahrhunderts, Köln, Wien 1971 = Quellen und Darstellungen zur Hansischen Geschichte new ser. 16.

1032 Karl Schib, Geschichte der Stadt und Landschaft Schaffhausen, Schaffhausen 1972.

1033 Reinhard Schindler, Augusta Treverorum, in: Bonner Jahrbücher 172, 1972.

1034 Wilhelm Schleiermacher, Cambodunum-Kempton. Eine Römerstadt im Allgäu, Bonn 1972.

1035 Walter Schlesinger, Unkonventionelle Gedanken zur Geschichte von Schleswig/Haithabu, in: Aus Reichsgeschichte und Nordischer Geschichte, (ed.) Horst Fuhrmann, Hans Eberhard Mayer, Klaus Wriedt, Stuttgart 1972 = Kieler Historische Studien vol. 6.

(1069) Walter Schlesinger, (ed.), see under Vor- und Frühformen der europäischen Stadt ... (No. 1069).

1036 Jean Schneider, Sur le droit urbain de Toul au Moyen Age, in: Economies et Sociétés au Moyen Age. Mélanges offerts à Edouard Perroy, Paris 1973 = Publications de la Sorbonne. Ser. "Etudes" vol. 5.

1037 Roland Schönfeld, Regensburg im Fernhandel des Mittelalters, in: Verhandlungen d. Hist. Ver. f. Oberpfalz u. Regensburg 113, 1973.

1038 Heinrich Schoppmeyer, Paderborn als Hansestadt, in: Westfälische Zeitschrift 120, 1970.

1039 Werner Schultheiß, Das Bürgerrecht der Königs- und Reichsstadt Nürnberg. Beiträge zur Verfassungsgeschichte der deutschen Städte, in: Festschrift für Hermann Heimpel zum 70. Geburtstag, (ed.) Max-Planck-Institut für Geschichte, vol. 2, Göttingen 1972 = Veröffentlichungen des Max-Planck-Instituts für Geschichte 36/II.

1040 Berent Schwineköper, Topographische Grundlagen der Freiburger Stadtgründung, in: Freiburg im Mittelalter. Vorträge zum Stadtjubiläum 1970, (ed.) Wolfgang Müller, Bühl 1970 = Veröffentlichung des Alemannischen Instituts 29.

1041 Berent Schwineköper, Die ostsächsischen Städt zwischen Oberweser und mittlerer Elbe im Investiturstreit, Konstanz 1975 = Vorträge und Forschungen part 11.

1042 Anton Špiesz, Remeslo na Slovensku u obdobi existencie cechov (Das Handwerk in der Slowakei im Zeitalter der Zünfte), Bratislava 1972.

1043 De stadsrekeningen van Arnheim, (ed.) W. Jappe Alberts, Pt. 1: 1353–1377, Groningen 1967 = Rijksuniversiteit Utrecht, Teksten en Documenten uitg. door het instituut voor middeleeuwse geschiedenis V.

1044 De stadsrekeningen van Deventer (ed.) G.M. De Meyer and W. Jappe Alberts, Pt. 1: 1394–1400, Groningen 1968 = Rijksuniversiteit Utrecht, Teksten en Documenten uitg. door het instituut voor middeleeuwse geschiedenis VII.

1045 De stadsrekeningen van Doesburg betreffende de jaren 1400/1401 en 1402/1403, (ed.) R.A.D. Renting, Groningen 1964 = Rijksuniversiteit Utrecht, Fontes minores medii aevi XV.

1046 Die Stadt in der europäischen Geschichte. Festschrift Edith Ennen, (ed.) Werner Besch, Klaus Fehn, Dietrich Höroldt, Franz Irsigler, Matthias Zender, Bonn 1972.

1047 Stadt und Land in der Geschichte des Ostseeraumes. Wilhelm Koppe zum 65. Geburtstag, (ed.) Klaus Friedland, Lübeck 1973.

1048 Stadt und Ministerialität. Protokoll der IX. Arbeitstagung des Arbeitskreises für südwestdeutsche Stadtgeschichtsforschung Freiburg i. Br. 13.–15. November 1970, (ed.) Erich Maschke and Jürgen Sydow, Stuttgart 1973 = Veröffentlichungen d. Komm. f. gesch. Landeskunde in Baden-Württemberg ser. B Forschungen vol. 76.

1049 Die mittelalterliche Stadt in Bayern, (ed.) Karl Bosl, München 1974 = Zschr. f. bayer. Landesgesch. suppl. (ser. B) 6.

1050 Die Stadt des Mittelalters II, Recht und Verfassung, (ed.) Carl Haase, Darmstadt 1972 = Wege der Forschung 244.

1051 Die Stadt des Mittelalters III, Wirtschaft und Gesellschaft, (ed.) Carl Haase, Darmstadt 1973 = Wege der Forschung 245.

1052 Stadt und Stadtherr im 14. Jahrhundert. Entwicklungen und Funktionen, (ed.) Wilhelm Rausch, Linz 1972 = Beiträge zur Geschichte der Städte Mitteleuropas vol. 2.

1053 Deutscher Städteatlas, (ed.) Heinz Stoob, No. 1, Dortmund 1973.

1054 Rheinischer Städteatlas, No. 1, (ed.) Edith Ennen, Klaus Flink und Martin Müller, Bonn 1972. No. 2, (ed.) E. Ennen, Kl. Fehn, Kl. Flink, (ed.) as 1, Bonn 1974.

1054a Die Städte Vorarlbergs, (ed.) Franz Baltzarek and Joh. Pradel with help of Roman Sandgruber, Wien 1973 = Österreichisches Städtebuch vol. 3.

1055 Walter Stark, Lübeck und Danzig in der zweiten Hälfte des 15. Jahrhunderts. Untersuchungen zum Verhältnis der wendischen und preußischen Hansestädte in der Zeit des Niedergangs der Hanse, Weimar 1973 = Abhandlungen zur Handels- und Sozialgeschichte vol. 11.

(1069) Heiko Steuer, (ed.) see under Vor- und Frühformen der europäischen Stadt . . . (No. 1069).

1056 Jesko v. Steynitz, Mittelalterliche Hospitäler der Orden und Städte als Einrichtungen der sozialen Sicherung, Berlin 1970 = Sozialpolitische Schriften No. 26.

1057 Wilhelm Störmer, Die Gründung von Kleinstädten als Mittel herrschaftlichen Territorienaufbaus, gezeigt an fränkischen Beispielen, in: Bayerische Geschichte als Tradition und Modell. Festschrift für Karl Bosl zum 65. Geburtstag, (ed.) Friedrich Prinz, Franz-Josef Schmale, Ferdinand Seibt, München 1973 = Zschr. f. bayer. Landesgesch. 36, 1973.

(1053) Heinz Stoob, (ed.), see under Deutscher Städteatlas . . . (No. 1053) and E. Keyser (No. 1008a).

1058 Heinz Stoob, Zur Städtebildung im Lande Hohenlohe, in: Bayerische Geschichte als Tradition und Modell. Festschrift für Bosl zum 65. Geburtstag, (ed.) Friedrich Prinz, Franz-Josef Schmale, Ferdinand Seibt, München 1973 = Zschr. f. bayer. Landesgesch. 36, 1973.

1059 Heinz Stoob, Die Wachstumsphasen der Stadt Goslar bis zur Mitte des 13. Jahrhunderts, in: Harz-Zeitschrift 22/23, 1970/71.

1060 Studien betreffende de sociale strukturen te Brugge, Kortrijk en Gent in de 14e en 15e eeuw door Willem Blockmans, Ingrid De Meyer and others, Gent 1971 = Studia Hist. Gandensia 139.

(1019) Jürgen Sydow, (ed.), see under Städtische Mittelschichten ... (No. 1019).

(1048) Jürgen Sydow, (ed.), see under Stadt und Ministerialität ... (No. 1048).

1061 Jürgen Sydow, Neue Veröffentlichungen über die deutsche Städtegeschichte, XI, in: Bll. f. dt. Landesgesch. 107, 1971.

1062 György Székely, Die Lateiner und die Wallonen von Stuhlweißenburg im mittelalterlichen Ungarn, in: Székesfehévár Éuszázadai 2, 1972.

1063 Aachener Urkunden 1101–1250, (ed.) Erich Meuthen, Bonn 1972 = Publikationen d. Ges. f. Rhein. Geschichtskunde 58.

1064 Urkundenbuch der Stadt Düren 748–1500, vol. 1, Pt. 1, (ed.) W. Kaemmerer, Düren 1971 = Beiträge zur Geschichte des Dürener Landes 12.

1065 Adriaan Verhulst, Die Frühgeschichte der Stadt Gent, Gent 1972 = Studia Hist. Gandensia 174.

1066 Charles Verlinden, Marchands ou tisserands? A propos des origines urbaines, in: Annales. Economies, sociétés, civilisations 27, 1972.

1067 Hermann Vetters, Das Problem der Kontinuität von der Antike zum Mittelalter in Österreich, in: Gymnasium 76, 1969.

1068 Les villes du Massif Central, colloque de Saint-Etienne novembre 1970, Saint-Etienne 1971.

1069 Vor- und Frühformen der europäischen Stadt im Mittelalter. Bericht über ein Symposion in Reinhausen bei Göttingen in der Zeit vom 18.–24. April 1972, (ed.) Herbert Jankuhn, Walter Schlesinger, Heiko Steuer, Pt. 1, Göttingen 1973. Pt. II: Skandinavien, westslawisches ungarisches und rumänisches Gebiet, Göttingen 1974 = Abh. d. Akademie der Wissenschaften in Göttingen, Phil.-hist. Kl. 3. Ser. No. 83 and 84.

1070 Daniel Waley, The Italian city-republics, London 1969.

1071 J.P. Wild, Textile manufacture in the northern Roman provinces, Cambridge 1970.

1072 Sabine Wilke, Das Goslarer Reichsgebiet und seine Beziehungen zu den territorialen Nachbargewalten. Politische, verfassungs- und familiengeschichtliche Untersuchungen zum Verhältnis von Königtum und Landesherrschaft am Nordharz im Mittelalter, Göttingen 1970 = Veröffentlichungen des Max-Planck-Instituts für Geschichte 32.

1073 Zwei Jahrtausende Kölner Geschichte, (ed.) Hermann Kellenbenz, Köln 1975.

1074 Tibor Zalčík, Urbanizmus stredovékeho mestana Slovensku (Urbanismus der mittelalterlichen Stadt in der Slowakei), Bratislava 1973.

(1046) Matthias Zender, (ed.), see under Die Stadt in der europäischen Geschichte ... (No. 1046).

(959) Klaus Zernack, (ed.), see under Beiträge zur Stadt- und Regionalgeschichte Ost- und Nordeuropas ... (No. 959).

1075 Wolfgang Zorn, Augsburg, Geschichte einer deutschen Stadt, Augsburg ²1972.

Recent work

1076 Susan Reynolds, An introduction to the history of the medieval town, Oxford 1977.

Index

EUROPE IN THE MIDDLE AGES: Selected Studies

RICHARD VAUGHAN, General Editor